Writing the
Research Paper

A Handbook

Eighth Edition

Writing the Research Paper

A Handbook

Anthony C. Winkler

Jo Ray Metherell

WADSWORTH
CENGAGE Learning

Australia • Brazil • Japan • Korea • Mexico • Singapore • Spain • United Kingdom • United States

Writing the Research Paper:
A Handbook,
Eighth Edition
Anthony C. Winkler
Jo Ray Metherell

Publisher/Executive Editor:
Lyn Uhl

Acquisitions Editor:
Kate Derrick

Assistant Editor: Kelli Streiby

Editorial Assistant:
Elizabeth Reny

Media Editor:
Cara Douglass-Graff

Marketing Manager:
Stacey Purviance

Content Project Manager:
PreMediaGlobal

Art Director: Jill Ort

Print Buyer: Susan Spencer

Rights Acquisition Specialist:
Katie Huha

Production Service:
PreMediaGlobal

Photo Manager:
PreMediaGlobal

Cover Designer: Nesbitt
Graphics Inc./Alisha Webber

Cover Image: VEER

Compositor: PreMediaGlobal

For product information and
technology assistance, contact us at **Cengage Learning**
Customer & Sales Support, 1-800-354-9706

For permission to use material from this text or product,
submit all requests online at **www.cengage.com/permissions.**
Further permissions questions can be e-mailed to
permissionrequest@cengage.com

Library of Congress Control Number: 2010932459

ISBN-13: 978-0-495-79964-1

ISBN-10: 0-495-79964-5

Wadsworth
20 Channel Center Street
Boston, MA 02210
USA

Cengage Learning is a leading provider of customized learning solutions with office locations around the globe, including Singapore, the United Kingdom, Australia, Mexico, Brazil, and Japan. Locate your local office at: **international.cengage.com/region**

Cengage Learning products are represented in Canada by Nelson Education, Ltd.

For your course and learning solutions, visit
www.cengage.com

Purchase any of our products at your local college store or at our preferred online store **www.cengagebrain.com**

Contents

Preface   xix

1   Basic Information about the Research Paper

1a	Hatred of the research paper	3
1b	Definition of the research paper	3
1c	Format of the research paper	4
1d	Reasons for the research paper	5
1e	The report paper and the thesis paper	5
1f	Drafts of the research paper	6
1g	Writing the research paper: Steps and schedule	9

2   Choosing a Topic

2a	How to choose a topic	13
2b	Topics to avoid	15

     2b-1   Topics that are too big   15
     2b-2   Topics based on a single source   15
     2b-3   Topics that are too technical   15
     2b-4   Topics that are trivial   16
     2b-5   Topics that are too hot   16

2c	Narrowing the topic	17

3   The Library

3a	Layout of the library	21

     3a-1   The computer   21
     3a-2   Online full-text databases   23

3a-3   Microform indexes   24

3a-4   Stacks   24

3a-5   Reserve room or shelf   25

3a-6   Main desk   25

3a-7   Reserve desk   25

3a-8   Audiovisual room   25

3a-9   Microform room   26

3a-10   Newspaper racks   26

3a-11   Computer room   27

3a-12   Carrels   27

3b   Organization of the library collections   27

3b-1   The Dewey Decimal System   28

3b-2   The Cutter-Sanborn Author Marks   29

3b-3   The Library of Congress Classification System   30

3b-4   Classification of periodicals   31

3b-5   Classification of nonbooks   33

4 Using the Computer in Your Research

4a   Computers and the research paper   37

4b   The Internet   38

4b-1   The World Wide Web   38

4c   Online resources   38

4c-1   Databases   39

4c-2   Electronic journals   39

4c-3   Online public-access catalogs (OPACs)   39

4c-4   Blogs and social networks   40

4d   Researching with search engines   41

4d-1   Finding a search engine   42

4e   Usenet, Listserv, telnet, and gopher   42

4f   Evaluating Internet sources   43

4f-1   Where was the information found?   43

4f-2   Who wrote it?   44

4f-3   Who publishes it?   44

4f-4   What are the writer's sources?   44

4f-5   What tone does the writer use?   45

4f-6   What do the writer's contemporaries
have to say?   45

4f-7   What is the writer's motive?   45

4f-8   What is the context of the writer's
opinion?   45

4g   Running a search   46

4h   Useful Internet sites   47

5   Doing the Research

5a   What information to look for   51

5a-1   Single-fact information   51

5a-2   General information   51

5a-3   In-depth information   52

5b   Where to look for information   52

5b-1   General indexes   53

5b-2   Specialized indexes   54

5b-3   Using interviews and surveys   57

5b-4   Corresponding by e-mail   57

5b-5   Attending lectures, concerts, or art exhibits   58

5c   Assembling a working bibliography   58

5d   Selecting your sources: Skimming   60

5d-1   Primary and secondary sources   61

5d-2   Evaluating sources   61

5e   Note-taking   63

5e-1   Using the computer to take notes   64

5e-2   Using a copy machine to take notes   65

5e-3   Kinds of notes   65
a. The summary   65
b. The paraphrase   66
c. The quotation   66
d. The personal comment   68

5f   Plagiarism and how to avoid it   69

6   The Thesis and the Outline

6a   The thesis: Definition and function   **75**

6a-1   Formulating the thesis   76
6a-2   Rules for wording the thesis   77
6a-3   Placing the thesis   79
6a-4   Choosing a title   80

6b   The outline   **81**

6b-1   Visual conventions of the outline   81
6b-2   Equal ranking in outline entries   82
6b-3   Parallelism in outline entries   82
6b-4   Types of outlines   83
        a. The topic outline   83
        b. The sentence outline   84
        c. The paragraph outline   85
        d. Decimal outline notation   86

6c   Choosing an outline form   **87**

7   Transforming the Notes into a Rough Draft

7a   Preparing to write the rough draft: A checklist   **91**

7b   Writer's block   **91**

7c   Writing with a computer   **91**

7c-1   Overdoing it   92
7c-2   Using a spell-checker   92

7d   Using your notes in the paper   **92**

7d-1   Summaries and paraphrases   92
7d-2   Direct and indirect quotations   93
7d-3   Using brief direct quotations   94
7d-4   Using long quotations   95
7d-5   Using quotations from poetry   97
7d-6   Using a quotation within another quotation   98
7d-7   Punctuating quotations   98
7d-8   Handling interpolations in quoted material   99
7d-9   Using the ellipsis   99

7d-10   Overusing quotations   102

7d-11   Personal commentary   103

7e   How to use quotations to explore and discover   104

7f   Writing with unity, coherence, and emphasis   105

7f-1   Unity   105

7f-2   Coherence   106

7f-3   Emphasis   108

7g   Using the proper tense   108

7h   Using graphics in your research paper   109

7i   Writing the abstract   115

8 Revising Your Rough Draft

8a   Principles of revision   119

8a-1   Rereading your writing   119

8a-2   Revising the paper from biggest to smallest elements   119

8b   Revising the opening paragraph   120

8b-1   Revising the introduction   121

a. Use a quotation   121
b. Ask a question   121
c. Present an illustration   122

8b-2   Check that your paragraphs follow the sequence of topics in the thesis   122

8b-3   Revising the body paragraphs   123

8b-4   Check paragraph transitions   124

8c   Revising sentences for variety and style   125

8c-1   Revise sentences to use the active voice   126

8c-2   Revise to use an appropriate point of view   128

8c-3   Revise sexist language   129

8d   Revising words: Diction   130

8d-1   Revise diction for accuracy and exactness   131

8d-2   Revise the overuse of phrases for subjects instead of single nouns   132

8d-3   Revise redundant expressions   133

8d-4   Revise meaningless words and phrases   133
8d-5   Revise snobbish diction   134

8e   Rules for Writers. Not.   134

9   The MLA System of Documentation

9a   Parenthetical documentation: Author-work (MLA)   139

9a-1   What to document   140
9a-2   Guidelines for in-text citations   140

9b   Format for "Works Cited" (MLA)   144

9b-1   General order in references to books   145
a. Author   146
b. Title   147
c. Name of editor, compiler, or translator   147
d. Edition (other than first)   147
e. Series name and number   147
f. Volume number   148
g. Publication facts   148
h. Page numbers   149
i. Medium of publication   149

9b-2   Sample references to books   149
a. Book by a single author   149
b. Book by two or more authors   149
c. Book by a corporate author   149
d. Book by an anonymous or pseudonymous author   150
e. Work in several volumes or parts   150
f. Work within a collection of pieces, all by the same author   150
g. Collections: Anthologies, casebooks, and readers   151
h. Double reference—a quotation within a cited work   151
i. Reference works   151
j. Work in a series   151
k. Reprint   152
l. Edition   152
m. Edited work   152
n. Book published in a foreign country   152
o. Introduction, preface, foreword, or afterword   153
p. Translation   153
q. Book of illustrations   153
r. Foreign title   153

9b-3   General order in references to periodicals   153
a. Author   153
b. Title of the article   154
c. Publication information   154
d. Pages   155
e. Medium of publication   155

9b-4   Sample references to periodicals   155

a. *Anonymous author   155*
b. *Single author   155*
c. *More than one author   155*
d. *Journal with continuous or separate pagination   156*
e. *Monthly magazine   156*
f. *Weekly magazine   156*
g. *Newspaper   157*
h. *Editorial   157*
i. *Letter to the editor   157*
j. *Critical review   157*
k. *Published interview   157*
l. *Published address or lecture   158*

9b-5   References to electronic sources   158

9b-6   General order in references to electronic sources   158

9b-7   Sample references to electronic sources   159

a. *Abstract online or on CD-ROM   160*
b. *CD-ROM   160*
c. *Computer program   160*
d. *Corporate website   160*
e. *E-mail   160*
f. *FTP source   160*
g. *Gopher   160*
h. *Government website   161*
i. *Electronic mailing list   161*
j. *MOOs and MUDs (synchronous communication)   161*
k. *Online book   161*
l. *Online database   161*
m. *Online dictionary   161*
n. *Online encyclopedia   162*
o. *Online magazine article—author listed   162*
p. *Online magazine article—no author listed   162*
q. *Telnet   162*
r. *Usenet   162*
s. *Website—author listed   162*
t. *Website—no author listed   162*

9b-8   Sample references to nonprint materials   162

a. *Address or lecture   162*
b. *Artwork   163*
c. *Film, videotape, or DVD   163*
d. *Interview   164*
e. *Musical composition   164*
f. *Radio or television program   165*
g. *Sound recording (compact disc or tape)   165*
h. *Performance   166*

9b-9   Sample references to special items   167

a. *Artwork, published   167*
b. *The Bible and other sacred writings   167*
c. *Classical works in general   167*

d. *Dissertation   168*
e. *Footnote or endnote citation   168*
f. *Manuscript or typescript   168*
g. *Pamphlet or brochure   169*
h. *Personal letter   169*
i. *Plays   169*
j. *Poems   170*
k. *Public documents   171*
l. *Quotation used as a source   172*
m. *Report   173*
n. *Table, graph, chart, map, or other illustration   173*

9c   Content notes   174

9c-1   **Content note explaining a term   175**

9c-2   **Content note expanding on an idea   175**

9c-3   **Content note referring the reader to another source   175**

9c-4   **Content note explaining procedures   175**

9c-5   **Content note acknowledging help   176**

9c-6   **Content note consolidating references   176**

9d   Finished form of the MLA paper   176

9d-1   **Appearance   176**

9d-2   **Title page   176**

9d-3   **Abstract   177**

9d-4   **Pagination and headings   177**

9d-5   **Spacing of text   178**

9d-6   **Font   178**

9d-7   **Illustrations, tables, and other graphics   178**
a. *Tables   179*
b. *Other illustrative materials   180*

9d-8   **Use of numbers   183**

9d-9   **Bibliography (titled "Works Cited")   183**

9e   Peer review checklist   184

9f   Submitting your paper electronically   184

10   The APA System of Documentation

10a   Parenthetical documentation: Author-date (APA)   187

10a-1   **Examples of APA in-text citations to books   188**
a. *One work by a single author   188*
b. *Subsequent references   188*

c. *One work by two authors* *188*
d. *One work by three to five authors* *189*
e. *Work by six or more authors* *189*
f. *Corporate author* *190*
g. *Works by an anonymous author or no author* *191*
h. *Authors with the same surname* *191*
i. *Two or more works in the same parentheses* *191*
j. *References to specific parts of a source* *192*
k. *Personal communications* *192*
l. *Citation as part of a parenthetical comment* *193*

10a-2 **Avoiding clutter in the text**   **193**

10b **Format for "References" (APA)**   **193**

10b-1 **General order for books in "References"**   **194**

10b-2 **Sample references to books**   **195**
a. *Book by a single author* *195*
b. *Book by two or more authors* *195*
c. *Edited book* *195*
d. *Translated book* *196*
e. *Book in a foreign language* *196*
f. *Revised edition of a book* *196*
g. *Book by a corporate author* *196*
h. *Multivolume book* *197*
i. *Unpublished manuscript* *197*

10b-3 **General order for periodicals in "References"**   **197**

10b-4 **Sample references to periodicals**   **198**
a. *Journal article, one author* *198*
b. *Journal article, up to six authors* *198*
c. *Journal article, paginated anew in each issue* *198*
d. *Journal with continuous pagination throughout the annual volume* *199*
e. *Magazine article, magazine issued monthly* *199*
f. *Magazine article, magazine issued on a specific day* *199*
g. *Newspaper article* *199*
h. *Editorial* *200*
i *Letter to the editor* *200*
j. *Review* *200*

10b-5 **Sample references to electronic sources**   **200**
a. *Abstract online* *201*
b. *CD-ROM* *201*
c. *Computer program* *202*
d. *Corporate website* *202*
e. *E-mail* *202*
f. *FTP source* *202*
g. *Gopher* *202*
h. *Government website* *202*
i. *Electronic mailing list (Listserv)* *203*
j. *MOOs and MUDs (synchronous communication)* *203*

k. *Online book* 203
l. *Online database* 203
m. *Online dictionary* 203
n. *Online encyclopedia* 203
o. *Online magazine article—author listed* 204
p. *Online magazine article—no author listed* 204
q. *Telnet* 204
r. *Usenet* 204
s. *Website—author listed* 205
t. *Website—no author listed* 205
u. *Message posted to a group* 205

10b-6   Sample references to nonprint materials   205

a. *Motion picture* 205
b. *Audio recording (cassette, record, tape, compact disc)* 206

10b-7   Sample references to special items   206

a. *Government documents* 206
b. *Legal references* 207
c. *A report* 208

10c   Writing the abstract   **208**

10d   Finished form of the paper   **209**

10d-1   Two kinds of APA papers: The theoretical and the empirical   209

10d-2   Appearance of the final copy   210

a. *Outline* 210
b. *Title page* 210
c. *Abstract* 211
d. *Text* 212
e. *Content notes and endnotes* 212
f. *Illustrations: Tables and figures* 212
g. *Use of numbers* 214
h. *Using the right tense* 214
i *Bibliography (titled "References")* 217

10e   Peer review checklist   **218**

10f   Submitting your paper electronically   **218**

11   The Traditional System of Documentation (CMS)

11a   Footnotes and endnotes   **221**

11a-1   Formatting of notes   221

11a-2   Rules for numbering the notes   223

11a-3   Sample footnote references to books   224

a. *Single author   225*
b. *More than one author   225*
c. *Work in several volumes or parts   225*
d. *Collections: Anthologies, casebooks, and readers   226*
e. *Double reference—a quotation within a cited work   226*
f. *Edition   226*
g. *Translation   227*

11a-4   Sample footnotes for periodicals   227

a. *Anonymous author   227*
b. *Single author   227*
c. *More than one author   227*
d. *Journal with continuous pagination in the annual volume   227*
e. *Journal with separate pagination for each issue   228*
f. *Monthly magazine   228*
g. *Weekly magazine   228*
h. *Newspaper   228*
i. *Editorial   229*
j. *Letter to the editor   229*

11b   Subsequent references in footnotes and endnotes   229

11c   Electronic sources   230

11d   Finished form of the paper   231

11d-1   Abstract   232

11d-2   Pagination and text format   232

11d-3   Content or reference notes   232

11d-4   Illustrations: Tables and figures   233

a. *Tables   233*
b. *Other illustrative materials   233*

11d-5   Use of numbers   234

11d-6   Bibliography   235

11e   Peer review checklist   235

11f   Submitting your paper electronically   236

12 Sample Student Papers

12a   Paper using author-work documentation (MLA)   239

12b   Paper using author-date documentation (APA)   251

12c   Paper using footnote documentation (CMS)   265

APPENDICES

A   Mechanics

A1   Numbers and dates   271

A1-a   Percentages and amounts of money   271
A1-b   Inclusive numbers   272
A1-c   Roman numerals   272
A1-d   Dates   272

A2   Titles   273

A2-a   Titles in italic   273
A2-b   Titles in quotation marks   275
A2-c   Titles within titles   277
A2-d   Frequent references to a title   277

A3   Italic and underlining   277

A4   Names of people   278

A5   Hyphenating words   279

A6   Spaces and punctuation marks   280

A7   Foreign-language words   280

A8   Abbreviations   281

A8-a   Commonly used abbreviations   281
A8-b   The Bible   285
A8-c   Shakespeare   287
A8-d   Days and months   287
A8-e   States and U.S. territories   288
A8-f   Publishers' names   288
A8-g   Abbreviations   291

A9   Spelling   291

B   General and Specialized References, an Annotated List

B1   A list of general references   293

B1-a   Sources that list books   293
B1-b   Sources that list periodicals and newspapers   294
B1-c   Sources about general knowledge   297

B1-d   Encyclopedias   297

B1-e   Sources about words: Dictionaries   297

B1-f   Works about places   299

B1-g   Works about people   299

B1-h   Resources about government publications   302

B1-i   Sources about nonbooks (nonprint materials)   303

B2   A list of specialized references   306

B2-a   Art   306

B2-b   Business and economics   308

B2-c   Dance   310

B2-d   Ecology   311

B2-e   Education   311

B2-f   Ethnic studies   312

B2-g   High technology   314

B2-h   History   315

B2-i   Literature   317

B2-j   Music   320

B2-k   Mythology, classics, and folklore   322

B2-l   Philosophy   323

B2-m   Psychology   324

B2-n   Religion   325

B2-o   Science   326

B2-p   Social sciences   327

B2-q   Women's studies   327

Credits   329
Index   333

Preface

The eighth edition of *Writing the Research Paper: a Handbook.*

Writing the Research Paper: A Handbook is a book designed to be consulted not read. A regular book builds from topic to topic in a steady accumulation of ideas and facts. This book, in contrast, treats each topic as an independent unit. You do not need to understand the material in Chapter 2 to progress to Chapter 3. When you want information on, say, how to document a website, you simply go to the appropriate chapter or section of the book and copy the model given there. An exhaustive index and table of contents take a reader instantly to where the particular material on a particular subject is to be found. Whether the student chooses to hop from topic to topic, like a feeding butterfly, or to burrow like a determined mole through every explanation depends on the individual. *Writing the Research Paper: a Handbook* can be used either way. In 1979 when the first edition was published, we wrote that "no part of this book is dependent for continuity upon another," adding, a few sentences later, that the aim was for students to use "as much of the book as they need, or as little." That is still the basic principle behind this book.

This eighth edition of *Writing the Research Paper: a Handbook* makes no assumptions about its potential users. No other prerequisites are required to use this book other than enrollment in a class that requires the writing of a research paper. Whatever the student needs to know about how to use the library or how to explore a search engine for ideas on a particular subject will be found in this new edition.

This new edition was made necessary by changes in the protocols of research paper writing and documentation made in 2009 by both the Modern Language Association (MLA) and the American Psychological Association (APA). Most of these changes were admittedly microscopic, but they nevertheless have to be observed. Every new trait or shift in style, now the law of the land of research, is faithfully covered here with many examples. We have added a new paper written in MLA style and updated the APA example. The CMS paper has also been tweaked to reflect changes, even minor ones, in the *Chicago Manual of Style.*

In this edition, we finally bid goodbye to the familiar card catalog that had come down to us through the ages. In earlier editions we felt obliged to pay lip service to what was in its day the best classification technology available. This edition, however, concentrates on the computer and the vast opportunities for research it has bestowed on the researcher, professional or amateur.

We have rearranged some of the earlier chapters merely as an extension of the logic of the presentation rather than of any compelling necessity. The particulars do not really matter, and the book is not altered in any way by these shifts. Everything you need to know about the research paper is still present here in a non-sequential way.

In revising for the eighth time a book that is known for its simplicity of presentation, we have become conscious of the fact that sometimes we occasionally provide too much information on a topic, making it seem more complex than it is. We have been very careful in this edition to thin out overly dense explanations and to provide, in the words of one poplar TV detective, "just the facts, Ma'am" The student does not need to know how a search engine works in order to use it, for example, and many instances of this kind of simplification will be found scattered throughout the text, making *Writing the Research Paper: a Handbook,* eighth edition even more accessible and useful than its predecessors.

The eighth edition retains the use of vignettes that illustrate the wonders and marvels that research has bequeathed the human race over the centuries. Illustrations preceding each chapter also help enliven the ponderous reputation that research has, fairly or unfairly, accumulated. The spiral binding makes the book easier to open and lie flat for consulting in tight places.

Finally, we have spent most of our time doing what every editor knows is the most unappreciated work because it is the least visible—namely, the word for word and line by line editing of text. Every word, sentence, paragraph, and page of this edition has been aerated by the most painstaking editorial pen we can wield with benefits which, if not plainly obvious to the reader, will be implicit in the increased clarity throughout the text. The spectacle of a felled tree in a garden will immediately draw the eye; however, the sight of a laboring gardener kneeling in the dirt to dig up a patch of dandelions suggests nothing but unglamorous toil and drudgery that only a few would appreciate. Appreciated or not, we have done the necessary weeding to make this book the best edition ever.

A textbook is a collaborative effort. This one is no exception. Among the many people, some unnamed, who contributed suggestions for this edition, we would like to acknowledge the excellent help of our editors, who encouraged us to reach for creative ideas while remaining focused and on course: Lyn Uhl, Senior Publisher, Kate Derrick, Acquisitions Editor, Elizabeth Reny, Editorial Assistant, Kelli Strieby, Senior Assistant Editor, and Trish O'Kane, Project Manager.

To them we extend our heartfelt thanks. The blame for everything wrong we reserve for ourselves:

We also wish to acknowledge the following reviewers whose insightful suggestions helped shape this edition, with special thanks to Scott Douglass, *Chattanooga State Technical Community College*, and Linda Smoak Schwartz, *Coastal Carolina University:*

Arnold J. Bradford, *Northern Virginia Community College*

Nancy Erickson, *DeVry University*

Billie Ertel, *Indiana Business College*

Marcia Hines, *Minnesota School of Business*

Thomas Hoberg, *Northeastern Illinois University*

L. Adam Mekler, *Morgan State University*

Michael Minassian, *Broward Community College*

Rebecca Mitchell, *University of California, Santa Barbara*

Minna Seligson, *Briarcliffe College*

John O. Silva, *LaGuardia Community College*

Anthony C. Winkler and JoRay Metherell

The Earth and its human inhabitants are not at the center of the universe.

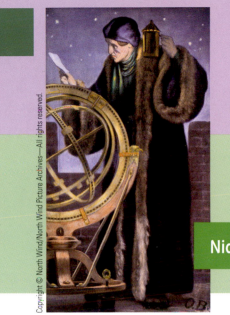

Nicolaus Copernicus

Nicolaus Copernicus (1473–1543), a Polish astronomer, used his research into planetary movement to write a book that revolutionized philosophy and theology. After constant observation of the skies, he published his masterpiece, *De Revolutionibus Orbium Coelestium* (1543), in which he argued that the earth orbited the sun and not vice versa. His ideas formed the basis of the heliocentric (sun-centered) Copernican system in which the sun was thought to be stationery and the planets its encircling satellites. This revolutionary conception broke sharply with the ancient Ptolemaic system, which pictured earth and humans as the centerpiece of creation. Approved by the church, the Ptolemaic view of the universe caused mariners navigation problems and was unreliable in calculating accurate time for one good reason: it was flatly wrong. Yet to embrace the Copernicus picture, which removed the earth from the center of creation, was for centuries after the publication of *De Revolutionibus Orbium Coelestium* regarded as mortal sin. With the passing of the generations, however, researchers have deposited the Ptolemaic universe into the rubbish bin of history, where it lingers as a sidewalk curiosity like last year's Christmas tree. Honest research not only finds truth, it also tends to be self-correcting.

1 Basic Information about the Research Paper

1a Hatred of the research paper

1b Definition of the research paper

1c Format of the research paper

1d Reasons for the research paper

1e The report paper and the thesis paper

1f Drafts of the research paper

1g Writing the research paper: Steps and schedule

FAQ

1. How can I make writing a research paper more enjoyable? *See 1a.*

2. Why is format so important? *See 1c.*

3. What does a first draft look like? *See 1f.*

4. What is the difference between the report paper and the thesis paper? *See 1e.*

5. How can I avoid being late with my paper? *See 1g.*

6. Why are research papers assigned, anyway? *See 1d.*

Writing the
Research Paper

A Handbook

1a Hatred of the research paper

Let's be frank with one another: you hate the research paper. You think it an assignment that is both picky and tedious. Wrestling with the correct format of a footnote drives you loopy. The tone of voice you think you must use in writing the research paper makes you sound papal—but you know only too well that you are only you, not the Pope. That, in a nutshell, is how you really feel about the research paper.

Millions of students—current as well as past—feel exactly as you do. Yet for all the anxiety that the research paper provokes, it has outlasted generations of its haters. Obviously it must be good for something, or else it would have been swept away long, long ago.

In fact, the research paper is an excellent tool for learning about a topic of your choice. Writing it will expose you to the rigors of research, acquaint you with the protocol of making correct citations to sources consulted, and teach you how to forge a mishmash of researched opinions into a single, coherent viewpoint. Of course, it is possible that your instructor will assign a specific topic for your paper, but typically topic choice is left up to the writer. Finding and shaping the final topic is usually regarded as a test of the student's judgment. The student who chooses a vast topic, such as wars throughout the ages, has taken on too big a job. On the other hand, the student who chooses to write on the history of the tire iron is proposing a topic that is too small.

Writing a research paper also has practical effects that could help you in later life. Research is research, and the techniques you learn from writing a research paper about, say, why the poetry of Edgar Allan Poe was so appealing in his day, will also apply to writing a business paper about, say, why a certain product isn't selling today. In both instances you would be researching causes. The research paper, in other words, is not art for art's sake; it's art for your sake (unless your name is Art). And the research paper, as bizarre as this sounds, can also be fun.

But you must make it fun. The first step in doing that is to choose a subject you genuinely like. You may even discover an interest in a subject that you didn't know you had. Research into any subject tends to lead to self-reflection. As you learn about your subject, whatever it may be, you also get glimpses into your own heart. Self-discovery of this kind is not unusual among students searching for a research topic. For some students the experience becomes a turning point in their lives that leads to permanent career changes. Remember, too, that a topic that might seem humdrum to you might to some readers come as a bolt of revelation. For example, a student from Afghanistan never wrote about her country until an instructor pointed out the fascination a paper on the customs and traditions of the Afghan people might hold for American readers.

1b Definition of the research paper

Research comes from the Middle French word *rechercher,* meaning "to seek out." Writing a research paper requires you to seek out information about a subject, take a stand on it, and back it up with the opinions, ideas, and views

1c

of others. What results is a printed paper variously known as a term paper or library paper, usually between five and fifteen pages long—most instructors specify a minimum length—in which you present your views and findings on the chosen subject.

1c   Format of the research paper

The research paper is a formal work that must abide by the rules of scholarly writing. These rules are simply an agreed-on way of doing things—much like etiquette, table manners, or rules of the road. For instance, in literary articles recently published you are likely to run across passages similar to this one:

> Brashear considers Tennyson to be at his best when his poetry is infused with "that tragic hour when the self fades away into darkness, fulfilling all of the poet's despairing pessimism" (18).

Formatting tip

The period always goes after the parenthetical reference at the end of a sentence.

This citation uses parenthetical documentation, a style favored by the MLA. The author of the quotation is introduced briefly; the quotation is cited; and a page reference is supplied in parentheses. In the alphabetized bibliography of the article appears this listing:

> Brashear, William. *The Living Will*. The Hague: Mouton, 1969. Print.

MLA tip

Here is the MLA formula for citing a book:

Inverted name of writer. *Title of Book*. Place of publication: Name of publisher, Year of publication. Medium of publication.

This sort of standardization makes it easier to write a scholarly paper as well as to read one. Part of your baptism of scholarship is to become familiar with the major citation styles used by different disciplines—most of which are covered in this book. Your instructor no doubt will tell you what documentation style to use. Once you know that, you can concentrate on mastering that style and ignore the others.

1d   Reasons for the research paper

One obvious reason for the research paper is that writing it forces you to learn lots about your chosen subject. Sifting through the pros and cons of opinions on any subject is a priceless learning experience. Another reason is that writing the paper teaches you the conventions of scholarly writing, among them the accepted styles of documentation and the ethics of research.

A third reason is that you will become familiar with the library through the "learning by doing" method. Even the simplest library is an intricate storehouse of information, bristling with indexes, encyclopedias, and abstracts. How to seek out from this maze of sources a single piece of information is a skill you learn by actual doing. Writing a research paper may also mean interviewing experts about your subject and blending their ideas with your own distinct point of view. In short, you, like everyone else, can profit from knowing how to do research.

There are other benefits as well. Writing the research paper is an exercise in logic, imagination, and common sense. As you chip away at the mass of data and information available on your chosen topic, you learn

- ☐ How to track down information
- ☐ How to organize
- ☐ How to use the Internet in your research
- ☐ How to discriminate between useless and useful opinions
- ☐ How to summarize
- ☐ How to budget your time
- ☐ How to conceive of and manage a research project from start to finish

1e   The report paper and the thesis paper

Papers assigned in colleges are one of two kinds: the report paper or the thesis paper. The report paper summarizes and reports your findings on a particular subject. You neither judge nor evaluate the findings; you simply relate them in a logical sequence. For instance, a paper that describes the opinions of experts in the debate over global warming is a report paper. Likewise a paper that chronologically narrates the final days of Hitler is a report paper.

Unlike the report paper, the thesis paper takes a definite stand on an issue. A thesis is a proposition or point of view that you are willing to argue against or defend. A paper that argues for the legalization of stem cell research is a thesis paper. So is a paper that attempts to prove that air bags save lives. Here are several more examples of topics that might be treated in report papers and thesis papers:

Report paper: How the Beatles got started as a rock group.

Thesis paper: The Beatles' lyrics gave hope to a disenchanted youth during the 1960s and 1970s.

Report paper: A summary of the theories of hypnosis.

Thesis paper: Hypnosis is simply another form of Pavlovian conditioning.

Report paper: The steps involved in passage of federal legislation.

Thesis paper: Lobbyists wield disproportionate influence on federal legislation.

Instructors are more likely to assign a thesis paper than a report paper, for obvious reasons: Writing a thesis paper requires you to exercise judgment, evaluate evidence, and construct a logical argument; writing a report paper does not.

1f   Drafts of the research paper

Whether your paper is a report paper or a thesis paper, experience over the years has shown that producing a good paper takes a minimum of three drafts. Many writers, your authors among them, do many drafts, umpteen at least. Three drafts, in other words, are the barest minimum.

Each draft is a separate stage in the progress of the paper. The first draft should be rough and much scribbled over, and should show definite signs of the wear and tear that inevitably come with composition. If your first draft isn't beat-up, you're either a miraculous writer or one who does not understand a basic truth about writing: First drafts are supposed to be messy. They are supposed to show signs of major rewriting and the back-and-forth movement of composing. In academic circles, that movement is called recursive, meaning that the writer goes back and forth over the material in the process of finding the right words to express ideas on paper. You might write a paragraph, stop, go back to the first sentence and change it, and then add the beginning of a second paragraph before pausing to rewrite some more of the first paragraph. Writers do not write as the crow flies, in a straight line, but rather as the bee does, buzzing back and forth, in fits and starts. If you find yourself writing this way, you're not being amateurish or inept; you're working exactly as writers typically do.

Here is an example of a first draft of an actual student paper:

means

~~A good definition for~~ conformity is being compliant with the standard

≡   mainstream society

and expected behavior and ways of ~~the general population. This is to say that~~

~~conformity is the expected behavior that is generally followed and accepted~~

~~by mainstream society.~~ In contrast any behavior that deviates from what is

expected is considered none conformity. A nonconformist is a person who ~~is~~

~~in the opposition to or~~ rejects the established ~~known~~ norms or customs ~~that~~

ordinarily   *by society*

~~are ordinary~~ followed. However, blindly accepting the conformist's traditions

and fashions is often to be narrow-minded because there are many traditions

that are flaws. In order ~~for us~~ to be self-reliant we must ask ourselves if we

agree with the standards and traditions that most of society blindly follows.

accepted

Still, certain norms ~~that are conformed to~~ are needed to maintain order; these

~~certain~~ norms are everyday laws and nondeviant behavior. ~~In~~ three works--

"Mending Wall" by Robert Frost, *Antigone* by Sophocles, and "Dead Man's

reveal

Path" by Chinua Achebe-- ~~there are~~ varying degrees of individualism in the

different characters. These characters call into question authority, tradition,

and laws. ~~This brings about the question of weather the battle is about non-~~

~~conformity vs. conformity, or individualism vs. society's traditions and blindly~~

~~accepted ideas.~~

     The speaker in "Mending Wall" is a New England farmer whose neighbor

believes that "good fences make good neighbors." Whenever part of his rock wall

collapses, he calls his neighbor, and they jointly walk the line to repair the holes.

The speaker realizes that this wall is unnecessary because "He is all pine and I am

apple orchard." In other words, there are no cows to wander into each other's

whose ancestors built walls; therefore, he, too, will mend a wall.

territory. But the neighbor is a blind conformist

Typical of first drafts, this one looks messy and scribbled over. Our point—
and it cannot be made too often—is that you should not feel discouraged if your
first drafts are messy. That's the way they're supposed to be. After you have corrected your first draft, it becomes your second draft. Here is the student's second
draft as corrected:

     Conformity means being compliant with the standard and expected

behavior of mainstream society. In contrast, any behavior that deviates from

what is expected is considered none conformity. A nonconformist is a person

who rejects the established norms or customs ordinarily followed by society.

However, blindly accepting the conformist's traditions and fashions is often to

ed

be narrow-minded because ~~there are~~ many traditions ~~that~~ are flaws. In order

to be self-reliant, we must ask ourselves if we agree with the standards and traditions that most of society blindly follows. Still, certain accepted norms are needed to maintain order; these norms are everyday laws and nondeviant behavior. Three works--"Mending Wall" by Robert Frost, *Antigone* by Sophocles, and "Dead Man's Path" by Chinua Achebe--reveal varying degrees of individualism in the different characters. These characters call into question authority, tradition, and laws.

The speaker in "Mending Wall" is a New England farmer whose neighbor believes that "good fences make good neighbors." Whenever part of the rock wall collapses, he calls his neighbor, and they ~~jointly~~ *together* walk the line to repair the ~~holes~~ *breaches*. *between the neighbors' properties* The speaker realizes that this wall is unnecessary because "He is all pine and I am apple orchard." In other words, there are no cows to wander into each other's territory. But the neighbor is a blind conformist whose ancestors built walls; therefore, he, too, will mend a wall. *Like his father and grandfather before him, he holds to the traditions that well-defined property lines make good neighbors. He never questions the reason for such a tradition . . .*

> **Scheduling tip**
>
> Research paper assignments have a way of creeping up on you. To avoid being ambushed by an overdue assignment, start working on the paper as soon as it is assigned. Once you get started, make a schedule and stick to it.

Ordinarily, as the example shows, writers make fewer and smaller changes in a second draft than in a first. But writing is nothing if not unpredictable, and many writers have found themselves in the odd position of totally rewriting a paper because they were unhappy with a second draft. The point is that the process of writing is rarely smooth, often messy, and seldom predictable; and inevitably it's recursive. Expect this kind of chaos when you write, and you won't be surprised.

The third and final draft is the one you submit. At this stage you're likely to think that your work is done. It may not be. Even the final draft might be ripe for change. If from this discussion you get the idea that the work of writing is never really done, you would not be entirely wrong. Sooner or later, of course, every scribbler must put down the pen and turn over the goods. Still, it is common for writers, on rereading a work written many years earlier, to get the itch to write it again. That's why many professional writers make it a point never to reread their published works.

Here is the final draft as it was submitted to the instructor:

Conformity means being compliant with the standard and expected behavior of mainstream society. In contrast, any behavior that deviates from what is expected is considered nonconformity. A nonconformist is a person who rejects the established norms or customs ordinarily followed by society. However, blindly accepting the conformist's traditions and fashions is often to be narrow-minded because many traditions are flawed. In order to be self-reliant, we must ask ourselves if we agree with the standards and traditions that most of society blindly follows. Still, certain accepted norms are needed to maintain order; these norms are everyday laws and nondeviant behavior. Three works--"Mending Wall" by Robert Frost, *Antigone* by Sophocles, and "Dead Man's Path" by Chinua Achebe--reveal varying degrees of individualism in the different characters portrayed. These characters call into question authority, tradition, and laws.

The speaker in "Mending Wall" is a New England farmer whose neighbor believes that "good fences make good neighbors." Whenever part of the rock wall between the neighbors' properties collapses, he calls his neighbor, and together they walk the line to repair the breaches. The speaker realizes that this wall is unnecessary because "He is all pine and I am apple orchard." In other words, there are no cows to wander into each other's territory. But the neighbor is a blind conformist whose ancestors built walls; therefore, he, too, will mend a wall. Like his father and grandfather before him, he holds to the tradition that well-defined property lines make good neighbors. He never questions the reason for such a tradition. . . .

1g Writing the research paper: Steps and schedule

It is impossible to produce a schedule that exactly matches every student's research-paper assignment. But generally there are seven distinct steps in the process, requiring you to submit at least five hand-ins over a period of five weeks. With some variations, many instructors observe this schedule:

1g

What You Must Do	What You Must Produce	When It Is Due
1. You must select a topic that is complex enough to be researched from a variety of sources but narrow enough to be covered in 10 or so pages.	Two acceptable topics, one of which the instructor will approve	At the end of the first week
2. You must do the exploratory scanning and reading of sources on your topic.		At the end of the second week
3. You must gather information on your topic and assemble it into some usable sequence.	Notes, a thesis statement, and an outline (APA format requires an abstract instead of an outline)	At the end of the third week
4. You must draft a thesis statement expressing the major idea behind your paper.		
5. You must outline the major parts of your paper.		
6. You must write a rough draft of the paper arguing, proving, or supporting your thesis with information uncovered by your research. You must acknowledge all borrowed ideas, data, and opinions.	A rough draft of the paper	At the end of the fourth week
7. You must prepare a bibliography listing all sources used in the paper and you must write the final draft.	The paper, complete with bibliography	At the end of the fifth week

The printing press brings reading material to ordinary people.

Johannes Gutenberg

We realize how indebted humankind is to Johannes Gutenberg (1400?–1468) when we consider that before his time, ordinary citizens did not have access to books or periodicals, but were dependent on the oral tradition of knowledge. Gutenberg is credited with inventing the first printing machine using hand-set movable type. All characters were of equal height, and the printing was done on handmade paper. Gutenberg was trained as a goldsmith, but he became a partner in a printing plant, where he experimented with movable type. The masterpiece of his press was the Mazarin Bible (1455), which allowed many readers to study the Bible firsthand. Other quality printed materials from his press also contributed significantly to the technology of human communication. It is impossible to calculate the profound effects Gutenberg's invention, had on the eventual democratizing of societies throughout the world, by spreading the influence of learning.

2   Choosing a Topic

2a	**How to choose a topic**
2b	**Topics to avoid**
2c	**Narrowing the topic**

FAQ

1. What topics should I avoid? *See 2b.*

2. How can I be sure that my paper can adequately cover my topic? *See 2b-1.*

3. How can I narrow a topic? *See 2c.*

4. Why shouldn't I choose a topic like abortion or the death penalty? *See 2b-5.*

2a   How to choose a topic

Writing a good research paper is not rocket science. It is not as difficult as calculus, and not as complex as physics. If you follow our advice and carefully observe the particular steps we suggest, you'll produce a good paper you enjoyed writing and will probably learn something about your subject at the same time.

No single step is as important to the whole process of writing a research paper as the choice of a topic. You're like a traveler who is choosing where to go. If it's someplace you like, you'll enjoy getting there. If it turns out to be a place you don't like, getting there will make you miserable. Ideally you should choose a topic that interests you, that is complex enough to need several research sources, and that will not bore—or talk down to—your reader.

- Pick a topic you like, are curious about, are an expert on, or are genuinely interested in. It can be anything from fighting obesity in children and teenagers to the effects of televising war. Whatever the topic, be it historical, controversial, or literary, your choice must satisfy two requirements: it must be approved by your instructor; and, most of all, it must appeal to you.

- If you are utterly at a loss for a topic and cannot for the life of you imagine what you could write ten whole pages on, go to the library and browse. Pore over books, magazines, and newspapers. Better yet, if your library has one, use its online public-access catalog (OPAC), a modern version of the card catalog, to search for ideas. An OPAC can locate any book in the library by author, title, and subject. For example, let's say you want to write a paper on a topic about children. Here's what you do:

  1. Type the subject *children* into the OPAC terminal. The following subtopics are displayed on the computer screen:

     Childbirth (psychological aspects)
     Child language
     Childlessness
     Child rearing—United States
     Children employment

  2. The list goes on and on. Explore ideas that you're drawn to and eventually you'll end up with a suitable topic. One student who investigated the possibility of writing a research paper about children ended up with the topic "Grammar and Communication among preschool children." OPACs are not only useful but also easy to use, with some of them summarizing the contents of books while also indicating availability.

- Your librarian can direct you to other electronic storage sources. CD-ROMs, for example, can store vast amounts of information on any topic. The entire works of Shakespeare could easily fit on a single CD-ROM. Any information in a CD-ROM file can be printed out easily for further study.

- If you still can't find a suitable topic, it's time to fire up the computer and search the Internet for ideas. (See Chapter 5 for advice on using the Internet.)

2a

For example, we used one of the most popular search engines, Google, and did a search for "research paper topics." In less than ten seconds we had 200,000,000 hits with suggestions ranging from Affirmative Action to Health Care Reform to Global Warming. More specifically, if you were interested in doing a paper on fictional detectives, you could enter this topic in a search engine. It might lead you to a link that never occurred to you, namely, Black Fictional Detectives. That could result in an intriguing paper.

☐ An encyclopedia is also an incredibly rich source of possible topics. Browse through the entries until you find an appealing subject. Check the two-volume *Library of Congress Subject Headings (LCSH)* for a heading that appeals to you. You're looking for a general idea that can be whittled down to a specific topic (see 2c). Many libraries have an encyclopedia online or on CD-ROM. Searching it online is fast and easy. There's also an encyclopedia available at www.encyclopedia.com. Searching it is free.

> **Caution tip**
>
> Many Internet sites offering to help you write a term paper are actually websites for research paper vendors. Don't be tempted to buy a paper! Many instructors use software that can detect papers purchased online. If you're found out, you'll be in big trouble, facing a flunking grade for the bootleg paper and even possible expulsion from school. Buying a paper is like hoping to get into shape by having a friend do your exercises for you.

☐ Take your time searching for a topic. Don't settle on the first idea that pops into your head. Think it over. Ask yourself whether you would enjoy spending five weeks reading and writing about that topic. If you have your doubts, keep looking until you hit on an idea that excites you. All of us are or can be excited about something. Whatever you do, don't make the mistake of choosing any old topic. Choose carelessly now, and you'll pay later in boredom. Choose carefully, and you'll be rewarded with the age-old excitement of research.

☐ One of the best ways to find and narrow a topic is to ask yourself questions about your general interests. The idea is to probe until you hit a nerve. You might begin by asking yourself some general questions: What do I want to write about? What particular subject interests me? What do I really like? If you have no immediate answer, keep asking the questions. Once you have an answer, use it to ask another, more focused question. For example, if your answer to "What do I really like?" is *literature,* you can then ask, "What kind of literature?" By this process, you gradually narrow your range of writing options. It's simple, and it works. All you need is a moment of reflection.

☐ Your search for a topic will most likely involve textual sources. That is what you would expect from a research paper. But there is another source you might look at in your search for a topic: namely, images. With computers and printers becoming so widely available, student writers have begun to incorporate images in their research papers. Many also use images to discover topics for a paper. For example, one student was inspired by a photograph of a polar bear stranded on a small island of ice to write a paper on the effects of global warming on Arctic wildlife. If, after looking through the usual written sources, you still can't find a topic, try thumbing through a picture book you might find on a coffee table. You may be pleasantly surprised at your findings.

2b Topics to avoid

Some topics present unusual difficulties; others are simply a waste of time. What follows is a summary of topics to avoid.

2b-1 Topics that are too big

Reference sources that multiply like flies; a bibliography that grows like a weed; opinions, data, and information that come pouring in from hundreds of sources—these are signs that indicate a topic that is too big. The solution is to narrow the topic without making it trivial. For example, "The Influence of Greek Mythology on Poetry," can become "Greek Mythology in John Keats' Ode to a Nightingale." "India in the Age of the Moguls" could be narrowed to "Royal Monuments of India during the Age of the Moguls."

2b-2 Topics based on a single source

The research paper is intended to expose you to the opinions of different authorities, to a variety of books, articles, and other references. If a topic is so skimpy that all the data on it come from a single source, say, a compelling biography, you're defeating the purpose of the paper. Choose only topics that are broad enough to be researched from multiple sources and are not dominated by the opinions of a single writer.

2b-3 Topics that are too technical

Writing about things that are technical often requires a vocabulary that might sound to your instructor like gobbledygook and be dismissed as a "snow job." Also, the skills that a research paper should teach are better learned in a paper on a general topic. Naturally, whether your paper is too technical depends on the class for which it is written. Ask your instructor. A topic like "Heisenberg's Principle of Indeterminacy as It Applies to Sub particle Research" is fine for a physics class but a dubious choice for a class in writing. Stick to topics that don't demand special knowledge of a particular subject and that are broad enough to be understood by any educated reader.

2b-4   Topics that are trivial

Your judgment must steer you away from trivial topics. The safest bet is also the most sensible one: Again, ask your instructor. Here are some topics that might strike some instructors as too trivial: "The Use of Orthopedic Braces for Dachshunds Prone to Backaches," "The Cult of Van Painting in America," "The History of the Tennis Ball," "How to Get Dates When You're Divorced," and "How to Diaper an Unruly Baby."

Sometimes a topic is trivial because it is obvious. For instance, everyone agrees that walking is good aerobic exercise, but the subject is so tame that unless you're a really good writer, a paper on the subject will likely fall flat. Likewise, a paper on growing carrots in your backyard as a hedge against the possibility of a worldwide carrot shortage is not likely to inspire you to do your best writing.

2b-5   Topics that are too hot

A topic that still smells of gunpowder from being hotly debated in the arena of public opinion is best avoided. There are at least two good reasons to stay away from such topics: First, it often is difficult to find unbiased sources on them; second, the information that is available usually comes from newspapers and magazines whose speculative reporting can make your documentation seem flimsy. Intellectually solid papers will reflect opinions taken from a variety of sources—books, periodicals, reference volumes, specialized indexes, and various electronic sources—which require a topic that has weathered both time and scholarly commentary.

If you find yourself being drawn into a hothouse of conflicting opinions on the topic, our advice is that you abandon it for another that is less controversial. At the very least you should try to locate an equivalent topic that has withstood the test of time and write about that instead. So, for example, instead of writing about a revolutionary war that broke out yesterday in some Baltic state, in the Middle East, or in Africa, you might turn your attention to a well-documented equivalent, say, the Castro revolution in Cuba, or the revolution for independence under Bernardo O'Higgins in Chile. Instead of writing a paper on whether or not the 2009 piracy of the cargo ship *Maersk* off the Coast of Somalia was properly handled by the U.S. President, you could write a research paper on the Golden Age of Piracy, focusing on such fascinating characters as Edward Thatch, Thomas Austin, and other pirates in history.

> **Search tip**
>
> Let your initial search for sources help you narrow your topic. If that search turns up a severe lack of sources—both in the library and on the Internet—consider tackling another topic. In other words, avoid any topic so rare that you have to spend all of your time chasing down sources.

2c   Narrowing the topic

No python knows the exact dimensions of its mouth, but any python instinctively knows that it cannot swallow an elephant. Experiment with your topic: Pursue one train of thought, and see where it leads. Does it yield an arguable thesis? Pare down and whittle away until you have something manageable. Bear in mind the length of your paper versus the size of your topic. Most research papers are about ten pages long—some books have longer prefaces. Following are a few examples of the narrowing you will have to do.

General Subject	First Narrowing	Second Narrowing
Mythology	Beowulf	The oral tradition in Beowulf
Migrant workers	California migrant workers	Major California labor laws and their impact on Mexican migrant workers
Theater	Theater of the Absurd	Theater-of-the-Absurd elements in *Who's Afraid of Virginia Woolf?*
John F. Kennedy	John F. Kennedy's cabinet	The contribution of Averill Harriman as U.S. ambassador to Russia
Russia	The Bolshevik Revolution of 1917	The role of Leon Trotsky in revolutionary Russia
China	Chinese agriculture	The effect on China of its agricultural policies during the past 10 years
Indians	Famous Indian fighters	Major Rogers's Rangers during the Indian wars
Nature's carnivores	Parasites	The ichneumon wasp and its parasitic hosts
Educational psychology	Psychological testing in schools	The Thematic Apperception Test (TAT) and its present-day adaptations

The first attempt at narrowing a subject usually is easier than the second, which must yield a specific topic. Use trial and error until you have a topic you like. Further narrowing may occur naturally after you are into the actual research. Remember that whatever subject you choose must be approved by your instructor. So before you become too involved in narrowing the subject, be sure that its basic concept has your instructor's blessing.

The peanut makes it to the big leagues.

George Washington Carver

Born as a slave around 1864, George Washington Carver will always be identified with the peanut. He is credited with improved crop management of the peanut and with demonstrating its many varied applications and uses. Carver was bought by German farmer Moses Carver from slave traders for a racehorse worth $300. He was educated by walking nine miles a day to get to school. Graduating high school, he was rejected by several colleges because of his race, but eventually gained admittance to the Tuskegee Institute, where he continued his research into peanuts. In his lifetime, his fame was worldwide, and through his influence the peanut became the main agricultural product in Alabama. Carver died in 1943, leaving most of his fortune to the Tuskegee Institute.

3 The Library

3a   **Layout of the library**

3b   **Organization of the library collections**

FAQ

1. How are books classified in a library? *See 3b.*

2. Where have all the index cards gone? *See 3a.*

3. What are PACs and OPACs? *See 3a-1.*

4. Are any databases available without a fee? *See 3a-2.*

5. What are stacks? *See 3a-4.*

3a Layout of the library

Basic architectural design differs from one library to the next, but certain facilities are standard. All modern libraries are equipped with computers available to students, photocopy machines, and a connection to the Internet, whether through a dedicated telephone line or high speed cable modem. Most modern libraries have phased out the use of card catalogs—drawers crammed with 3 × 5 cards indexing the library's collection—and have replaced them with the computer.

3a-1 The computer

Gone from most libraries is the horse and buggy card catalog, its place taken by the digital computer. In the blink of an eye, the computer can locate a subject, and its related titles can be displayed. Students who have personal computers can often gain remote access to their library's central computer through an assigned password. In effect, this arrangement makes the holdings of a library open to students twenty-four seven. Many freshmen students who were born into a world of computers cannot even begin to imagine the astounding gain in efficiency these machines have made to the researcher. But since that is the universal story whose tagline is a smug, "you don't know how easy you have it," we'll go ahead and say it here. After all, it is the natural observation of one generation to another; we heard it from our parents; you will say it to your own children.

> **Online search tip**
>
> If you want to know if a certain book is available for purchase or still in print, go to www.amazon.com and key in the title or author. Here, online, is an amazing collection—the equivalent of *Books in Print*—accessible in just a few clicks of your mouse.

In addition to cataloging and organizing the collection of a library, computers used in most libraries are also linked to useful databases. These computerized systems are known as *public-access catalogs* (PACs) or *online public-access catalogs* (OPACs); their databases list titles of articles and essays as well as full text material to which the user has easy access, either to print out as a hard copy or to read on the screen. (For more on databases, see 5c-1.)

Access to a growing number of college libraries is available online. For example, the library of the Georgia State University in Atlanta allows students, and others, to search its online card catalog as well as several databases from any

3a

Figure 3-1   A university library's home page

computer connected to the Internet. The library's home page, which is probably similar to the home page of your own college library, is reproduced in Figure 3-1 above.

To search for a book in the GSU Library, we simply typed in the title of one of our books, *Rhetoric Made Plain*. The response—almost immediate—is shown in Figure 3-2. It not only gives information about the book; it also displays the call number, the book's availability, and its location in the library. With this online service, a user can also search the Union Catalog, a database that contains information about the holdings of virtually every major college library in Georgia. And the system permits access to a variety of databases through the Galileo system (see 5c-1). Ask your librarian about the facilities available in your library.

Most libraries belong to a consortium of libraries linked through a network that allows access to the holdings of other members. If one college library doesn't have a particular title, you can most likely find it in the collection of another. If your library doesn't own a certain title, ask your librarian about the possibility of

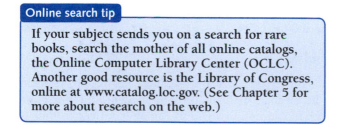

Georgia State University
Law - University Library

University Library General Collection books with Call Numbers PT-PZ and R-Z are now in storage. Please use the Request Form for retrieval.

New Search Heading Results Title Results Previous Search Request My Account GIL Universal Catalog GALILEO Preferences Book Bag Other Databases Other Libraries Help Exit

Institution Name: Georgia State University Libraries
Search Request: Keyword Relevance Search = +Rhetoric +Made +Plain
Search Results: Displaying 1 of 1 entries

◀ Previous   Next ▶

Brief Display   Full Display   More Like This   Technical Display

Relevance: ▌▌▌▐
Author: Winkler, Anthony C.
Title: Rhetoric made plain / Anthony C. Winkler, Jo Ray McCuen.
Edition: 4th ed.
Publisher: San Diego : Harcourt Brace Jovanovich, c1984.
Description: xv, 455 p. : ill. ; 24 cm.
Notes: "Select list of reference works": p. 273-286.
Subject(s): English language --Rhetoric.

Location: University Library General Collection
Call Number: PE1408 .W6197 1984
Univ Lib Request Form: For PT-PZ and R-Z GENL collection books, click here.
Univ Lib Request Form: For Non-Q bound periodicals, click here.
Number of Items 1
Status: Not Charged

◀ Previous   Next ▶

Record Options
Select Download Format Full Record ▾ Format for Print/Save
Enter your email address: Email
Save results for later: Save To Bookbag

New Search   Quick Search   Previous Searches   Request   GALILEO   Preferences   Bookbag   Expanded Search   Other Libraries   Help   Exit

GIL Record Error?
Use our GSU GIL Catalog Record Error Reporting Form.

Figure 3-2   The results of a database search

an interlibrary loan from a member of the consortium. Remember, however, that getting a book or periodical from another library may take several days, which could slow down your research project.

> **Online search tip**
>
> If your subject sends you on a search for rare books, search the mother of all online catalogs, the Online Computer Library Center (OCLC). Another good resource is the Library of Congress, online at www.catalog.loc.gov. (See Chapter 5 for more about research on the web.)

3a-2   Online full-text databases

The most useful databases offer the full text of an article or book rather than an index that sends you scurrying through the library. Different libraries subscribe to different databases, so your first order of business as a researcher is to find out which databases are available in your school library. Other databases available on the Internet without a subscription fee can be found by using any search engine.

(For more on search engines, see 5d.) Here are some useful databases found in most libraries:

1. *Oxford English Dictionary*
2. *Encyclopedia Britannica*
3. *American National Biography*
4. *The Grove Dictionary of Art Online*
5. *Routledge Encyclopedia of Philosophy*

3a

Some databases cover many years; others index only relatively recent information, generally over the past ten years. Databases also vary in scope of coverage: Full-text databases provide entire articles that can be printed out; others provide only abstracts—summaries of articles. Following are some popular full-text databases.

HighWire Press: Sponsored by Stanford University, HighWire Press (www.highwire.stanford.edu), contains many free journals in the life sciences, physical sciences, social sciences, and medicine.

Merlot: Multimedia Educational Research for Learning and Online Teaching: Merlot (www.merlot.org/merlot/index.htm) offers a selection of materials in thirteen "communities," subject areas ranging from biology to world languages, all free. A warning, though: the materials are not subject to peer review, so you should be wary of the information in them. (For more on how to evaluate an electronic source, see 5f.)

Project Gutenberg Electronic Public Library: Started by Michael Hart in 1971, Project Gutenberg (www.promo.net/pg) aims to make available online books that are in the public domain—meaning, as a rule of thumb, books published before 1923. The ambitious goal of the project was to have 10,000 books online by the end of 2001. At the close of that year, however, the system had 4,161 e-texts online—still a substantial number. New titles are expected to be added at the rate of 100 per month.

3a-3   Microform indexes

Online sources are gradually replacing the once-popular microform, a system that stored magazines and newspapers on a small single sheet of film (*microfiche*) or a roll of film (*microfilm*). In addition to an OPAC, some libraries continue to use microform indexes for both periodicals and their permanent book collections. Systems vary from one library to another. Most depend on microfilm readers that allow for a fast scan or a slow search. A microfiche storage system is also used to catalog articles published in major national newspapers. Either system (or both) may be available in your library. Ask the librarian.

3a-4   Stacks

The *stacks* are the shelves on which books and periodicals are stored in the library. The stacks can be *open* or *closed*. If the stacks are open, you may roam at will among the shelves and handle the books; if the stacks are closed, you must obtain books from a clerk by listing the title of each book, its author, and its call number on a request slip. Closed stacks are more common at larger libraries; in smaller libraries the stacks are often open.

3a-5   Reserve room or shelf

Encyclopedias, indexes, gazetteers, and other works that are ordinarily consulted for information rather than read from cover to cover are stored in the reference room or on the reference shelf. Usually large and unwieldy, these volumes are generally available for use only within the library; they cannot be checked out. Many are also available either online or on CD-ROM. If you need help, ask the reference librarian.

3a

3a-6   Main desk

The main desk functions as an information center as well as a checkout counter for books. Librarians and clerks stationed here are trained to help a researcher find material or track down difficult sources. Library personnel can be of invaluable assistance; if you are confused or lost, don't be afraid to ask them for help. Many libraries employ a full-time librarian to supervise the reference section and to help students find the right reference material.

> **Library tip**
>
> The reference librarian can be the researcher's best resource. This person usually has a wealth of information at hand and can be of invaluable help. Some libraries even offer a reference librarian's service over the telephone or via e-mail.

3a-7   Reserve desk

Reserve books are kept at the reserve desk. Books on reserve are available for use only in the library and only for a limited time, generally for an hour or two. Instructors often place on reserve any book or magazine essential to their lectures or courses. When the demand for a book exceeds the supply, the book often is placed in the reserve collection, which in many libraries is listed in a separate reserve catalog.

3a-8   Audiovisual room

Cassettes, tapes, music CDs, DVDs, picture slides, filmstrips, and other nonbook media are stored in an audiovisual room and generally indexed by whatever conventional filing system the library uses (see 3b-1 and 3b-3). The audiovisual librarian can help you locate this kind of material. Often the audiovisual room adjoins an equipment area where students can listen to tapes or watch a film. Some libraries, replete with extensive new audiovisual hardware, now call themselves *media centers* instead of *libraries*.

3a-9   Microform room

This is the room in which microfilm and microfiche are stored. But as we said, microform is an obsolete technology that is being gradually replaced.

3a-10   Newspaper racks

3a

Many libraries subscribe to major national and foreign newspapers. Current issues generally are displayed on long wooden clamps, known as *newspaper racks*, that hold and store the newspapers. Often the racks are surrounded by comfortable chairs in which you can sit and read. Typical newspapers found in these racks include the *New York Times, Washington Post, Los Angeles Times, Wall Street Journal, London Times, Manchester Guardian, Hindustan Times*, and even some newspapers written in foreign languages such as *Die Zeit* (German) or *Le Monde* (French). A useful Internet source for online newspapers is the Internet Public Library, available at www.ipl.org/reading/news. Figure 3-3 is a printout showing the impressive range of the library's collection.

Here are some guidelines for tracking down news sources not displayed on the library racks:

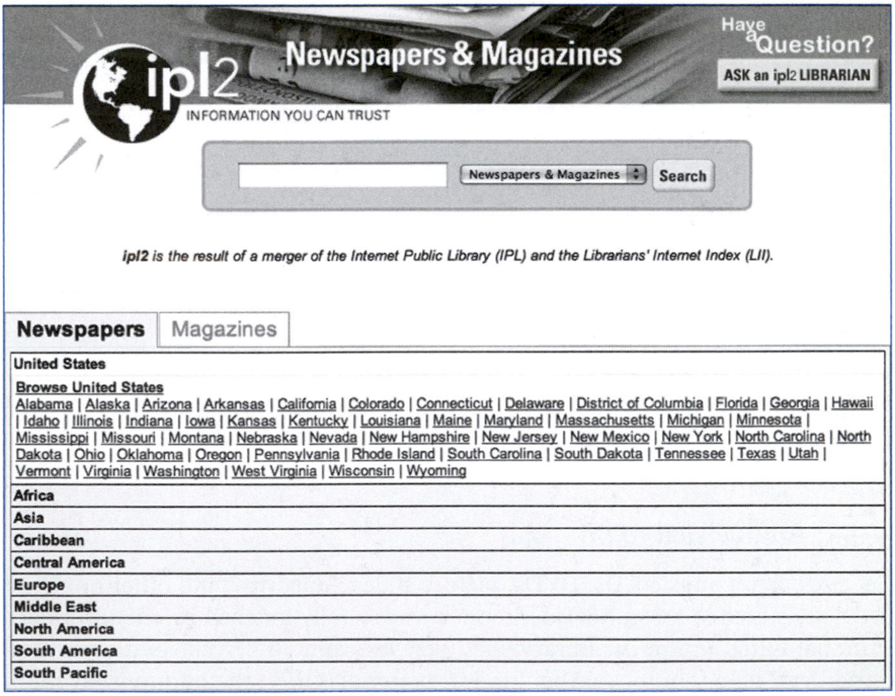

Figure 3-3   An online newspaper collection

1. Check www.newspapers.com. Use this source to find almost any newspaper in the United States.

2. Check CNN Interactive at www.cnn.com. This is an excellent source for information on current events.

3. Check the CQ Weekly at public.cq.com. Consult this source when you want to find out about congressional activities in Washington, D.C.

4. Check CSPAN Online at www.c-span.org. Use this source to find information about public affairs, government activities, and politics.

5. Check U.S. News Online at www.usnews.com. This site provides free in-depth essays or articles on current political issues.

Other online sources exist for individual newspapers to which your library might subscribe. Check with your librarian. For more on newspaper research, see 4c-1, 4h, and 5b-1.

3a-11 Computer room

Computer equipment is available in most libraries, either free or at a reasonable rental rate. Typically, software has been installed for word processing and Internet access. If your library has a computer room, ask your librarian about the policies for using the equipment: there may be a sign-up sheet and time limits per user, for example.

3a-12 Carrels

Carrels are small, semi-enclosed desks equipped with bookshelves and designed to provide students with a quiet, insulated nook for reading or researching. The carrel section of a library is set aside for students intent on serious scholarship. Some libraries even impose fines on students caught misusing this area. Carrels generally can be reserved by upper-class students for either a semester or an entire school year; the remaining carrels are distributed among lower-division students on a first-come, first-served basis.

3b Organization of the library collections

Even the great libraries of antiquity, like the ones in Nineveh in the sixth century B.C. and in Alexandria in the third century B.C., searched constantly for more efficient systems of organizing their collections. Clay tablets were grouped by subject and stored on shelves; papyrus rolls were stacked in labeled jars. Knowledge has grown so enormously, and classification systems have become so complex, that today librarians are trained extensively in classifying books. The two major classification systems now used by libraries are the Dewey Decimal System and the Library of Congress Classification System.

3b-1   The Dewey Decimal System

Devised in 1873 by Melvil Dewey and first put to use in the library of Amherst College, the Dewey Decimal System divides all knowledge (fiction and biography excepted) into ten general categories:

000–099	General Works
100–199	Philosophy and Psychology
200–299	Religion
300–399	Social Sciences
400–499	Language
500–599	Pure Science
600–699	Technology (Applied Sciences)
700–799	The Arts
800–899	Literature
900–999	History

Each of these ten general categories is subdivided into ten smaller divisions. For example, the category "Literature" (800–899) is divided further into these subcategories:

800–809	General Works (about literature)
810–819	American Literature
820–829	English Literature
830–839	German Literature
840–849	French Literature
850–859	Italian Literature
860–869	Spanish Literature
870–879	Latin Literature
880–889	Greek and Classical Literature
890–899	Literature of Other Languages

And the subcategory "English Literature," for example, is divided into ten even-narrower groups:

820	English Literature (general)
821	Poetry
822	Drama
823	Fiction
824	Essays
825	Speeches
826	Letters

827   Satire and Humor

828   Miscellany

829   Minor Related Literature

An endless number of more-specific headings are easily created through the addition of decimal places. For instance, from the category "English Drama" (822), the more specific heading "Elizabethan" is devised: 822.3. The addition of another decimal place creates an even more specific category for the works of Shakespeare: 822.33.

Fiction and biography are classified in a special way under the Dewey Decimal System. Fiction is marked with the letter F and biography with the letter B. Fiction is alphabetized by author, biography by subject. For example, "F-Pas" is the classification of a novel by Boris Pasternak; "B-C56" is one of the several biographies of Sir Winston Churchill.

The obvious advantage of the Dewey Decimal System is the ease with which it yields specific categories to accommodate the rapid proliferation of books. Probably for this reason, the system is currently used in more libraries throughout the world than are all other systems combined.

3b-2   The Cutter-Sanborn Author Marks

The Dewey Decimal System is generally used in conjunction with the Cutter-Sanborn Author Marks, devised originally by Charles Ammi Cutter and later merged with a similar system independently developed by Kate Sanborn. The Cutter-Sanborn Author Marks system distinguishes between books filed under an identical Dewey decimal number. In the early days of the Dewey system, books with the same Dewey decimal number were simply shelved alphabetically by author. But as more and more books were published, alphabetical shelving became impossibly difficult, leading eventually to the invention of the author marks.

The author marks enhance alphabetical shelving by assigning a number to every conceivable consonant-vowel or vowel-consonant combination that can be used to spell the beginning of an author's surname. These numbers are published in a table that alphabetically lists the various combinations and assigns each a number. For instance, the G section of the Cutter-Sanborn Table lists the following combinations and numbers:

Garf	231	Garn	234
Gari	232	Garnet	235
Garl	233	Garni	236

So, for example, to assign an author mark to the book *Double Taxation: A Treatise on the Subject of Double Taxation Relief,* by Charles Edward Garland, a librarian (1) looks up the combination of letters in the Cutter-Sanborn Table closest to the spelling of the author's surname—in this case "Garl," with the number 233; (2) places the first letter of the author's surname before the number; and (3) places after the number the first letter or letters of the first important word in the title. The author mark for this book is G233d. The call number of the book is its Dewey decimal number plus its author mark:

336.294

G233d

Similarly, the book *Religion and the Moral Life,* by Arthur Campbell Garnett, has a Dewey decimal number of 170 and an author mark of "G235r," giving the following call number:

170

G235r

Under this dual system, a book is shelved first by sequence of its Dewey decimal number and then by sequence of its author mark. To find any title, a student must first locate the Dewey decimal category on the shelf and then identify an individual book by its author mark.

3b-3   The Library of Congress Classification System

The Library of Congress Classification System is named for the library that invented it. Founded in 1800, the Library of Congress at first simply shelved its books by size. Its earliest catalog, issued in 1802, showed the United States as the owner of 964 books and 9 maps. By 1812, the nation's collection had increased to 3,076 books and 53 maps. By 1897, when the library finally acquired its own building, the collection had grown to half a million items and was increasing at the staggering rate of 100,000 items a year. The library had acquired such a vast collection that a new system was necessary for classifying it. Published in 1904, the Library of Congress Classification System has grown immensely in popularity and is now widely used, especially by larger libraries.

The system represents the main branches of knowledge with 21 letters of the alphabet. These branches are divided further by the addition of letters and Arabic numerals up to 9,999, allowing for a nearly infinite number of combinations. The system is therefore especially useful for libraries with enormous collections. Here is a list of the general categories:

A	General Works
B	Philosophy, Psychology, Religion
C	Auxiliary Sciences of History
D	History: General and Old World
E–F	History of America
G	Geography, Anthropology, Recreation
H	Social Sciences
J	Political Science
K	Law
L	Education
M	Music

N	Fine Arts
P	Language and Literature
Q	Science
R	Medicine
S	Agriculture
T	Technology
U	Military Science
V	Naval Science
Z	Bibliography, Library Science, Information Resources

These general categories are narrowed by the addition of letters. Numerous minute subdivisions are possible. "Language and Literature" (designated "P") is subdivided into other categories, among them the following:

P	Philology and Linguistics: General
PA	Greek and Latin Philology and Literature
PB	Celtic Languages and Literature
PC	Romance Languages (Italian, French, Spanish, and Portuguese)
PD	Germanic (Teutonic) Languages

The addition of numerals makes possible even more minute subdivisions within each letter category. From the general category "P"—"Language and Literature"—is derived the more specific category "Literary History and Collections," designated "PN." The call number "PN 6511" indicates works dealing with "Oriental Proverbs;" "PN 1993.5 U65," on the other hand, is the call number for a book about the history of motion pictures in Hollywood.

The classification under this system proceeds from the general to the specific, with longer numbers assigned to more-specialized books. Like the Dewey Decimal System, the Library of Congress system uses an author number to differentiate books shelved within a specific category. To locate a book with a Library of Congress classification, you must first find the subject category on the shelf and then track down the individual title by its author number. Two printed volumes titled *Library of Congress Subject Headings (LCSH)* are available in most libraries. These books use subject headings to group materials on the same or a similar topic under one term. You may find it helpful to look up your topic in the LCSH.

3b-4   Classification of periodicals

Periodicals and newspapers are classified differently from books. Current issues are usually shelved alphabetically by title and are accessible to the public. (Some libraries shelve current issues by call number.) Back issues, either bound in book form or reproduced on microfilm, are stored elsewhere—usually in a special section of the library to which the public may or may not be admitted, depending on whether the stacks are open or closed.

3b

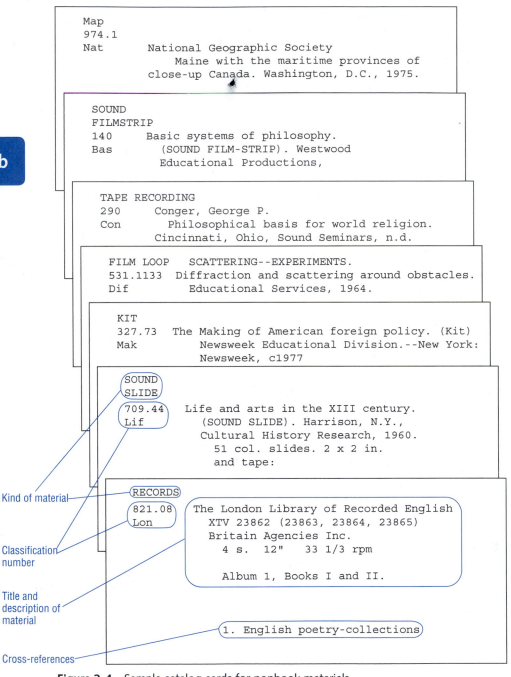

Map
974.1
Nat   National Geographic Society
               Maine with the maritime provinces of
           close-up Canada. Washington, D.C., 1975.

SOUND
FILMSTRIP
140   Basic systems of philosophy.
Bas   (SOUND FILM-STRIP). Westwood
             Educational Productions,

TAPE RECORDING
290   Conger, George P.
Con   Philosophical basis for world religion.
           Cincinnati, Ohio, Sound Seminars, n.d.

FILM LOOP   SCATTERING--EXPERIMENTS.
531.1133   Diffraction and scattering around obstacles.
Dif   Educational Services, 1964.

KIT
327.73   The Making of American foreign policy. (Kit)
Mak   Newsweek Educational Division.--New York:
           Newsweek, c1977

SOUND
SLIDE
709.44   Life and arts in the XIII century.
Lif   (SOUND SLIDE). Harrison, N.Y.,
           Cultural History Research, 1960.
             51 col. slides. 2 x 2 in.
             and tape:

RECORDS
821.08   The London Library of Recorded English
Lon   XTV 23862 (23863, 23864, 23865)
           Britain Agencies Inc.
             4 s.   12"   33 1/3 rpm

             Album 1, Books I and II.

           1. English poetry-collections

Kind of material

Classification number

Title and description of material

Cross-references

Figure 3-4   Sample catalog cards for nonbook materials

3b-5   Classification of nonbooks

Nonbook materials—films, microfilms, recordings, news clippings, sheet music, reproductions of masterpieces, transparencies, slides, programmed books, and other audiovisual material—may be listed either in the general catalog or as a special collection. No hard-and-fast rule exists for classifying this kind of material. Figure 3-4 on the previous page shows several examples. Ask your librarian how nonbooks are catalogued.

Most instructors consider the library to be students' most reliable guide to research papers that draw on the published work of experts. In fact, many instructors require that at least part of each research paper reflect the use of sources actually found in the library. Making you familiar with the local library is one aim of the research paper.

3b

Electricity changes cities into modern metropolises.

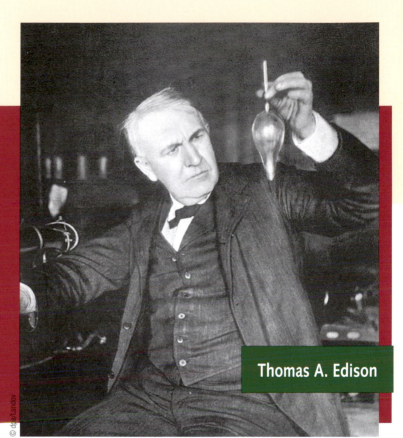

Thomas A. Edison

© dpa/Landov

Thomas Edison (1847–1931) has become America's best-known and most prolific inventor. During his lifetime, he patented over one thousand inventions, including the microphone and the phonograph. His most dramatic invention was the incandescent lamp with a carbon filament (1875), which later became the light bulb as we know it and quickly replaced candles or oil lamps. Along with the light bulb, he also invented a system for distributing light and power, including generators, motors, light sockets, underground conductors, and safety fuses. Although Edison had little formal education, he did enormous research on his inventions. Edison's laboratory and other buildings associated with his career have been reconstructed in Greenfield Village, Michigan, a historical park connected with the Henry Ford Museum.

4 Using the Computer in Your Research

4a Computers and the research paper

4b The Internet

4c Online resources

4d Researching with search engines

4e Usenet, Listserv, telnet, and gopher

4f Evaluating Internet sources

4g Running a search

4h Useful Internet sites

FAQ

1. How have computers changed the writing of research papers? *See 4a.*

2. Are the Internet and the World Wide Web the same thing? *See 4e.*

3. What are the three types of search engines? *See 4d-1.*

4. What is a database? *See 4c-1.*

5. What is a blog? *See 4c-4.*

6. What is a Listserv? *See 4e.*

7. How can I judge the merit of an Internet source? *See 4f.*

4a   Computers and the research paper

Most significant inventions in human history are credited to one or two people with whom their name is closely identified—Edison with the light bulb or Ford with the assembly line spring to mind as examples. But while the computer does have some ancestral history traceable back to the laboratory, no unanimity exists about its inventor. Some historians give credit to Scotsman John Napier (1550–1617), inventor of logarithms and of *Napier's bones*, a working abacus; some to Charles Babbage (1792–1871), the English inventor of the Difference Engine and the Analytical Engine; and still others to Blaise Pascal (1623–1662), French mathematician and inventor of the Pascaline, a mechanical calculator.

No matter what its origin, the computer is indispensable to the research paper writer because of its two strong points: its ability to work as a word processor; and its capacity to store vast quantities of information that is also instantly retrievable.

Most of us are familiar with the computer in its function as a word processor. Formatting the research paper—from footnoting to the bibliography—is done by word processing software. Because a computer can calculate far in advance of printing how much space is needed on every specific page, the writer does not have to count lines at the bottom of the page for footnotes nor manage the indentation of bibliographic entries.

In the bad old days, mistakes were often corrected by daubing a syrupy white fluid known as "liquid paper" over the typo and then typing the correction on top of the smudge giving the paper a untidy look. Nowadays mistakes are corrected on the screen of the computer and the finished product is handled by the printer. With the use of voice recognition software, such as Dragon NaturallySpeaking, the writer who is not a good typist can even dictate the paper to the computer.

The capacity of the computer for storing a vast quantity of instantly retrievable material has also made it useful to the researcher. With the emergence of the Internet and the widespread acceptance of search engines, the word "browsing" has taken on a whole new meaning. Through the magic of electronics, a researcher can now search the text of a thousand page book for any word or phrase and find it instantly. Five hundred clerks manually combing through a text at the same time could do no better.

The computer has also changed the process of research in other practical ways:

- In some quarters, computers have done away with note cards. Many students prefer to make notes on their laptops, where they can use the cut-and-paste function to easily and accurately transfer notes to the emerging paper. This procedure eliminates the possibility of error in transcribing handwritten notes from the cards onto the paper.

- In some schools, instructors prefer the submission of papers by e-mail to the traditional submission of hard copy. The upshot: You don't have to be physically present to turn in a paper; you can submit it from, say, a beach in Jamaica.

☐ The whole laborious business of research, of digging for primary and secondary sources, has been speeded up enormously by the use of computers and the easy access they offer to full-text databases.

4b   The Internet

The Internet, or net, is a planetary brain without a skull. It consists of untold millions of computers called hosts connected by a common protocol or way of "talking" that enables them to communicate. In the early days, computers were connected to a network through a modem and a telephone line. Today, much faster connections are available through a high-speed cable modem or a digital subscriber line (DSL). The introduction of Wi-Fi in 1997 added to the mix a wireless technology connecting computers worldwide. More and more businesses such as motels and restaurants offer free Wi-Fi connections to their patrons with laptops, fueling what is already a stupendous growth.

4b-1   The World Wide Web

Although the terms *Internet* and *World Wide Web* are often used interchangeably, they are not the same thing. The World Wide Web, or Web, is part of the Internet. Also part of the net are Usenet (a bulletin board for special-interest discussion groups), e-mail, and file transfer protocol (FTP). The web, as you will find out, uses a specialized vocabulary. But it is not one that you need to understand to use the web. For example, knowing that *http* is webspeak for *hypertext transfer protocol* or that *URL* refers to *uniform resource locator* and is technobabble for an address at the web, will not help you find essays on the work of American poet Charles Bukowski. But it might help you sound cool among a group of geeks.

Computers are idiot savants ("learned idiots"): They do exactly what you tell them to do. That means you must reproduce Internet addresses without the slightest deviation. A comma used in the wrong place will cause your search to fail. The better way to transcribe a web address is to copy and paste the URL—better still, to use a link. (A link is a reference to another site or document. It is sometimes called a hot link because clicking on the link will take you directly to the other document.)

4c   Online resources

The Internet is a treasure trove of data, facts, statistics, images, opinions, speculations, graphics, and viewpoints—everything that comes under the general heading of information. The best sources of this readily available material are databases, electronic journals, online public-access catalogs (OPACs), and blogs.

4c-1   Databases

A *database* is a collection of data organized and stored electronically for easy retrieval. Typically, databases are available through a fee-based membership, which for many students will be too costly, or, more commonly, through a local public or college library. One of the most attractive features of a database is that it can be searched in several ways, usually by keyword, author, or title. A popular database to which many libraries subscribe is InfoTrac® College Edition, which indexes an incalculable number of articles and titles.

Some states maintain vast databases that can be accessed with a password available at local libraries. One example is the Galileo system of Georgia (http://www.galileo.usg.edu/scholar/dekalb-pl/subjects/). The databases in the Galileo system are vast and varied. They include encyclopedias; business directories; government publications; thousands of magazines and scholarly journals that are fully indexed; the full text of many of these articles; dictionaries; corporate reports; and more. This digital library of Georgia is linked to library catalogs and even contains some full-text books—known as e-books. Galileo can also be accessed for information found in Spanish databases. Ask your librarian about the databases available in your library.

4c-2   Electronic journals

Electronic journals are serial publications that can be accessed by a computer through the Internet. Many libraries subscribe to electronic journals on a variety of disciplines and subjects. One website, the Directory of Open Access Journals (DOAJ, www.doaj.org) catalogs thousands of journals and alphabetized articles covering a wide range of topics.

Most of the material you use in a research paper will probably exist in a database. Many databases store the electronic equivalent of printed journals whose content has been subject to peer review and is therefore trustworthy. (Peer review means that the article has been gone over by a panel of experts in the author's field and judged publishable.) Some electronic journals, however, are strictly that: They have no print equivalent. Depending on who publishes them, they vary widely in trustworthiness and have to be individually evaluated. (For more on how to judge an electronic source, see 4f.)

4c-3   Online public-access catalogs (OPACs)

Many library catalogs are available on the web. Go to www.libdex.com, which takes you to LibDex, an index to 17,900 libraries worldwide. You can search for the catalog of a particular library by keyword or name.

Another useful public-access catalog is the Online Computer Library Center (OCLC), a nonprofit membership organization that includes many thousands of libraries in more than 76 countries. Its interlibrary loan service was introduced in 1979 and has since processed millions of requests from thousands of libraries worldwide. You can access this catalog through your school library, which most likely is a member, or through a public library that subscribes to the service. If you need a specialized publication that your library does not have, check the OCLC catalog. In many libraries this catalog is listed under the title "WorldCat." A free version of WorldCat can be found at www.worldcatlibraries.org. Although not as extensive as the subscribed catalog, it is still a good tool for the researcher, and it is free.

4c-4   Blogs and social networks

4c

Blogging and *tweeting* sound like words that belong in a sci-fi movie, not in a textbook describing two of the hottest trends lately to appear on the Net. Short for *weblog*—like the log of a ship's captain—a *blog* is a personal website maintained by an individual and reflecting its owner's point of view. Blogs may include images, text, and conversations. With their links to other websites, as well as the capacity to accommodate feedback from readers, blogs have been described as personal interactive diaries. The first blog appeared in 1997. Although blogs vary widely in focus, tone, and personality and make no bones about reflecting the subjective point of view of their owners, they have this in common: they multiply like houseflies. As of this writing, some estimates put the number of blogs at over 50 million.

Twitter is one of many social networking sites whose members are tied together by common interests, ideas, ambitions, or goals. You can post information or messages known as *tweets* on the site for other members to read. Since its debut in 2006, Twitter has averaged more than 55 million visits per month. With a text limit of 140 characters, Twitter asks one question, "What are you doing?" Users of Twitter reply in their own vocabulary. Twitter has the same function as did the old-fashioned message boards on which people would scribble personal messages. The difference is that now the message is accessible far more widely.

Social networks vary in their membership rules, some requiring newcomers to formally enroll with the submission of a brief biography, others asking for nothing more than an Internet name and identity. Since the site is a virtual one, the person on the other end of the keyboard with whom you are chatting could be anyone in any part of the world, your neighbor next door or someone a continent away. A surprising number of friendships have resulted in contacts initially made through social networks and later developed into face-to-face meetings that ended in other intimacies, including marriage. Many networks use the resources of such well-known sites as *MySpace*, which tells the world all about you; *Facebook*, which has a similar function; and *Twitter*, where you can start a discussion by posting an opinion to which other members react.

"Social networking" has taken on increased importance on the Internet. This new way of communicating—whose most important current sites are Facebook, MySpace, Twitter, and YouTube—has formed thousands of communities of souls who like each other's company to the exclusion of random Internet users. You may decide to open a Facebook or MySpace website, and then allow only chosen friends access to it. YouTube, which has become a mass medium for TV news videos, became successful because it was a platform for easily sharing video content

among intimate friends. As social networking expands to include a global audience, the jury is still out on whether usefulness will ever catch up with technology. In other words, a thousand years from now, will one be able to do more on
these sites than leave a note to one's spouse to call the plumber about the clogged
toilet on the moon cabin?

How is social networking related to your research paper writing? It shouldn't
be. Although television news is permeated by blogs, tweets, and YouTube reports
that help to identify crimes, revolutions, and natural disasters, networks are still
too much in flux and unsupervised to be of use in your research paper. Moreover,
blogging or tweeting is often a form of bad writing because bloggers or tweet-
ers rarely take the time to review or edit their postings; instead, they let their
thoughts flow like interior monologues. Just because you write on Twitter doesn't
mean you're free to write like a twit.

To sum up, information available on the Internet through databases, electronic journals, and blogs is easy to use and to retrieve. However, many instructors regard these sources as suspect because verifying their accuracy is difficult
and sometimes even impossible. Many instructors therefore limit the number of
electronic sources that can be cited in any one paper. The problem with Internet
sources is that many of them are not subjected to peer review but are simply adrift
on a tide of speculation. Some databases are impeccable sources, but others are
not. All researchers are advised to exercise caution in using electronic sources.

4d   Researching with search engines

A search engine is a program that searches the web for specific words related
to your topic. Search engines are supported by advertisers and cost nothing to
use. To search for a specific subject, type keywords into the search box of your
chosen search engine site and click on Search or Go. Articles (a, an, the) are not
keywords; neither are prepositions (of, in, to, for). And certain connectors—and,
or, not—have special meanings (see 4d-1). Most search engines—Yahoo!, Google,
and AltaVista, for example—are case insensitive. Entering keywords in upper- or
lowercase produces the same results. The results of the search, called hits, are
ranked by the frequency with which a keyword occurs in a document.

Search engines, in reply to your query or topic, will return the titles of the
essays, books, and other sources that deal with your topic. The hits will be highlighted, allowing you to click on them for more information. If the hit is a full-
length article stored in a database, clicking on the highlighted title will take you
right to the source. If it is simply the title of a book, you will be given enough
publication details to look up the volume in the library.

> **Research tip**
>
> Read the instructions for the search engine
> you're using.

4d-1   Finding a search engine

Basically, there are three types of search engines: manual, robotic, and metasearch. Yahoo! uses a manual search engine. It searches directories and subcategories that have been compiled by humans. Google, on the other hand, is a robotic search engine. At this writing it has indexed billions of pages, far more than its competitors. At its heart is a "spider," software designed to crawl the web and scan its untold number of pages. A metasearch engine searches and compiles the top listings of other search engines. MetaCrawler is an example of a metasearch engine. By default it searches a few other search engines—you can choose otherwise—among them Google, Yahoo! Search, MSN Search, Ask, About, and LookSmart.

For a comprehensive listing and rankings of search engines, go to Windweaver, www.windweaver.com/searchlinks.htm

Some search engines have a wide net and cover a broad range of topics. Others have a narrow focus and specialize in indexing literature and other material from a specific subject area, say, education. If you wish to see what is available in a particular subject area you've chosen to write about, use a search engine.

4e   Usenet, Listserv, telnet, and gopher

What most of us use on the Internet is really the World Wide Web. But the web is only one part of the Internet, although it is the most useful for the typical researcher. Other parts of the Internet are Usenet, electronic mailing lists, telnet, and gopher. These are older technologies that are being rapidly replaced by the more colorful and graphical web.

Usenet, created in 1979 by three graduate students from Duke, began as a series of electronic bulletin boards on which anyone could post a question or message and to which anyone else with a computer could reply. Eventually, separate bulletin boards—called discussion forums or newsgroups—evolved for separate topics.

Listserv and similar software manage the electronic mailing lists of discussion groups. Once you subscribe to a mailing list, every message posted on it is automatically sent by e-mail to you and all other subscribers. One such service likens itself to a call-in radio show on which exchanges are done entirely by e-mail. Individual lists are devoted to specific topics or hobbies; and, as is the case among Usenet discussion groups, some lists are moderated and others are not.

Telnet is a protocol for connecting computers on the Internet. Many large databases use telnet as an access system. Today many sites that were formerly restricted to telnet are now available on the web.

Gopher is an old-fashioned system of searching the Internet. Most gopher files are now accessible on the web. For student-researchers, these terms hold more historical value than practical value.

4f   Evaluating Internet sources

The Internet is a vast public library that has no librarian. No one monitors the accuracy of information posted on it. No one looks over others' shoulders to ensure that every contributor plays fair and tells the truth. It is possible for anyone with a peeve to post anything on the Internet and try to pass it off as fact. We found one website that claimed to be a global collection of national anthems, but had the words of several anthems wrong. In short, there are umpteen sources on the Internet whose content is suspect. Given its unsupervised nature, the unavoidable question is, How can you trust what you read on the Internet?

The answer is, sometimes you can't. When an Internet source is suspect, your best choice is to drop it from your bibliography. This may seem a drastic step to take, but it is better than to leave the reader wondering about the authenticity of your sources.

1. If you can't trace the source—whether primary or secondary—drop it from your list of references.

2. If your source is an outdated statistic that was found in an unlikely place, cut it.

3. Stick to sources with stable hyperlinks or URLs. An Internet source that has the moving record of a nomad is suspect.

4. Beware of sources identified with a <com> tag on the Internet. The com. tag tells practically nothing about a source.

Many formulas for evaluating sources are available. Most are based on common sense. Your scrutiny of a suspect source should be based on asking yourself the following questions about it.

4f-1   Where was the information found?

Some websites are maintained by hobbyists with an ax to grind; some by world-renowned universities; others by companies primarily interested in promoting their products. The trick is to learn how to tell the good Internet sites from the bad. The first step is to know who founded and maintains the site—information that is part of the site's domain name.

All Internet sites are classified by their domain names, which reflect who maintains them. Following are the most common domains:

Com	A commercial organization
Edu	An educational institution
Gov	A nonmilitary government agency or department
Mil	The military
Net	A network administrator
Org	A nonprofit organization (not educational or governmental)

A site maintained by the government or a reputable educational institution is likely to be more impartial and trustworthy than one privately developed by, say, an adoring fan. So, for example, the URL www.consumerreports.org, which is the address of Consumer Reports, tells you that the site is maintained by a nonprofit organization, in this case Consumers Union.

Of course, this is not to say that a site developed by a commercial organization or even an individual is necessarily a bad source of information. But knowing who is behind a site at least gives you a better idea of the likely quality of its information.

4f-2   Who wrote it?

The question of who wrote the material you are citing must also be factored into your assessment of the material's trustworthiness. Is the author identified? Are the author's credentials listed? Is the author qualified to write on the topic? You can verify the credentials and qualifications of an author by checking their biography sources either online or in the library.

The question of unknown authorship is one very good reason that many instructors will not allow *Wikipedia* to be cited as a source of authority, although it is very popular with students. Wikipedia bills itself as a free-authorship encyclopedia, which means that anyone can contribute to its content. In theory, this is a fine, democratic idea; in reality, this policy opens the door to nearly limitless abuse and a staggering potential for misinformation. For formal research, no writer would choose to stake a serious argument on such a suspect source. The words of the prophets might well be written on the subway walls, as the song goes; but in academia that idea is romantic twaddle that just doesn't cut it.

4f-3   Who publishes it?

Somewhere in most online magazines is a paragraph describing what they are about. If a magazine you're thinking of citing as a source declares that it was "founded to wage war against the small-mindedness of the establishment and the petty bureaucrats whose influence in society is vastly overdone," you would be smart to question its editorial evenhandedness. Such a combative statement should make you wonder whether the editors of the magazine have an ax to grind that would strongly bias their reporting.

4f-4   What are the writer's sources?

If a writer declares some incident is true without offering corroboration, the prudent researcher should ask, "Did it really happen?" In one online magazine we came across an article in which the writer described a woman who was being hounded by right-wing extremists. After investigating the writer's background, we were convinced that without corroboration, we could not take the story at face value.

4f-5   What tone does the writer use?

What we're looking for in a writer's tone is evidence of respect for the research process and for the opinions of others. We're especially wary of writers who express their views in a belligerent tone.

4f-6   What do the writer's contemporaries have to say?

The majority is not always right; in fact it often is wrong. History has taught us that lesson repeatedly. So don't reject material just because a writer has a unique point of view or takes an unpopular position that flies in the face of conventional wisdom.

But some writers stubbornly maintain positions that are wrong. For example, we came across an Internet source that painted a rosy picture of friendly relations between the Arawak and Carib Indians, the major tribes occupying the West Indies at the arrival of Christopher Columbus. Yet, according to most historians, the two tribes were constantly at war. Indeed the Caribs were known for eating their Arawak captives—a consuming relationship, yes, but hardly friendly.

One of the problems with Internet material is that much of it is not subject to peer review. As we pointed out in 4c-2, peer review is a healthy safeguard against wrongheaded ideas. It is almost universally practiced by reputable electronic journals, most of which are published or maintained by sites with ".edu" in their domain name. Seldom, however, is this useful filter applied to run-of-the-mill Internet sites. In the absence of peer review, you would be smart to question the accuracy of an electronic source.

4f

4f-7   What is the writer's motive?

A writer may hold a certain point of view or a particular opinion for motives that have nothing to do with research. Sometimes those motives are clear; at other times they are not. A writer who has been fired by a prominent magazine, for example, is hardly likely to be objective about his former employers. A whistleblower is not likely to draw rave reviews from the people he ratted on. Biographer Marchette Chute decided that she could not trust John Smith's story about being rescued by Pocahontas. When Smith published the tale, he was broke and down on his luck and hoping that the story of his sensational rescue would make his book a best-seller. Most historians agree with Chute that Smith's story of his rescue by Pocahontas is a myth.

Before you cite any source in a research paper, you should ask yourself whether the writer's content is dictated by some political or personal motives.

4f-8   What is the context of the writer's opinion?

Context refers to the environment in which an opinion is formed. Some subjects, mainly in the sciences and social sciences, are sensitive to context; others are not. The literary opinions of an eighteenth-century critic, for example, may seem old-fashioned to us but are not changed materially by the context of the twenty-first century. On the other hand, the fiery proclamations made by one side or the other about the Vietnam War while it was raging must be weighed in the context of the stormy times. Even a relatively recent subject can be context sensitive. For example, if you cite 1994 statistics on the life expectancy of AIDS patients, your data would be wrong. Between 1994 and 1999, deaths from AIDS in the United States declined by seventy percent because of the efficacy of new drugs.

The bottom line is this: Evaluating Internet sources is basically an exercise in editorial judgment. If you can't identify the writer of source material, or the writer's tone is angry, the material is suspect. That's sound advice, of course, whether the source is online or bound in gold leaf and roosting on your library shelf.

4g Running a search

When you're ready to begin a search, experiment with different ways of framing your search questions. The computer doesn't care if you ask a stupid question or an intelligent one. In the worst-case scenario, you're likely to get back the response, "No items found." But you're far more likely to get more hits than you can sort out than too few. For example, a student assigned a paper on "Fictional Protagonists with Psychological Problems" entered the entire title in Google and got back 13,300 hits.

Here is an example from an actual search. The student, a senior at a large metropolitan state university, was researching a paper on the anti-suffrage movement. Using IxQuick.com he entered "Women's anti-suffrage movement." He got twenty-five hits, ranked in order of relevance and almost all useful.

The student was drawn to one hit—a monograph by Susan E. Marshall titled *Splintered Sisterhood* (Madison: University of Wisconsin Press, 1997). A reading of the blurb showed the book covered his topic exactly. He printed out the description of the book and later learned it was available in his college library. Following a chain of links led him to a website, The Women's Suffrage Movement Project, which in turn linked him to positions of the anti suffragists. In a matter of seconds, he was well on his way to gathering sources maintained by sites with ".edu" in their domain name.

Next, he went to InfoTrac College Edition and typed in "Susan E. Marshall." The search returned two hits, one of which was a book review that cited two other books, *Women Against Women* by Jane Jerome Camhi (Brooklyn, NY: Carlson, 1994); and Thomas J. Jablonsky's *The Home, Heaven and Mother Party* (Brooklyn, NY: Carlson, 1994). So now he not only had the names of three authors and their works, he also had leads to other sources.

By now you should be getting the idea. After less than five minutes at the computer, our student had references to three books and numerous journal sources, some of which were available online in full text. All the student did was type women's antisuffrage movement into the search engine, which did all the legwork.

This example is subject to our cautions about material taken off the Internet (see 4f). But it clearly shows the amazing power of the computer as a research tool. The student had not even tapped into the databases of his local library, which would have been the logical next step. Your authors can remember the horse-and-buggy days, when after hours of slogging through a library's collection, they might turn up a pitiful one or two sources. Those were not the good old days. These are.

> **Documentation tip**
>
> Don't use any documenting format found on the Internet unless it's been approved by your instructor.

4h

4h   Useful Internet sites

Anyone who has ever surfed the net soon accumulates a list of favorite sites. The sites noted below should be particularly useful when you have to write a research paper. Bear in mind that the Internet is a volatile place, where the only constant is change. It's possible that some of these sites may have vanished by the time you read this book.

A useful site is the Bible concordance (word index) available through the University of Virginia's site, at *etext.virginia.edu/relig.browse.html*. On the site are versions of the Bible that can be accessed and searched electronically—a feature that is especially useful if you are doing research on a religious topic. Other online databases, some of which are open to the public, are also available from the University of Virginia at *etext.virginia.edu*

You'll find an electronic encyclopedia on the web at *www.encyclopedia.com*. The thousands of articles here make the site a handy reference for preliminary search, on a variety of topics. The Internet Public Library (*www.ipl.org*) is a useful site for any researcher and has many links to other sources of information and help. Remember, too, to use the search engine of your choice to find sources that can help you every step of the way in writing your research paper. For example, using IxQuick.com, we typed in "grammar help" and immediately turned up sixty-seven sites offering online help with common grammatical problems.

Another useful reference site is Refdesk (*www.refdesk.com*), an enormous collection of reference materials, with a comprehensive series of links leading to a variety of good sources. For example, its dictionary collection includes links to the venerable Oxford English Dictionary as well as to Merriam-Webster's website. Under one roof, you'll find almanacs, guides, and newspapers and a stewpot of services, from the atomic clock to a subject index of facts.

Finally, don't overlook the Internet for help in documenting the sources you cite in your paper. By typing "MLA" in the search box of Yahoo!, we were able to locate several sites that offered advice on documentation. Some of those sites were maintained privately; some were offered by junior colleges and other institutions. But all claimed to have up-to-date and accurate information on how to document sources. No doubt by the time this book reaches print, many more sites will be available just a telephone call and a few keystrokes away, thanks to the miracle of the computer.

4h

"Hello, Hello!" The telephone allows long-distance conversation.

Alexander Graham Bell

Always fascinated by sound and electricity, Alexander Graham Bell conceived of transmitting speech by electric waves and experimented endlessly with that notion. His first complete sentence by telephone, "Mr. Watson—Come here—I want to see you," spoken to his assistant, is now famous the world over. At the Philadelphia Centennial Exposition in 1876, the telephone was introduced to the world. After a long, complicated litigation about patent rights, in which Bell's claims were upheld by the U.S. Supreme Court, the Bell Telephone Company was formed and later separated into several companies that continue to operate today.

5 Doing the Research

5a   What information to look for

5b   Where to look for information

5c   Assembling a working bibliography

5d   Selecting your sources: Skimming

5e   Note-taking

5f   Plagiarism and how to avoid it

FAQ

1. Where can I start looking for information on my topic? *See 5b.*

2. What exactly is plagiarism? *See 5f.*

3. What are the three broad categories of sources? *See 5a.*

4. What is a general index? *See 5b-1.*

5. What is a specialized index? *See 5b-2.*

6. What is the difference between a working bibliography and a final bibliography? *See 5c.*

7. Where should I start my search if my paper is about a novel? *See 5.*

8. How can I get through a large number of references without reading every one of them? *See 5d.*

9. What are primary and secondary sources of evidence? *See 5d-1.*

10. How do I evaluate sources of evidence? *See 5d-2.*

11. How many notes should my paper have? *See 5e-1.*

12. What are the four kinds of notes? *See 5e-5.*

5a What information to look for

The sources you actually cite as supporting references in your paper typically consist of essays; book chapters; magazine, newspaper, or journal articles; treatises; pamphlets; and tape or disk transcriptions. These materials may be in printed, electronic, or photographic form. Exactly what kind of material you need to look for depends on the topic, thesis, and even the point of view you use in the paper.

In the beginning of your search, your aim is to find sources. By the end, you are arguing with some sources and agreeing with others, while evaluating them all for relevance and scholarly worth. Being able to tell the quality of one source from another is a sign that you have mastered your topic well enough to have formed your own opinions on it. But that stage comes later; for now, your task is to locate sources on your topic—which is why you are headed for the library.

Generally speaking, all sources can be grouped into three broad categories: single-fact information, general information, and in-depth information.

5a-1   Single-fact information

Single-fact information answers specific questions of fact: In what year was Osama bin Laden born? Who assassinated Julius Caesar? What percentage of students admitted to Harvard Medical School in 2005 were foreign born? How many cantons does Switzerland have? How did the early Ethiopians avoid malaria? What is a tsunami?

Answers to these and similar questions can be found in dictionaries, almanacs, encyclopedias, magazines, even telephone books. To get the answers to single-fact questions, you also can ask your reference librarian, who is highly trained in information management, storage, and retrieval. Many libraries even have a reference librarian available to answer queries over the telephone.

5a-2   General information

General information provides an overview of a subject or a particular topic. For example, if you were writing a paper on Zionism—the movement to create a Jewish national state in Palestine—the *Columbia Encyclopedia* would be a good source of general information to answer these broad questions: When did the movement start? What brought it about? Who were its leaders? Where does the movement stand today?

Encyclopedias and other general-information sources usually are found in a reference room or section in most college libraries. (For guidelines about how to select general-information sources, see 5d.) Some libraries subscribe to online encyclopedia databases that make the search for information even easier. Others have an encyclopedia available on CD-ROM.

5a-3   In-depth information

In-depth information is found in sources that cover a topic in detail. For example, *Admiral of the Ocean Sea* by naval historian Samuel Eliot Morison provides in-depth information about the voyages, life, and times of Christopher Columbus. *The Soul of a New Machine* by Tracy Kidder gives an in-depth look at the process of building a new computer system. In-depth information is mainly found in books because many topics are too complex to be detailed in any other form. But essays and articles can also be useful sources of in-depth information, especially about new or particularly focused topics. Use a search engine to find relevant material on your research paper topic.

Research papers typically blend all three kinds of information—single-fact, general, and in-depth—the proportion of each varying with the nature and complexity of a particular topic. The facts you need to back up what you're contending will not line up neatly in formation and come marching to your attention like bullied sheep. Almost at any stage, it is likely that you'll be trying to find everything from single-fact information to general information to in-depth information. Research, particularly at the beginning of a paper, can be chaotic. The problem is, at this early stage, you're not sure what information you need. Perhaps you haven't even arrived at the final wording of your thesis. Don't despair. Fumbling around in the early stages of writing is a necessary part of the learning process.

5b   Where to look for information

The more libraries become electronic, the more they begin to seem alike. Today, even modest country libraries will have various online databases available to help the researcher. (See Chapter 4 for information on how to do electronic searches.) We suggest the following steps as you begin your search for information:

- ☐ Ask your librarian about online databases that might help you find information about your possible topic. Using the experts in your library to help you with your research is a smart move.

- ☐ Look up your topic in an online encyclopedia. Many encyclopedia articles, in addition to being good sources of information, will often suggest related subheadings worth exploring.

> **Research tip**
>
> Try *Encarta*, an encyclopedia available in many libraries on CD-ROM. It offers many useful links to the World Wide Web.

- ☐ At the risk of being overwhelmed, you could check the Library of Congress's online catalog for books on your subject at www.catalog.loc.gov.

☐ Consult Appendix B of this book for an annotated listing of useful reference sources.

☐ Run a search of your topic in one of the search engines recommended in Chapter 5 (see 5d-4). Google (www.google.com) is a good beginning. All you do is type a name or subject into the search engine's window, then sit back and see how much information pops up.

☐ Check the bibliography at the end of encyclopedia articles.

☐ Search the computerized library catalog under the subject heading as well as any suggested cross-listings. (See 3a-1 for how to use library catalogs.)

☐ Check *Book Review Digest* for summaries of reviewed books. This reference is often available online through a commercial database.

☐ For definitions of technical or controversial terms, check a standard dictionary, or go to www.dictionary.com. You can also use a search engine to find other online dictionaries.

☐ Check *Who's Who* for information about noteworthy people. This resource often is available on a database.

☐ For information about countries and other places, consult gazetteers and atlases.

5b

In addition to the library catalog and general references—encyclopedias, for example—the various indexes to published information are useful sources to consult at the beginning of your research. Basically the indexes are classified under two broad headings: general and specialized. In many libraries, these indexes are available on CD-ROM or from other computerized sources.

5b-1   General indexes

A general index catalogs information published in magazines, newspapers, and journals. Up-to-date information on a subject can be found in recently published magazines like *Time, Newsweek, U.S. News and World Report, National Geographic, Harper's, Psychology Today,* and *Ebony;* newspapers like the *New York Times,* the *Washington Post,* the *Wall Street Journal,* and the *Atlanta Constitution;* and journals like the *Kenyon Review, Scientific American,* and the *Quarterly Review of Biology.* Magazines and newspapers typically cover topical subjects; journals have a narrower, more specialized focus. Articles in these publications are indexed in either bound general indexes or computerized databases. Some of these indexes not only list the published article but also provide an abstract or summary of it; a few databases actually provide the full text.

The trend nowadays is for general indexes to be stored and presented electronically through a database. Indexes so arranged are easier to access, to say nothing of quicker, than indexes presented in bound volumes. A case in point is *The Readers' Guide to Periodical Literature.* Bound volumes of this index are virtually unavailable, with most libraries switching to the easier-to-manage electronic version. Figure 5-1 on the next page is a representation of a typical

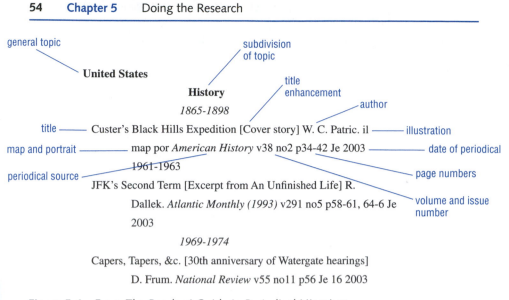

general topic

subdivision
of topic

United States

History

title
enhancement

author

1865-1898

title —— Custer's Black Hills Expedition [Cover story] W. C. Patric. il —— illustration

map and portrait ———— map por *American History* v38 no2 p34-42 Je 2003 ———— date of periodical

periodical source 1961-1963

page numbers

JFK's Second Term [Excerpt from An Unfinished Life] R.

Dallek. *Atlantic Monthly (1993)* v291 no5 p58-61, 64-6 Je

volume and issue
number

2003

1969-1974

Capers, Tapers, &c. [30th anniversary of Watergate hearings]

D. Frum. *National Review* v55 no11 p56 Je 16 2003

Figure 5-1   From *The Readers' Guide to Periodical Literature*

electronic entry from the *Readers' Guide*. We have added our editorial annotations as explanations of the different entry elements. Ask your librarian whether or not the library subscribes to a database that contains this index.

Many online databases, however, index only recently published material. The *Readers' Guide,* for example, goes back to 1983 for selective publications. To conduct research on topics before 1983 will require consulting the bound volume, if you can find it. Some database indexes, such as the Galileo system, are developed and maintained by a state government for use by residents of the state. Other such systems no doubt exist in other states. You should always ask your research librarian about the databases to which your local library subscribes.

Magazine Index catalogs articles from twice as many magazines as the *Readers' Guide,* but its listings begin only in 1976. A current version lists articles for just the last five years. Articles are arranged by both subject and author.

Indexes to newspapers are invaluable for tracking down news articles about a subject. Usually an index gives the exact location of each article, an indication of its length, and a brief summary of the content. Articles are listed by subject. Figure 5-2 is a sample entry from the *New York Times Index.* The complete back file of the *New York Times* can be accessed by a Google search for "New York Times Article Archives." These archives contain over three million articles. Figure 5-3 is a sample listing from a newspaper database.

5b-2   Specialized indexes

Specialized indexes catalog information on specific subjects. For example, the *Social Sciences Index* is a useful source for articles in the social sciences; for material on the humanities or education, the *Humanities Index* and the *Education Index*

ProQuest

| Basic | Advanced | Topics | Publications | My Research 0 marked items |

Databases selected: ProQuest Newspapers

Results – powered by ProQuest® Smart Search

Narrow your results by: Topic   About

Corrections
Republican Party (company/org)
Iraq War-2003
Ratings & rankings

Presidential electic
Tournaments & ch
Settlements & dan
Financial performa

1-8 of 56 (sorted by number of documents)

230 documents found for: *New York Times; Late Edition (East Coast); New York, N.Y., Apr 12, 2007* » **Refine Search** | **Se**

Mark all   0 marked items: Email / Cite / Export

1. **$101 Million Payout in '03 Parking Deck Collapse**
New York Times (Late Edition (East Coast)). New York, N.Y.: Apr 12, 2007. ; p. B.3

Full text   Abstract

2. **2 Bombs Set by Unit of Al Qaeda Kill 23 in Algeria**
Craig S. Smith, Said Chitour contributed reporting from Algiers.. **New York Times (Late Edition (East Coast)).**

Full text   Abstract

3. **4 Women in Assault Case Say They Acted in Defense**
Anemona Hartocollis. **New York Times (Late Edition (East Coast)).** New York, N.Y.: Apr 12, 2007. ; p. B.3

Full text   Abstract

4. **4 Years On, the Gap Between Iraq Policy and Practice Is Wide; [News Analysis]**
David e. Sanger. **New York Times (Late Edition (East Coast)).** New York, N.Y.: Apr 12, 2007. ; p. A.12

Full text   Abstract

5. **A Bad Choice, a Quick Exit; [Editorial]**
New York Times (Late Edition (East Coast)). New York, N.Y.: Apr 12, 2007. ; p. A.20

Full text   Abstract

6. **A Better Wi-Fi Not Quite Up To Its Promises**
David Pogue. **New York Times (Late Edition (East Coast)).** New York, N.Y.: Apr 12, 2007. ; p. C.1

Full text   Abstract

7. **A Compact Cellphone With a Full Bag of Tricks**
John Biggs. **New York Times (Late Edition (East Coast)).** New York, N.Y.: Apr 12, 2007. ; p. C.8

Full text   Abstract

8. **A Line Divides Art and Life. Erase It at Your Own Risk.; [Review]**
Richard Eder. **New York Times (Late Edition (East Coast)).** New York, N.Y.: Apr 12, 2007. ; p. E.6

Full text   Abstract

9. **A Music Device That Can Play, Oh, 2 Million Songs or So**
Stephen C. Miller. **New York Times (Late Edition (East Coast)).** New York, N.Y.: Apr 12, 2007. ; p. C.8

Full text   Abstract

Figure 5-2   From the *New York Times Index*

5b

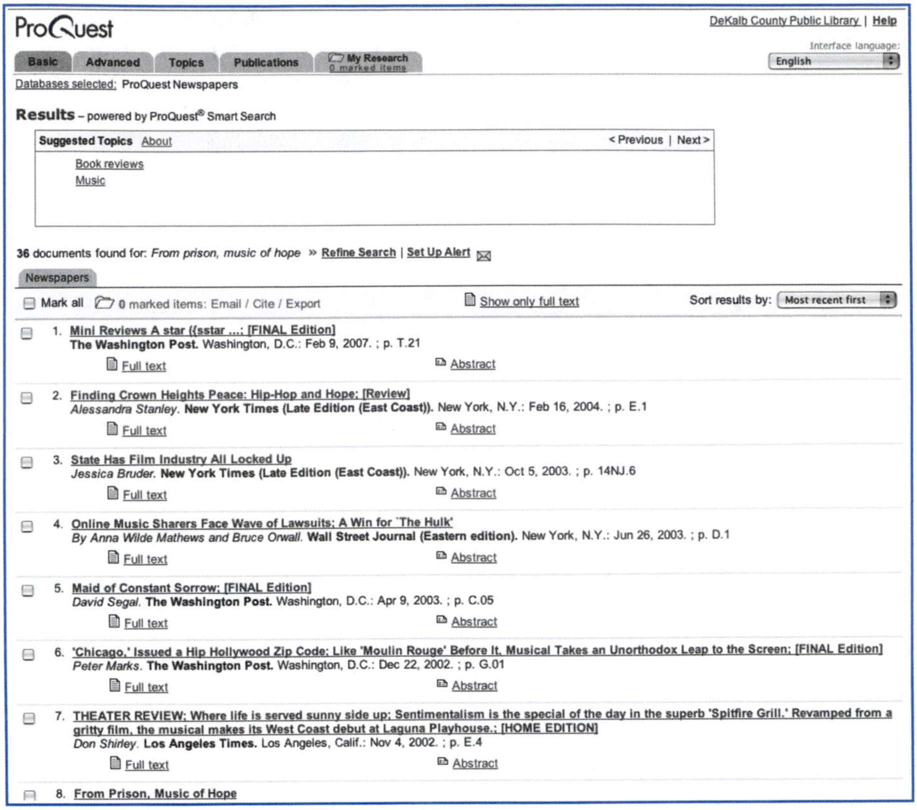

Figure 5-3   Search results from a newspaper database. Image published with permission of ProQuest-CSA LLC. © 2007, ProQuest-CSA LLC; all rights reserved. Further reproduction is prohibited without permission.

are good choices. Other specialized indexes are listed in Appendix B. Ask your librarian to direct you to the index most appropriate to your subject and to help you interpret its listings.

> **Research tip**
>
> To find an index that specializes in your subject, enter *index to [name of subject]* on the World Wide Web window or in a search engine.

Choosing the right index takes editorial judgment. If you are researching, say, the political influences on art, you could consult *Art Index,* which is available online in some databases. *Art Abstracts* is another useful online index on the subject. For a paper on child abuse, you might consult *Psychological*

Abstracts, which is likewise available online through your local library. The *Social Sciences Citation Index* is an excellent source of information on any social science topic, such as, say, the Kurd population in Iraq. When available online, these and similar indexes allow keyword searches that can, in a blink, uncover a host of material on any topic. If an index comes in old-fashioned technology, otherwise known as a *book,* its topics are typically alphabetically arranged. But before you begin the plodding, you'd be smart to ask your librarian if there is an electronic equivalent.

5b-3 Using interviews and surveys

Most of the information you use in your papers will come from books or periodicals. But these are not the only sources of information. Interviews with some of the many experts found on campus can be another important source of information on virtually every topic. Many students overlook this important source. But it's a fact that one geology professor is worth at least his or her weight in books and often can refer you to other sources (books, journals, and magazines) that you might have overlooked.

If you do decide to use interviews in your paper, be sure you consult only experts in the field of your topic. An *expert* is someone who is acknowledged as an authority in a particular subject or who has had a unique experience with it. An example of the second kind of expert is the survivor of an airliner crash. If you're writing a paper about airline safety, the experience of an actual crash survivor can be used to add personal testimonial evidence to your thesis. Naturally, before you quote an expert, you have to establish his or her credentials. Doing so, however, can be touchy. The trick is to determine an expert's credentials without appearing to subject him or her to a third degree. One way to do that is to ask the expert for a *curriculum vitae*—the academic equivalent of a résumé. Then you can copy the credentials you need to establish the expert's legitimacy.

A survey can also add another dimension to your paper, especially if you're writing about a topic in psychology or the social sciences. If you were doing a paper on the effect of deregulation on the price of natural gas in your community, surveying homeowners about what they're paying for gas under the new system could be very useful. Admittedly, not all papers can benefit from a survey. If you think your particular subject can, be sure to get your instructor's approval before you go to the trouble of making the survey.

5b-4 Corresponding by e-mail

E-mailing an expert and asking the right questions is an efficient way of getting information. In your e-mail, be sure to identify yourself and your research project, and to ask specific, pointed questions so that the expert knows what you're getting at and can answer quickly. Most teachers or other experts in a field are willing to help students who seem serious and diligent. Here is a sample e-mail to a student's church minister:

5b

Dear Reverend Osborne: I am a freshman student at Butte Community College and am writing a paper on the success of church members who have joined one of the Maranatha projects to build churches in third-world countries. Since I know that you have sponsored several such projects, I would like to ask you some questions that would help my research:

- What motivates most students to join Maranatha?
- How much time is involved in a typical building project?
- Who pays for the student's trip to the target area?
- What are the students' general responses after finishing a project? (Did they find it worth the effort? Were they inspired to continue to be altruistic, or did they burn out?)

Please accept my sincere appreciation for your time.

Sincerely,

Gabriella Lopez

Gabriella Lopez

5b-5   Attending lectures, concerts, or art exhibits

A famous lecturer, artist, or musician passing through your campus or town may be used as a unique citation on your chosen topic. Such visits are usually announced in the local newspaper. For instance, if you are writing a paper on the lyrics of contemporary country music, and Tim McGraw is giving a concert in a nearby city, you might want to attend this performance and take careful notes about the themes and stories in the singer's repertoire. If the visitor is a lecturer, try to get a CD or hard copy of the lecture that you can cite. For an art exhibit, take notes on what you see and, if available, obtain a brochure about the artist. Whatever you do, don't forget to make a bibliographic card linked to your notes so you can make an accurate citation of the source when you write the paper.

5c   Assembling a working bibliography

The *bibliography* is a list of sources on the research topic. The *working bibliography* is made up of those sources that you consulted for information; the *final bibliography* is an alphabetical list of the sources you actually used in the paper.

You assemble the working bibliography as you scan the reference material for information on the subject. Jot down promising sources on 3 × 5 cards—we

Location of source

Library call number

947.08

P

College library

Pares, Bernard.

The Fall of the Russian Monarchy.

New York : Knopf, 1939.

Bibliographic entry

Annotation stating why source may be useful

Chapter 5 deals with Rasputin's rise in Russian politics and the ministers' reaction to him. Chapter 13 is a description of Rasputin's murder by Yusupov and conspirators.

Figure 5-4   Sample bibliography card

5c

call them *bibliography cards.* The cards should contain information about possible sources along with a brief note about why they are likely to be useful (Figure 5-4).

Some instructors don't require that cards be used to create a working bibliography; they simply want students to have one, however it's compiled. Others insist that cards be used in the form described here.

Even though your inclination may be to compile your bibliographic references using a laptop computer, photocopier, material downloaded from the web, or a combination of those, there are persuasive reasons for using old-fashioned bibliography cards. The first is that you know exactly where your bibliographic references are located. Second, you can shuffle the cards to put your citations in any order you like. (Try shuffling a laptop entry with a photocopied source.) Third, you're less likely to lose citations stored on cards than splattered in a scattershot fashion here and there. The bibliography card system may be ancient, but its ease of use and convenience actually make the note-taking phase of your research easy to do. (See 5e-4 for how to take notes.) If you have a choice, use the bibliography cards.

Each source actually used will be recorded on two kinds of cards: the title on the smaller bibliography card; notes from the source on the larger note card—either handwritten or pasted up from your computer notes. A source you check but don't use will appear only on the working bibliography card. After you decide not to use a source, you can place its card in the inactive pack.

The process is simple:

- ☐ Record each source in ink on a separate 3 × 5 card.
- ☐ Use the same format on the bibliography cards that you will use later in the final bibliography. If you do that, you can prepare the final bibliography by

simply copying from the cards the titles you actually use. List the following basic information on each card:

Name of author(s)

Title of work

Facts of publication

Page(s) of information

☐ In the upper right-hand corner of the card, write the name of the library or place where you found the source—for example, "Main city library," "County Museum," or "Uncle Jim's library."

☐ In the upper left-hand corner of the card, cite the library call number of the source, so that you can find it easily even if it's been reshelved. If you are using an electronic source, make accurate note of the full URL (Internet address).

Generally, you will end up with many more sources in the working bibliography than are listed in the final bibliography. This is as it should be. Many sources are consulted, but few chosen. False starts and dead ends are to be expected. Books will lure you in with a promising title and table of contents, but once skimmed will prove to be too technical, dated, or beside the point. As a researcher, you must ignore irrelevant sources, tracking down only those articles, essays, and books that promise to be useful.

5d   Selecting your sources: Skimming

Seldom will you have the time to read every book or article written about your subject. Instead you'll do what the experienced researcher does—skim a source to determine its usefulness. If an initial skimming indicates that the source is helpful and to the point, you can read it carefully later. If the source appears to be dated, irrelevant, or otherwise useless, then you should set it aside and follow more promising leads. But don't destroy the bibliography card of the discarded source: you may change your mind and want to return to it later.

Skimming, like most skills, improves with practice. Here are some hints on how to skim a piece of writing for major ideas:

☐ In a book, glance at the preface. That's where the author usually states what the book is about. Likewise, the afterword often recounts the author's major ideas.

☐ Look up your research subject in the index of the book. Frequently you can tell from the number of pages devoted to the subject whether or not the book is likely to be useful. For instance, if you are looking in an English history book for information on Jack Sheppard, the eighteenth-century criminal, and see from its index that it contains only one page about him, you probably should move on to another source.

☐ Read the chapter headings. Often they reveal what each chapter is about. Subheadings also can tell you a lot about the major ideas in a book.

☐ Read the first and last two sentences in a paragraph to find out what information it contains. Generally the main idea of a paragraph is stated in its initial sentences and summed up in its final sentences.

☐ Glance at the opening paragraph of an article, essay, or book chapter. Often the author's thesis is stated in the first paragraph or two.

> **Source tip**
>
> The thesis of an article is often listed in a sub-heading under the title.

☐ Glance at concluding paragraphs in an article, essay, or book chapter. Often these final paragraphs sum up the discussion and restate major ideas.

☐ Run your eye down the page, reading every fourth or fifth sentence, to get a fair idea of what the material is about.

5d

5d-1   Primary and secondary sources

The judgments or conclusions in your paper must be backed by supporting evidence, which consists mainly of two kinds: *primary* and *secondary sources*. *Primary sources* are original writings by an author, documents, artifacts, laboratory experiments, or other data that provide firsthand information. A literary paper about an author might quote letters, memoirs, an autobiography, novels, short stories, plays, and personal notes by the author as primary sources of evidence.

Secondary sources are writings, speeches, and other documents *about* a primary source. The opinions of critics are important secondary sources. An experiment is a primary source; commentary on it by others is a secondary source. Making a picky distinction between these two is not necessary. It is only necessary to know that your papers should consist of both kinds of evidence.

5d-2   Evaluating sources

All sources are not created equal. They vary in quality of scholarship, force of argument, and accuracy of detail. Some sources are scholarly, useful, and accurate; others are worthless, silly, and misleading.

For example, a student writing a paper on human evolution would be grievously mistaken in taking the fossil remains of the Piltdown Man to be the missing link—no matter how many library sources say so. In a brief burst of glory, the Piltdown Man was hailed as the missing link in human evolution. Many articles and books in the library still make this claim, though their authors would now dearly love to retract them, because the Piltdown Man has been exposed as a hoax. Although anthropologists know all about the Piltdown Man's checkered career, a student-researcher might not. All fields are littered with errors preserved in the collections of libraries. Yet the student-researcher, who is often a novice in the subject, must discriminate between error and truth in the writings of experts, which is tricky but not impossible.

Fortunately, there are some commonsense ways of evaluating sources of evidence:

5d

☐ *Choose sources that cover your particular subject in depth.* For instance, if you were writing a paper on John Quincy Adams's presidential achievements in opposing slavery, a journal article on Adams's mission to Russia from 1781 to 1783 would be of little use because it is beside the point. But a helpful source would be Adams's own diaries or one of the definitive biographies about him that discuss his attitude toward slavery. In other words, choose only material that hits the proverbial nail on the head of your topic, ignoring any material that merely comes close.

☐ *Recognize the point of view in sources.* An article titled, "How Marriage Counseling Can Undermine Already-Fragile Relationships" obviously does not have the same point of view as one titled, "Active Listening Has Become a Successful Tool in Marriage Counseling." The first is against marriage counseling; the second seems to favor it. Often the title and opening paragraph of a work immediately reveal the writer's point of view, which may or may not coincide with your own.

☐ *Verify one opinion against another.* No one who has conscientiously researched the literature on human fossils would be duped by the early claims on behalf of the Piltdown Man, because those claims have been thoroughly discredited in later writings. In any given field, authors often comment on the work of their peers. The diligent researcher soon sees a consensus of opinion among experts that can be used to judge the reputation of an author or source.

☐ *Note the date of the evidence.* In certain fields of knowledge—particularly the natural and social sciences—conclusions change rapidly. In researching any topic, therefore, you should attach the greatest importance to the most recent data. Even traditional subjects, such as drug abuse or weight control, require that you use the most recent publications or electronic sources. If two sources differ only in date, cite the later one as your authority. Moreover, be aware that journals, although more difficult to read than magazines, usually contain more accurate and up-to-date sources. Magazines tend to be more general; journals more specialized.

☐ *Exercise your editorial judgment.* Try to evaluate the logic and likely authenticity of any source you intend to use. For example, if you are doing a paper on the possible existence of UFOs, you can and should analyze the testimony of alleged eyewitnesses. Common sense and keen attention to detail are the chief requirements for evaluating this kind, as well as many other kinds, of evidence. You need to train yourself to see contradictions, ironies, or out-and-out errors in the presentation of an argument.

☐ *Check your evaluations against those of professionals.* For example, the opinions of literary critics can give you an idea of how experienced readers respond to a certain novel. *The Book Review Digest* is a good source for critical opinions on books. You also can check the credentials of an author or expert in any of the various biographical dictionaries or *Who's Who* to judge how much weight to give his or her evaluation.

☐ *Beware of statistics.* You should question the credibility of any source that cites statistics. Exaggerated numbers are often tossed carelessly around in arguments and debates. To assert that "millions of minority youths walk the streets of Atlanta, unemployed" is to be figurative rather than factual. Be particularly wary of alleged numbers and statistics from which conclusions are drawn. Here are reliable references to find or check statistics:

TO FIND	CHECK THIS SOURCE
General statistics	*World Almanac; Current Index to Statistics (electronic)*
Statistics about the United States	*Statistical Abstract of the United States,* with links to prior years and a historical edition (electronic)
World statistics	United Nations *Demographic Yearbook; UNESCO Statistical Yearbook* (electronic)
Public opinion polls	Gallup Poll (electronic); *Public Opinion Online* (electronic)
Census statistics	U.S. Census Bureau website (electronic)

5e Note-taking

Eventually the information you've uncovered through research must be turned into notes. Many students nowadays use computers to organize and save notes for later editing and incorporation into a rough draft, but dinosaurs that we are, we still recommend 4 × 6 note cards, which can be added to, deleted, or reshuffled during the initial drafting. Bear in mind, as you read and take notes, that a research paper should contain a variety of material taken from different sources. It is not enough to write down your own ideas and speculations, ignoring everyone else's opinions on the subject. Your own ideas should be derived from information uncovered on the subject through research, and a reader should be made aware not only of your conclusions but also of your evidence and reasoning.

☐ Use 4 × 6 cards for note-taking. Large enough to accommodate fairly long notes, 4 × 6 cards are also unlikely to be confused with the smaller bibliography cards.

☐ Write in ink rather than pencil so that the cards can be shuffled without blurring the notes.

☐ Write down only one idea or quotation on each card. Cards with only a single note can be put in any sequence simply by shuffling. If a note is so long that two cards have to be used, staple them together.

☐ Identify the source of the note in the upper left-hand corner of the card. Because the bibliography card already lists complete information on the source, use only the author's last name or keywords from the title followed by a page number. For example, use "Fülöp-Miller 10," or "Holy Devil 10," to identify a note taken from page 10 of *Rasputin, the Holy Devil* by René Fülöp-Miller.

☐ Jot down in the upper right-hand corner of the card a general heading for the information the card contains. These headings make it easy to organize the notes by shuffling the cards. (Write the heading in pencil so that it can be changed.)

5e-1   Using the computer to take notes

For note-taking, some students prefer to use their laptops instead of cards. If that's okay with your instructor, then by all means go ahead. You can use two approaches: (1) You can download material and print it out, highlighting the passages you find particularly useful. (2) You can keep electronic sources in your computer, organizing them by folders and files, and later use the copy-and-paste function to transfer quotations into your rough draft. Some neatnik students like this system because it spares them from having cards scattered all over their desks, with the attendant risk of losing some.

Using your computer to take notes is especially handy for filing your ideas by the major entries of your outline. For instance, if a research paper on civil disobedience covers famous writers who favored that tactic, you might create a folder titled, "Pro–Civil Disobedience." Within that general folder, you could nest individual files about writers like Plato, Henry David Thoreau, Walter Lippmann, and Martin Luther King, Jr., who all advocated civil disobedience under certain circumstances. But for this system to work, you had better be prepared to organize carefully.

If you do use your computer for note-taking, we recommend that you devise some sort of labeling system to keep strict track of your notes and where you found them. One simple thing you can do is number each note sequentially. Another is to insert beside the note more or less the same information that you would have scribbled on a note card. After the note, or before if you prefer, type in parentheses either the complete name of the source or enough key words from its title to identify it. After the title of the source, put the relevant page number— where in the book or article or other source the material appears. Because you have a bibliography card on every source you do use, you don't need to have the complete reference listed here. But, if you don't use bibliography cards, then you might as well identify the source of each note with a complete bibliographic citation. If you do that, you save yourself having to retype the citation later. All you have to do is copy and paste the note into the bibliography.

5e-2   Using a copy machine to take notes

Many students nowadays don't use note cards at all, preferring to simply photo-copy pages from books or magazines. The popularity of this latest note-taking system is easily seen in the long lines at the library copy machines. Copying no doubt is easier than laboriously scribbling down information about a book or a quotation from one, but in some ways it is also more confusing and harder than using note cards. Most students who prefer copying to using note cards do not use bibliography cards unless an instructor requires them. Many instructors, in fact, do; but a few instructors do not, which means that if you do not carefully note from where you copied a source, you are likely to end up with an orphaned page.

Yet it's easy to see why some students prefer copying to note-taking. On the face of it, copying is easier. You simply place the page on the copy machine plate, insert a coin, press a button—and you have your source. Photocopying seems a painless alternative to scribbling down notes on a card. Better yet, if you own a text scanner or have access to one, you can first copy and scan any page and then simply paste any passage from it into your paper. Nothing could be simpler. Compared to that process, taking notes on a card and transcribing the information into a paper is definitely work from the Stone Age.

A couple of suggestions if you are in the mood to use a copy machine rather than to copy by hand:

1. Always write down details about the source on the top of the page immediately after copying it. Get in the habit of photocopying the source's pages that include the necessary bibliographic information.

2. Be neat about the pages you copy. Pages are bigger and messier than note cards, and many students who copy end up with a tangled snarl of unmanageable pages, some of which they hopelessly mix up. Nothing is more frustrating than having to trek back to the library to look up information you already found once but somehow lost.

5e-3   Kinds of notes

The notes you gather from your research must blend into the body of your paper to provide documentation in support of your thesis. These notes are of four kinds: the summary, the paraphrase, the quotation, and the personal comment.

a. The summary

A *summary* is a condensation of significant facts from an original piece of writing. A chapter is condensed into a page, a page into a paragraph, or a paragraph into a sentence, with the condensation in each case retaining the essential facts of the original. Consider the summary in Figure 5-5 of an eight-page description of Rasputin.

Common sense should govern your use of the summary. Some facts need to be quoted in detail, but others do not and can be just as effectively summarized. For instance, the summary shown in Figure 5-5 was for a paper on Rasputin that dealt mainly with the historical truth about the man, not with his physical

5e

appearance. So it was enough for the student to summarize certain of Rasputin's features that made him both repulsive and attractive. In another context, say, in a paper on the physical disfigurement of famous people, it might have been necessary for the student to quote generously from the eight-page description.

b. The paraphrase

The *paraphrase* restates a passage in approximately the same number of words as the original, using the syntax and vocabulary of the paraphraser. It is the most common form of note writing in research papers.

Paraphrasing achieves two purposes: first, it shows that you have mastered the material well enough to be able to rephrase it; second, it gives your paper an even, consistent style because both original material and source material are cast in your own words. Here is a short passage from *The Fall of the Russian Monarchy* by Bernard Pares. The passage has been paraphrased in Figure 5-6.

> Meanwhile Rasputin, as he appears to have done earlier, disappeared into the wilds of Russia. Here too he was true to an historical type. Always, throughout Russian history, there had been stranniki or wanderers who, without any ecclesiastical commission, lived in asceticism, depriving themselves of the most elementary of human needs, but gladly entertained by the poor wherever they passed. Some of them went barefoot even throughout the winter and wore chains on their legs. This self-denial gave them a freedom to address as peasant equals even the Tsars themselves, and there are many instances of their bold rebukes scattered over Russian history.

c. The quotation

A *quotation* reproduces an author's words exactly as they were spoken or written, preserving even peculiarities of spelling, grammar, and punctuation. Use of an

---

Fülöp-Miller 3–10.   Rasputin's appearance

Rasputin's appearance was a combination of coarse, unkempt peasant burliness and mystical, poetic religiosity. He was at once repulsive and attractive. Strangers who met him were first disgusted by such details as his pock-marked skin and his dirty fingernails, but inevitably they came under the spell of his urgent, probing blue eyes.

Figure 5-5   Sample note card containing a summary

Pares 134–35.   *Rasputin as nomad, ca. 1902*

*For some time Rasputin became like the well-known stranniki,
ascetics who, without official priestly license, wandered all over
Russia, depending on the poor for food and shelter. Some of the
nomads even walked barefoot in the freezing Russian winter
with chains clinking around their legs. This kind of self-denial
bestowed on them the peculiar right to address even a Tsar as
their equal. In this role of half priest–half beggar, Rasputin
roamed the wilds of Russia.*

Figure 5-6   Sample note card containing a paraphrase

occasional quotation is justified where the authority of the writer is being evoked
or where the original material is so splendidly expressed as to be altogether ruined
by summary or paraphrase. If the quotation contains a misspelled word or other
error, reproduce it faithfully, adding [sic] beside it to indicate that the error is not
yours but the source's.

Student papers tend to overuse quoted material (so much so that many teachers automatically regard excessive quotations as a sign of padding). A good rule
of thumb is to limit quoted material to no more than 10 percent of the total paper.
Another good rule of thumb is to quote only when the authority of the writer is
needed or when the material simply cannot be paraphrased or summarized.

Figure 5-7 shows a note card with a quotation. To place quotations on note
cards, follow these rules:

- ☐ Put quotation marks around the quotation.
- ☐ Introduce the quotation or place it in proper context.
- ☐ Copy quotations exactly as they are written.

Occasionally a summary or paraphrase is combined with a quotation on a
note card, the key phrases or words from the original source used to add literary
flavor or authenticity to the note. Following is an original passage from *The Fall
of the Russian Monarchy*. The note card in Figure 5-8 combines a paraphrase with
a quotation from this source.

> Nothing is more untrue than the easy explanation that was so often given, that
> he became the tool of others. He was far too clever to sell himself to anyone.
> He did not ask for presents and had no need; he had only to accept all that was
> showered upon him, and that he did briefly and almost casually, in many cases at
> once passing on the largess to the poor; his position was that of one who plun-
> dered the rich for the poor and was glad to do it.

Fülöp-Miller 366.   The murder of Rasputin

Farewell letter from Empress Alexandra to the murdered
Rasputin:

   "My dear martyr, grant me your blessing to accompany me
   on the sorrowful road I have still to tread here below. Remember us in Heaven in your holy prayers. Alexandra."

Figure 5-7   Sample note card containing a quotation

5e

Pares 140, 144.   Rasputin's generosity to the poor

Some critics have accused Rasputin of becoming "the tool of
others" in order to acquire expensive personal gifts or other
material advantage. Nothing could be further from the truth.
Rasputin was "too clever to sell himself to anyone." He did not
need to. All he had to do was sit back and accept all the
luxuries offered to him by high society. And, in fact, one of his
favorite roles was that of a Russian Robin Hood, who "plundered
the rich for the poor" by taking gifts and immediately passing
them on to people in need.

Figure 5-8   Sample note card containing a paraphrase and quotations

d. The personal comment

Personal comments are ideas, conjectures, or conclusions that occur to you during
the research. These notes generally are used to explain a fuzzy statement, stress
a particular point, draw a conclusion, clarify an issue, identify an inconsistency,
or introduce a new idea. Jot down the ideas as they dawn on you. If the personal
comment deals with material on another card, staple the two cards together. An
example of a personal comment is shown in Figure 5-9.

Personal Comment   The Tsarina's initial attraction to Rasputin

It became clear, from all accounts describing the first meeting between Alexandra and Rasputin, that initially this peasant monk gained entrance to the Tsarina's confidence by offering hope for the health of her hemophiliac son, at a time when she was utterly sunk in grief and despair. In the grip of maternal terror, she <u>wanted</u> to believe that God had sent a simple peasant to perform miracles.

Figure 5-9   Sample note card containing a personal comment

5f   Plagiarism and how to avoid it

Plagiarism is the act of passing off another's words and ideas as your own. In a cosmic sense, the process of learning is made up of countless tiny crimes of plagiarism because we all borrow freely from one another. No generation speaks a language of its own invention; few people actually create the proverbs and sayings they utter daily. The mother who tells her child, "A thing of beauty is a joy forever," is plagiarizing from the poet John Keats; the father who warns his son, "Hell hath no fury like a woman scorned," has plagiarized from the playwright William Congreve. A teacher who encourages students to turn in their research papers early by telling them that "the early bird gets the worm" is plagiarizing from Benjamin Franklin. Innumerable other examples can be given to show how we freely and openly borrow ideas and expressions from one another.

Blatant plagiarism, however, involves the deliberate stealing of someone else's words and ideas, generally with the motive of earning undeserved rewards. A student who copies a friend's paper is guilty of blatant plagiarism. Likewise, a student who steals an idea from a book, rewords it, and then passes it off as an original thought has committed an act of plagiarism.

Under the conventions of writing research papers, you must acknowledge the source of any idea or statement not truly your own. This acknowledgment is made in a note specifying the source and author of the borrowed material. All summaries, paraphrases, or quotations must be documented; only personal comments can remain undocumented. In sum, to avoid plagiarism you must do the following:

- ☐ Provide a note for any idea borrowed from another.
- ☐ Place quoted material in quotation marks.

☐ Provide a bibliography entry at the end of the paper for every source used in the text or in a note.

Not every assertion can be documented, nor is it necessary to document what is common knowledge. For instance, it is commonly known that the early settlers of America fought wars with the Native Americans—an assertion that any student could safely make without documentation. Similarly, a student could write, "For centuries it was universally accepted in most parts of the world that inequalities of social status were ordained by God. Thus, both the earl in his castle and the peasant in his hut believed that God wanted them there." Since the tremendous gap between the rich and powerful and the poor and powerless of past ages is well known, this statement would not be considered plagiarism. As a rule, a piece of information that shows up in five or more sources can be considered general knowledge. Proverbs and sayings of unknown origins also are considered general knowledge and do not have to be documented.

The following, however, must be accompanied by a citation specifying author and source:

5f

☐ Any idea derived from a known source

☐ Any fact or data borrowed from the work of another

☐ Any especially clever or apt expression, whether or not it says something new, that is taken from someone else

☐ Any material lifted verbatim from the work of another

☐ Any information that is paraphrased or summarized and then used in a research paper

> **Source tip**
>
> It's not the length of the writing that determines whether you give credit to a source; it's the use of its phrasing or ideas.

Plagiarism in student papers is often an honest mistake. Most of the time, a student—in the crush of writing to meet a tight deadline—simply forgets to cite a source. Sometimes the student makes the mistake of thinking that the material is common knowledge and needs no documentation. To illustrate plagiarism in different degrees, we have reproduced a passage from a book, followed by three student samples, two of which are plagiarized.

Original passage   Alexander III died on 20 October, 1894, and was succeeded by his son Nicholas. The new emperor was more intelligent and more sensitive than his father. Both those who knew him well, and those who had brief and superficial contact with him, testify to his exceptional personal charm. The charm was, however, apparently associated with weakness and irresolution. Nicholas appeared to agree with the last person he had talked to, and no one could tell what he would do next.

Student version A (plagiarized)

When Alexander III died on October 20, 1894, he was succeeded by his son Nicholas, who was more intelligent and more sensitive than his father. People who knew him well and also some who knew him only superficially testify that he was exceptionally charming as a person. This charm, however, was associated with weakness and an inability to make decisions. Nicholas always seemed to agree with the last person he had talked to, and no one could predict what he would do next.

5f

The preceding is an example of outright plagiarism. No documentation of any sort is given. The writer simply repeats the passage almost verbatim, in effect taking credit for writing it.

Though documented with a footnote, the passage below is still plagiarism because the student has changed only a word or two of the original, without doing a paraphrase:

Student version B (plagiarized)

When Alexander III died on October 20, 1894, he was succeeded by his son Nicholas, who was more intelligent and more sensitive than his father. People who knew him well, and also some who knew him only superficially, testify that he was exceptionally charming as a person. This charm, however, was associated with weakness and an inability to make decisions. Nicholas always seemed to agree with the last person he had talked to, and no one could predict what he would do next.[3]

3. Hugh Seton-Watson, *The Russian Empire, 1801-1917*, vol. 3 of *The Oxford History of Modern Europe* (Oxford: Oxford UP, 1957), 547.

And here is an acceptable use of the material. The original is paraphrased properly and its source documented with a footnote:

Student version B (not plagiarized)

Emperor Nicholas II, who came to the throne of Russia following the death of his father, Alexander III, was apparently a man of exceptional personal charm and deep sensitivity. Ample testimony has come to us from both intimate as well as casual acquaintances, indicating that indeed he possessed a magnetic personality. However, the general consensus is that he was also a man who lacked the ability to make hard decisions, preferring to agree with the last person he had seen, and thus making it impossible to predict what he would do next.[3]

3. Hugh Seton-Watson, *The Russian Empire, 1801-1917*, vol. 3 of *The Oxford History of Modern Europe* (Oxford: Oxford UP, 1957), 547.

5f

One last caution. Students who would never think to borrow material from a printed source often take freely from electronic sources. That is plagiarism. We admit that it can be difficult citing sources on the web. Many sites don't name authors; others don't number pages; still others have finger-busting Internet addresses. But all systems of citation now have conventional ways of documenting material from electronic sources. See 9b, 10b, and 10d.

> **Note-taking tip**
>
> It will be easier to transpose your notes into the first draft of your paper if you make them in well-developed, complete sentences.

Human thoughts and emotions become subjects of study.

Sigmund Freud

There was a time when the human mind was considered a mystery, but today much has been learned about the way our brains function. Sigmund Freud, a Viennese doctor, is considered one of the most important pioneers of modern psychology. By studying the unconscious, he laid the groundwork for psychoanalysis. While practicing medicine in the 1880s, he found out that he could help hysterical patients by having them, under hypnosis, recall traumatic incidents in their lives. He also developed the technique of free association, whereby patients could talk about emotionally charged aspects of their lives. Freudian theory, although often criticized for its emphasis on sex, has deeply influenced anthropology, education, art, and literature.

6 The Thesis and the Outline

6a	The thesis: Definition and function
6b	The outline
6c	Choosing an outline form

 FAQ

1. What is a thesis? *See 6a.*
2. Where should I place the thesis? *See 6a-3.*
3. Why should a thesis be a single sentence? *See 6a-1 and 6a-2.*
4. How do I come up with a title? *See 6a-4.*
5. What's the difference between a topic outline and a sentence outline? *See 6b-4a and 6b-4b.*
6. Once I begin writing, can I change my outline? *See 6c.*
7. What is a paragraph outline? *See 6b-4c.*

The thesis: Definition and function

The thesis is a statement that summarizes the central idea of the paper. By convenience and custom, the thesis is usually the last sentence of the opening paragraph, as it is in the following example:

The Bilingual Child

Several million children in the United States are admitted to public school every year without having the fluency in English required to succeed in the early grades. These children speak Spanish, Vietnamese, Korean, Japanese, Armenian, Arabic, or some other language in their homes and neighborhoods. Because of their lack of language preparedness, some of them have had to repeat first grade--occasionally more than once. As a consequence, bilingual programs were created in many public school systems. Students forced into these programs had much of their schoolwork translated for them by teachers familiar with their home culture and language. *Contrary to the hopes of bilingual-education advocates, the latest research indicates that bilingual programs confuse children and slow them down in achieving the goal of learning English.*

The italicized sentence is the thesis—the central idea that the writer intends to argue. After readers have read through this first paragraph, the aim of the paper is abundantly clear to them; they know what to anticipate.

The thesis serves at least three functions. First, it establishes a boundary around your subject that discourages you from wandering aimlessly. Often we are tempted to stray from the point when we write. We begin by intending to write a paper about Rasputin's place in history, and then stumble onto some fascinating fact about Russian monasteries and want somehow to work it in. With a clear thesis before us, however, we are less likely to be sidetracked. Formulated before the actual writing begins, the thesis commits us to argue one point, discuss one subject, clarify one issue. So committed, we will not leapfrog from topic to topic, nor free-associate from one minor point to another.

Second, the well-rounded thesis can chart an orderly course for the paper, making it easier to write. Consider this thesis:

Two defects in the design of the *Titanic* contributed to its sinking: its steering was sluggish and unresponsive, even for a ship of its immense size, and its traverse bulkheads, which should have made it virtually unsinkable, did not extend all the way up to its deck.

The course before you is as plain as day: First, the sluggish steering of the *Titanic* must be discussed and clarified with appropriate facts and details; second, the design of the ship's traverse bulkheads must be dealt with and the defect thoroughly explained. Your job is easier because the thesis conveniently divides your paper into two parts, establishing not only the topics to be discussed but also their sequence. It is better and easier by far to write about this thesis than to write randomly about the sinking of the *Titanic*.

Third, the thesis gives the reader an idea of what to expect, making the paper easier to read. Textbooks have elaborate chapter headings and section headnotes just for this purpose. Newspaper stories are headlined and captioned for a similar reason. It is easier to read virtually anything if we have an anticipation that narrows and focuses our attention. A paper without a thesis creates no such anticipation and so is more difficult to follow.

6a-1   Formulating the thesis

There is no chicken-and-egg mystery about which comes first—the notes or the thesis. You cannot formulate a thesis unless you know a great deal about your subject. Ordinarily, then, you are well into your research and notes before you can formulate the thesis. Of course this is only a guess, not a rule. Writing is not a cookie-cutter business, and papers are not written in a lockstep fashion.

One thing is certain: For your thesis, you are looking for a central idea that summarizes the information you have gathered, along with your own opinions on the subject. This idea must be expressed in one sentence. Think of your thesis as the statement you would scribble down if you were asked to sum up the heart of your paper in a single sentence.

Consider, for instance, a paper on Rasputin. The student, after much reading and note-taking, discovers that despite his diabolic reputation, Rasputin did some good. Specifically she discovers that (1) Rasputin had intense religious feelings; (2) he had a passionate desire for peace in Russia; and (3) he was deeply devoted to his family and friends. She summarizes her findings about Rasputin in the following thesis:

> After six decades of being judged a demoniacal libertine, Rasputin now
>
> deserves to be viewed from another point of view--as a man who was
>
> intensely religious, who passionately desired peace for Russia, and who
>
> was deeply devoted to his family and friends.

Notice that this thesis specifies exactly what the writer has to do and what information she needs to do it. To begin with, she will have to document Rasputin's reputation as a demoniacal libertine. Having done that, she will have to support her three contrary assertions: that Rasputin was intensely religious, that he passionately desired peace, and that he was deeply devoted to his family and friends. The thesis, moreover, suggests exactly the kind of information that the student needs to write the paper. First, she must cite historical opinion that portrays Rasputin as a demoniacal libertine. Second, she must produce anecdotal material, eyewitness accounts, biographical opinions, and similar evidence that support her contrary assertions about Rasputin.

6a-2   Rules for wording the thesis

Properly worded, the thesis should (1) be clear, comprehensible, and direct; (2) predict major divisions in the structure of the paper; and (3) commit you to an unmistakable course, argument, or point of view. The thesis on Rasputin is clear, implies a four-part division in the structure of the paper, and obligates the writer to argue a single proposition: that Rasputin was judged harshly by history. Likewise, the thesis on the *Titanic* disaster is clear and direct, divides the paper into two principal parts, and commits the writer to a single argument: that the ocean liner sank because of defects in steering and in the bulkheads. What follows is a series of rules to guide you in properly wording your thesis.

☐ *The thesis should commit you to a single line of argument.* Consider this example:

6a

Poor   The Roman theater was inspired by the Greek theater, which it imitated,

and eventually the Romans produced great plays in their *theatrons*, such

as those by Plautus, who was the best Roman comic writer because of

his robustness and inventiveness

This thesis threatens to wrench the paper in two directions: It commits the student to cover both the origins of Roman theater and the theatrical career of Plautus, one of Rome's greatest comic playwrights. This dual thesis came about because the student laboriously had accumulated two sets of notes—one on the origins of Roman theater and another on the career of Plautus—and was determined to devise a thesis that would allow the use of both. The result is this curiously dual thesis that skews the paper in two contrary directions. Persuaded to relinquish the notes on the origins of the Roman theater and to focus the paper entirely on the career of Plautus, the student drafted the following thesis:

Better   Because of his robust language and novel comic plots, Titus Maccius

Plautus can be considered the best Roman comic playwright, and his

plays are still successfully staged today.

The paper now is committed to a single line of argument, and its focus therefore is vastly improved.

☐ *The thesis should not be worded in figurative language.* The reasoning behind this rule is obvious: Figurative language is too indefinite, too hazy to express the central idea of a paper. For example:

Poor   Henry James is the Frank Lloyd Wright of the American novel.

No doubt the writer knows exactly what he means by this allusion, but its significance is murky to a reader. The following, plainly expressed thesis is vastly better:

Better   The novels of Henry James have internal consistency because of the way he unifies his themes, patterns his episodes, and orders his images.

☐ *The thesis should not be worded vaguely.* Vagueness, like figurative language, may tantalize, but it does not inform. Moreover, a paper with a vague thesis is a paper without direction and is all the more difficult to write. Consider this thesis:

Poor   Cigarette smoking wreaks havoc on the body.

Doing a paper on a thesis like this truly puts any writer to the test. The thesis suggests no direction, provides no structure, proposes no arguments. Contrast it with this improved version:

Better   Cigarette smoking harms the body by constricting the blood vessels, accelerating the heartbeat, paralyzing the cilia in the bronchial tubes, and activating excessive gastric secretions in the stomach.

Now the writer knows exactly what points to argue and in what order.

☐ *The thesis should not be worded as a question.* A thesis worded as a question does not give you the obligatory direction that a statement does. Here is an example:

Poor   Who makes the key decisions in U.S. cities?

This sort of question makes a good starting point for research. Indeed, most research begins with a question in the mind of the researcher. But the eventual thesis should not be your original question; it should be the answer uncovered in your research:

Better   Key decisions in large U.S. cities are made by a handful of individuals, drawn largely from business, industrial, and municipal circles, who occupy the top of the power hierarchy.

☐ *The thesis should be a single, concise, easily understood sentence.* It should function as an accurate thumbnail sketch of the paper and should be short enough to be expressed on a postcard. If your thesis is more than a single sentence, if it is wordy and hard to understand, your paper is likely to be wordy and hard to understand as well. A weak thesis generally leads to a weak paper; a strong thesis to a strong paper. This is not a universal truth, but more often than not it is true. The thesis that is long and knotty is likely to muddle you and send your paper flying off in different directions. Meanwhile, the reader struggling to fathom your paper's thesis is even less likely to make sense of its contents. Here is a muddled thesis:

Poor   Despite the fact that extensive time consumed by television detracts from homework, competes with schooling more generally, and has contributed to the decline in the Scholastic Aptitude Test score averages, television and related forms of communication give the future of learning its largest promise, the most constructive approach being less dependent on limiting the uses of these processes than on the willingness of the community and the family to exercise the same responsibility for what is taught and learned this way as they have exercised with respect to older forms of education.

☐ The passage is difficult to unravel. A whole paper based on this thesis would be equally unclear. Here is an improved version:

Better   Although numerous studies acknowledge that the extensive time spent by students watching television has contributed to a decline in Scholastic Aptitude Test scores, leading educators are convinced that television holds immense promise for the future of learning, provided that the family and the community prudently monitor its use.

☐ To paraphrase an old saying, "Like thesis, like paper." A muddled, incoherent thesis will generate an equally muddled and incoherent paper.

6a-3   Placing the thesis

Some variation in placement of the thesis does exist, but most instructors distinctly prefer the thesis as the final sentence of the initial paragraph. Following are three examples of theses—the italic sentences—introduced in this customary place.

Thesis

He is a vagabond in aristocratic clothing--shabby but grand. As he scurries along in his cutaway and derby hat, aided by a cane, he is obviously a tramp, but a tramp with the impeccable manners of a dandy. He is willing to tackle any job but seldom does it properly. He often falls in love, but usually the affair sours in the end. His only enemies are pompous people in places of authority. The general public adores him because he is everyman of all times. Charlie Chaplin's Tramp has remained an international favorite because he is a character with whom the average person can empathize.

Thesis

A quarter of a million babies are born each year with birth defects. Only 20 percent of those defects are hereditary. Most could have been prevented: They are the tragic results of poor prenatal care. An unfavorable fetal environment, like that produced by malnutrition in the mother or by her use of drugs, is a primary cause of many kinds of birth defects.

Thesis

Theodor Seuss Geisel wrote and illustrated zany children's books, usually in verse, under the pseudonym "Dr. Seuss." He wrote twenty-six best-sellers over a period of thirty years, and they are all still in print. In story after story, this author creates a topsy-turvy world where the normal becomes aberrant and the aberrant normal. The simple vocabulary and rhyming lines of Dr. Seuss's books make them easy for children to read, but the author's illustrations are primarily responsible for the imaginative flair in his work.

6a-4   Choosing a title

No magic formula exists on how or when to title your paper. The title, however, should be clear, specific, and informative. If possible, include in it some key words from the subject of your paper. Here are examples, good and bad:

Not clear	An Admirable Animal
Clear	The Courage of Turtles
Not specific	Child Beauty Pageants
Specific	The JonBenet Case: How a Child Beauty Queen Was Murdered

Not informative	Razzle-Dazzle in Egypt
Informative	Tutankhamen's Tomb and Its Dazzling Contents

Usually, your thesis is a good source for a title. Consider this example:

Thesis	The imposition of sharia law on non-Muslims living in Western societies inevitably leads to resentment and political unrest.
Title	Sharia Law in Non Muslim Societies

6b   The outline

An outline is an ordered list of the topics covered in a paper. It is useful to both writer and reader. The writer who writes from an outline is less likely to stray from the point or to commit a structural error—overdeveloping one topic while skimping on another, for example. The reader, in turn, benefits from the outline in the form of a complete and detailed table of contents.

6b-1   Visual conventions of the outline

The conventions of formal outlining require that main ideas be designated by Roman numerals (I, II, III, IV, and so on). Sub-ideas branching off from the main ideas are designated by capital letters (A, B, C, D, and so on). Subdivisions of these sub-ideas are designated by Arabic numerals (1, 2, 3, 4, and so on). And minor ideas are designated by lowercase letters (a, b, c, d, and so on). Here is an example of the proper form of an outline:

6b

I. Main idea

   A. Sub-idea

   B. Sub-idea

      1. Division of a sub-idea

      2. Division of a sub-idea

         a. Minor idea

         b. Minor idea

II. Main idea

The presumption behind this arrangement is obvious: You do not merely generalize; you support your contentions and propositions with examples and details. Indeed, that is exactly what you are expected to do—to make assertions that are supported by concrete examples and specific details. If you have not been diligent in gathering specific facts about your topic, this deficiency will now be painfully obvious. Notice that every subdivided category must have at least two sections because it is impossible to divide anything into fewer than two parts. An outline that divides the subject into three or four levels—that is, down to examples or details—generally is adequate for most college-level research papers. If further subdivisions are necessary, the format is as follows:

I.

   A.

      1.

        a.

           (1)

              (a)

The basic principle remains the same: Larger ideas or elements are stacked to the left, with smaller ideas or elements to the right.

6b-2   Equal ranking in outline entries

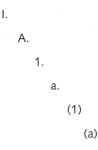

The logic of an outline requires that each entry be based on the same organizing principle as another entry of equal rank. All capital-letter entries consequently must be equivalent in importance and derived from the same organizing principle. Notice the absence of equal ranking in the following example:

   I.   Rousseau gave the people a new government to work toward.

      A. It would be a government based on the general will.

      B. The new government would serve the people instead of the people serving

         the government.

      C. The people tore down the Bastille.

Entry C is out of place because it is not of equal rank with entries A and B. A and B are sub-ideas that characterize the new government proposed by Rousseau; C is a statement that describes the revolt of the French people against the old government.

6b-3   Parallelism in outline entries

The clarity and readability of an outline are improved if its entries are worded in similar grammatical form. Notice the lack of parallelism in the following outline:

   I.   The uses of the laser in the military

      A. For range finding

      B. For surveillance

      C. To illuminate the enemy's position

Entries A and B consist of the preposition "for" followed by a noun, whereas entry C is worded as an infinitive phrase. C should be reworded to make it grammatically like entries A and B:

    I.   The uses of the laser in the military

        A. For range finding

        B. For surveillance

        C. *For illuminating the enemy's position*

The outline now is easier to read because its entries are parallel.

6b-4   Types of outlines

The three main types of outlines are the topic outline, the sentence outline, and the paragraph outline. Never mix or combine the different formats in a paper: Use one type of outline exclusively.

a. The topic outline

The topic outline words each entry as a phrase, breaking down the subject into major subheadings. Topic outlines are particularly useful for outlining relatively simple subjects. Here is a topic outline of the paper on Rasputin:

Rasputin's Other Side

Thesis: After six decades of being judged a demoniacal libertine, Rasputin now deserves to be viewed from another point of view--as a man who was intensely religious, who passionately desired peace, and who was deeply devoted to his family and friends.

    I.   The ambiguity of the real Rasputin

        A. His birth

        B. Popular historical view

           1. His supporters

           2. His detractors

    II. Rasputin's religious feelings

        A. His vitality and exuberance

        B. His simple peasant faith

    III. Rasputin's desire for peace in Russia

        A. His concern for the Russian underdog

           1. His loyalty to the peasantry

           2. His opposition to anti-Semitism

        B. His opposition to all wars

6b

IV. Rasputin's gentle, compassionate side

    A. His kindness to the Romanovs

    B. His love for family

Notice that the thesis of the paper is a separate entry immediately after the title. It is also customary to omit introduction and conclusion entries.

b. The sentence outline

The sentence outline uses a complete sentence for each entry. (Some instructors allow the entries to be worded as questions, but most prefer declarative sentences.) Sentence outlines are especially well suited for complex subjects. Here is a sentence outline of the paper on Rasputin:

Rasputin's Other Side

Thesis: After six decades of being judged a demoniacal libertine, Rasputin now deserves to be viewed from another point of view--as a man who was intensely religious, who passionately desired peace, and who was deeply devoted to his family and friends.

I.   The real Rasputin is difficult to discover.

    A. The birth of Rasputin coincided with a shooting star.

    B. The popular historical view of Rasputin portrays him as primarily evil.

       1. Supporters called him a spiritual leader.

       2. Detractors called him a satyr and charged that his depraved faithful were merely in awe of his sexual endowments.

II. Rasputin had intense religious feelings.

    A. He was both vital and exuberant.

    B. He had a simple peasant faith in God.

III. Rasputin's passionate desire for peace in Russia revealed itself in several ways.

    A. He was concerned for the Russian underdog.

       1. He wanted a tsar who would stand up for the peasantry.

       2. He spoke out boldly against anti-Semitism.

    B. Because of his humanitarian spirit, he was opposed to all wars.

6b

IV. Rasputin had a gentle, compassionate side.

    A. He showed great kindness to the Romanovs.

    B. Maria Rasputin tells of her father's love for his family.

c. The paragraph outline

The paragraph outline records each entry as a complete paragraph, in effect producing a condensed version of the paper. This form is useful mainly for long papers whose individual sections can be summarized in whole paragraphs; it is seldom recommended by instructors for ordinary college papers. Here is the Rasputin paper in the form of a paragraph outline:

Rasputin's Other Side

Thesis: After six decades of being judged a demoniacal libertine, Rasputin now deserves to be viewed from another point of view--as a man who was intensely religious, who passionately desired peace, and who was deeply devoted to his family and friends.

I.   Rasputin himself always attached great significance to the fact that at the time of his birth, a shooting star was seen streaking across the horizon. He considered the phenomenon to be an omen that he was fated to have influence and special powers. The popular historical view of Rasputin paints him primarily as evil. In his day, however, he attracted numerous supporters, who thought of him as their spiritual leader. But he also had many detractors who called him a satyr and accused his followers of sexual depravity.

II.   Rasputin had intense religious feelings. He was so filled with vitality and exuberance that he could stay awake until the early hours of the morning, dancing and drinking in frenzied religious fervor. He did not have the theology of a sophisticated church cleric; instead he expressed his religion in the simple terms of a Russian peasant.

III.   Rasputin's passionate desire for peace in Russia revealed itself in several ways. For instance, he was concerned for the Russian underdogs, for the peasants and the Jews, always encouraging the tsar to protect these unfortunate groups. And, his humanitarian and pacifist nature made him a determined opponent of all wars.

IV.   Rasputin had a gentle, compassionate side. He was completely devoted to the tsar's family and was known to have had a calming influence on the hemophiliac son of the tsar. Maria Rasputin gives a glowing report of her father's kindness and love.

d. Decimal outline notation

Other outline forms use various methods of indenting, labeling, and spacing. One form that has been gaining favor in business and science is the decimal outline. Based on the decimal accounting system, this outline form permits an unlimited number of subdivisions through the simple addition of another decimal place. Here is the body of the Rasputin paper notated in the decimal outline form:

Rasputin's Other Side

Thesis: After six decades of being judged a demoniacal libertine, Rasputin now deserves to be viewed from another point of view--as a man who was intensely religious, who passionately desired peace, and who was deeply devoted to his family and friends.

1. The ambiguity of the real Rasputin
    1.1. His birth
    1.2. Popular historical view
        1.2.1. His supporters
        1.2.2. His detractors
2. Rasputin's religious feelings
    2.1. His vitality and exuberance
    2.2. His simple peasant faith
3. Rasputin's desire for peace in Russia
    3.1. His concern for the Russian underdog
        3.1.1. His loyalty to the peasantry
        3.1.2. His opposition to anti-Semitism
    3.2. His opposition to all wars
4. Rasputin's gentle, compassionate side
    4.1. His kindness to the Romanovs
    4.2. His love for family

Notice that the decimal outline form uses the same indentation pattern as other outlines, with larger ideas stacked to the left and smaller ideas to the right.

6b

6c Choosing an outline form

Which kind of outline should you use? If you are a beginning writer, and if your research has uncovered much detail on your subject, don't hesitate: Use a detailed sentence outline. Develop it at least down to the third level—the level of Arabic numerals. In doing so, you actually erect a kind of scaffolding for the essay. To write the rough draft, you simply transcribe from the outline, fill in the blanks, insert transitions and connectives—and you have a paper.

The main entries of a sentence outline should be the topic sentences of various paragraphs. Its details should be exactly the kind you intend to use to support the topic sentence. As an example, here is a sentence outline of the first paragraph from a paper on Agatha Christie's fictional sleuth, Hercule Poirot:

I.   Poirot's unique personality and character set him apart from other fictional detectives.

   A. His physical appearance was unique.

      1. He was five feet four inches tall, had a black handlebar mustache, an egg-shaped head, and catlike eyes that grew greener as the solution to a crime drew near.

      2. He wore a black coat, pin-striped pants, a bow tie, shiny black boots, and, usually, a coat and muffler.

Here is the paragraph as it appeared in the paper:

> Poirot's unique personality and character set him apart from other fictional detectives. One of the memorable features of his personality and character was his physical appearance. He was "a diminutive five foot four inches tall and slender."[7] His hair was an "unrepentant" black, neatly groomed with hair tonic. His upper lip displayed his pride and joy and his more distinctive feature, a small black handlebar mustache.[8] He had catlike eyes that grew greener as the solution to a crime drew near and a head the shape of an egg. Thus Poirot has been referred to as a "mustachioed Humpty Dumpty."[9] This "extraordinary looking little man, who carried himself with immense dignity," almost always wore the same outfit, consisting of a black jacket, striped pants, a bow tie, and, in all but the hottest weather, an overcoat and muffler. He also wore patent leather boots that almost always displayed a dazzling shine.[10]

Notice the close correspondence between the outline and the developed paragraph. First, the main entry of the outline is exactly the same as the topic sentence of the paragraph. Second, sub-idea A is fleshed out and used in the paragraph to introduce the details that follow. Third, the details in the outline are used nearly word-for-word in the paragraph. Naturally there is more material in the paragraph than in the outline, which is not surprising because the second is a shorthand version of the first.

If you are going to be following an outline as you write, this kind is especially useful. Once drafted, it becomes a condensed version of the paper. Any paragraph is easy to write when you know exactly what its main point must be and what details it should contain. That kind of information is provided by the detailed sentence outline.

Your computer will prove to be a useful tool for writing both your outline and your essay. In fact, most word-processing programs offer an outlining feature that has several formats with automatic numbering or lettering.

6c

> **Outlining tip**
>
> **If you intend to experiment with different kinds of outlines, create a separate file for each one so you can pick and choose among the various versions.**

Not all instructors require a formal outline for a research paper. Indeed, not all writers would benefit from making one. Some writers compose organically and do not like to be hemmed in by a predefined plan. Others like to have a visible scaffolding for their papers. The point is, if your instructor does not require an outline and you do not feel you would benefit from making one, then simply sit down and begin writing the paper. On the other hand, if an outline would help you write a paper but is not required, go ahead and outline to your heart's content. If given a choice between outlining and not outlining, do what suits you. The idea is to write the best paper you can, not the best outline.

Finally, we don't want to leave you with the impression that the movement from thesis to outline to final paper is always neat, predictable, and certain. It is anything but. Writing, as we've said before, is a messy business. It leaves behind a litter of scrawled-over papers and almost never proceeds in a straight, unbroken line. For example, you could begin by drafting an outline and find to your dismay that the actual paper you write turns out to be considerably different from what you outlined. If that should happen to you, simply change the outline while being comforted by the thought that it has happened at one time or another to every writer. In fact, it is a healthy sign: It shows that once inspired, you were smart enough to write freely, that you weren't hog-tied by misplaced loyalty to an outline. When it comes to writing, almost nothing occurs in an ideal way, and every paper is accompanied by a good deal of fumbling, false starts, dead ends, and unexpected departures from plans. Expect complications, and your outlook as you tackle your paper will be healthily realistic.

Penicillin saves lives.

Alexander Fleming

Formed in mold, penicillin was the first antibiotic to be used in the treatment of human bacterial infections. First observed by Scottish biologist Alexander Fleming in 1928, this "mold" became extremely effective in curing syphilis, gangrene, meningitis, pneumococcal pneumonia, and other infections that usually led to death. Despite hundreds of other antibiotics discovered in recent years, penicillin still remains an important part of antibiotic therapy.

7 Transforming the Notes into a Rough Draft

7a Preparing to write the rough draft: A checklist

7b Writer's block

7c Writing with a computer

7d Using your notes in the paper

7e How to use quotations to explore and discover

7f Writing with unity, coherence, and emphasis

7g Using the proper tense

7h Using graphics in your research paper

7i Writing the abstract

FAQ

1. What should I do before I write my rough draft? *See 7a.*

2. Should I rely on a spell-checker? *See 7c-2.*

3. What is the string of pearls effect? How can I avoid it? *See 7d-10.*

4. Are my own ideas relevant to my paper, or should my paper reflect only "official" references? *See 7d-11.*

5. How do I know if a quote is a long quotation? *See 7d-4.*

6. What is an indirect quotation? *See 7d-2.*

7. What is the difference between a summary and a paraphrase? *See 7d-1.*

8. What does unity mean? *See 7f-1.*

9. How do I know which tense to use? *See 7g.*

10. How do I use the ellipsis? *See 7d-9.*

11. When is it appropriate to use graphics? *See 7h.*

12. Do I have to write an abstract? *See 7i.*

7a   Preparing to write the rough draft: A checklist

The following is a practical checklist of things you should do before beginning to write the rough draft:

1. Formulate a thesis. If you do not have one written down, you should at least have a main idea for your paper. The thesis will emerge as you write.

2. Go over your notes, picking out only material relevant to your thesis. Bear in mind that thousands of papers are ruined every year by writers who try to cram in every single note, no matter whether or not it is pertinent. You must exercise editorial judgment—based on your thesis—about which notes you use.

3. Organize your notes in the order of their appearance in the paper. If you took our advice and used note cards, you can easily rearrange them. If you saved the notes in your laptop, you can cut and paste them in sequence, complete with bibliographic citations.

4. Write an outline or abstract of the paper, breaking down the thesis into an ordered list of topics. Juggle the topics until they are arranged in the most logical and emphatic order. If necessary, rephrase your thesis to give a more definite structure to the paper.

Once you have formulated the thesis, sorted your notes, and drafted the outline or abstract, you are ready to begin writing the rough draft. Work from the outline and your notes. Take advantage of the built-in dictionary and thesaurus that are available in your word-processing program or those that are easily accessible online.

7b   Writer's block

Writer's block, in our view, is a misnamed condition. A writer is not a pipe through which water flows and which can be blocked by a pebble. All writer's block means is that you haven't found the right topic or you're expressing a point of view or opinion in which you don't truly believe. The writer who is enthusiastic about a topic and is eager to express an opinion on it never becomes blocked. Being blocked is a condition suffered mainly by writers who have no love for their topic.

Of course, it is possible for writers to judge their work so harshly that everything they write seems to them to be awful. The solution to this condition was proposed by the poet William Stafford who, when asked if he ever developed writer's block, replied, "Never. I just lower my standards." So if you should come down with "writer's block," lower your standards enough to get something rough down on paper. Once you have that rough draft, you can always refine it through editing.

7c   Writing with a computer

For the writer, the computer is a godsend; for the scholar it can be a nightmare. Writing with a computer virtually eliminates holographic manuscripts—meaning handwritten manuscripts showing the actual changes made by the writer. Few documents are as revealing of the process of composition as a handwritten manuscript. But that is the scholar's loss, not the writer's.

7c-1   Overdoing it

One danger of the trackless changes of a word processor is the temptation to over-revise, to redo the paper over and over with little or no improvement in each successive version. Indeed, an earlier draft sometimes proves to have the best flow, a discovery often made after that draft has already been erased and lost. For this reason, we encourage students to save the earlier draft just in case it turns out to be better than a later one.

When writing the paper, do not use fancy fonts to dress up your work. These are usually much harder to read than a plain font. Also, do not resort to extravagances such as excessive capitalization to underscore a point.

7c-2   Using a spell-checker

Spell-checkers are dictionary smart but context dumb. They can catch the misspelling of a word, but none can tell you whether or not you have used a word correctly. Here is a classic example:

> Bee fore wee rote with checkers
> Hour spelling was inn deck line.
> But now when wee dew have a laps,
> Wee are not maid too wine.

> And now bee cause my spelling
> Is checked with such grate flare,
> Their are know faults in awl this peace,
> Of nun eye am a wear.

If you run this poem through your spelling checker, it will not flag a single word, proving again that there is no substitute for the human eye.

7d   Using your notes in the paper

Notes, meaning quotations and paraphrases or summaries as well as your own personal observations, must be embedded in the text where they belong and tied into the context of the discussion with a reference. Using notes properly is essential to the success of the paper. Properly tied into the text, the note represents the extent and nature of your research efforts. You'll want to be sure that the progress of your paper is logical and that you haven't left out some important material (see also 7f).

7d-1   Summaries and paraphrases

A summary is a condensation of an idea. A paraphrase is a restatement of an idea using approximately the same number of words as in the original. The sources of summaries and paraphrases must be given in the body of the paper, either in running text or in parentheses. Here is an example of a paraphrase used without mention of its source in the text:

> When the court life of Russia died out at the imperial palace of Tsarskoe Selo, all kinds of political salons suddenly made their appearance in various sections of St. Petersburg. Although these new salons became the breeding ground for the same kinds of intrigues, plots, counterplots, and rivalries that had taken place at the imperial palace, somehow their activities seemed dwarfed, and their politics lacked the grandeur and dazzle that had accompanied the political style at the palace (Fülöp-Miller 101).

In this case, parenthetical documentation of the paraphrase is sufficient. However, if you want to state a paraphrase more emphatically, or to throw the weight of an expert behind the summary, you should mention the source in the text:

> As Hugh Seton-Watson points out in the preface to his book on the Russian empire, most people tend to forget that the Russian empire was multinational and therefore peopled with many non-Russian citizens, most important of whom were the Polish (ix).

The summary here is more emphatic because it is coupled with the name of the authority whose work is summarized.

7d-2 Direct and indirect quotations

A direct quotation is the exact reproduction of someone else's words. An indirect quotation reports what someone said or wrote but not in the exact words of the original. Direct quotations usually appear in quotation marks; indirect quotations never do. Study the following examples:

Direct quotation	J. K. Galbraith makes the following statement: "In the Affluent Society no useful distinction can be made between luxuries and necessaries."
Indirect quotation	J. K. Galbraith suggests that in an affluent society, people don't make any useful distinction between luxuries and necessities.
Direct quotation	After defining the *qasida* as a "pre-Islamic ode," Katharine Slater Gittes comments: "These wholly secular odes glorify the Bedouin life, the life of the wanderer."

Indirect
quotation

According to Katharine Slater Gittes, the main purpose of the *qasida*, a pre-Islamic ode, is to glorify the life of the Bedouin wanderer.

Research paper writers typically use a mix of both direct and indirect quotations to avoid the choppy style that results from a string of direct quotations alone. This blend maintains the continuity of the writer's own style, giving the text a smoother flow.

Direct quotations must be reproduced with the exact phrasing, spelling, and punctuation of the original. Any modification made in a quotation—no matter how minor—must be indicated either in a note placed in square brackets within the quotation or in parentheses at the end of the quotation:

Milton was advocating freedom of speech when he said, "Give me the liberty to know, to think, to believe, and to utter *freely* [emphasis added] according to conscience, above all other liberties" (120).

Quotations must blend logically into surrounding sentences so as not to produce an illogical or mixed construction. The following quotation is blended poorly:

Chung-Tzu describes a sage as "suppose there is one who insists on morality in all things, and who places love of truth above all other values" (58).

Here is the same quotation properly integrated into the sentence:

Chung-Tzu describes a sage as "one who insists on morality in all things, and who places love of truth above all other values" (58).

7d-3   Using brief direct quotations

Brief quotations (four lines or less) can be introduced with a simple word or phrase. Look for the highlighted phrases in these sentences:

Betty Friedan admits that it will be quite a while before women know "how much of the difference between women and men is culturally determined and how much of it is real."

"God is the perfect poet," said Browning in "Paracelsus."

Vary your introductions to quotations. If you introduce one quotation with "So-and-so says . . . ," try something different for the next, perhaps "In the opinion of at least one critic . . . ," or "A view widely shared by many in the field affirms that , . ."

If the quotation is grammatically part of the sentence in which it occurs, the first word of the quotation does not need to be capitalized, even if it is capitalized in the original:

Original
quotation

"Some infinitives deserve to be split." ·

Bruce Thompson

Quotation
used as part
of a sentence

Bruce Thompson affirms what writers always have suspected, namely that "some infinitives deserve to be split."

Moreover, if a quotation is used at the end of a declarative sentence, it is followed by a period whether or not a period is used in the original:

Original
quotation

"Love is a smoke rais'd with the fume of sighs;…"

Shakespeare

Quotation
used as part
of a sentence

In Act I Romeo describes love as "a smoke rais'd with the fume of sighs."

7d-4   Using long quotations

Unlike quotations of four lines or less, longer quotations need to be introduced by a sentence, placed in context, and explained. Moreover, long quotations must be set off from the text. Here's how:

- ☐ Introduce the quotation with a colon (unless the quotation runs on from the text—that is, finishes a thought started in the text).
- ☐ Do *not* leave an extra line space between the text and the start of the quotation. Double-space everything.
- ☐ Indent the quotation ten spaces from the left margin of the page.
- ☐ In a quotation of two or more paragraphs, indent the first line of each paragraph an additional quarter inch or three spaces as in this example:

The final paragraphs of "A Rose for Emily" bring to a horrifying climax all the elements of Gothic horror that have pervaded the story:

No extra
space above
quotation in
double-spaced
paper.

Opening
sentence of
first paragraph
indented 0.25
inch or
3 spaces.

For a long while we just stood there, looking down at the profound and fleshless grin. The body had apparently once lain in the attitude of an embrace, but now the long sleep that outlasts love had cuckolded him. What was left of him, rotted beneath what was left of the nightshirt, had become inextricable from the bed in which he lay; and upon him and upon the pillow beside him lay that even coating of the patient and biding dust.

Body of
quotation
indented
1 inch or
10 spaces
from margin.

Opening sentence of second paragraph indented as in first paragraph.

> Then we noticed that in the second pillow was the indentation of a head. One of us lifted something from it, and leaning forward, that faint and invisible dust dry and acrid in the nostrils, we saw a long strand of iron-gray hair.

If the quotation runs just one paragraph or the first line of the quotation is not the start of a paragraph, no extra indentation is needed:

In his novel *Lady Chatterley's Lover*, D. H. Lawrence creates a mesmeric and ritualistic effect as he describes the love scene between Mellors and Connie:

> But he drew away at last, and kissed her and covered her over, and began to cover himself. She lay looking up to the boughs of the tree, unable as yet to move. He stood and fastened up his breeches, looking round. All was dense and silent, save for the awed dog that lay with its paws against its nose. He sat down again on the brushwood and took Connie's hand in silence. (150)

Lawrence has created a trancelike mood that conveys the symbolic importance of this scene.

7d

☐ Quotations that are set off with an indentation are not set within quotation marks. (But quotation marks are used in long quotations around dialogue, titles of essays, titles of poems, and foreign phrases.)

☐ Do not leave an extra line space between the end of the quotation and the text that follows it.

Quotation tip

Conventions used by various styles to handle long quotations:

1. Definition of a long quotation:
   MLA: Any quotation longer than 4 lines.
   APA: Any quotation longer than 40 words.
   CMS: Any prose quotation of 8 or more lines; any poetry quotation of 2 or more lines.

2. Indentation:
   MLA: 10 spaces or 1 inch.
   APA: 5 spaces or 0.5 inch.
   CMS: 10 spaces or 1 inch.

> 3. Quoted material longer than one paragraph:
> MLA: Indent first lines of all paragraphs
> 3 spaces or 0.25 inch.
> APA: Indent first lines of all paragraphs but
> the first 5 spaces 0.5 inch.
> CMS: Indent first lines of all paragraphs (we
> recommend 5 spaces).

7d-5   Using quotations from poetry

Unless the stanzaic line needs to be preserved for stylistic emphasis, short passages of poetry should be in quotation marks and incorporated into the text. Verse quotations of two or three lines can also be part of the text, but separate the lines by a slash and leave a space on each side of the slash:

> "The raven's croak, the low wind choked and drear, / The baffled stream, the
>
> gray wolf's doleful cry" are typical Romantic images used by William Morris to
>
> create a mood of idle despair.

Verse quotations of more than three lines are formatted much like long prose quotations: They are introduced with a colon; they are separated from the text (above and below) by regular double-spacing; and they are indented one inch or ten spaces from the left margin. Do not add quotation marks that do not appear in the original poem. Notice also that no quotation marks are used at the start or the end of each quotation. The spatial arrangement of the original poem (indentation and spacing within and between lines) should be accurately reproduced:

> In the following lines from "You Ask Me Why, Tho' Ill at Ease," Tennyson
>
> expresses the poet's desire for freedom to speak out:
>
> > It is the land that freemen till,
> >
> > > That sober-suited Freedom chose,
> >
> > > The land, where girt with friends or foes
> >
> > A man may speak the thing he will.

A quotation beginning in the middle of a line of verse should be reproduced exactly that way, not shifted to the left margin:

> As Cordelia leaves her home, exiled by Lear's folly, she reveals full insight into
>
> her sisters' evil characters:
>
> > > I know you what you are;
> >
> > And like a sister am most loath to call
> >
> > Your faults as they are nam'd. Love well our father:

To your professed bosoms I commit him:

But yet, alas, stood I within his grace,

I would prefer him to a better place.

(*Lr*.1.1.272-77)

7d-6   Using a quotation within another quotation

Use single quotation marks to enclose a quotation within another brief quotation:

Rollo May is further exploring the daimonic personality when he states that "in his essays, Yeats goes so far as to specifically define the daimonic as the 'Other Will.'"

For quotations within long indented quotations, use double quotation marks:

In his essay "Disease as a Way of Life," Eric J. Cassell makes the following observation:

As the term "diarrhea-pneumonia complex" suggests, infants in the Navajo environment commonly suffered or died from a combination of respiratory and intestinal complaints that are not caused by any single bacterium or virus.

7d

7d-7   Punctuating quotations

The rules for punctuating quotations are few and simple:

☐ Place commas and periods inside the quotation marks:

"Three times today," Lord Hastings declares in Act 3, "my foot-cloth horse did stumble, and started, when he look'd upon the Tower, as loath to bear me to the slaughter-house."

☐ Place colons and semicolons outside the quotation marks:

Brutus reassures Portia, "You are my true and honourable wife, as dear to me as are the ruddy drops that visit any sad heart"; consequently, she insists that he reveal his secrets to her.

☐ Place question marks and exclamation points inside the quotation marks if they are part of the quotation, but outside if they are not:

King Henry asks, "What rein can hold licentious wickedness when down the

hill he holds his fierce career?"

But:

Which Shakespearean character said, "Fortune is painted blind, with a muffler

afore her eyes"?

7d-8   Handling interpolations in quoted material

Personal comments or explanations within a quotation must be placed in square brackets (not parentheses). The word *sic* in square brackets means that the quotation has been copied exactly, errors and all.

The critical review was titled "A Cassual [sic] Analysis of Incest and Other

Passions."

The *sic* indicates that *Cassual* is reproduced exactly as it is spelled in the original. Here is an explanatory interpolation also set off in square brackets:

Desdemona answers Emilia with childlike innocence: "Beshrew me if I would

do such a wrong [cuckold her husband] for all the whole world."

7d

7d-9   Using the ellipsis

The ellipsis—three dots with a space before and after each dot—is used to indicate the omission of material from a quotation. Omissions are necessary when only a part of the quotation is relevant to your point. Use of the ellipsis, however, does not free you from the obligation to remain faithful to the intent of the author's original text. The following example shows how the misuse of the ellipsis can distort an author's meaning:

Original   Faulkner's novels have the quality of being lived, absorbed,
                remembered rather than merely observed.

                                                Malcolm Cowley

Misused   Malcolm Cowley further suggests that "Faulkner's novels have the
quotation
                quality of being . . . merely observed."

Ellipsis tip

A period is not the same as the dot of an ellipsis. Ellipsis dots have a space between them. A period follows a word with no space between.

If you are quoting no more than a fragment, and it is clear that something has been left out, no ellipsis is necessary:

Malcolm Cowley refers to Faulkner's "mythical kingdom."

But when it is not clear that an omission has been made, the ellipsis must be used. These are the rules:

☐ *Omissions within a sentence are indicated by three spaced dots:*

Original   Mammals were in existence as early as the latest Triassic, 190 million years ago, yet for the first one hundred and twenty million years of their history, from the end of the Triassic to the late Cretaceous, they were a suppressed race, unable throughout that span of time to produce any carnivore larger than cat-size or herbivore larger than rat-size.

Adrian Desmond

7d

Quotation   Adrian Desmond, arguing that dinosaurs were once dominant over mammals, points out that "mammals were in existence as early as the latest Triassic . . . yet for the first one hundred and twenty million years of their history . . . they were a suppressed race, unable throughout that span of time to produce any carnivore larger than cat-size or herbivore larger than rat-size."

Two omissions are made in the quotation, and both are indicated by an ellipsis of three spaced dots.

☐ *Omissions at the end of a sentence use a period followed by three spaced dots:*

Adrian Desmond, arguing that the dinosaurs were once dominant over mammals, points out that for millions of years the mammals were "a suppressed race, unable throughout that span of time to produce any carnivore larger than cat-size. . . ."

Notice that the first dot is a period. It is placed immediately after the last word with no intervening space.

If the ellipsis is followed by parenthetical material at the end of a sentence, use three spaced dots and place the sentence period after the final parenthesis:

> Another justice made the following, more restrictive, statement: "You have the right to disagree with those in authority . . . but you have no right to break the law . . ." (Martin 42).

☐ *Omissions of a sentence or more also are indicated by four dots; however, a complete sentence must both precede and follow the four dots.* Here's an example:

Original	*Manuscript Troana* and other documents of the Mayas describe a cosmic catastrophe during which the ocean fell on the continent, and a terrible hurricane swept the earth. The hurricane broke up and carried away all towns and forests. Exploding volcanoes, tides sweeping over mountains, and impetuous winds threatened to annihilate humankind, and actually did annihilate many species of animals. The face of the earth changed, mountains collapsed, other mountains grew and rose over the onrushing cataract of water driven from oceanic spaces, numberless rivers lost their beds, and a wild tornado moved through the debris descending from the sky.
	Immanuel Velikovsky

Unacceptable use of four dots to mark the omission	That species of animals may have been made extinct by some worldwide catastrophe is not unthinkable. "According to *Manuscript Troana*. . . . The face of the earth changed, mountains collapsed, other mountains grew and rose over the onrushing cataract of water driven from oceanic spaces, numberless rivers lost their beds, and a wild tornado moved through the debris. . . ."

The quotation is unacceptably used because the fragment "According to *Manuscript Troana*" is placed before the four dots. Here is an acceptable use:

> That species of animals may have been made extinct by some worldwide catastrophe is not unthinkable. Immanuel Velikovsky states that "*Manuscript Troana* and other documents of the Mayas describe a cosmic catastrophe. . . . The face of the earth changed, mountains collapsed, other mountains grew and rose over the onrushing cataract of water driven from oceanic spaces, numberless rivers lost their beds, and a wild tornado moved through the debris. . . ."

Complete sentences are reproduced before and after the four periods, satisfying the convention.

☐ *Omissions of long passages—several stanzas, paragraphs, or pages—are marked by a single line of spaced dots:*

Speaking through the prophet Amos, the God of the Israelites warns sternly:

> For you alone have I cared
>
> among all the nations of the world;
>
> therefore will I punish you
>
> for all your iniquities.
>
> . . . .
>
> An enemy shall surround the land;
>
> your stronghold shall be thrown down
>
> and your palaces sacked.

☐ *Omissions that immediately follow an introductory statement require no ellipsis:*

Acceptable	In Booth's fantastic mind, his act was to be "the perfect crime of the ages and he the most heroic assassin of all times."
Not acceptable	In Booth's fantastic mind, his act was to be … "the perfect crime of the ages and he the most heroic assassin of all times."

Although an omission has been made in the beginning of the quotation, the use of an ellipsis following the introductory statement is unnecessary.

7d-10 Overusing quotations

No passage in the paper should consist of a long string of quotations. A mixture of summaries, paraphrases, and quotations is smoother and easier to read; moreover, a mixture gives the impression that you've done more in your paper than simply patch together bits and pieces from books and articles. Here is an example of a paragraph crammed with too many quotations:

> According to McCullough, "the groundswell of public opinion against the Japanese started in the early 1900s" (191). This is when the United States Industrial Commission issued a report stating that the Japanese "are more servile than the Chinese, but less obedient and far less desirable" (Conrat 18). At about the same time, the slogan of politician and labor leader Dennis

Kearney was "the Japs must go!" (Daniels 10). The mayor of San Francisco wrote that "the Japanese cannot be taken into the American culture because they are not the stuff of which American citizens are made" (9-10). In 1905, writes McCullough, "the Japanese and Korean Expulsion League held its first meeting and spawned many other such similar organizations" (102).

Here is an improved version, which deftly turns many of the quotations into summaries and paraphrases, resulting in a cleaner, less cluttered paragraph:

The anti-Japanese movement in America goes back to the turn of the century, when the United States Industrial Commission claimed that the Japanese "are more servile than the Chinese, but less obedient and far less desirable" (Conrat 18). At about the same time, the slogan of politician and labor leader Dennis Kearney was "The Japs must go!" while the mayor of San Francisco insisted that it was impossible for the Japanese to assimilate into American culture and that they were "not the stuff of which American citizens are made" (Daniels 9-10). In this xenophobic atmosphere, the Japanese and Korean Expulsion League was formed in 1905, and a number of other anti-Japanese societies followed (McCullough 102).

Notice, by the way, that the improved version contains fewer references than the original. The blend of summaries, paraphrases, and quotations not only reduced clutter, but also cut down on the number of notes by combining references from the same source into a single sentence and under a single note. By this deft blending, you also avoid "the string of pearls effect," that is, having one quotation follow another in rapid succession.

7d-11 Personal commentary

In your research, you no doubt will arrive at your own ideas and opinions about the topic—that's a part of learning and one of the reasons teachers assign research papers. A good paper is made up not only of other writers' ideas, but also of your own, backed by solid evidence. Some of your own opinions appear as personal comments in your notes, but others occur to you as you write the first draft. For instance, one student, writing a paper arguing that the present grading system in universities does not help learning, incorporated this personal note into her paper:

7d

> The University of California at Santa Cruz does not use GPAs, bell curves, or class ranking to judge a student's academic ability. Instead, it uses a pass/no pass system accompanied by the instructor's narrative comments on the student's work. Yet, UCSC is often praised for its atmosphere of fostering learning for learning's sake and encouraging students to try new fields of knowledge without risking a bad transcript.

The student's opinion was based on evidence gained after visiting a friend at the university.

Without personal notes like these, your paper might seem wholly strung together from the ideas of others, with nothing of your own in it. Be sure that your rough draft reveals your own points of view, your own beliefs, and your own conclusions.

7e How to use quotations to explore and discover

Your role in the research paper is not simply to cite a parade of authority opinions; it is also to react to them according to your personal theories and views. Authority opinion should be used to support or confirm your own viewpoint, not to replace it. If you agree with an opinion, say so and why. On the other hand, if you disagree, state the case for your disagreement. In writing the research paper, you must claim your seat at the banquet table of opinion as an intellectual equal. The thesis should reflect your own views or speculations on the topic, and the authorities you cite should never be given more credence than your personal judgment.

What we have described is, of course, an ideal that often is undone by the timidity of student-researchers. Many students feel that they cannot or should not doubt authority, much less debate its views. But that is exactly what you must do if your research paper is going to be original. You must assert your opinion; you must react to the research; you must say why you think it right or wrong. Consider an example from a paper arguing that boxing should be banned because its only objective is to injure an opponent. Early on in the paper the student cites Joyce Carol Oates's famous essay "On Boxing":

> To turn from an ordinary preliminary match to a "Fight of the Century," like those between Joe Louis and Billy Conn, Joe Frazier and Muhammad Ali, Marvin Hagler and Thomas Hearns, is to turn from listening or half-listening to a guitar being idly plucked to hearing Bach's *Well-Tempered Clavier* perfectly executed, and that too is part of the story's mystery: so much happens so swiftly and with such heart-stopping subtlety that you cannot absorb it except to know that something profound is happening and it is happening in a place beyond words.

So angered was the student by the quotation that he follows it with this satirical commentary:

> One can only imagine the deviant mind that can draw a parallel between the
>
> divine music of Bach and the bestial antics of professional boxers. How can one
>
> compare hands that break skulls, detach retinas, crush spleens, and cause fatal
>
> injuries, to hands that create musical chords to soothe human souls and trans-
>
> port people away from pain to a sphere of peace and pleasure?

No formula exists for judging ideas; the process will always be oddball and grounded in personal values. Research should inform our best decisions and influence our values, but there will always be issues over which sincere people disagree. As the writer of research papers, you should not be afraid to defend what you believe or to disagree with those with whom you differ.

7f Writing with unity, coherence, and emphasis

The primary rule of writing the research paper is that your notes must be blended smoothly into the natural flow of the paper. Paraphrases, summaries, indirect quotations, and allusions must be edited for smoothness. Quotations, of course, have to be used verbatim, must not be altered in any way, and yet must be made to fit into the context of the paper. Transitions between ideas should be logical and smooth. The paper should not seem a patchwork of unrelated snippets. In sum, you must observe the rhetorical principles of unity, coherence, and emphasis.

7f

7f-1 Unity

The rhetorical principle of unity means that a paper should stick to its chosen thesis without rambling. If the thesis states that Japanese art influenced French impressionism, the paper should cover exactly that subject and nothing more. If the thesis proposes to contrast the lifestyles of inner-city residents and suburb dwellers, the paper should pursue just that comparison, ignoring all side issues, no matter how fascinating you find them. To write a unified paper might require you, as one English teacher put it, to "kill your babies." Every writer has had to commit such editorial murder of a favorite image, word, phrase or sentence that simply didn't fit.

To observe the principle of unity, you simply have to follow the lead of your thesis. Properly drafted, the thesis predicts the content of the paper, controls its direction, and obligates you to a single purpose. You introduce only material relevant to your thesis, suppressing the urge to dabble in side issues or to stray from the point. Such single-mindedness will produce a unified paper that is easy to read.

7f-2   Coherence

If unity means "sticking to the point," coherence means "sticking together." To make your writing coherent, you must think of the paragraph as expressing a single idea to which the individual sentences contribute bits of meaning. Here are four suggestions to help you write coherent paragraphs:

☐ *Repeat key words or use clear pronouns.* Either repeat key words or make certain that the pronouns you use clearly hark back to them. In the passage that follows, notice how the key word *villain* is either repeated or replaced by a pronoun clearly referring to it:

The villain in science fiction movies is always the personification of evil. One way this concentration of evil is achieved is by surrounding the villain with numerous henchmen. Without henchmen, the villain would appear much less powerful. To accentuate his villainy, he surrounds himself with ruthless storm troopers, evil robots, slime monsters, or whatever. With these associates by the villain's side, the eventual triumph of the hero over the villain takes place against a backdrop of overwhelming odds.

Repetition of the word *villain* and use of the pronouns *he, himself,* and *his,* which refer to *villain,* provide a common thread connecting all five sentences.

☐ *Use parallel structures.* The deliberate repetition of certain words, phrases, or clauses in a paragraph can give sentences a cohering rhythm and harmony, as the repetition of *can* and a verb does in this example:

Fleas of various species can jump 150 times their own length, can survive months without feeding, can accelerate 50 times faster than the space shuttle, can withstand enormous pressure, and can remain frozen for a year and then revive.

☐ *Use transitional markers.* Transitional markers are words or phrases used to assert the relationships between the sentences of a paragraph. Common among these markers are the conjunctions *and, or, nor, but,* and *for.* Other, lengthier connectives also are used to ensure coherence. Consider the highlighted words in this passage:

The type-A person is forever nervous about coming events--always wanting success but fearing failure. As an illustration consider Howard Hughes, the brilliant entrepreneur. He started a car industry with good potential, but shut it down overnight because his automobile was not perfect. Such rashness is typical of type-A people, who often set themselves up for failure because their best efforts never seem good enough. In contrast to type As, type Bs pride themselves on their optimism and relaxed attitude. Type Bs are the kind of people who study hours for an exam and do poorly, yet they still feel good about themselves because they did all that was possible.

Transitional markers add to the coherent and smooth development of the ideas in a paragraph. Here are some of the most common transitional markers and how they are used:

Adding: *furthermore, in addition, moreover, similarly, also*

Opposing: *however, though, nevertheless, on the other hand, unlike*

Concluding: *therefore, as a result, consequently*

Exemplifying: *for example, for instance, to illustrate, that is*

Intensifying: *in fact, indeed, even, as a matter of fact*

Sequencing: *first, second, finally, in conclusion, to sum up, in short*

☐ *Use a transitional sentence.* One common way to make the transition from one paragraph to the next is to open the second paragraph with a straddling sentence. This is a sentence that stands with one foot on the paragraph that is just ending and the other on the one that is just beginning. Here is an example of the use of a transition sentence that straddles two paragraphs:

7f

> Anyone with an interest in biography soon becomes interested in Boswell's *Life of Johnson*. It stands next to other biographies as Shakespeare stands beside other playwrights: towering above them all. For more than two centuries it has been continuously in print, and in that time it has won innumerable admirers. No other biography has given so much pleasure; no other biography has created such a vivid central character. It has become a truism that, as a result of Boswell's extraordinary book, Samuel Johnson is better known to us than any other man in history.

Straddle sentence ———

> As well as being a famous and much loved book, the *Life of Johnson* is a work that raises fundamental questions about the nature of biography itself. Is it possible for a biographer to fully understand what it is like to be another human being? However careful and diligent the writer, can biography be accurate, that is, faithful to life? Everybody

knows "Dr. Johnson," or so we think; but is the man we know from the pages of Boswell's book the same Johnson who strode the streets of London 250 years ago? Is biography science or art? History or fiction?

Boswell's Presumptuous Task, Adam Sisman

7f-3   Emphasis

The rhetorical principle of *emphasis* requires the expression of more important ideas in main or independent clauses and of less important ideas in subordinate or dependent clauses. In sum, emphatic writing attempts to rank ideas through grammatical structure. Here's an example of a piece of writing that is not emphatic:

Poor emphasis

The gifted child is a high achiever on a specific test, either the Otis or Binet I.Q. test. These tests are usually administered at the end of the second grade. They determine the placement of the child in third grade. These tests are characterized by written as well as oral questions, so that the child has the opportunity to be creative.

The grammatical treatment of ideas is altogether too democratic. A reader simply cannot distinguish between important and unimportant ideas because they are both expressed in a similar grammatical structure. Here is the same passage made emphatic:

Improved emphasis

A child is considered gifted if the child has achieved a high score on a specific test—the Otis or Binet I.Q. test, for example. Characterized by written as well as oral questions so that the child has the opportunity to be creative, these tests are administered at the end of the second grade to determine the proper placement of the child in third grade.

By placing subordinate ideas in subordinate clauses, the writer achieves a focus that's missing from the unemphatic version.

7g   Using the proper tense

MLA and CMS styles use the present tense to cite a work (e.g., "Leaver *suggests*"). APA style requires the past or present perfect tense to cite a work (e.g., "Gomez, Haggart, and Franz *have noted*"). Papers in the humanities usually are written in the present tense because their comments have universal significance that makes them true now or then. Here is an example:

> *Cold Mountain* is the grueling account of the journey of a Civil War soldier home
>
> to his sweetheart, Ada. In this, his first novel, the author reveals remarkable
>
> insight into human loneliness and the changes wrought by war.

Although the novel itself was published 1997, the comments about it are in the present tense because they continue to be true today.

Papers in the social sciences and certain of the life sciences use the APA style. They usually are written in the past or present perfect tense because most of the time the writers are indicating the results of studies or experiments that took place in the past. But exceptions do exist. Look at this student example:

> Benson (1997) reported that one in five women was destined for breast cancer.
>
> His study is considered accurate and has been the basis for extensive reevalua-
>
> tion of women's disease prevention.

As the example indicates, the APA style requires the past tense (*reported, was*) for sources cited but the present tense (*is*) for generalizations and conditions that remain true today. It requires the present perfect tense (*has been*) for experiments or conditions that have been reported and are still valid.

7h

7h Using graphics in your research paper

The ease with which graphics can be downloaded from the Internet or scanned from books and periodicals has changed the look of the modern student research paper. Students nowadays routinely include illustrations in their research papers. A paper on ancient Mesopotamian art might include an illustration of some typical pottery or cave drawing from that period. A paper on infant mortality, or on shifts in the housing market, might feature a pie chart, a block table, or some graph to emphasize a point. If you have the expertise, many computers allow the creation of tables, line graphs, or pie charts on your own. Or you may prefer to download such items from various electronic sources.

> **Graphic tip**
>
> Don't use graphics just to fill up pages in your paper. Only use them when they add significantly to the content of your work.

Here are some electronic sources for graphics you can download and use in your paper:

Artwork	Library of Congress Exhibitions, lcweb.loc.gov/exhibits
Population statistics	U.S. Census Bureau, www.census.gov
Federal government information	USA.gov (the U.S. government's official web portal), www.usa.gov
The latest in disease control	National Institutes of Health, www.nih.gov

Here are some general rules to which you should pay attention:

1. Place your graphics as close as possible to their introduction. Don't separate text from artwork by pages.

2. Know the difference between figures and tables. A table presents information systematically, usually by columns. Any illustration that is not a table is a figure, such as a blueprint, chart, line drawing, map, or other artwork. Tables use the heading "Table" at the top of the illustration; figures use the heading "Fig." at the bottom of the illustration. All figures as well as tables must be numbered consecutively. (See the samples that follow.)

3. Provide the source (book, periodical, agency, or URL) for any illustrations used. (See samples that follow.)

4. Full-color art is acceptable if you have a color printer, but the headings and explanations should be in black print.

5. Always explain the table or figure before you show it in your text.

6. Make your explanations as brief and clear as possible.

(For how to document graphics, see Chapter 9, 10, or 11 for the documentation system you are using.)

The following are some sample illustrations of what a student might typically use.

■ For a paper on the Middle East conflict up to September 11, 2001:

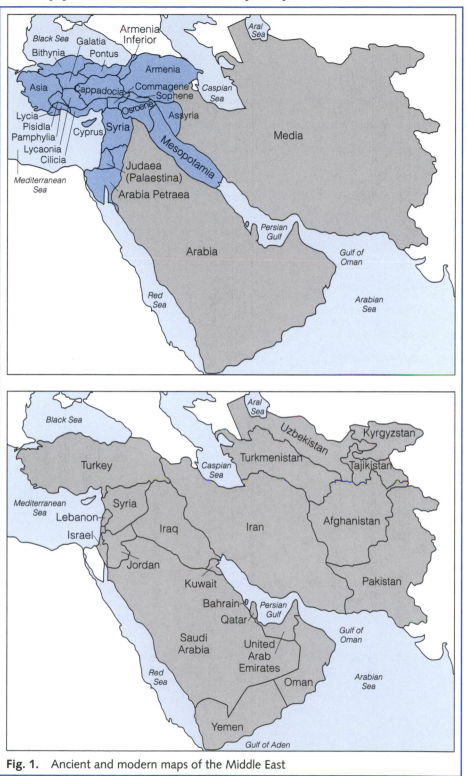

Fig. 1. Ancient and modern maps of the Middle East

7h

☐ For a paper concerning infant mortality due to mothers smoking:

Table

Exposure to environmental tobacco smoke: Percentage of children ages 0–6 living in homes where someone smokes regularly by race, Hispanic origin, and poverty status, 2003

Characteristic	Percentage
All	
Total	10.6
Race and Hispanic origin*	
White, non-Hispanic	11.1
Black, non-Hispanic	14.2
Other, non-Hispanic	12.3
Hispanic	3.8
Household poverty status	
Below 100% Poverty	21.8
100–199% Poverty	18.4
200% Poverty and Above	6.7

Source: U.S. Environmental Protection Agency, Indoor Environments Division, *National Survey on Environmental Management of Asthma and Children's Exposure to Environmental Tobacco Smoke.*

7h

For a paper on ancient Greek art:

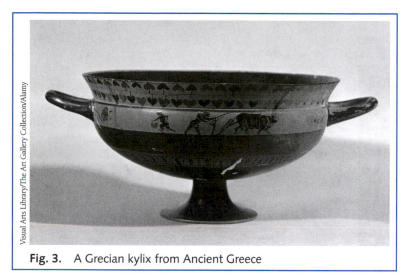

Visual Arts Library/The Art Gallery Collection/Alamy

Fig. 3. A Grecian kylix from Ancient Greece

For a paper on the work in anthropology of Mary Leakey:

Arco Images/Arco Images GmbH/Alamy

Fig. 4. A bone discovered by Mary Leakey in Tanzania

7h

☐ For a paper on the financial difficulty young couples face in trying to buy a house in the last decade:

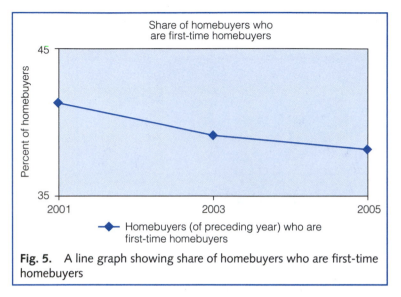

Fig. 5.   A line graph showing share of homebuyers who are first-time homebuyers

7h

☐ For a paper on Robert Penn Warren's poem "Evening Hawk":

Fig. 6.   A large hawk on the wing

7i   Writing the abstract

An abstract—a summary of the major ideas contained in your research paper—is for papers written in the APA style. Although the abstract replaces an outline, we suggest for the sake of logical progression and balance in the paper that you write from an outline, even if you are not required to submit one. Writing the abstract in coherent paragraphs is relatively easy if you have outlined your paper. To produce a smooth abstract you need only link and condense the main ideas of the outline with appropriate commentary.

In writing the abstract, use no more than one page (about 120 words). (Remember that the whole point of abstracting is to condense.) The abstract always falls on page 2, the page after the title page. It should have a running head and page number. Center the title "Abstract" (without quotation marks) one inch from the top of the page.

The abstract should meet the following criteria:

1. Reflect accurately the purpose and content of your paper
2. Explain briefly the central issue or problem of your paper
3. Summarize your paper's most important points
4. Mention the major sources used
5. State your conclusions clearly
6. Be coherent so that it is easy to read
7. Remain objective in its point of view

Here is an example from a student paper:

Vitamins 2

Abstract

Until recently, the official view on healthful eating was that anyone who ate

a normally balanced diet did not need vitamin supplements. However, recent

research by a team at Trinity College in England and at Brigham and Women's

Hospital in Boston concludes that certain vitamins, especially the vitamins

A, B, C, D, and E (also called antioxidants), can help prevent such serious

diseases as heart failure, diabetes, depression, flu, and eye problems. The

conclusion of this research is that although vitamins cannot substitute for good

eating habits, plenty of exercise, and not smoking, the findings do strengthen

the argument for adding vitamins as a nutritional supplement.

Human beings start flying like birds.

The Wright Brothers

Human beings have always envied eagles and seagulls for their ability to flap their wings, sail on high, and dodge through the air. Orville and Wilbur Wright, two brothers from Dayton, Ohio, had their interest in flying aroused by the German engineer Otto Lilienthal's glider flights. Both excellent engineers, the brothers used the facilities of the bicycle repair shop and factory they owned for a place to experiment with flying. On December 17, 1903, they made the first controlled, sustained flight in a power-driven airplane, near Kitty Hawk, North Carolina. After this astounding accomplishment, they continued their work in Dayton and built several biplanes. Their record-breaking flights earned them world recognition, and in 1909 the U.S. government accepted their planes for army use.

8 Revising Your Rough Draft

8a	Principles of revision
8b	Revising the opening paragraph
8c	Revising sentences for variety and style
8d	Revising words: Diction
8e	Rules for writers. Not.

FAQ

1. How many times should I reread my writing? *See 8a-1.*

2. How should I proceed in my revision? *See 8a-2.*

3. How can I spice up my introductions? *See 8b-1.*

4. Can I refer to myself in the paper as "I"? *See 8c-2.*

5. What is sexist language? *See 8c-3.*

6. What are meaningless words and phrases? *See 8d-4.*

7. What is the active voice and why should I use it? *See 8c-1.*

8. How do I revise the body paragraphs? *See 8b-3.*

9. What are redundant expressions? *See 8d-3.*

10. Why shouldn't I use a big word if I know one? *See 8d-5.*

8a · Principles of revision

Revision is partly a psychological and partly a mechanical process. All writers who wish to write well must learn how to revise their work. Take the sentence you just read. It is not what we first wrote, but what we ended up with after revision. Originally, we wrote this: "Every writer who wishes to write well must learn to revise his work." The problem with that sentence is that its use of the pronoun "his," by typecasting every writer as a man, is sexist. We could have changed this sentence to read "Every writer who wishes to write well must learn how to revise their work." But that would have meant using a plural pronoun, "their," to take the place of a singular noun, "every writer." If this were an informal paper, that usage would be perfectly acceptable. However, a formal research paper is held to stricter standards of grammar, and many instructors would regard such a construction as wrong. This kind of adaptation of language and grammar to fit a particular audience is what we mean when we say that revision is partly psychological.

The process of revision is also partly mechanical. As you comb over the first draft, you will no doubt find misstatements of opinions and errors of facts. Grammatical mistakes made in the heat of composing will suddenly become apparent. You'll find instances of poor word usage. A better way of phrasing an idea will occur to you. Some paragraphs will seem tedious and overstuffed with details. Others will strike you the very opposite way—as too thin and requiring shoring up with more data. All these miscues and mistakes, big and little, will occur to you during the revision process. As veteran writers have said, "There is no writing; there is only rewriting."

8a-1 Rereading your writing

"The last act of writing must be to become one's own reader," said John Ciardi, the American poet. All revision is based on repeated rereading of the first draft. Dedicated writers are fanatic about rereading their material. One novelist claimed he revised every page 20 times; another boasted that he went over every line he wrote at least 150 times. Our own efforts at revising fall somewhere between those two numbers.

How often should you go over your rough draft as you revise it? Certainly, the typical student cannot go over the material 30 times or 150 times or even 10 times. Nor can the busy instructor. But most writing teachers agree that the research paper writer should go over the text a minimum of three times.

8a-2 Revising the paper from biggest to smallest elements

Many instructors recommend that in their revision, students work from the biggest elements to the smallest. This is, on the whole, good advice because it makes the act of revision methodical. Bear in mind, however, that just because you're focusing on finding mountains is no excuse for ignoring mole hills. If, in your first revision pass you discover a small fry, such as a misspelled word, by all means correct it even though you're after bigger fish.

8b   Revising the opening paragraph

Check your opening paragraph to see whether your beginning is sprightly enough to draw in your reader. Check the thesis to be sure that it is not muddled or vague. Your thesis, which typically is the final sentence of the first paragraph, should clearly explain what your paper proposes to argue, assert, or do. Here's an example of a muddled opening:

> Most women think that they will be victimized by men and that this is a normal state of affairs; therefore it is important that women fight back by standing up for themselves. They must refuse to play second fiddle to men. On the other hand, given the present distribution of power and privilege, women are bound to be tinged by the historical leftovers of inequality. In order to get along in the world, they will have to show a certain amount of admiration for men and a willingness to accommodate them. My paper is an attempt to demonstrate that this is a backward tactic.

This introduction has too many themes: Women are victimized by men; women should stand up to men; women's roles are still affected by the inequality of the past; to get along in the world, women must show a willingness to accommodate men. The student was advised to focus her research on, and develop, one point. Here's her rewritten introduction:

> Today our society enforces femininity by certain unspoken threats, and if a woman tests the limits of her gender beyond a certain point, she will lose the approval of women as well as men. For example, if she is viewed as pushy, assertive, aggressive, and selfish, she may lose her job, her boyfriend, and alienate her family. Moreover, a woman who dares to oppose this patriarchal system risks being perceived as both unfeminine and undesirable. That is why some women have resigned themselves to playing a narrowly prescribed role in this male-dominated drama. But this unacknowledged principle of surrender to masculinity has become too costly for women of this generation to continue engaging in it.

With the thesis now plainly stated in the last sentence, the introduction is clear and sharp.

8b-1   Revising the introduction

Opening paragraphs usually consist of two sections: an introduction and a thesis. The introduction is made in the initial sentences; the thesis is, traditionally, the final sentence of the paragraph. Because it gives the reader a first glimpse of what's to come, the introduction is critically important to the paper. A sprightly and attractive introduction will entice your reader to read on and to want more. A drab introduction will have the opposite effect. Beginnings are limited only by the writer's imagination. You may find a boost in three time-honored strategies for beginning a paper: Use a quotation, ask a question, or present an illustration.

a. Use a quotation

Beginning the paper with a quotation that your opening remarks either support or refute has the advantage of immediately plunging into the topic. The quotation can be a well-known saying or any especially apt comment. A dictionary of familiar quotations is available in the reference section of all libraries, with quotations listed by subject headings. Be sure that the quotation you use is applicable to the topic and that it leads naturally to your thesis. In this introduction the quotation suggests that civil servants should be trained professionals:

> "There are some things we can no longer afford—above all we can no longer afford to do without highly trained government officials." These words are found in the diary of Felix Frankfurter, chief justice of the United States under Franklin Delano Roosevelt. Frankfurter's warning that government jobs cannot be left to amateurs who are appointed because they gave money to a president's election campaign or otherwise curried favor with the candidate is even truer today than it was sixty years ago.

Quotation tip

Go to any search engine and type in "dictionary of quotations." Then follow the links to a gold mine of quotations.

b. Ask a question

Asking a question has the advantage of allowing you to steer the discussion in exactly the direction you want to go. Here's an example from a paper advocating expanded welfare assistance to single mothers with children:

> Would you really want to exchange places with a mother on welfare because she gets for free money that others earn? Before you say yes, consider the case of Joan Smith. She washes her clothes in a bathtub. She travels everywhere by

8b

bus or foot. She lives with rickety furniture in an apartment that rattles every time trucks drive by. Shootings that endanger her children's lives are common in her neighborhood. She feels disgraced because she is poor and dependent on the public dole. The irony of her situation is that she is bright and filled with intellectual curiosity. She could go to college if only someone would pay her way. I believe in a welfare system that helps single mothers with dependent children improve their lives by offering them a free education so that they can pursue a career that will eventually help them get off welfare and live with independent dignity.

c. Present an illustration

Anecdotes or examples that illustrate a point are popular openings for both sermons and papers. Start your paper with a riveting illustration, and your reader will eagerly follow you. Here is an example from a paper arguing that the original versions of fairy tales, although more gruesome than the modern ones, also were harmless and more appealing:

> When Cinderella's wicked stepsisters saw the prince holding up the glass slipper during the ball and looking eagerly for the girl who could wear it, they sliced off their heels and toes in an effort to make that slipper fit. This scene appears in the original version of "Cinderella." It is rather grisly, but typical of many fairy tales before they were sanitized to omit the more gruesome details for fear they might scare children or harden them to torture, torment, and mayhem. But modern research by a number of leading psychiatrists and psychologists reveals that coping with imaginary evil, including violence, is healthy for children and does not turn them into neurotic or cold-blooded adults.

Aptly chosen, the right anecdote or example can be an effective introduction for your research paper.

8b-2   Check that your paragraphs follow the sequence of topics in the thesis

The topic sentences of your paragraphs must follow the same sequence as the points of your thesis. If the thesis announces that it will cover a, b, and c, your topic sentences must appear in that same sequence. Consider this thesis:

Although drugs do effectively lower cholesterol and reduce the risk of heart attack or stroke, many have serious side effects that include headache and muscle pain, severe allergic reactions that affect breathing, and even permanent damage to the liver and inflammation of the pancreas.

As you thumb through the paper, however, you find its paragraphs covering this sequence of topics:

1. An introduction to cholesterol-reducing drugs that lower the risk of heart attack and stroke
2. Headache as a side effect
3. Muscle pain as a side effect
4. Pancreatic inflammation as a side effect
5. Liver damage as a side effect
6. Allergic reactions that affect breathing

The paragraphs have the topics in a different sequence than was announced in the thesis. Jumbling the sequence of topics makes the paper harder to read. If you do not cover the topics in the order promised by your thesis, you need to either rewrite the thesis or shuffle the paragraphs so that the two sequences match.

8b-3   Revising the body paragraphs

By body paragraphs we mean those in the middle of the paper where the argument is at its thickest. Don't make these paragraphs so compact and dense as to choke the reader with details. A long paragraph forces the reader to swallow information in one big gulp. It's better that the information be organized in tidbits of shorter paragraphs. Here is an example:

8b

Sexual harassment has declined by 20 percent this year. So states the Equal Employment Opportunities Commission (EEOC), a federal agency that upholds all federal laws prohibiting job discrimination. How can this statistic be true? Have people changed their characters or basic instincts? Have women become less squeamish about being touched by male fellow workers, or have men stopped "hitting on" females because men have decided to revert to Victorian morality and manners? As a student, I was determined to shed some light on what was happening in our society, so I went on my personal investigation. Well, here is what I found out when I checked with the personnel managers of two companies for which I work: The most important information I received was that men have become more sensitive to women's need to be respected because the media has exposed much about sexual harassment. Following the Clarence Thomas and Anita Hill sexual harassment case back in 1991, all kinds of seminars or workshops on sexual harassment were offered. Men have been warned that the legal consequences of touching women inappropriately may be loss of job or even jail time.

Here is the same information served up in smaller paragraphs:

Sexual harassment has declined by 20 percent this year. So states the Equal Employment Opportunities Commission (EEOC), a federal agency that upholds all federal laws prohibiting job discrimination. How can this statistic be true? Have people changed their characters or basic instincts? Have women become less squeamish about being touched by male fellow workers, or have men stopped "hitting on" females because men have decided to revert to Victorian morality and manners?

As a student, I was determined to shed some light on what was happening in our society, so I went on my personal investigation. Well, here is what I found out when I checked with the personnel managers of two companies for which I work. The most important information I received was that men have become more sensitive to women's need to be respected because the media has exposed much about sexual harassment. Following the Clarence Thomas and Anita Hill sexual harassment case back in 1991, all kinds of seminars or workshops on sexual harassment were offered. Men have been warned that the legal consequences of touching women inappropriately may be loss of job or even jail time.

8b-4   Check paragraph transitions

In Chapter 7 we discussed techniques of ensuring smooth transitions between paragraphs (see end of verified). If we liken your essay to a train, the individual paragraphs would be separate boxcars of meaning. They must be linked to one another not only by simple sequence, but also by the locomotion of a common theme, idea, or argument. You achieve this linkage by the use of transitional markers and sentences. You should check that your paragraphs are truly coupled together rather than simply sitting side by side.

8c   Revising sentences for variety and style

Variety is easy to recognize and define. It means a mixture that is not monotonous. Style, on the other hand, is not that easy to pinpoint. Its presence in a piece of writing is unmistakable but not showy. Like tact, style is conspicuous in its absence but subtle in its presence. A passage that monotonously uses the same kind of sentence over and over again is not only boring, it is also without style. Here is an example of what we mean:

Monotonous   Poetry is regarded by many as the highest literary art form. Poetry is

seen nowadays as an unpopular form. Poetry used to be read very

widely by the middle classes. Poetry no longer enjoys that distinction

and today is hardly read by anyone.

Notice that the writer begins each sentence with the same word, *poetry*. Moreover, every sentence is more or less the same length. Writers sometimes deliberately write several similar sentences in a row for emphasis. But this writer is being lazy, not emphatic, and the result of the repetition is monotony. The problem is easily fixed by simply combining some sentences or beginning some others with a different word:

Varied   Poetry is regarded by many as the highest literary art form. Nowa-

days, however, it has become unpopular. Whereas poetry used to be

read very widely by the middle classes, today it hardly is ever read by

anyone.

We do not like to begin more than two sentences in a row with the same word; and we do not like to end more than two sentences in a row with the same word, either. If we find ourselves using many short sentences in a row, we deliberately interrupt the monotony by making the next sentence longer. Our aim is to write a succession of sentences that do not appear cut from a cookie cutter. If you find yourself using several sentences of the same kind in a row, go back over the material and change them for the sake of variety.

Here is a summary of ways to vary your sentences:

☐ Learn to juxtapose short and long sentences. Follow several short sentences with a long one:

The name "Christopher" meant nothing. Felice paid no attention. She ignored

the call. But because the speaker, who turned out to be an elderly gentleman,

was gracious in his comments about the tragedy of war, she listened.

☐ The first three sentences are short; the last one is long.

8c

☐ Learn to subordinate. Most of us write compound sentences almost without thinking. But subordinating one clause to another requires thoughtful effort. It means that you must place lesser thoughts "sub," or below, the main idea.

Coordinate	I arrived at Yankee Stadium, and the first inning was already underway.
Subordinate	The first inning was already under way when I arrived at Yankee Stadium.

The fact that the inning was already under way is the more important idea and belongs in the main clause.

Coordinate	The car still runs well, but it is not worth selling.
Subordinate	The car, which still runs well, is not worth selling.

The fact that the car is not worth selling is the more important idea and belongs in the main clause.

☐ Learn to use parallel constructions. A parallel construction is one that uses grammatically similar elements to express ideas. Here are two examples:

Not parallel	The king stood on the balcony. Then he decided to wave at the crowd. Later he also shook hands with the foreign minister.
Parallel	The king stood on the balcony, waved at the crowd, and shook hands with the foreign minister.

Notice that all verbs are active and in the past.

Not parallel	He traveled by bus, by ship, and he took a plane.
Parallel	He traveled by bus, by ship, and by plane.

8c-1   Revise sentences to use the active voice

Verbs have two voices—active and passive. In the active voice the subject acts: "Jim wrote those letters." In the passive voice, the subject is acted upon: "Those letters were written by Jim." Whenever you can, use the active voice in your writing. That the passive voice makes a writer seem objective is a myth. What the passive voice does is make your writing sound textbookish and stilted. In bureaucratic or political writing, the passive voice is often used to shield the person responsible for an action: "Two laws protecting illegal aliens were passed." The person proposing those laws is hidden from the reader's view.

Consider the following excerpt from a student's paper on the Great Pyramid at Giza:

Passive
Who built the Great Pyramid? When? How? Throughout history students of archaeology have been baffled by these questions. All sorts of mystical theories have been propounded by Egyptologists, but it has been concluded by most experts today that the Great Pyramid was built by Egyptian citizens using the simplest of tools and technology

Notice the directness and vigor of the passage when it's recast in the active voice:

Active
Who built the Great Pyramid? When? How? Throughout history these questions have baffled students of archaeology. Egyptologists have propounded all sorts of mystical theories, but most experts today have concluded that the Great Pyramid was built by Egyptian citizens using the simplest of tools and technology.

Two exceptions call for the passive voice: (1) for an occasional change of pace—to add an inviting pleat in an otherwise seamless bolt of writing, and (2) for the sake of focus, especially when the action is more important than the actor. For example, look at the last sentence of the passage. Because the Great Pyramid is the focus of both the research and the passage, it deserves the emphasis it receives from the passive construction. Compare the last passage with the following:

Who built the Great Pyramid? When? How? Throughout history these questions have baffled students of archaeology. Egyptologists have propounded all sorts of mystical theories, but most experts today have concluded that Egyptian citizens, using the simplest of tools and technology, built the Great Pyramid.

Recasting the final sentence in the active voice removes the pyramid from center stage and replaces it with "Egyptian citizens." But the focus of the paragraph is on the Great Pyramid, not on Egyptian citizens. The passive voice in this instance is more emphatic.

A third reason to use the passive voice is to avoid sexism. For instance, it is better to write, "The laboratory was kept sterile at all times," than to use the awkward "He or she [meaning the technician] kept the laboratory sterile at all times." (See 8c-3.)

8c

8c-2   Revise to use an appropriate point of view

Research papers consist mainly of information found in books, periodicals, and other sources that you incorporate into your writing. In the past, most instructors insisted that research papers be written only from the third-person point of view, in an attempt to keep the writing objective. The first-person point of view was thought suitable only for personal writing—topics like the favorite, "How I Spent My Summer Vacation." Here are examples of the two points of view:

First-person point of view   In my research I found that the most extreme negative criticism of Jefferson Davis places the full weight of the Southern defeat on his head.

Objective point of view   Research indicates that the most extreme negative criticism of Jefferson Davis places the full weight of the Southern defeat on his head.

Today many prestigious journals have relaxed their rules. Authors routinely use the "I" or "we" point of view to report research data or draw attention to their findings, as the following examples show:

> For several weeks before I showed up, field archaeologists, mapping specialists and other workers had been collecting bits and pieces those ancients left behind—tiny corncobs, animal bones, stone tools, arrowheads. It's tedious work, as I find out when I'm assigned to help Betsy Marshall, a spry 76-year-old volunteer and former schoolteacher.
>
> Grace Lichtenstein,
> *Smithsonian,* May 2002

> A complicating feature of marriage transactions in complex societies is that there may be variability by social status, wealth, region, or ethnic group. Where this problem has arisen in coding for this study, we selected the preferred form of the dominant stratum or ethnic group within the society.
>
> Alice Schlegel and Rohn Eloul,
> *American Anthropologist,* June 1988

Which brings us to the question: Should you ever use the first-person point of view ("I" or "we") in your research papers, and if so, when?

If your instructor bans any but the third-person point of view, that, of course, is the point of view you have to use. Should your instructor not specify, you should ask. All other things being equal, a safe rule of thumb is this: Use the first-person point of view only for expressing your personal comments, judgments, or experiences. Otherwise use the third-person point of view. Here are some examples:

First person   I have tested these assumptions on a body of data gathered from three anthropologists.

> To produce a better fit with reality, I have made the following adjust-ments in my interpretations of the findings.
>
> Thus I theorized that . . .
>
> My findings indicated the exact opposite.

If you do use only the third-person point of view, at least try not to sound stuffy.

8c-3   Revise sexist language

In your writing, watch for language that reflects the values and biases of a male-dominated society. An example:

> A doctor should always look after the best interest of his patients.

This sentence makes a sexist assumption: that every doctor is a man. Hundreds and thousands of sentences like this can well lead us to the delusion that to be a doctor, you must be a man. Not only is this severely limiting; it is also false.

Publishers today encourage the use of sex-neutral nouns and pronouns in place of those that automatically and inaccurately specify sex, usually male. We urge you to do likewise. You could easily rewrite the preceding sentence a number of ways. For example, use plural nouns and pronouns:

> Doctors should always look after the best interest of their patients.

Here are two other fixes:

> A doctor should always look after the best interest of his or her patients.
>
> A doctor should always look after the best interest of patients.

All three sentences express the same idea but without the male bias.

Among the various solutions to sexist language that have been proposed over the years is the introduction of a new, nonsexist pronoun, *thon*—short for "that one"—to be used in place of *he* or *him* when the person's gender is not identified. So, for example, instead of writing

> A doctor should always look after the best interest of his patients,

you would write,

> A doctor should always look after the best interest of thon's patients.

8c

And instead of writing

> When a police officer comes, I will ask him.

you would write,

> When a police officer comes, I will ask thon.

This particular construction solves the problem of the automatic use of *he* and *him* to refer to some unknown third person who could very well be female. The idea is not new. *Thon* was first proposed in 1858, and it has yet to catch on.

A solution that some writers have hit on is to alternate between *she* and *he*, rather than the automatic *he*. Some writers even invert customary usage and write *she* where *he* once would have been used. But it strikes us that substituting one kind of sexism for another is not the best solution. With a little effort, any writer worth thon's salt can figure out how to express virtually any idea without resorting to sexist constructions.

Another common trick is to use the passive voice to hide the subject's gender.

> As soon as the doctor arrives, the nurse will notify him.

> Upon arrival, the doctor will be notified by the nurse.

Many jokes have been made about awkward words coined, so the wits say, to avoid sexist language. "Personhole" and "huperson" come to mind as classics of their kind, supposedly a replacement for "manhole" and "human." But sexist language is no laughing matter. And it does not belong in a research paper.

8d   Revising words: Diction

Word choice and usage comes under the heading of *diction*. Some people seem to think that when it comes to word choice, bigger is always better. But using a word just because it is big is a bad idea. You're better off using words for their exactness, appropriateness, and accuracy than for their size. The only time a bigger word is a better choice is when it is more accurate. In any case, the final decision to use this word over that should be based on the audience for whom you're writing. If you're doing a research paper for a history class, you could probably justify writing this sentence:

> The professor wrote a biography of the political leader that some critics called
>
> a *hagiography*.

Most readers would not know offhand the meaning of this word—it's an uncommon word that means treating a subject like a saint. But in the context of the sentence it is a useful word with no exact single-word equivalent. You can use a big word if it is suitable to your meaning and you have every expectation that your audience will understand it. Otherwise, you should use several small words to plug the gap made by the omission of your big word.

8d-1 Revise diction for accuracy and exactness

The best writing is concise and to the point. It uses a vocabulary appropriate to the subject. If you know your topic well, you will be exact in writing about it. Your readers will know exactly what you mean because you will tell them without being vague or fuzzy. You'll use the right technical terms and pile on details when necessary. Notice the difference between the following two paragraphs, taken from the first and second drafts of a student paper on the origin of Indian castes:

Inexact   The occupations of the four major castes were spelled out in the *Laws of Manu*: The Brahmin were the highest, the Kshatriyas came second, the Vaishyas followed, and the Sudras were at the bottom of the pile.

The vagueness of this passage results partly from the writer's mistaken assumption that readers would be familiar with the general divisions of Indian castes and partly from the writer's not knowing the caste divisions well. When the instructor pointed out that more information was needed, the student produced this revision:

More exact   The occupations of the four major castes were spelled out in the *Laws of Manu*: The Brahmin were to teach, interpret the Vedas (holy scriptures), and perform the required ritual sacrifices. The Kshatriyas were to be the warriors and social governors (even kings). The Vaishyas were to tend the livestock and to engage in commerce in order to create wealth for the country. As for the Sudras, they were to become the servants of the three higher castes--doing their bidding without malice or resentment.

8d

The added detail makes the writer's style seem surer and more confident.

Use as many words as you need to make your point—no more, no less. Most of all, if you don't know what you're talking about, don't try to snow your reader with words. Exactness adds to clarity by getting rid of jargon and padding, of any words that do not add significantly to meaning.

Here's an example:

Not concise   In early 1970 the National Aeronautics and Space Administration conducted an investigation to find funds from Congress for this new concept of a reusable space vehicle. The administration decided that the establishment of a careful approach on its part was an important necessity because some members of Congress would doubtless show a strong opposition to the replacement of the expendable Saturn rockets that had carried the Apollo astronauts to the moon. There was tremendous precision and careful documentation in the preparation and submission of the request to Congress.

Concise   In the early 1970s, the National Aeronautics and Space Administration (NASA) decided to see if Congress would fund its new concept of a reusable space vehicle. The administration approached the problem carefully, because some congressional members had already opposed replacing the expendable Saturn rockets that had carried the Apollo astronauts to the moon. A precise and well-documented request was submitted to Congress.

The first version is fuzzy because the main ideas are expressed in lumpy phrases: "conducted an investigation" instead of "decided to see"; "decided that the establishment of a careful approach on its part was a necessity" instead of "approached the problem carefully"; and "the replacement of" instead of "replacing."

8d

8d-2   Revise the overuse of phrases for subjects instead of single nouns

The heavy use of long phrases for subjects is a characteristic of bureaucratic writing. Here are several examples of sentences that are hard to read because they use phrases instead of single nouns as subjects. The phrase used as a subject is highlighted. Rewriting the sentences to simplify the subject makes them more concise.

Phrase subject   The ratification of the agreement by the board requires a vote of a majority.

Simplified subject and introductory sentence   To ratify the agreement, the board needs a majority vote.

Or

The board needs a majority vote to ratify the agreement.

Phrase subject   The anthropological study of the Incas used computers.

Simplified   The Incas were studied with computers.
subject

Or

Computers were used to study the Incas.

8d-3 Revise redundant expressions

Redundant expressions are unnecessary words used to repeat what has already been said. Here is an example:

> During that time period the park area was populated with Indians who were
>
> sullen in appearance and made a living by working with silver metal.

That "time" is a "period," "park" an "area," "sullen" an "appearance," and "silver" a "metal" is clear from common knowledge and the context of the sentence. It is enough to write this:

> During that time the park was populated with Indians who looked sullen and
>
> made a living by working with silver.

8d

8d-4 Revise meaningless words and phrases

Meaningless words and phrases, used as fillers, blur a style. Consider the highlighted words in the following passage:

> The problem of world hunger is by and large a matter of business and politics.
>
> Basically the two become virtually entwined until for all intents and purposes
>
> they cannot be addressed separately in any given city or country.

Getting rid of the filler words clarifies the idea:

> The problem of world hunger is a matter of business and politics. The two
>
> become entwined until they cannot be addressed separately in any city or
>
> country.

8d-5   Revise snobbish diction

Snobbish diction consists of words used not to clarify but to impress. One writer submitted this dense patch:

> A person desirous of an interview must be cognizant of the fact that the interviewer may have dozens of other candidates to evaluate. A smart candidate endeavors to utilize the time wisely, facilitating the interviewer in ascertaining the candidate's qualifications.

Replacing the highlighted words with their more common equivalents results in a sharper and less pompous style:

> A person wanting an interview must be aware that the interviewer may have dozens of other candidates to evaluate. A smart candidate tries to use the time wisely, helping the interviewer find out the candidate's qualifications.

Language tip

It is easier to recognize pompous language when you hear it than when you read it silently. Read your paper aloud and listen to the language.

8e   Rules for writers. Not.

Here is a fun list of the sort of revisions writers most often make in their work. You can use it to guide your hand in revising your paper and to be amused while doing so.

1. Verbs has to agree with their subjects.
2. Prepositions are not words to end sentences with.
3. And don't start a sentence with a conjunction.
4. It is wrong to ever split an infinitive.
5. Avoid clichés like the plague. (They're old hat.)
6. Also, always avoid annoying alliteration.
7. Be more or less specific.
8. Parenthetical remarks (however relevant) are (usually) unnecessary.
9. Also too, never, ever use repetitive redundancies.
10. No sentence fragments.
11. Contractions aren't necessary and shouldn't be used.

12. Foreign words and phrases are not apropos.

13. Do not be redundant; do not use more words than necessary; it's highly superfluous.

14. One should NEVER generalize.

15. Don't use no double negatives.

16. Eschew ampersands & abbreviations, etc.

17. One-word sentences? Eliminate.

18. Analogies in writing are like feathers on a snake.

19. The passive voice should never be used.

20. Eliminate commas, that are, not necessary. Parenthetical words however should be enclosed in commas.

21. Never use a big word when a diminutive one would suffice.

22. DO NOT use exclamation points and all caps to emphasize!!!

23. Use words correctly, irregardless of how others use them.

24. Understatement is always the absolute best way to put forth earth-shaking ideas.

25. Use the apostrophe in it's proper place and omit it when its not needed.

26. If you've heard it once, you've heard it a thousand times: Resist hyperbole; not one writer in a million can use it correctly.

27. Puns are for children, not groan readers.

28. Go around the barn at high noon to avoid colloquialisms.

29. Even if a mixed metaphor sings, it should be derailed.

30. Who needs rhetorical questions?

31. Exaggeration is a billion times worse than understatement.

32. Do not put statements in the negative form.

33. A writer must not shift your point of view.

34. Place pronouns as close as possible, especially in long sentences of ten or more words, to their antecedents.

35. Writing carefully, dangling participles must be avoided.

36. If any word is improper at the end of a sentence, a linking verb is.

37. Take the bull by the hand and avoid mixing metaphors.

38. Avoid trendy locutions that sound flaky.

39. Everyone should be careful to use a singular pronoun with singular nouns in their writing.

40. Always pick on the correct idiom.

41. The adverb always follows the verb.

42. Be careful to use the homonym.

43. Proofread carefully to see if you any words out.

Marie Curie wins the 1903 Nobel Prize.

© Associated Press

Marie Curie

From an early age, Marie Curie (born Maria Sklodowska on November 7, 1867, in Warsaw, Poland) was captivated by the mysteries of mathematics and physics. She was known by her friends for having a formidable memory and an obsession with work, often neglecting to eat or sleep while she was studying. She is the only person ever to win two Nobel Prizes in different fields of science—physics (1903) and chemistry (1911). In 1895, she married the famous Pierre Curie, and together they studied radioactive materials, particularly pitchblende, from which uranium is extracted. Today she is revered for pioneering research in nuclear physics and cancer therapy and for the discovery of radium and polonium.

9 The MLA System of Documentation

9a Parenthetical documentation: Author-work (MLA)

9b Format for "Works Cited" (MLA)

9c Content notes

9d Finished form of the MLA paper

9e Peer review checklist

9f Submitting your paper electronically

FAQ

1. How many times do I need to document my sources? *See 9a.*

2. What should I document? *See 9a-1.*

3. What do I do if I don't mention the authority in my text? *See 9a-2.*

4. In my text, how do I cite a work within a collection? *See 9b-2f, g.*

5. Is there a way I can indicate line breaks when I am citing poetry within my text? *See 9a-2.*

6. What are some ways to vary my introduction of authors? *See 9a-2.*

7. What do the "publication facts" for a book include? *See 9b-1g.*

8. How do I handle a newspaper source in "List of Works Cited"? *See 9b-4h.*

9. What is the URL of an electronic source? What are angle brackets? *See 9b-6.*

10. What does "date of access" for an electronic source mean? How important is it? *See 9b-6.*

11. Should I include an outline even if it is not required? *See 9d.*

12. If I want to use a photo in my paper, how should I handle it? *See 9d-7.*

The Modern Language Association, sponsor of the MLA style, is an association of over 30,000 American and international scholars and writers in a hundred countries. MLA was founded in 1883 as a group advocating the study of literature and modern languages. Today its style is widely used by literature and language scholars worldwide.

The MLA style requires every source you use be documented twice: first in an in-text citation in the body of the work and then in an entry in the bibliography at the end of the paper. The in-text citation specifies the source while the bibliography entry lists its complete publication details.

For example, a student writing a paper alludes to an episode in a novel by Denise Chavez. Here is her in-text citation.

> In her novel *Face of an Angel, Denise Chavez* suggests that a waitress serves
> her clients in a variety of roles: efficient servant, clairvoyant, arbitrator, and
> confidante (271).

The student has identified the source in the text, naming both the writer and the title and giving, in parentheses, the page number being cited. This is a typical parenthetical citation. But it is not the only way the citation could have been handled:

> A waitress plays many roles as she waits on her clients: efficient servant, clairvoy-
> ant, arbitrator, and confidante (Chavez 271).
>   Author   Page number

Whichever form is used, the full Chavez reference will also appear as an entry in the bibliography, titled "Works Cited," at the end of the paper. Here is the formula that is typically used to document a book:

9a

> name of author inverted (period) + title of book or work italicized (period) +
> city of publication (colon) + publisher + year of publication (period) +
> medium of publication.

Here are the details of this particular work, written out:

> Chavez, Denise. *Face of an Angel*. New York: Warner, 1994. Print.

Notice that there is a period after the author's name; a period after the title; a colon after the city; a comma after the publisher's name; and a period after the year of publication. The punctuation marks used are a period, a period, a colon, a comma, a period, and a period. This formula, with some minor variations we will note later, is applicable to virtually all citations you might list in "Works Cited."

9a-1   What to document

General knowledge, common sayings, and self-evident opinions do not need to be documented. The rule of thumb is this: If the idea or opinion is of the kind that any well-read person is likely to know, then no documentation is necessary. For instance, the assertion that the Nazi regime under Hitler committed atrocities against the Jews requires no documentation because it is common knowledge. But if you quote from eyewitness accounts of those atrocities, you must acknowledge them both within the text of your paper and in a bibliographic entry. Consider the difference between these two assertions:

- On September 11, 2001, the World Trade Center towers in New York and the Pentagon in Washington, D.C., were attacked by suicide terrorists flying hijacked commercial airplanes.

- The medieval and barbaric Taliban regime in Afghanistan was destroyed by the heroic actions of the U.S. Marines stationed at Camp Rhino, outside Kandahar, Afghanistan (Ebrahamian 95).

The first statement needs no documentation because the tragedy of September 11, 2001, is so vividly etched on the world's consciousness that it has become painful common knowledge. On the other hand, that the actions of a specific Marine outpost brought down the Taliban regime—even if widely regarded today as true—is not common knowledge; it is opinion. As time passes and historians have a chance to do their work, we will begin to understand which military units and battles were decisive in the war against the Taliban. For the time being we can only speculate. So the second assertion, which is not your own, must be documented as the opinion of a particular source.

9a

> **Documentation tip**
>
> If you're ever indecisive about whether or not to document, it is better to err on the side of too much rather than too little. Plagiarizing is still a greater sin than being overcautious.

9a-2   Guidelines for in-text citations

1. *Keep it brief:* Keep your parenthetical references as brief as possible—give only the information needed to clearly identify a source. For instance, the statement "Wharton understood the snobbishness of New York high society and depicted it with a steady view" needs no parenthetical citation if your "Works Cited" includes only one work by Wharton. For your reader's convenience, however, you can identify the novel used to support your claim:

Wharton's *House of Mirth* is ample proof that the author understood the snobbishness of New York high society and depicted it with a steady view.

2. *Introduce the authority:* Introduce paraphrases or quotations by giving the authority's name. Use both the first name and the surname the first time the authority is cited:

Robert M. Jordan suggests that Chaucer's tales are held together by seams that are similar to the exposed beams supporting a Gothic cathedral (237-38).

Subsequent citations simply use the authority's surname:

Jordan further suggests . . .

3. *Identify the source:* Wherever possible, identify what makes the source important:

Noam Flinker, lecturer in English at Ben-Gurion University of the Negev in Israel, an authority on biblical literature, repeatedly suggests . . .

4. *Mention both author and work:* If you can do so smoothly, mention both the author and the work in your introduction:

In his essay "Criticism and Sociology," David Daiches insists that "sociological criticism can help to increase literary perception as well as to explain origins" (17).

5. *Document parenthetically if the authority is not mentioned:* If you do not mention the authority behind a paraphrase or quotation in your text, place this information in parentheses:

Democracy is deemed preferable to monarchy because it protects the individual's rights rather than his property (Emerson 372).

6. *Material by two or three authors:* When referring to material written by two or three authors, mention the names of all authors:

Christine E. Wharton and James S. Leonard take the position that the mythical figure of Amphion represents a triumph of the spiritual over the physical (163).

9a

Or

Eugene Gafner, James Frazier, and Walter W. Milligan edited a series of short

novels because they believed it was time to pump new blood into an anthol-

ogy of modern novellas (24).

Subsequent text references would refer simply to "Wharton and Leonard" or to "Gafner, Frazier, and Milligan."

7. *Material by more than three authors:* For a work with more than three authors or editors, use the first name followed by *et al.* or *and others* (no comma following the name):

G. B. Harrison et al. provide an excellent overview of the best in English litera-

ture in *Major British Writers*.

8. *Anonymous author:* When a work is listed as anonymous, mention that fact in the text and place in parentheses the title of the work from which the piece was taken (or an abbreviated version if the title is very long):

Another anonymous poem, "Trees" (*Driftwood* 130-31), also damns the city

for its thoughtless pollution of the environment.

9. *No author:* When a work has no author, cite the first two or three significant words from the title:

Spokane's *Spokesman Review* ("Faulkner Dies") gets at the heart of America's

greatest fiction writer when it states that . . .

10. *More than one work by the same author:* When more than one work by the same author is referred to in the paper, use a shortened version of the title in each citation. The following passage is an example of how to handle two works by the same author:

Feodor Dostoevsky declares that the "underground" rebel is representative of

our society (*Underground* 3). He seems to confirm this view in Raskolnikov's

superman speech (*Crime* 383-84), where he identifies . . .

11. *Work in a collection:* When citing a work in a collection, state the name of the person who wrote the opinion you are citing:

Lionel Trilling's "Reality in America" does not consider V. L. Parrington a great

intellect.

Place the title of the piece within quotation marks.

12. *Multivolume works:* When referring to a specific passage in a multivolume work, give the author, the volume number followed by a colon and a space, and the page reference:

Other historians disagree (Durant 2: 25).

When referring to an entire volume, give the name of the author followed by a comma, and then the abbreviation *vol.* followed by the volume number:

Other historians disagree (Durant, vol. 2).

13. *Double reference*—a quotation within a cited work:

As Bernard Baruch pointed out, "Mankind has always thought to substitute energy for reason" (qtd. in Ringer 274).

14. *Short passages of poetry:* When you are incorporating short passages of poetry into your text, follow these rules:
- ☐ Set off the passage with quotation marks.
- ☐ Use a slash (with a space before and after the slash) to indicate line breaks.
- ☐ Place the proper documentation in parentheses immediately following the quotation, inside the period because the reference is part of your basic sentence. The reference should be to the lines of the poem. Here is an example:

Byron's profound sense of alienation is echoed in canto 3 of *Childe Harold's Pilgrimage*: "I have not loved the World, nor the World me: / I have not flattered its rank breath, nor bowed / To its idolatries a patient knee" (190-91).

15. *Use Arabic numerals:* Use Arabic numerals for books, parts, volumes, and chapters of works; for acts, scenes, and lines of plays; and for cantos, stanzas, and lines of poetry.

IN-TEXT CITATIONS

volume 2 of *Civilization Past and Present*

book 3 of *Paradise Lost*

part 2 of *Crime and Punishment*

act 3 of *Hamlet*

chapter 1 of *The Great Gatsby*

NOTE: The words *volume, book, part, act,* and *chapter* do not need to be capitalized.

9a

16. *Vary your introductions:* As you write the paper, you will find a number of ways to introduce authors and their works. In places you'll find it easier and more elegant to mention the source in your text. In others, mentioning the writer's name will seem the more natural alternative. Here are some possibilities:

In text	Lionel Trilling, the noted critic and editor, has championed this idea (108).
In parenthetical citation	Although it has had its detractors, the idea has been championed by at least one prominent critic (Trilling 108).
In text	In *The Coming of Age*, Simone de Beauvoir contends that the decrepitude accompanying old age is "in complete conflict with the manly or womanly ideal cherished by the young and fully grown" (25).
In parenthetical citation	This attitude is central to the archetypal approach of interpreting poetry (Fiedler 519).

9b Format for "Works Cited" (MLA)

MLA calls the bibliography "Works Cited," and in it you will list every source you actually used in your paper, in alphabetical order by surname of the first author. Here are the rules for preparing the "Works Cited" page.

1. Use a new page for your "Works Cited" page.

2. Alphabetize the surnames of cited authors. Remember that nothing always precedes something. For instance, Rich, Herman B., comes before Richmond, D. L. Alphabetize the prefixes *M'*, *Mc*, and *Mac* literally, not as if they were all spelled *Mac*, and disregard the apostrophe. MacKinsey precedes McCuen, and MacIntosh precedes M'Naughton.

3. If the name of an author includes an article or a preposition—for example, *de, la, du, von,* or *van*—and the prefix is part of the surname, then alphabetize according to the prefix (Von Bismarck comes before Vonnegut). If the prefix is not part of the surname, treat it as part of the first and middle names (Bruy, Cornelis J. de). When in doubt, consult the biographical section of Merriam-Webster's *Collegiate Dictionary* (2003).

4. Put single-author entries before multiple-author entries beginning with the same surname:

Hirsch, E. D.

Hirsch, E. D., and O. B. Wright.

5. Entries by the same author or authors in the same order are arranged alphabetically by title, excluding *A, An,* or *The.* Use a row of three hyphens followed by a period to replace the name of the repeated author(s):

Kissinger, Henry Alfred. *The Necessity for Choice.*

---. *Nuclear Weapons and Foreign Policy.*

Note that the three hyphens may not be used if any author names differ from the previous entry. Thus, the three hyphens are never used along with names of different authors.

6. Alphabetize works by authors with the same surname by the first letter of the first name:

Butler, Alban

Butler, Samuel

7. Alphabetize corporate authors—associations, government agencies, institutions—by the first significant word of the name. Use the full name, not an abbreviation:

Brandeis University (not B.U.)

Southern Asian Institute (not SAI)

8. Place a parent body before a subdivision:

Glendale Community College, Fine Arts Department

9. If a work is anonymous, move its title into the author's place, and alphabetize it by the first significant word in the title.

10. Alphabetize legal references by the first significant word:

Marbury v. Madison

National Labor Relations Act

9b

9b-1   General order in references to books

The basic template for an MLA citation is the one we gave you earlier:

name of author inverted (period) + title of book or work underlined (period) +

city of publication (colon) + publisher + year of publication (period) +

medium of publication.

Center the title "Works Cited" (without quotation marks) on a new page with a one-inch top margin and double spacing throughout. Put the page number in the upper right-hand corner of your paper one-half inch from the top. Begin the first entry flush with the left margin and subsequent lines indented one-half inch, a format known as a hanging indent. See Figure 9-1.

a. Author

The name of the author comes first, alphabetized by surname and followed by a period. If a book has more than one author, invert the name of only the first and follow it with a comma:

> Brown, Jim, and John Smith.

For more than three authors, use the name of the first followed by *et al.*:

> Foreman, Charles, et al.

Or you may list all names as they occur in full:

> McCuen, Jo Ray, Anthony Winkler, Cathy Perrits, and Becky Bailey.

In some cases the name of an editor, translator, or compiler is cited before the name of an author, especially if the actual editing, translating, or compiling is the subject of discussion (see 9b-1c).

9b

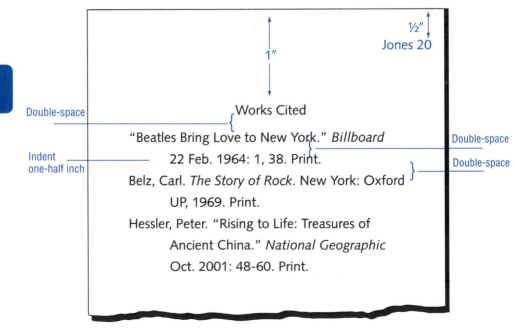

Figure 9-1   Sample "Works Cited" page, MLA style

b. Title

Cite the title exactly as it appears on the title page. A period follows the title unless the title ends with some other punctuation mark. Book titles are italicized. Chapter titles are set off in quotation marks. The initial word and all subsequent words (except for articles and prepositions) in the title are capitalized. Ignore any unusual typographical style (all-capital letters, for example) or any peculiar arrangement of capital and lowercase letters, unless the letters form an acronym or the author is known to insist on such typography. Separate a subtitle from the title by a colon:

D. H. Lawrence: His Life and Work.

c. Name of editor, compiler, or translator

The name(s) of the editor(s), compiler(s), or translator(s) is given in normal order, preceded by *Ed.* (for "Edited by"), *Comp.* (for "Compiled by"), or *Trans.* (for "Translated by"):

Homer. *The Iliad.* Trans. Richmond Lattimore.

If the editing, compiling, or translating is emphasized in your text discussion, place the name of the editor, compiler, or translator first—followed by a comma and then *ed. (eds.), comp. (comps.),* or *trans.* (notice the periods). For example, if you are drawing attention to the translator, use the following format:

Text citation:

The colloquial English of certain passages is the product of Ciardi's translation.

"Works Cited" entry:

Ciardi, John, trans. *The Inferno.* By Dante Alighieri. New York: NAL, 1961. Print.

d. Edition (other than first)

Cite the edition being used if it is other than the first. Use Arabic numerals (3rd ed.) with no other punctuation. Always use the latest edition of a work unless you have some specific reason of scholarship for using another:

Harmon, William. *A Handbook to Literature.* 10th ed. Upper Saddle River, NJ:

Prentice, 2006. Print.

e. Series name and number

Give the name of the series, without quotation marks and not italicized, the number of the work in the series in Arabic numerals, and a period:

Stewart, Joan Hinde. *Colette.* Boston: Twayne, 1983. Print. Twayne's World

Authors Ser. 679.

9b

f. Volume number

In an entry that refers to all of the volumes of a multivolume work, cite the number of volumes after the title or editor:

> Durant, Will, and Ariel Durant. *The Story of Civilization*. 10 vols. New York:
>
> Simon, 1968. Print.

An entry for only selected volumes cites the volumes actually used after the title. Then the total number of volumes may be listed after the publication facts or omitted:

> Durant, Will, and Ariel Durant. *The Story of Civilization*. Vols. 2 and 3.
>
> New York: Simon, 1968. Print. 10 vols.

For multivolume works published over a number of years, show the total number of volumes, the range of years, and specific volumes if not all of them were used:

> Froom, LeRoy Edwin. *The Prophetic Faith of Our Fathers*. 4 vols. Washington, DC:
>
> Review and Herald, 1950-54. Print.
>
> Froom, LeRoy Edwin. *The Prophetic Faith of Our Fathers*. Vol. 1. Washington, DC:
>
> Review and Herald. Print. 4 vols. 1950-54.

g. Publication facts

Indicate the place, publisher, and date of publication for the work you are citing. A colon follows the place, a comma the publisher, a period the date, and a period the medium of publication. MLA allows you to shorten the publisher's name as long as it is clear: Doubleday (for Doubleday & Company), McGraw (for McGraw-Hill), Little (for Little, Brown), Scott (for Scott, Foresman), Putnam's (for G. Putnam's Sons), Scarecrow (for Scarecrow Press), Simon (for Simon & Schuster), Prentice (for Prentice Hall).

9b

Other rules:

☐ If more than one place of publication appears, give the city shown first on the book's title page. If the city is well-known, the state is not needed.

☐ If more than one copyright date is given, use the latest unless your study focuses on an earlier edition. (A new printing does not constitute a new edition. For instance, if the title page bears a 1975 copyright date but a 1978 fourth printing, use 1975.)

☐ If no place, publisher, date, or page numbering is provided, insert *N.p., n.p., n.d., or N. pag.*, respectively (notice the capitalization). *N. pag.* explains to the reader why no page numbers are provided in the text citation. If the source contains no author, title, or publication information, supply in brackets whatever information you can obtain:

Dickens, Charles. *Master Humphrey's Clock*. London: Bradbury and Evans, n.d. Print.

Farquart, Genevieve. *They Gave Us Flowers*. N.p. 1886. Print.

Photographs of Historic Castles. [St. Albans, England]: N.p., n.d. N. pag. Print.

h. Page numbers

Bibliographical entries for books rarely include a page number; however, entries for shorter pieces appearing within a longer work (articles, poems, short stories, and so on, in a collection) should include a page reference. In that case, supply page numbers for the entire piece, not just for the page or pages cited in the text:

Daiches, David. "Criticism and Sociology." *Literature in Critical Perspective*.

Ed. Walker K. Gordon. New York: Appleton, 1968. 7-18. Print.

i. Medium of publication

Publications come in many forms, and the medium of publication (*Print, Web, CD-ROM, LP, Audiocassette*, and so on) is included in the entries.

9b-2   Sample references to books

Name of author inverted (period) + title of book or work italicized (period) +

city of publication (colon) + publisher + year of publication (period) +

medium of publication.

a. Book by a single author

Kingsolver, Barbara. *The Poisonwood Bible*. New York: Harper, 1999. Print.

b. Book by two or more authors

Frank, Francine, and Frank Anshen. *Language and the Sexes*. Albany, NY: State U

of New York P, 1983. Print.

Brown, Ruth, et al. *Agricultural Education in a Technical Society: An Annotated*

Bibliography of Resources. Chicago: American Library Assn., 1973. Print.

c. Book by a corporate author

American Institute of Physics. *Handbook*. 3rd ed. New York: McGraw, 1972. Print.

NOTE: If the publisher is the same as the author, repeat the information, as shown here:

Defense Language Institute. *Academic Policy Standards*. Monterey: Defense

Language Institute, 1982. Print.

9b

d. Book by an anonymous or pseudonymous author

No author listed:

> *Current Biography*. New York: Wilson, 1976. Print.

If you are able to research the author's name, supply it in brackets:

> [Stauffer, Adlai]. *Cloudburst*. Knoxville: Review and Courier Publishing Assn.,
>
> 1950. Print.

The name of an author who writes under a pseudonym (or nom de plume) also may be given in brackets:

> Eliot, George [Mary Ann Evans]. *Daniel Deronda*. London: Martin Secker, 1919. Print.

e. Work in several volumes or parts

When citing the whole multivolume work:

> Wallbank, T. Walter, and Alastair M. Taylor. *Civilization Past and Present*.
>
> 2 vols. New York: Scott, 1949. Print.

When citing a specific volume of a multivolume work:

> Wallbank, T. Walter, and Alastair M. Taylor. *Civilization Past and Present*. Vol. 2.
>
> New York: Scott, 1949. Print. 2 vols.

When citing a multivolume work whose volumes were published over a range of years:

> Froom, LeRoy Edwin. *The Prophetic Faith of Our Fathers*. 4 vols. Washington:
>
> Review and Herald, 1950-54. Print.

When citing a multivolume work with separate titles:

> Jacobs, Paul, Saul Landen, and Eve Pell. *Colonials and Sojourners*. New York:
>
> Random, 1971. Vol. 2 of *To Serve the Devil*. Print. 4 vols.

f. Work within a collection of pieces, all by the same author

> Selzer, Richard. "Liver." *Mortal Lessons*. New York: Simon, 1976. 62-77. Print.
>
> Johnson, Edgar. "The Keel of the New Lugger." *The Great Unknown*. New
>
> York: Macmillan, 1970. 763-76. Vol. 2 of *Sir Walter Scott*. Print. 3 vols.

NOTE: List the chapter or titled section in a book only when it demands special attention.

9b

g. Collections: Anthologies, casebooks, and readers

> Welty, Eudora. "The Wide Net." *Story: An Introduction to Prose Fiction*. Eds.
>
> Arthur Foff and Daniel Knapp. Belmont: Wadsworth, 1966. 159-77. Print.

h. Double reference—a quotation within a cited work

Whenever possible, take material from the original source, but when the original source is not available, then you may use a secondary source. If the material is a quotation, use the abbreviation "qtd. in" before the indirect source cited in your parenthetical reference:

> In his work *History of the Reformation*, John Knox states that when Queen
>
> Elizabeth I died, "all men in England lamented that the realm was left without
>
> a male to succeed" (qtd. in Fraser 3).

Only the secondary source is listed in the "Works Cited":

> Fraser, Antonia. *Mary Queen of Scots*. New York: Dell, 1969. Print.

i. Reference works

Treat an article in an encyclopedia or dictionary the way you would a piece in a collection, but do not cite the editor of the work. If the article is signed, give the author first. (Often the author is identified by initials that are clarified in a ledger at the end of the volume.) If no author is listed, give the title first. If the encyclopedia or dictionary arranges articles alphabetically, you may omit volume and page numbers.

(i) Encyclopedias

> Ballert, Albert George. "Saint Lawrence River." *Encyclopaedia Britannica*. 1963 ed.
>
> Print.
>
> "House of David." *Encyclopedia Americana*. 1974 ed.
>
> Berger, Morroe, and Dorothy Willner. "Near Eastern Society." *International*
>
> *Encyclopedia of the Social Sciences*. 1968 ed. Print.

(ii) Dictionaries and annuals

> "Barsabbas, Joseph." *Who's Who in the New Testament*. 1971. Print.
>
> "Telegony." *Dictionary of Philosophy and Psychology*. 1902. Print.

j. Work in a series

(i) Numbered series

> Auchincloss, Louis. *Edith Wharton*. Minneapolis: U of Minnesota P, 1961. Print.
>
> University of Minnesota Pamphlets on American Writers 12.

(ii) Unnumbered series

>   Miller, Sally. *The Radical Immigrant*. New York: Twayne, 1974. Print.
>
>   Immigrant Heritage of America Series.

k. Reprint

To cite a reprint, follow the title with the date of the original publication, and end the citation with the year of the reprint and the medium of publication.

>   Babson, John J. *History of the Town of Gloucester, Cape Ann. Including the*
>
>   *Town of Rockport*. 1860. New York: Peter Smith, 1972. Print.
>
>   Thackeray, William Makepeace. *Vanity Fair*. London, 1847-48. New York:
>
>   Harper, 1968. Print.

l. Edition

>   Perrin, Porter G., and Jim W. Corder. *Handbook of Current English*. 4th ed.
>
>   Glenview, IL: Scott, 1975. Print.
>
>   Rowland, Beryl, ed. *Companion to Chaucer: Studies*. New York: Oxford UP,
>
>   1979. Print.

m. Edited work

If the work of the editor(s) rather than that of the author(s) is being discussed, place the name of the editor(s) first, followed by a comma and then by *ed.* or *eds.:*

>   Craig, Hardin, and David Bevington, eds. *The Complete Works of Shakespeare*.
>
>   Rev. ed. Glenview, IL: Scott, 1973. Print.

If you are stressing the text of the author(s), place the author(s) first:

>   Clerc, Charles. "Goodbye to All That: Theme, Character, and Symbol in
>
>   *Goodbye, Columbus." Seven Contemporary Short Novels*. Ed. Charles
>
>   Clerc and Louis Leiter. Glenview, IL: Scott, 1969. 106-33. Print.

n. Book published in a foreign country

>   Ransford, Oliver. *Livingston's Lake: The Drama of Nyasa*. London: Camelot,
>
>   1966. Print.
>
>   Vialleton, Louis. *L'origine des êtres vivants*. Paris: Plon, 1929. Print.

NOTE: Titles of foreign-language books are in lowercase except for the initial letter and proper nouns.

9b

o. Introduction, preface, foreword, or afterword

Davidson, Marshall B. Introduction. *The Age of Napoleon*. By J. Christopher

Herold. New York: American Heritage, 1963. Print.

p. Translation

Symons, John Addington, trans. *Autobiography of Benvenuto Cellini*. By

Benvenuto Cellini. New York: Washington Square, 1963. Print.

q. Book of illustrations

Janson, H. W. *History of Art: A Survey of the Major Visual Arts from the Dawn*

of History to the Present. With 928 illustrations, including 80 color plates.

Englewood Cliffs, NJ: Prentice and Abrams, 1962. Print.

r. Foreign title

Use lowercase lettering for foreign titles except for the first word and proper
names:

Vischer, Lukas. *Basilius der Grosse*. Basel: Reinhard, 1953. Print.

Supply a translation of the title or city if it seems necessary. Place the English version in brackets (not italicized) immediately following the original:

Bruckberger, R. L. *Dieu et la politique* [God and politics]. Paris: Plon, 1971.

Print.

9b-3   General order in references to periodicals

Bibliographic references to periodicals list items in the order below.

name of author inverted (period) + title of article (in quotation marks followed

by a period within the quotation mark) + name of periodical (omitting

any introductory *a, an,* or *the*) + series number or name (if relevant) +

volume number and/or issue number + date of publication or work

(colon) + inclusive page numbers (period) + medium of publication

consulted (period) + supplemental information (period)

a. Author

List the author's surname first, followed by a comma and then by the first name or
initials. If there is more than one author, follow the same format used for books
(see 9b-1a and 9b-2).

b. Title of the article

List the title in quotation marks, followed by a period inside the end quotation mark unless the title itself ends in a question mark or exclamation point.

c. Publication information

List the name of the periodical, italicized, omitting any introductory article (*A, An, The*), followed by a space and a volume and/or number; then by a space and the year of publication in parentheses; and then by a colon, a space, and page numbers for the entire article, not just for the specific pages cited. End with the medium of publication and a period. Take the information directly from the periodical, not from any other source. Usually the information appears on the cover or title page of the periodical.

In addition to the volume number, the periodical also may have an issue number (Number 4), a month, or a season (Fall). The issue number follows the volume number, separated by a period (4.2 means volume 4, issue 2). Some scholarly journals have no volume numbers, numbering issues only. In those cases, treat the issue number the way you would a volume number:

> Layne, Linda L. "Breaking the Silence: An Agenda for a Feminist Discourse of
>
> Pregnancy Loss." *Feminist Studies* 23 (1997): 289-93. Print.

For journals paginated anew in each issue, insert the issue number following the volume number, separated by a period:

> Beets, Nicholas. "Historical Actuality and Bodily Experience." *Humanitas* 2.1
>
> (1966): 15-28. Print.

Some journals use a month or season designation in place of an issue number:

> McInnis, Douglas. "The Plight of the Bumble Bee." *Popular Science* 251 (Nov. 1997):
>
> 75-80. Print.

Magazines that are published weekly or monthly require only the date, without a volume number:

> Biema, David van. "Opus Dei." *Time* 24 Apr. 2006: 52-63. Print.
>
> Newman, Richard J. "Tougher Than Hell." *U.S. News & World Report* 3 Nov. 1997:
>
> 42-49. Print.

Newspapers require the page number, which may include a section letter. If the section or part is numbered, add *sec.* or *pt.* before that number.

9b

Harbin, John. "Training Session Spreads the Mission of HonorAir." *Times-News*

[Hendersonville, NC], 22 Mar. 2007, 1B. Print.

Rumberger, L. "Our Work, Not Education, Needs Restructuring." *Los Angeles*

Times, 24 May 1984, pt. 2: 5. Print.

NOTE: If the newspaper title doesn't include the place name, add it in brackets after the title as in the Harbin entry.

d. Pages

If the pages of the article are scattered throughout the issue (for example, pages 30, 36, 51, and 52), use one of the following formats:

30, 36, 51, 52	Pages 30, 36, 51, and 52 (This is the most precise method and should be used when only three or four pages are involved.)
30+	Beginning on page 30

e. Medium of publication

See explanation in 9b-1i, page 149.

9b-4 Sample references to periodicals

a. Anonymous author

"Elegance Is Out." *Fortune* 13 Mar. 1978: 18. Print.

b. Single author

Kluger, Jeffrey. "The Nuke Pipeline." *Time* 17 Dec. 2001: 40-45. Print.

c. More than one author

Hillenbrand, Barry, and Jeff Jacobson. "Heartland." *Modern Maturity* Jan./ Feb. 2002:

34-43. Print.

After the first author, all authors are listed with first names first. If three authors have written the article, place a comma after the second author. Join the second and third authors by *and*, preceded by a comma:

Kennedy, Craig H., Shuklas Smith, and Dale Fryxell. "Comparing the Effects of

Educational Placement on the Social Relationships of Intermediate School

Students with Severe Disabilities." *Exceptional Children* 64 (Fall 1997):

31-47. Print.

If more than three authors have collaborated, list the first author's name, inverted, followed by a comma and *et al.*

> Enright, Frank, et al.

Or you may list all names as they occur in full:

> McCuen, Jo Ray, Anthony Winkler, Cathy Perrits, and Becky Bailey.

d. Journal with continuous or separate pagination

Note that current MLA guidelines no longer make a distinction between journals that are numbered continuously (e.g., Vol. 1 ends on page 208, Vol. 2 starts on page 209) or numbered separately; that is, each volume starts on page 1. No matter how the journal is paginated, all of them must contain volume *and* issue numbers. One exception are journals with issue numbers only; simply cite the issue numbers alone as though they are volume numbers (see Layne entry on page 154).

> Paolucci, Anne. "Comedy and Paradox in Pirandello's Plays." *Modern Drama*
>
> 20.2 (1977): 321-39. Print.
>
> Cappe, Walter H. "Humanities at Large." *Center Magazine* 11.2 (1978): 2-6. Print.
>
> Mangrum, Claude T. "Toward More Effective Justice." *Crime Prevention*
>
> *Review* 5.1: 1-9. Print.

e. Monthly magazine

Do not give the volume and issue numbers even if they are listed:

> Swerdlow, Joel L. "Changing America." *National Geographic* Oct. 2002:
>
> 43-55, 60-61. Print.

NOTE: Notice the split reference. The article is printed consecutively on pages 43 through 55 and then continues on pages 60 and 61. Another way to handle articles that do not appear on consecutive pages is to cite the first page followed by a plus sign, leaving no intervening space (see 9b-3d):

> Miller, Mark Crispin. "The New Wave in Rock." *Horizon* Mar. 1978: 76+. Print.

f. Weekly magazine

> Gopnik, Adam. "Improvised City." *New Yorker* 19 Nov. 2001: 88-91. Print.

If the article has no author, begin with the title:

> "Philadelphia's Way of Stopping the Shoplifter." *Business Week* 6 Mar. 1972:
>
> 57-59. Print.

9b

g. Newspaper

Tagliabue, John. "Threat of Nuclear Terror Has Increased." *New York Times* 2 Nov.

2001: B4. Print.

("B4" stands for section B, page 4 of the newspaper.)

List the edition and section of the newspaper if specified:

Southerland, Daniel. "Carter Plans Firm Stand with Begin." *Christian Science*

Monitor 9 Mar. 1978, western ed.: 1, 9. Print.

If the section or part is labeled with a numeral rather than a letter, then the abbreviation *sec.* or *pt.* must appear before the section number. For example, see the unsigned editorial below.

h. Editorial

Signed:

Futrell, William. "The Inner City Frontier." Editorial. *Sierra* 63.2 (1978): 5. Print.

Unsigned:

"Criminals in Uniform." Editorial. *Los Angeles Times* 7 Apr. 1978, pt. 2: 6. Print.

i. Letter to the editor

Payne, Steven. Letter. *Time* 3 Nov. 2001: 10. Print.

j. Critical review

Andrews, Peter. Rev. of *The Strange Ride of Rudyard Kipling: His Life and*

Works, by Angus Wilson. *Saturday Review* 4 Mar. 1978: 24-25. Print.

Rev. of *Charmed Life*, by Diane Wynne Jones. *Booklist* 74 (Feb. 1978): 1009. Print.

Daniels, Robert V. Rev. of *Stalinism: Essays in Historical Interpretations*, ed.

Robert C. Tucker. *Russian Review* 37 (1978): 102-03. Print.

"Soyer Sees Soyer." Rev. of *Diary of an Artist*, by Ralph Soyer. *American Artist*

Mar. 1978: 18-19. Print.

9b

k. Published interview

Leonel J. Castillo, Commissioner, Immigration and Naturalization Service.

Interview. "Why the Tide of Illegal Aliens Keeps Rising." *U.S. News &*

World Report 20 Feb. 1978: 33-35. Print.

I. Published address or lecture

Trudeau, Pierre E. "Reflections on Peace and Security." Address to Conference

on Strategies for Peace and Security in the Nuclear Age. Guelph, ON, Can.

27 Oct. 1983. Rpt. in *Vital Speeches of the Day* 1 Dec. 1983: 98-102. Print.

9b-5   References to electronic sources

No uniform standard has emerged for citing electronic sources. To add to the dilemma, electronic materials are not as stable and permanent as are print materials. In this section, we treat electronic sources as closely as possible to print sources, with the addition of facts about electronic publication and access information.

When you cite electronic sources, your primary aim is not to follow some tedious format but to provide enough information for the reader to find your citation and verify its accuracy. The citation that conforms exactly to a specific format but leads the reader to the wrong source is like the bridegroom who wears the right clothes but shows up at the wrong wedding. Following the correct format is important only because doing so usually results in an accurate citation.

9b-6   General order in references to electronic sources

Online material often requires a bibliographic citation slightly different from other references. Here is the usual template. Not all items will appear in every electronic citation.

(1) Name of author or editor. (2) Title of piece in quotation marks, or, if a book

or magazine or journal, italicized. (3) Publication information on any print

and/or electronic source. (4) Title of the Internet site. (5) Medium of pub-

lication consulted (Web). (6) Access date (7) URL, if needed, enclosed in

angle brackets (< >).

1. *Author, editor, etc.:* List last name first as you would with a print source. In the case of an electronic source, the author could be the website developer or programmer. If no author is identified, lead with the title or the name of the electronic source you're citing. If a source has more than one author, list all the names in normal order.

2. *Title:* For shorter works, like essays or poems, place title in quotation marks. Titles of longer works—plays or novels, for example—are continuously underlined except for the final period. If there is no title, insert the name of the database or website you're citing.

9b

3. *Publication information for any print source:* Include place, the name of the publisher or the sponsoring organization, and the year of publication.

4. *Title of the Internet site* (whether a database, online journal, or other).

5. Medium of publication (Web).

6. *Date of access:* This is especially important because electronic sources change rapidly. The reader should know exactly when you consulted the source. Use just a word space (no period) between the date of access and the URL.

7. *URL:* MLA does not require the URL unless it is necessary to guarantee access or your instructor requires one; usually a title will suffice for an Internet search. You should enclose the complete URL (Internet address; see 5b-3) within angle brackets (< >), followed by a period. If the URL is lengthy and complicated, give the URL of the home or search page and the links or keywords needed to find the page, preceded by *Path* or *Keywords.*

Figure 9-2 is an example of a citation to an online book that has been published in print.

Two rules will help you cite online sources correctly. First, the last element before the beginning of the URL (marked with an opening angle bracket) should always be the date of access followed by a period. Second, all MLA citations of a URL end with a closing angle bracket followed by a period. These observations do not apply to material cited from storage on a permanent medium, a CD-ROM, for example.

9b-7 Sample references to electronic sources

The following are models of some of the most common electronic sources you might consult for a paper.

NOTE: Remember that MLA uses angle brackets (< >) to enclose the URL.

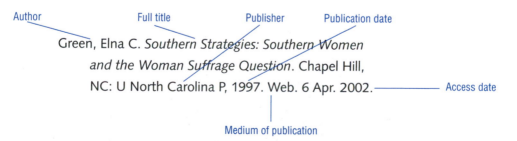

Figure 9-2 Citation for an online book published in print

a. Abstract online or on CD-ROM

Bourg, S. N. "Sexual and Physical Aggression within a Dating/Acquaintance Relationship: Testing Models of Perpetrator Characteristics." *Current Research*. July 2001. Abstract. Web. 23 May 2002.

Gawrych, George W. "Jihad in the 20th Century." *Military Review*. 75.5 (1995): 33-39. Abstract. *Historical Abstracts*. ABC-CLIO. Fall 1997 update. CD-ROM.

b. CD-ROM

"Baylor, Elgin." *Microsoft Encarta Reference Library 2002*. Seattle: Microsoft Corp., 2002. CD-ROM.

c. Computer program

Dragon NaturallySpeaking. Computer software. Version 9, preferred ed. for Windows. Nuance Communications, Inc. 2006. CD-ROM.

d. Corporate website

IDG, Inc. "Report: Job Cuts in 2001 Reach Nearly 2 Million." Web. Jan. 2002. 25 Feb. 2002. <http://idg.net/>.

e. E-mail

Personal:

McCuen, Jo Ray. "Re: Airline Security." Message to author. 13 Oct. 2006. E-mail.

Posted to an online discussion group:

Underman, Norris. "Elizabeth Gaskell's Villages." 22 Oct. 2009. <news:humanities.lit.authors. Gasskell>.

f. FTP source

For a list of web abbreviations, see 5b-2.

Mathews, J. Preface. *Numerical Methods for Mathematics, Science, and Engineering*. 2nd ed. N.p.: Prentice Hall, 1992. Web. 8 June 1999. <ftp://ftp.ntua.gr/pub/netlib/textbook/index.html>.

g. Gopher

at Jordan, Z. Pallo. "Telecommunications Green Paper." The Ministry of Posts, Telecommunications and Broadcasting. Web. 7 July 1995. 5 Jan. 2002. <www.gopher.com/gopher/ws/index>

9b

h. Government website

Library of Congress. "Official U.S. Executive Branch Web Sites." Web. 9 July
  1999. 8 Sept. 2002.

i. Electronic mailing list

Pyatt, Elizabeth J. "Re: Everson Typography." The Celtic Linguistics List.
  24 Sept. 2001. Web. 10 June 2002. <http://listserv.linguistlist.org/
  cgi-bin/wa?A2=ind0109&L=celtling&D=1&F=&S=&P=83>.

j. MOOs and MUDs (synchronous communication)

"Basic MOO Building Commands." Miami U (Oxford, Ohio). Web. 15 Sept.
  2002.

k. Online book

Green, Elna C. *Southern Strategies: Southern Women and the Woman*
  Suffrage Question. Chapel Hill, NC: U North Carolina P, 1997. Web.
  3 Jan. 2005.

Hawthorne, Nathaniel. *Twice-Told Tales*. Ed. George Parsons Lathrop. Boston:
  Houghton, 1883. Web. 16 May 2006.

Keats, John. *Poetical Works*. 1884. *Bartleby.com: Great Books Online*. Ed. Steven
  van Leeuwen. Web. 2002. 5 May 2002. <http://www.bartleby.com/>.

l. Online database

Journal article:

Curry, Michael R. "Toward a Geography of a World without Maps: Lessons
  from Ptolemy and Postal Codes." *Annals of the Association of American*
  Geographers 95.3 (2005): 680-91. *Blackwell Synergy*. Web. Sept. 26, 2006.

Newspaper article:

Thomson, David. "Dietrich at 100: The Camera's Truest Lover." *New York Times*
  23 Dec. 2001. Research Library at Proquest. Galileo. Web. 6 Mar. 2002.

m. Online dictionary

"Pawky." *Webster's New World Dictionary*. Merriam-Webster, 1988. eLibrary.
  Web. 23 July 2002. <www.elibrary.com>.

n. Online encyclopedia

"James Boswell." *The Columbia Encyclopedia*, 5th ed. eLibrary. 1 Jan. 1993.

   Web. 28 July 2002. <www.elibrary.com>.

o. Online magazine article—author listed

Peterson, Scot. "Business: The Smaller the Better." *ZDNet News* 18 Dec. 2001.

   Web. 5 Jan. 2002.

p. Online magazine article—no author listed

"Men's Shavers: How to Choose." *Consumer Reports* January 2007. Web.

   1 Apr. 2007.

q. Telnet

Asimov, Isaac. "Of butterflies and the origin of the species." *San Francisco*

   Chronicle. 22 May 1991. Web. 5 Jan. 2002. <www.telnet.org> or, more

   directly, <http://www.sfgate.com>.

r. Usenet

Peterson, Bo. "Re: Bob Marley discography." 11 Jan. 1994. Web. 5 Jan. 2006.

   <www.usenet.com>.

s. Website—author listed

Graser, Sara. "Kissing Charles Bukowski." *Oyster Boy Review* 13. Summer

   2001. Web. Apr. 2007.

t. Website—no author listed

Jamaica Tourist Board. Official Site of the Jamaica Tourist Board. 2000-2001.

   Web. 3 Jan. 2002.

9b-8   Sample references to nonprint materials

Because nonprint materials come in many forms and with varied information, you should provide as much information in references to them as is necessary for retrieval. Often the title or topic is sufficient.

a. Address or lecture

In citing an oral presentation, give the speaker's name, the title of the presentation (if known) in quotation marks, the sponsoring organization, the location, and the date. At the end, note the appropriate descriptive label (Address, Keynote speech, Reading, or Forum, for example).

Beach, Bert B. "Religious Liberty and Human Rights—with Special

Considerations for the Problems of Minority Churches." Academy

of Rottenburg-Stuttgart Diocese. Weingarten, Germany. 28 Nov. 1997.

Address.

Fearing, Michael. Professional Retirement Club. Bishop, CA. 15 Mar. 1997.

Seminar.

Witt, Alexandra. "On Being a News Anchor at MSNBC." Veloris Lang Lecture.

Glendale, CA. 5 Jan. 2006. Lecture.

To cite a reprint of an address or lecture appearing in a periodical, see 9b-41.

b. Artwork

To cite a painting or sculpture, state the artist's name first. Italicize the title of the work. Then name the medium (Oil on canvas, Lithograph on paper, etc.). When possible, name the institution or private collection that houses the work. Follow that name with a comma and the city.

Angelico, Beato. *Madonna dei Linaioli*. Tempera on wood. Museo di San

Marco, Firenze.

Alicia Quaini. *Pink Flowers in a Vase*. Oil on canvas. Franco and Anna Collec-

tion, Buenos Aires.

If you use a photograph of a painting or sculpture, show not only the institution or private owner and the city, but also the complete publication information for the source in which the photograph appears. Include the page, slide, figure, or plate number if relevant. Here is an example:

Saint-Grudens, Augustus. *Adams Memorial*. Photograph. Rock Creek Cem-

etery, Washington, D.C. *Art through the Ages*. By Helen Gardner. New

York: Harcourt, 1980. 797. Print.

See also 9b-9.

c. Film, videotape, or DVD

Film citations usually begin with the title, italicized. They should include the director's name, the name(s) of the leading actor(s), the distributor, and the year released. End with the medium.

The Turning Point. Dir. Herbert Ross. Perf. Anne Bancroft, Shirley MacLaine,

Mikhail Baryshnikov, and Leslie Brown. Twentieth Century-Fox, 1978. Film.

Information on the producer, writer, and size or length of the film also should be supplied if they are relevant to your study. If you are discussing a particular individual's contribution, begin with that person's name:

> Mathews, Tom, writ. *Mad City*. Dir. Costa Gavras. Perf. Dustin Hoffman, John
>
> Travolta, Alan Alda, and Mia Kirshner. Warner Brothers, 1997. DVD.
>
> Joanou, Phil, dir. *Gridiron Gang*. Perf. Kevin Dunn and Leon Rippy. Columbia
>
> Pictures, 2006. Laser disc.

d. Interview

Citations of interviews should specify the kind of interview, the name (and, if pertinent, the title) of the person interviewed, and the date of the interview:

> Carpenter, Edward, librarian at the Huntington Library, Pasadena. Telephone
>
> interview. 2 Mar. 1999.
>
> Moasser, Dr. Mark. Medical consultation. 26 June 2006.

e. Musical composition

To cite a musical composition, begin with the composer's name. Italicize the title of an opera, a ballet, or a piece of instrumental music identified by name, but do not italicize or enclose in quotation marks an instrumental composition identified by form, number, and key.

> *Opera:*
>
> Mozart, Wolfgang. *The Abduction from the Seraglio*.

> *Instrumental music identified by name:*
>
> Brahms, Johannes. *Variations on a Theme by Handel*.

> *Instrumental composition identified by form, number, and key:*
>
> Liszt, Franz. Sonata in B Minor.

> *When to cite in text:*

Whenever possible, cite the title of the composition in your text. For instance:

> Bach's *Well-Tempered Clavier* is a principal keyboard . . .

However, when opus numbers would clutter the text, cite the composition more fully in "Works Cited":

> Grieg, Edvard. Minuet in E Minor, op. 7, no. 3:

9b

Published scores are treated like books:

> Brahms, Johannes. *Three Intermezzi for the Piano, Op. 117*. 1892. New York:
>
> > Schirmer, 1926. Print.

f. Radio or television program

Citations should include the title of the program (italicized), the network or local station, and the city and date of broadcast. If appropriate, the title of the episode is listed in quotation marks before the title of the program; the title of the series, neither italicized nor in quotation marks, comes after the title of the program. The names of the writer, director, narrator, performers, and producer also can be supplied if they are important to your discussion:

> *Diving for Roman Plunder*. Narr. and dir. Jacques Cousteau. KCET, Los Angeles.
>
> > 14 Mar. 1978. Television.
>
> "Episode 1." *Bramwell III*. Masterpiece Theatre. Perf. Jemma Redgrave. KCET,
>
> > Los Angeles. 9 Nov. 1997. Television.
>
> *The Third Twin*. Writ. Ken Follett. CBS, New York. 9 Nov. 1997. Radio.

g. Sound recording (compact disc or tape)

For commercially available recordings, cite the following: the composer, conductor, or performer; the title of the recording or of the work(s) on the recording; artist(s); manufacturer; catalog number (optional); and year of issue (if not known, use n.d.). Which person is cited first depends on your emphasis. In general, italicize titles of recordings, but do not italicize or enclose in quotation marks the titles of musical compositions identified only by form, number, and key (see the Bach entry that follows). Indicate the medium, neither italicized nor enclosed in quotation marks, after the date.

> Bach, Johann Sebastian. Toccata and Fugue in D Minor; Toccata, Adagio,
>
> > and Fugue in C Major; Passacaglia and Fugue in C Minor. Johann
> >
> > Christian Bach.
>
> Sinfonia for Double Orchestra, op. 18, no. 1. Cond. Eugene Ormandy.
>
> > Philadelphia Orchestra. LP. Columbia, MS 6180, n.d. CD.
>
> Beatles, The. "I Should Have Known Better." *The Beatles Again*. Apple
>
> > Records, SO-385, n.d. Audiocassette.

If you are citing a specific song or piece, place the title in quotation marks:

> Vivaldi, Antonio. "The Spring." *The Four Seasons*, Op. 8, Nos. 1-4. Print.

9b

Here are some other examples:

> Burr, Charles. Jacket notes. *Grofe: Grand Canyon Suite*. Columbia, MS 6003,
>
> n.d. LP.
>
> Dwyer, Michael. *Readings from Mark Twain*. 15 Apr. 1968. LP. Humorist
>
> Society. San Bernardino.
>
> Eagle, Swift. *The Pueblo Indians*. Caedmon, TC 1327, n.d. CD.
>
> *Shakespeare's Othello*. With Paul Robeson, José Ferrer, Uta Hagen, and Edith
>
> King. Columbia, SL-153, n.d. CD.
>
> Wilgus, D. K. *Irish Folksongs*. 9 Mar. 1969. DVD. U of California, Los Angeles,
>
> Archives of Folklore. T7 69-22.

h. Performance

Performances (plays, operas, ballets, concerts) are cited in the form used for films, with added information on the theater, city, and date of the performance. For operas, concerts, or dance productions you may also want to cite the conductor (cond.) or choreographer (chor.). If the author, composer, director, or choreographer is emphasized in your paper, supply that information first.

This citation emphasizes the play:

> *Barrymore*. By William Luce. Dir. Gene Saks. Perf. Christopher Plummer. Music
>
> Box, New York. 18 Sept. 1997. Performance.

This citation emphasizes the author:

> Durang, Christopher. *Beyond Therapy*. Dir. John Madden. Perf. John
>
> Lithgow and Dianne Wiest. Brooks Atkinson, New York. 26 May 1982.
>
> Performance.

This citation emphasizes the conductor:

> Conlon, James, cond. *La Bohème*. By Giacomo Puccini. With Renata Scotto.
>
> Metropolitan Opera. Metropolitan Opera House, New York. 30 Oct.
>
> 1977. Performance.

This citation emphasizes the guest performers:

> Domingo, Placido, and Norah Amsellem. *Carmen*. By Georges Bizet. Cond.
>
> James Levine. Metropolitan Opera. Metropolitan Opera House, New York.
>
> 23 Sept. 1997. Performance.

9b

This citation emphasizes the choreographer:

> Baryshnikov, Mikhail, chor. *Swan Lake*. By Peter Ilyich Tchaikovsky. American
>
> Ballet Theatre, New York. 24 May 1982. Performance.

9b-9 Sample references to special items

No standard form exists for every special item you might use in your paper. Again, as a general rule, arrange the information in your bibliographic entry in the following order: author, title, place of publication, publisher, date, and any other information that could help with retrieval. Some examples of common citations follow.

a. Artwork, published

> Healy, G. P. A. *The Meeting on the River Queen*. White House, Washington, DC.
>
> Illus. in *Lincoln: A Picture Story of His Life*. By Stefan Lorent. Rev. and enl. ed.
>
> New York: Harper, 1957. Print.

To cite a work of art you have experienced, see 9b-8b.

b. The Bible and other sacred writings

The convention of using italics or quotation marks for titles does not apply to the names of sacred writings, such as the Bible, Talmud, Koran, or Upanishads. These names appear without italicizing or quotation marks when used within the text.

When referring to the Bible, cite the book and chapter in the text (the verse, too, can be cited when necessary):

> The city of Babylon (Rev. 18.2) is used to symbolize an evil society in . . .
>
> or
>
> In Rev. 18:2 the city of Babylon is used as a symbol of evil in a society that . . .

In the "Works Cited," specify which version:

> *The Bible*, Rev. Standard Version . . .

c. Classical works in general

In your text, when you refer to classical works that are subdivided into books, parts, cantos, verses, and lines, specify the appropriate subdivisions:

> Francesca's speech in *The Inferno* (5.118-35) is poignant because . . .
>
> Ovid makes claims to immortality in the last lines of *The Metamorphoses*
>
> (3.Epilogue).

9b

In the "Works Cited," these references appear as follows:

> Alighieri, Dante. *The Inferno*. Trans. John Ciardi. New York: NAL, 1961. Print.
>
> Ovid. *The Metamorphoses*. Trans. and introd. Horace Gregory. New York:
>
> > NAL, 1958. Print.

d. Dissertation

If the paper has not been published, place the title in quotation marks, and identify the work with *Diss.*:

> Cotton, Joyce Raymonde. "*Evan Harrington*: An Analysis of George Meredith's
>
> > Revisions." Diss. U of Southern California, Los Angeles, 1968. Print.

If the paper has been published, treat the dissertation like a book, but include the label *Diss.*, and state where and when the dissertation was originally written:

> Cortey, Teresa. *Le rêve dans les contes de Charles Nodier*. Diss. U of California,
>
> > Berkeley, 1975. Washington, DC: UP of America, 1977. Print.

e. Footnote or endnote citation

A bibliographic reference to a footnote or endnote in a source takes the following form:

> Faber, M. D. *The Design Within: Psychoanalytic Approaches to Shakespeare*.
>
> > New York: Science House, 1970. Print.

In other words, no mention is made of the note. But mention of the note should be made in the text:

> In Schlegel's translation, the meaning is changed (Faber 205, n. 9).

The reference is to page 205, note 9, of Faber's book.

f. Manuscript or typescript

A bibliographic reference to a manuscript or typescript from a library collection should provide the following information: the author, the title (italicized) or a description of the material, the form of the material (MS for "manuscript," TS for "typescript"), and any identifying number. If possible, give the name and location of the library or institution where the material is kept. For example:

> Chaucer, Geoffrey. *The Canterbury Tales*. MS. Ellesmere E126C9. Huntington
>
> > Library, Pasadena.

9b

Cotton Vitellius. MS. A. SV. British Museum, London.

The Wanderer. MS. Exeter Cathedral, Exeter.

g. Pamphlet or brochure

Citations of pamphlets or brochures should conform as nearly as possible to the format used for citations of books. Give as much information about the pamphlet as is necessary to help a reader find it. Italicize the title:

Calplans Agricultural Fund. *An Investment in California Agricultural Real*

Estate. Oakland: Calplans Securities, n.d. Print.

h. Personal letter

Published:

Wilde, Oscar. "To Mrs. Alfred Hunt." 25 Aug. 1880. Letter. *The Letters of Oscar*

Wilde. Ed. Rupert Hart-Davis. New York: Harcourt, 1962. 67-68. Print.

Unpublished:

Thomas, Dylan. Letter to Trevor Hughes. 12 Jan. 1934. TS. Dylan Thomas

Papers. Lockwood Memorial Library, Buffalo.

Personally received:

Highet, Gilbert. Letter to the author. 15 Mar. 1972. TS.

i. Plays

(i) Classical play

In your text, provide parenthetical references to act, scene, and line(s) of the play:

Cleopatra's jealousy pierces through her words:

What says the married woman? You may go;

Would she had never given you leave to come:

Let her not say 'tis I that keep you here;

I have no power upon you; hers you are. (1.3.20-23)

The reference within parentheses in the right-hand margin is to Act 1, Scene 3, lines 20 to 23. In "Works Cited," the play is cited this way:

Shakespeare, William. *Antony and Cleopatra. The Complete Works of*

Shakespeare. Ed. Hardin Craig and David Bevington. Rev. ed. Glenview,

IL: Scott, 1973. 1073-1108. Print.

NOTE: When the play is part of a collection, list the pages that cover the entire play.

(ii) Modern play

Many modern plays are published in book form:

> Miller, Arthur. *The Crucible*. New York: Bantam, 1952. Print.

When a play has been republished as part of a collection, cite it like this:

> Chekhov, Anton. *The Cherry Orchard*. 1903. *The Art of Drama*.
>
> Ed. R. F. Dietrich, William E. Carpenter, and Kevin Kerrane. 2nd ed.
>
> New York: Holt, 1976. 134-56. Print.

NOTE: The page reference is to the entire play.

j. Poems

(i) Classical poem

> Lucretius [Titus Lucretius Carus]. *Of the Nature of Things*. Trans. William Ellery
>
> Leonard. *Backgrounds of the Modern World*. New York: Scott, 1950.
>
> 343-53. Vol. 1 of *The World in Literature*. Ed. Robert Warnock and
>
> George K. Anderson. 4 vols. 1950-51. Print.

Or, if published in one book:

> Alighieri, Dante. *The Inferno*. Trans. John Ciardi. New York: NAL, 1961. Print.

(ii) Modern poem

Modern poems are usually part of a larger collection (anthology or magazine):

> Moore, Marianne. "Poetry." *Fine Frenzy*. Ed. Robert Baylor and Brenda Stokes.
>
> New York: McGraw, 1972. 372-73. Print.
>
> Wetzsteon, Rachel. "Lawyers on the Left Bank." *New Yorker* 11 Aug. 2003:
>
> 70. Print.

NOTE: Cite all of the pages on which the poem appears.

If the poem has been published as a book, use the following format:

> Byron, George Gordon, Lord. *Don Juan*. Ed. Leslie A. Marchand. Boston:
>
> Houghton, 1958. Print.

9b

k. Public documents

As a general rule, follow this order: government; body; subsidiary bodies; title of document (italicized); identifying code; and place, publisher, and date of publication. Most publications by the federal government are printed by the Government Printing Office, which is abbreviated GPO.

(i) The Congressional Record

A citation to the *Congressional Record* requires only the title, date, page(s), and medium.

> *Cong. Rec.* 15 Dec. 1977: 19740. Print.

(ii) Congressional publications

> United States. Cong. House. Committee on Foreign Relations. *Hearings on*
> *S. 2793, Supplemental Foreign Assistance Fiscal Year 1966—Vietnam.*
> 89th Cong., 2nd sess. Washington: GPO, 1966. Print.
>
> United States. Cong. Joint Economic Committee on Medical Policies and Costs.
> *Hearings.* 93rd Cong., 1st sess. Washington: GPO, 1973. Print.
>
> United States. Cong. Senate. Permanent Subcommittee on Investigations of
> the Committee on Government Operations. *Organized Crime—Stolen*
> *Securities.* 93rd Cong., 1st sess. Washington: GPO, 1973. Print.

(iii) Executive branch publications

> United States. Dept. of Commerce. Bureau of the Census. *Statistical Abstracts*
> *of the United States.* Washington: GPO, 1963. Print.
>
> United States. Dept. of Defense. *Annual Report to the Congress by the*
> *Secretary of Defense.* Washington: GPO, 2006. Print.
>
> United States. Dept. of Education. National Commission on Excellence in
> Education. *A Nation at Risk: The Imperative for Educational Reform.*
> Washington: GPO, 1983. Print.
>
> United States. Office of the President. *Environmental Trends.* Washington:
> GPO, 1981. Print.

(iv) Legal documents

When citing a well-known statute or law, a simple format in a text citation suffices; no bibliographical entry is needed.

9b

The Federal Trade Commission Act of 1914.

(15 USC 78j(b), 1964)

(US CC art. 9, pt. 2, par. 9-28)

(US Const. art. 1, sec. 2)

When citing a little-known statute, law, or other legal agreement, provide all of the information needed for retrieval:

"Agreement between the Government of the United States of America

and the Khmer Republic for Sales of Agricultural Commodities." *Treaties*

and Other International Agreements. Vol. 26, pt. 1. TIAS No. 8008.

Washington: GPO, 1976. Print.

Names of legal cases are abbreviated, and the first important word of each party is spelled out: Brown v. Board of Ed. stands for "Oliver Brown versus the Board of Education of Topeka, Kansas." Cases, unlike laws, are italicized in the text but not in the "Works Cited."

Text:

Miranda v. Arizona

"Works Cited" entry:

Miranda v. Arizona.

The following information must be supplied in the order listed: (1) name of the first plaintiff and the first defendant; (2) volume, name, and page (in that order) of the law report cited; (3) the place and name of the court that decided the case; and (4) the year in which the case was decided:

Richardson v. J. C. Flood Co. 190 A.2d 259. DC App. 1963. Print.

The citation means that the *Richardson v. J. C. Flood Co.* case can be found on page 259 of volume 190 of the Second Series of the *Atlantic Reporter.* The case was settled in the District of Columbia Court of Appeals in 1963.

For further information on the proper form for legal citations, consult *The Bluebook: A Uniform System of Citation,* 18th ed. (Cambridge, Mass.: Harvard Law Review Association, 1996).

I. Quotation used as a source

Text citations:

According to Oleg Grabar, . . . (qtd. in Gittes 238).

Dwight MacDonald said . . . (qtd. in Trimble 25).

"Works Cited" entries:

Gittes, Katharine Slater. "The Canterbury Tales and the Arabic Frame

Tradition." *PML* 98 (1983): 237-51. Print.

Trimble, John R. *Writing with Style: Conversations on the Art of Writing.*

Englewood Cliffs, NJ: Prentice, 1975. Print.

m. Report

Titles of reports in the form of pamphlets or books are italicized. When a report is included within a larger work, the title is set off in quotation marks. The work must be identified as a report:

The Churches Survey Their Task. Report of the Conference on Church,

Community, and State. London: Allen & Unwin, 1937. Print.

Luxenberg, Stan. "New Life for New York Law." Report on New York Law

School. *Change* 10 (Nov. 1978): 16-18. Print.

n. Table, graph, chart, map, or other illustration

If the table, graph, chart, or map has no title, identify it as a table, graph, map, or chart:

National Geographic Cartographic Division. Graph on imports drive into U.S.

market. *National Geographic* 164 (July 1983): 13. Print.

The descriptive label is not italicized or set off in quotation marks. If the table, graph, chart, or map has a title, use the title in quotation marks:

Benson, Charles S. "Number of Full-Time Equivalent Employees, by Industry,

1929-1959." Table. *The Economics of Public Education.* Boston:

Houghton, 1961. 208. Print.

This time the table has a title, so it is set off in quotation marks. (Notice the capitalization too.)

If you reproduce the table or other item in your paper, give the source in full as a footnote (see the discussion in 9d-7) and add an in-text reference using the number you give it in your paper:

In many industries the number of part-time employees exceeds the number of

full-timers (see table A.1).

If you do not reprint the item, its source is cited in text and in the "Works Cited" the same way that other information is.

We would urge you to bear in mind that the point of documentation is to tell your reader the source of a certain idea or fact used in your paper. It is not to satisfy a protocol that insists on a comma being used here or a colon there. These requirements are nothing more than window-dressing compared to your overall aim, which is to give a source credit that is due. Should you ever find yourself unable to remember the fine points of a documentation entry, keep in mind that your purpose is not to comply with protocol, but to pinpoint the source of borrowed material. Better you leave off ten commas than not carry out this one overriding purpose.

9c Content notes

Content notes consist of material that is relevant to your research but that does not need to interrupt the flow of your text. For example, here is the text, with an elevated number announcing the note:

> The centaur, being half horse and half man, symbolized both the wild and benign
>
> aspects of nature. Thus the coexistence of nature and culture was expressed.[12]

The note at the foot of the page adds information without interrupting the flow of the text:

> 12. It should be noted that the horse part is the lower and more animalistic
>
> area, whereas the human part is the upper, including the heart and head.

Content notes can consist of an explanation, additional information, reference to other sources, information about research procedures, or acknowledgment of special help.

The format of content notes is the same no matter which style of documentation you use in the paper. Some instructors insist that all content notes be gathered together on a page titled "Notes," placed after the text of the paper but before the "Works Cited." Other instructors want them placed at the foot of the appropriate page so that the reader can look down and read them as they occur. Observe the following rules when you're typing or keying in content notes:

- ☐ Indent the first line of each note one-half inch.
- ☐ Double-space content notes gathered at the end of the paper, but single-space those shown at the foot of a page. The examples shown here are double-spaced.
- ☐ The note should begin four lines below the text and should be identified by a numeral, followed by a period and then one space. Notes at the end of the chapter or at the end of the book are preferred to footnotes.
- ☐ Do not type a solid line between the text and the note. That would indicate a note continued from the previous page.
- ☐ Double-space between notes if there is more than one note at the foot of a page.

☐ Give complete documentation for content notes sources in the "Works Cited," not in the notes themselves. For instance, the following content note might appear in a biology paper:

> 10. Harvey disagrees with this aspect of Johnson's interpretation of handwriting (233).

In the "Works Cited" the full source is given:

> Harvey, O. L. "The Measurement of Handwriting Considered as a Form of Expressive Movement." *Quarterly Review of Biology* 55 (1980), 231-49. Print.

9c-1   Content note explaining a term

> 1. The *Rebellion of 1837* refers to December 1837, when William Lyon Mackenzie, a newspaper editor and former mayor of Toronto, led a rebellion intended to establish government by elected officials rather than appointees of the British crown.

9c-2   Content note expanding on an idea

> 2. This pattern of development was also reflected in their system of allocation: Only a small percentage of tax money was used for agriculture, whereas great chunks were apportioned to industry.

9c-3   Content note referring the reader to another source

> 3. For further information on this point, see King and Chang (124-35).

NOTE: The "Works Cited" must provide full documentation for this source:

> King, Gilbert W., and Hsien Wu Chang. "Machine Translation of Chinese." *Scientific American* 208.6 (1963): 124-35. Print.

9c-4   Content note explaining procedures

> 4. Participants were grouped according to their smoking history as never-smokers, cigar and/or pipe smokers exclusively, ex-cigarette smokers (smoked cigarettes regularly in the past but not within the year before the time of the interview), and current cigarette smokers (smoked cigarettes regularly at the time of the interview for at least one year).

9c

9c-5   Content note acknowledging help

> 5. The authors wish to acknowledge the help of the Montreal Children's Hospital in providing access to its Hewlett-Packard 3000 computer.

9c-6   Content note consolidating references

If a substantial part of your paper is based on several sources that deal with the same idea, consolidating the references into a single note can save space and reduce repetition.

> 1. For this idea I am indebted to Holland (32), Folsom (136-144), and Edgar (15-17).

9d   Finished form of the paper

Even though every style has its individual requirements, instructors vary in the conventions they expect students to observe in their written work. For example, MLA does not require a separate title page, which some instructors insist on. Other instructors do not require a separate title page but are adamant about an outline and will not accept a paper without one. The good news is that abiding by one style will automatically make it unnecessary for you to follow another. So before you submit your final paper, we strongly advise that you check the particular requirements of your instructor.

9d-1   Appearance

The paper should be neat and crisp, as it most likely will be if you use a computer to write it. Don't submit a handwritten paper unless your professor specifically permits it. Use 8½ × 11-inch paper that is heavy enough to withstand the instructor's corrections and comments. Don't staple the pages together or submit the paper inside a folder: Simply clip the pages together with a paper clip and hand in the paper. Do not use half sheets or strips of paper taped or stapled to the pages as these can get lost in handling.

NOTE: Be sure to give the paper a thorough proofreading before submitting it.

9d-2   Title page

MLA does not require a separate title page. Instead, the first page should start with your name, the name of the instructor, the name of the course, and the date. Each of these elements is a separate line flush with the left-hand margin of the page. The title of the paper goes below the date, centered, in title case (all major words capitalized). In the top right-hand corner of the page, insert a running head

9d

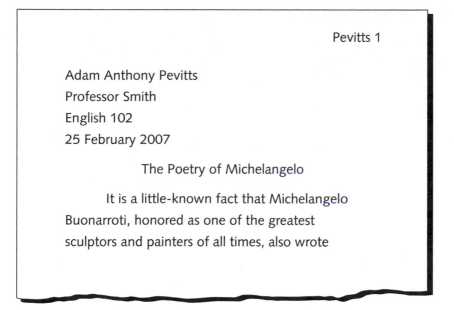

Pevitts 1

Adam Anthony Pevitts

Professor Smith

English 102

25 February 2007

The Poetry of Michelangelo

It is a little-known fact that Michelangelo
Buonarroti, honored as one of the greatest
sculptors and painters of all times, also wrote

Figure 9-3   Sample opening page, MLA style

(header) consisting of your last name, a space, and the page number. Figure 9-3 shows the opening-page treatment that MLA requires. If your instructor requires a title page, it counts as page 1, but it is not numbered.

9d-3   Abstract

A paper written with MLA documentation does not need a separate abstract.

9d-4   Pagination and headings

Number pages, including the first, consecutively in the upper right-hand corner of the paper. Use Arabic numerals (1, 2, 3). The MLA header starts with your last name, a space, and then the page number. No hyphens, parentheses, periods, or other characters follow the numbers. Endnotes and the "Works Cited" begin on new pages but are numbered in sequence from the body of the paper (see the student paper in 12a). Use lowercase roman numerals (i, ii, iii) to paginate the outline and any other material that precedes the body of the paper. The MLA title page is not numbered but is counted as "i" if an outline follows, and as "1" if no outline follows. If the title page is not separate, MLA counts the front page as "1."

If your paper contains sections, use headings either centered on the page or aligned with the left margin. Italicize but do not capitalize headings. Separate headings from the last line of the previous section by quadruple-spacing.

NOTE: A heading should always have at least two lines of text following it. If not, start the heading at the top of the next page.

9d-5   Spacing of text

Double-space the text, including quotations, content notes, and footnotes (see Figure 9-4).

Allow one-inch margins all around. Use a ragged right margin: Do not justify the text.

9d-6   Font

Use a font that is easy to read. MLA suggests a readable font, such as 12-point Times Roman. Script and other decorative typefaces are often difficult to read and so are not acceptable. If in doubt, consult your instructor.

9d-7   Illustrations, tables, and other graphics

Papers in many fields use tables, graphs, charts, maps, drawings, paintings, photographs, and other illustrations. A table presents information systematically, usually in columns, and is always labeled "Table." Any other kind of illustration

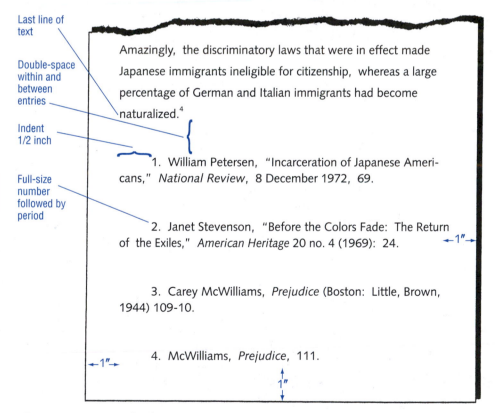

Figure 9-4   Format for footnotes

is labeled "Fig." or "Figure." The general rule is that illustrations should appear as close as possible to the part of the text that they illustrate. Or if the material requires an entire page, it should be placed in an appendix.

a. Tables

Tables should be titled and numbered above the table. Sources appear abbreviated, but must be cited in full in the "Works Cited." Tables should be numbered with Arabic numerals and titled at the top of the table:

Table 2

Significance of Differences between Mean Grade Point Averages of Male

Achievers and Underachievers from Grade 1 through 11

Capitalize both the word "Table" and the title as you would a book title: Do not use all capital letters. Place the table source and accompanying notes flush left at the bottom of the table (see 7h). If you don't list a source, a reader will assume that the table is your original work. Indicate notes to tables with superscript letters (lowercase) or symbols (asterisks and daggers) to avoid confusion with notes to the text. (Use one or the other consistently.) Figure 9-5 shows a sample original table.

Table 1	
Operating Expenses for Micah's House	
Educational Programs	
Trisomy 18 Online Campaign	$10,186,437
Public Outreach and Education	8,233,940
Research	6,783,271
Merchandise Program	1,334,423
Supporting Organization Activities	2,783,375
Membership Growth and Development	1,689,349
Management and General Expenses	511,689
Total Operating Expenses	**$31,522,484**

Figure 9-5   Sample table

b. Other illustrative materials

Other illustrations should be labeled "Fig." or "Figure" and numbered with Arabic numerals: Figure 3. Give each figure a title, using title case (capital and lowercase letters), placed under the illustration:

Fig. 12. The Development of the Alphabet

Put any notes and the abbreviated source flush left immediately below the caption. If no source is cited, a reader is going to assume that the illustration is your original work. Indicate notes to illustrations with superscript letters or symbols to avoid confusion with other note numbers in the text. Figures 9-6 through 9-10 on the following pages show several kinds of text illustrations.

If your illustrative material takes up a good share of the page, you may choose to place it on a separate page titled "Appendix." In your text you would simply write "See appendix." On the appendix page, center the word "Appendix" and place the illustration under it.

9d

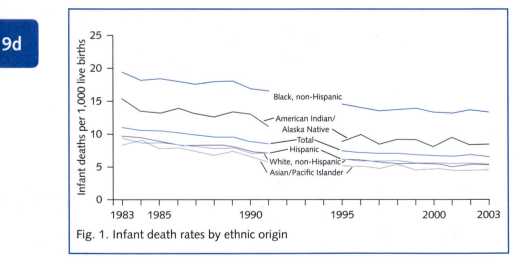

Fig. 1. Infant death rates by ethnic origin

Figure 9-6   Sample line graph

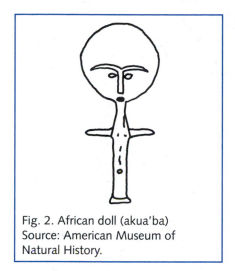

Fig. 2. African doll (akua'ba)
Source: American Museum of
Natural History.

Figure 9-7   Sample drawing

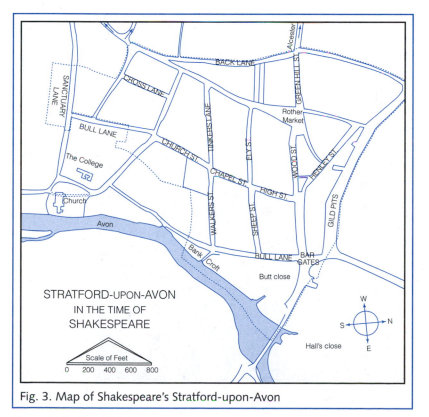

Fig. 3. Map of Shakespeare's Stratford-upon-Avon

Figure 9-8   Sample map

9d

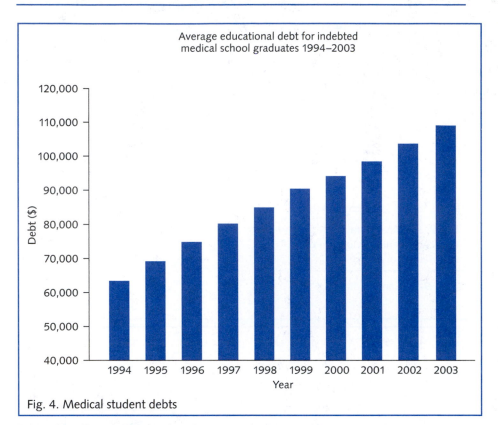

Average educational debt for indebted
medical school graduates 1994–2003

Fig. 4. Medical student debts

Figure 9-9   Sample bar graph

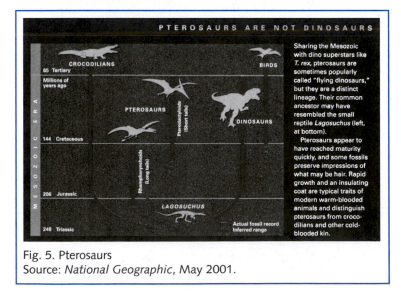

Fig. 5. Pterosaurs
Source: *National Geographic*, May 2001.

Figure 9-10   Sample graphic illustration

9d-8   Use of numbers

In dealing with numbers, most scholars observe the following rules:

- ☐ Use Arabic numerals for volumes, books, parts, and chapters of works; acts, scenes, and lines of plays; cantos, stanzas, and lines of poetry.

- ☐ In papers on subjects in which numbers are used infrequently, you may spell out numbers written in one or two words without accompanying symbols or abbreviations, and use numerals for others: five hundred, three thousand, two billion, 4½, 4.5, 101, 3,100, 7.1 million *or* 7,100,000, 5% *or* five percent, $2 *or* two dollars, 6 p.m. *or* six o'clock. Use the same style for symbols throughout the text of your paper.

- ☐ If the paper uses numbers frequently, as for a scientific or statistically supported thesis, use numerals with technical units of measure (2 millimeters) and for numbers that represent similar things, especially data presented together (4 respondents strongly supported the proposal and 22 opposed it). Spell out other numbers that can be written in one or two words, as explained above.

- ☐ In using numbers that indicate a range, give the second number in full for numbers through 99 (e.g., 4–8, 16–23, 80–99). In the MLA style, when using three digits or more, cite only the last two in the second number unless more digits are needed for clarity (e.g., 65–97, 120–30, but 3,877–906 and 3,907–4,223).

- ☐ Place commas between the third and fourth digits from the right, the sixth, and so on (e.g., 2,400; 5,000,000). Exceptions are page and line numbers, addresses, the year, and zip codes.

- ☐ Use the number 1, not the lowercase letter *l* or the uppercase letter *I*.

- ☐ In the following cases, use words to express numbers in your text:

  - ☐ Numbers less than ten, not used in measurements: five soldiers, six research papers.

  - ☐ Common fractions: one-fourth of the student body, a one-third majority.

  - ☐ Any number beginning a sentence: Three bulls galloped down the street.

  - ☐ 0 and 1 when used alone: He had zero dollars left; only one answer counted (but 1 out of 15 patients improved).

9d-9   Bibliography (titled "Works Cited")

The bibliography appears on a separate page at the end of your paper, under the centered heading "Works Cited" (not within quotation marks).

9d

9e Peer review checklist

Because two pairs of eyes usually are better than one, ask another student with good writing skills to go over your paper for clarity, consistency, focus, and mechanics. Here is a checklist the peer reviewer can use:

PEER REVIEW CHECKLIST

_____ 1. Does the title give the reader a clue to the subject of the paper?

_____ 2. Is the thesis clear and positioned properly (in the opening paragraph)?

_____ 3. Do the paragraphs support the thesis?

_____ 4. Does the paper move coherently from beginning to end?

_____ 5. Are sources introduced properly and cited correctly in the body of the paper?

_____ 6. Are quotations woven smoothly into the text?

_____ 7. Is the paper free of grammatical or mechanical errors?

NOTE: Just before you print out your final copy, always run the spelling checker too.

9f Submitting your paper electronically

Some instructors allow students to submit papers electronically—as an e-mail attachment, on a floppy disk, on a CD, or even on a web page. If you have the expertise to use any of these systems, always get approval from your instructor and follow his or her directions. Still, don't get so caught up by electronic publishing that you ruin your paper with bells and whistles at the expense of more traditional text that might have resulted in a better paper.

9f

The theory of relativity throws the world into a new age.

© dpa/Landov

Albert Einstein

A small German man with a Jewish background profoundly changed the world's view of time and space with a simple formula: $E = mc^2$. Today Albert Einstein is considered one of the most brilliant physicists of all time. In addition to exploring relativity, he also explained the photoelectric effect and studied the motion of atoms, on which he based his view of Brownian movement. In 1921 he won the Nobel Prize in physics. After the Nazis confiscated his property in Germany, he moved to the United States and became an American citizen. Although he persuaded President Franklin Delano Roosevelt to authorize development of the atomic bomb, he himself remained a confirmed pacifist.

10 The APA System of Documentation

10a Parenthetical documentation: Author-date (APA)

10b Format for "References" (APA)

10c Writing the abstract

10d Finished form of the paper

10e Peer review checklist

10f Submitting your paper electronically

FAQ

1. Why does the APA style stress the date over the page number in its citations? *See 10a.*

2. When is a page number necessary in APA citations? *See 10a-1j.*

3. How are the names of two authors joined when they appear in a parenthetical citation? *See 10a-1c.*

4. When is the Latin term *et al.* required in a citation? *See 10a-1d, e.*

5. What is the rule of thumb for abbreviating corporate authors in a citation? *See 10a-1f.*

6. What is the best way to avoid clutter when citing sources? *See 10a-2.*

7. What is the APA bibliography called? *See 10b.*

8. What is a "hanging indent"? *See 10b.*

9. Where can I find the correct form for listing a translated book in "References"? *See 10b-2d.*

10. What is the general order for references to periodicals? *See 10b-3.*

11. How do I distinguish between printed sources and electronic sources when citing them in "References"? *See 10b-5.*

12. How should I treat an e-mail in "References"? *See 10b-5e.*

The American Psychological Association's style—used by the social sciences, business, anthropology, and some of the life sciences—consists of parenthetical citations in the text, much like the style recommended by the MLA. However, unlike MLA, APA in-text citations mention the author (last name only) and the date of the cited publication, not the author and page number. Part of the reason for stressing the date over the page number is the nature of scientific research, which is time sensitive and can quickly become obsolete. Here is a typical APA in-text citation:

> Pollock (1994) has shown that a disturbance in the mother's initial contact with the infant can affect her decision or capacity to breast-feed her infant.

Or

> One study has shown that a disturbance in the mother's initial contact with the infant can affect her decision or capacity to breast-feed her infant (Pollock, 1994).

No page number is ever needed in the citation unless the source is used as a direct quote. Here are two examples:

No page number:

> The psychological response to defeat was often more dramatically expressed by the women of the South than by the men, as Mary Chestnut documents in her Civil War diary (Vann Woodward, 1981).

Page number necessary because of direct quote:

> The psychological response to defeat was often more dramatically expressed by the women of the South than by the men. Evidence of that comes from Mary Chestnut, who in her diary tells the story of a woman who "raved and dashed herself finally on the ground" when she heard about the fall of New Orleans (Vann Woodward 1981, p. 640).

In the second example, a page number must be cited because the text contains a direct quote. Notice the abbreviation *p.* (*pp.* if more than one page is cited). Your paper will then list the publication details of the source on a page titled "References" (APAs term for a bibliography):

Vann Woodward, C. (1981). *Mary Chestnut's Civil War.* New Haven:

Yale University Press.

APA also requires the "References" page to use a hanging indentation for its entries as well as italics—not underlining—for book titles, the names of magazines, and the like. See the sample entries in 10b.

10a-1 Examples of APA in-text citations to books

Here are some examples of the parenthetical documentation of the APA.

a. One work by a single author

The surname of the author and the year of publication are inserted in the text at the appropriate point:

> Leakey (2001) speculates that perhaps we have not yet found the perfect link
>
> between humans and apes.

> Or

> In a recent study (Leakey, 2001), paleoanthropologists focused on Kenya Man,
>
> a possible early hominid and ancestor of humankind.

> Or

> In a study published in 2001, Leakey described finding a skull in the Kenya
>
> desert that turned out to be a candidate for humankind's ancestor.

If the name of the author is given in the text, then cite only the year of publication in parentheses (first example). Otherwise, show both the author and the date of publication in parentheses (second example). If, however, both the year and the author are cited in the text discussion, then no parenthetical citation is necessary (third example).

b. Subsequent references

Subsequent references do not need to include the year so long as the study cannot be confused with other studies in your paper:

> In a more-recent study, Johnson (2002) found that children were more
>
> susceptible. Johnson also found that . . .

c. One work by two authors

When a work has two authors, always mention both names each time the reference occurs in your text. In naming two authors, join their names by *and* in the text but by an ampersand in a parenthetical citation.

> Much earlier, Grant and Change (1958) had discovered . . .

But

In a previous study of caged rats (Grant & Change, 1958), the surprising element

was . . .

d. One work by three to five authors

For works with three to five authors, mention all authors and the year of publication the first time the reference occurs. In subsequent citations include only the surname of the first author followed by *et al.* (not underlined or in italic and no period after *et*) and the year:

First citation:

Holland, Holt, Levi, and Beckett (1983) indicate that . . .

Subsequent citation:

Holland et al. (1983) also found . . .

An exception occurs when two separate references have the same first author and same date and so would shorten to the same reference. For example, Muskavitch, Baran, and Parker (2002) and Muskavitch, Baran, and Petrossian (2002) would both shorten to Muskavitch et al. (2002). In this case always cite both references in full to avoid confusion. Also, multiple-author citations in footnotes, tables, and figures should include the surnames of all authors in every citation.

e. Work by six or more authors

When a work has six or more authors, name only the surname of the first author followed by *et al.* (not underlined or italicized, and no period after *et*) and the year in the first as well as in subsequent citations. In "References," list the names of all authors. Again, if two separate references would shorten to the same form, list as many authors as are necessary to distinguish between the two references, followed by *et al.* For instance:

Verska, Sage, Finley, Attarian, and McBride (2006)

and

Verska, Sage, Bradley, Attarian, and McBride (2006)

would be cited in the text this way:

Verska, Sage, Finley, et al. (2006)

and

Verska, Sage, Bradley, et al. (2006)

NOTE: A comma precedes *et al.* following more than one name, but not following a single name.

10a

f. Corporate author

Sometimes a scientific work is authored by a committee, an institution, a corporation, or a government agency. The names of most corporate authors should be spelled out each time they appear as a source in your text. Occasionally, however, the name is spelled out in the first citation only and abbreviated in subsequent citations. The rule of thumb for abbreviating is that you must supply enough information in the text for a reader to locate the source in the references list. In the case of a long and difficult corporate name, you may use an abbreviation in subsequent citations as long as the name can be recognized and understood.

First citation in the text:

(National Institute of Mental Health [NIMH], 2005)

Subsequent citations:

(NIMH, 2005)

First citation in the text:

(Santa Barbara Museum of Natural History [SBMNH], 1999)

Subsequent citations:

(SBMNH, 1999)

If the name is short or an abbreviation would not be understood easily, spell out the name each time the reference occurs:

(Harvard University, 2006)

(Russell Sage Foundation, 2006)

(Bendix Corporation, 2006)

The names of all of these corporate authors are simple enough to be written out each time they are cited.

10a

NOTE: When using an acronym (words formed from the initial letters of other words), such as FEMA (the Federal Emergency Management Administration), AIDS (acquired immunodeficiency syndrome), PETA (People for the Ethical Treatment of Animals), or FBI (Federal Bureau of Investigation), be sure that you spell out the full name the first time you use the acronym unless it is commonly known, like TV, PC, IQ, or NATO. Here is an example from a student paper:

The Federal Emergency Management Administration (FEMA) was encouraged

to give money to victims of the fire.

g. Works by an anonymous author or no author

When the author of a work is listed as "Anonymous," use the word *Anonymous* in parentheses in the text, followed by a comma and the date:

(Anonymous, 2004)

In "References," the work should be alphabetized under A, for "Anonymous."

When a work has no author information, cite the first two or three words from the title of the book or article, followed by a comma and the year:

To obtain the tax benefits of a property exchange, the parties who started the

exchange must complete it ("First guarantee exchange," 2002).

One study shows that the number of women in their forties returning to college

continues to grow ("New educational horizons," 2002)--especially in urban areas.

In "References," works without authors are alphabetized according to the first significant word in the title. Articles (*the, a, an*), prepositions (*from, between, behind*), and pronouns (*this, those, that*) do not count.

Citations of statutes and other legal materials are treated like citations of works without authors: You cite the first few words of the reference and the year. Notice that court cases cited in the text must be in italic.

(*Baker v. Carr,* 1962)

(National Environmental Protection Act, 1970)

(Civil Rights Act, 1964)

h. Authors with the same surname

If your paper includes two or more authors with the same surname, include the authors' initials in all text citations even if the dates differ:

D. L. Spencer (1965) and F. G. Spencer (1983) studied both aspects of . . .

i. Two or more works in the same parentheses

Sometimes your paper may require that you cite two or more works supporting the same point. List the citations in the same order that they appear in "References," using the "References" guidelines (see 10b). The following rules will be helpful:

☐ List two or more works by the same author(s) by year of publication. If one work is in the process of being published, cite it last, using the words *in press:*

Research in the past two years (Ford & Beckham, 2000, 2002) has revealed many

potential . . .

10a

Or

Past studies (Murphy, 2005, 2006, in press) reveal . . .

☐ Identify different works by the same author that have the same publication date by a, b, c, and so on, added after the year in the "References" entries.

According to these studies (Sturgis, 2001a, 2001b, in press) the prevalent attitude is. . .

☐ List two or more works by different authors alphabetically according to the first authors' surnames. Use semicolons to separate the studies:

Three separate studies (Delaney & Rice, 1980; Rodney & Hollander, 1980; Zunz, 1981) tried to build on the same theory, but . . .

j. References to specific parts of a source

If you are giving your reader statistical information gathered from tables, charts, or graphs, be sure to cite the source in the body of the paper where you refer to the information. Anytime you refer to a specific quotation, figure, or table, you must supply the appropriate page, figure number, or table number:

(Spetch & Wilkie, 1983, pp. 15-25)

(Halpern, 1982, Fig. 2)

(Table 4.8, p. 2)

Notice that the words *page, pages,* and *figure* are abbreviated.

k. Personal communications

Personal communications include letters, memos, e-mail, and telephone conversations. Because readers cannot access them, personal communications have limited use for researchers and are not listed in "References." You cite them in your text only. Give the initials and the surname of the communicator, and the date on which the communication took place:

(A. Sorensen, personal communication, November 19, 2010)

Or

A. Sorensen (personal communication, November 19, 2010) quickly approved the entire research project.

10a

Or

In two separate e-mails, Dr. Kazanjian approved the protocol for this significant

autism research project (personal communication, November 19, 2005).

I. Citation as part of a parenthetical comment

When a citation appears as part of a parenthetical comment, use commas rather than brackets to set off the date:

(See Appendix A of Jenkins, 1983, for additional proof.)

10a-2 Avoiding clutter in the text

Many scholars use the APA system of documentation because it helps the reader identify authority and date immediately without looking to the bottom of the page or flipping to the end of the work. But you should guard against having so many references on one page that they make it unreadable. The following passage, for example, is cluttered with parenthetical information:

The protocol itself was faulty (Jacobson, 1995); thus the resulting research also

was seriously flawed (Lester, 1961; Masters, 1961; Zimmerman, 1960), and

millions of dollars in time and equipment were wasted (Smith, 1999).

To avoid this kind of congestion, some references can be given in the text:

In 1995 Jacobson acknowledged that the original protocol was faulty, so that

when Zimmerman (1960), Lester (1961), and Masters (1961) performed their

experiments, these, too, were flawed. The consequent loss of millions of dollars

in time and equipment has been well documented (Smith, 1999).

A prudent mixture of parenthetical and in-text references should be used when a page threatens to become engorged with citations.

10b Format for "References" (APA)

The APA bibliography is titled "References" and has its own formatting quirks. Figure 10-1 on the next page shows a typical entry. To prepare your APA references, do the following:

☐ Start the references on a new page.

NOTE: The page numbers in the reference list continue on from the text.

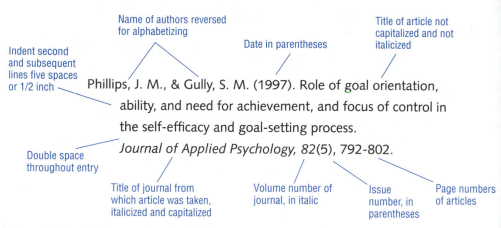

Figure 10-1 "References" entry (APA)

☐ Center the title "References" one double-space down from the running head.

☐ Double-space throughout the list.

☐ Cite only the sources you actually used in the paper, not sources you consulted.

☐ List titles by the same author chronologically, not alphabetically:

Rigby, R. L. (2008). . . .

Rigby, R.L. (2009). . . .

See additional guidelines for order in 10a-1i.

☐ Indent the second and subsequent lines of each entry five spaces or one-half inch (hanging indent).

☐ Place a period followed by one space between all of the elements in each entry. The two main exceptions are the colon between the place of publication and the publisher in citations to books, and the commas around the volume number for journals.

☐ Italicize the titles of books, periodicals, and volume numbers.

Study the reference examples in the rest of 10b.

10b-1 General order for books in "References"

Your references for books should contain the following elements in this order:

1. The name(s) of the author(s) in inverted order. Use only the initials of the first and middle names unless two authors mentioned in the paper have identical last names and initials. In the latter instance, the list of names is followed by a period.

2. The year of publication in parentheses, followed by a period.

3. The title of the book in italics with only the initial letter of the first word and proper nouns capitalized. (When a subtitle is separated from the title by a colon, the initial letter of the first word in the subtitle is also capitalized.)

4. The place of publication, followed by a colon.

5. The name of the publisher, followed by a period. (The name of the publisher is listed in as brief a form as is intelligible. Terms like Publisher, Co., and Inc. are omitted. But names of university presses and associations are spelled out.)

NOTE: The only time you need to indicate the state in which a work is published is when the city is not well known, for instance, Englewood Cliffs, NJ, or Mountain View, CA.

10b-2 Sample references to books

a. Book by a single author

Jones, E. (1931). *On the nightmare.* London: Hogarth.

Place a period after the author's name (the period following an initial serves this purpose), after the final parenthesis of the publication date, after the title, and at the end of the entry. Use a colon to separate the city of publication from the publisher.

b. Book by two or more authors

With two names, use an ampersand before the second name and a comma to separate the names:

Terman, L. M., & Merrill, M. A. (1937). *Measuring intelligence.* Cambridge,

MA: Riverside Press.

With three to six names, use an ampersand before the last name and use commas to separate the names (Bowen, B. M., Poole, K. J., & Gorky, A.). Give the surnames and initials of all authors, up to six. Separate the names with commas and use an ampersand between the last two names. If more than six authors are listed, use *et al.* to indicate the seventh and subsequent authors:

Johnson, T. H., Corbett, M., Benioff, M. F., Castuera, I. O., Nassiman, P.,

White, P. R., et al.

c. Edited book

Give the surname and initials of all editors up to six. For more than six editors, use *et al.* to indicate the seventh and subsequent editors. Insert *Ed.* or *Eds.* in parentheses after the name or names. Notice the period after the closing parenthesis:

10b

Friedman, R. J., & Katz, M. M. (Eds.). (1974). The psychology of depression:

Contemporary theory and research. New York: Wiley.

When referring to an article or chapter in an edited book, use the following form:

Waxer, P. (1979). Therapist training in nonverbal behavior. In A. Wolfgang

(Ed.), *Nonverbal behavior: Applications and cultural implications*

(pp. 221-240). New York: Academic Press.

Precede the name of the editor(s) with the word *In*. When an editor's name is not in the author position, do not invert his or her name. Place *Ed.* or *Eds.* in parentheses after the name(s), followed by a comma. The title of the article or chapter is not placed in quotation marks, and only the initial letter in the title, subtitle, and proper nouns are capitalized. Give inclusive page numbers for the article or chapter in parentheses after the title of the book. Precede the page number(s) with *p.* or *pp.*

d. Translated book

Place the name of the translator of a book (name not inverted) in parentheses after the book title; it is followed by a comma and *Trans.*, with a period after the end parenthesis:

Rank, O. (1932). *Psychology and the soul* (W. Turner, Trans.). Philadelphia:

University of Pennsylvania Press.

e. Book in a foreign language

Books in a foreign language are treated like books written in English, but the title is given in the foreign language with an English translation provided in brackets and not in italics.

Saint-Exupéry, A. de. (1939). *Terre des hommes* [Earth of men]. Paris: Gallimard.

f. Revised edition of a book

Give the edition (*Rev. ed.*, *4th ed.*, and so on) in parentheses following the title. Place a period after the final parenthesis:

Boulding, K. (1955). *Economic analysis* (3rd ed.). New York: Harper.

g. Book by a corporate author

When a book is authored by an organization rather than a person, the name of the organization appears in the author's place:

Committee of Public Finance. (1959). *Public finance.* New York: Pitman.

10b

When the corporate author is also the publisher, use the word *Author* in place of the publisher:

Commission on Intergovernmental Relations. (1955). *Report to the president.*

Washington, DC: Author.

Alphabetize group authors by the first significant word of the name.

h. Multivolume book

When citing a multivolume source, place the number(s) of the volume(s) actually used in parentheses immediately following the title. Use Arabic numerals for the volume number(s):

Reusch, J. (1980). Communication and psychiatry. In H. I. Kaplan,

A. M. Freedman, & B. J. Sadock (Eds.), *Comprehensive textbook of*

psychiatry: Vol. 1. Baltimore: Williams & Wilkins.

If a multivolume book was published over a number of years, list the years in parentheses following the author's name:

Brady, V. S. (1978-1982).

i. Unpublished manuscript

Treat an unpublished manuscript the way you would a book, but instead of writing the place of publication and publisher, write *Unpublished manuscript:*

Lopez, M.R. (2006). *Health problems of immigrants in San Bernardino County.*

Unpublished manuscript.

NOTE: For a publication of limited circulation, supply in parentheses, immediately after the title, an address where the publication can be obtained.

10b

10b-3 General order for periodicals in "References"

Entries for periodicals in your reference list should contain the following elements in the order shown:

1. Name(s) of author(s) in inverted order with only the initials of first and middle names.
2. Year of publication in parentheses, followed by a period. (For magazines issued on a specific day or month, give the year followed by a comma and then the month or the month and day.)

3. Title of article (no quotation marks or italics), with only the initial letter of the first word of the title and subtitle and proper nouns capitalized, followed by a period.

4. Name of the journal or magazine, in italics, with the first word and all other words of four letters or more capitalized, followed by a comma.

5. Volume number, in italics, followed by a comma. (Do not give volume numbers of periodicals issued on a specific date.)

6. Inclusive page numbers followed by a period (no *p.* or *pp.*).

10b-4 Sample references to periodicals

a. Journal article, one author

Harvey, O. L. (1980). The measurement of handwriting considered as a form

of expressive movement. *Quarterly Review of Biology, 55,* 231-249.

b. Journal article, up to six authors

Rodney, J., Hollender, B., & Campbell, M. (1983). Hypnotizability and phobic

behavior. *Journal of Abnormal Psychology, 92,* 386-389.

Use an ampersand preceded by a comma in front of the last author. Name each author up to six authors; use *et al.* for the seventh and subsequent authors (see 10b-2b). If the article has six or more authors, use this shortened form for in-text parenthetical citations:

(Unterseher et al., 2004).

See 10a-1 for more about in-text citations.

c. Journal article, paginated anew in each issue

Anderson, L. (2001). The overlooked factor in weight control. *Journal of*

Longevity, 71(12), 6-8.

If the journal begins each issue with page 1, supply the volume number in Arabic and italic, followed immediately (no space) by the issue number in Arabic and in parentheses, a comma, a space, and then the page number(s) and a period:

Reavey, P., Ahmed, B., & Magnumdar, A. (2006). How can we help when she

won't tell us what's wrong? *Journal of Community and Applied Social*

Psychology, 16(3), 171-188.

10b

d. Journal with continuous pagination throughout the annual volume

Most scholarly journals are paginated continuously throughout the year, so volume and page numbers are all that the reader needs to locate your source:

> Anthony, R. G., & Smith, N. S. (1977). Ecological relationships between
>
> mule deer and white-tailed deer in southeastern Arizona. *Ecological*
>
> *Monographs, 47,* 255-277.

e. Magazine article, magazine issued monthly

List the author(s), then the year and month of publication in parentheses, separated by a comma. Place a period after the end parenthesis. Give the title of the article without quotation marks and with only proper nouns and the first word of the title and of the subtitle capitalized, followed by a period. Next come the name of the magazine, in italics, with all major words capitalized, a comma, and finally the inclusive page numbers (no *p.* or *pp.*):

> Kernan, M. (2001, October). Head's up: From a computer-generated model, sculp-
>
> tors cast a bronze triceratops that looks like the real thing. *Smithsonian,* 34-36.

f. Magazine article, magazine issued on a specific day

List the author(s), followed by the year, a comma, the month, and the day of the month in parentheses, with a period following the closing parenthesis. Give the title of the article (no quotation marks), with only proper nouns and the first word of the title and subtitle capitalized, followed by a period. Then give the name of the magazine, in italics, with all major words capitalized, followed by a comma and inclusive page numbers (no *p.* or *pp.*):

> Kalfayou, M. (1997, November 5). As a woman sees it: Honk for domestic
>
> violence. *The American Observer,* 3.

NOTE: APA style retains the article (*The*) in the name of magazines and newspapers.

g. Newspaper article

Newspaper articles are treated like magazine articles issued on a specific day, with the exact date in parentheses following the author. Here, too, only the first word and proper nouns in the title are capitalized. The title of the newspaper is in italics and capitalized following APA style. Note the section and page(s) after the newspaper title. Use Arabic numerals throughout the entry, and use *p.* or *pp.* for "page(s)":

> Goodman, E. (1983, December 23). Bouvia case crosses the "rights" line. *Los*
>
> *Angeles Times,* p. B5.

10b

If the newspaper article has no author, begin with the title or headline of the article:

> When Social Security is a senior's only financial support.

Alphabetize works with no author by the first significant word in the title. The example above would be alphabetized on "social."
In your text, use a shortened version of the title in parentheses ("Social Security," 2005).

h. Editorial

> Guion, R. M. (1983). Comments from the new editor [Editorial]. *Journal of*
>
> *Applied Psychology, 68,* 547.

When citing an editorial, place the word *Editorial* in brackets, followed by a period, after the title of the editorial. If the editorial has no title, "[Editorial]" immediately follows the date. Otherwise, treat the entry like any other magazine or journal article.

i. Letter to the editor

> Redgrave, L. (2006, May/June). All the right movies [Letter to the editor]. *AARP,* p. 6.

NOTE: When the month of the magazine is given in parentheses after the author, use *p.* or *pp.* for "page(s)." Place *Letter to the editor* in brackets immediately following the title. If there is no title, place the bracket following the parenthetical date.

j. Review

Place *Review of* followed by the title of the work being reviewed in brackets immediately following the title of the review.

> Boorstein, J. K. (1983, November/December). On welfare [Review of the
>
> article Dilemmas of welfare policy: Why work strategies haven't worked].
>
> *Society,* pp. 120-122.

10b-5 Sample references to electronic sources

Under the APA style, a citation to an electronic source does not differ significantly in its basic elements or sequence from a citation to a printed source. What sets the electronic citation apart is the URL. According to APA, the following two rules are of great importance and should always be observed:

- ☐ Direct readers as closely as possible to the information being cited. Whenever possible, reference specific documents rather than home or menu pages.
- ☐ Provide addresses that work.

An electronic citation should consist of the following in the order shown:

1. Author, given the same way as any other citation, followed by a period.
2. The date of the document in parentheses. Use year-month-day format, with no abbreviations:

    (2007, February 25).

    Insert a period after the closing parenthesis.

3. Title with only the first word, the first word after a colon, and proper nouns capitalized. No quotation marks around article titles. Use italics for titles of books, periodicals, and microfilm.
4. The source—a database, website, or online magazine—in italics.
5. The word *Retrieved* followed by the date, followed by the word *from* and the complete URL. *Do not add a period at the end of the entry if the entry ends with a URL.*

Here is an example:

> Peterson, S. (2001, December 18). Business: The smaller the better. *ZDNet*
>
> *News*. Retrieved January 5, 2002, from http://www.zdnet.com/zdnn/
>
> stories/comment/0,5859,2833529,00.html

What follow are examples of the most common electronic sources.

a. Abstract online

Notice the addition of the word *Abstract* before *retrieved:*

> Bourg, S. N. (2001). Sexual and physical aggression within a dating/acquaintance
>
> relationship: Testing models of perpetrator characteristics. ProQuest. Abstract
>
> retrieved October 16, 2007, from http://proquest.umi.com/pqdlink?Ver
>
> =1&Exp=04-17-2012&FMT=7&DID=728459911&RQT=309&attempt=1&cfc=1

10b

b. CD-ROM

Provide an author (if available), the date of publication, the title of the work, and the name of the CD-ROM program or publication. Furnish edition or version numbers, and any other available publication information:

> Psychoanalysis. (2002). *Microsoft Encarta Reference Library* [CD-ROM]. Seattle,
>
> WA: Microsoft Corporation.

NOTE: No access date is needed for citations to CD-ROMs and other permanent storage media.

c. Computer program

> Dragon NaturallySpeaking (Version 9, preferred edition for Windows) [Computer software]. (2006). Burlington, MA: Nuance, Inc.

d. Corporate website

> IDG, Inc. (2001). *Report: Job cuts in 2001 reach nearly 2 million.* Retrieved January 4, 2002, from http://idg.net/

e. E-mail

According to the APA, e-mail and other personal communications that cannot be retrieved by readers should be cited in the text, not listed in the references. E-mail posted to an online discussion group is styled like this:

> McCuen, J. (2001, March 21). Give genius a chance [Msg 12]. Message posted to http://groups.google.com/groups?hl=en&threadm=efbc3534 .0201220323.5235319c%40posting.google.com&prev=/groups%3Fhl %3Den%26group%3Dhumanities.lit.authors.shakespeare

f. FTP source

See 5b-2 for a list of some abbreviations used on the Internet.

> Zeleznikar, A. P. (1997, March 2). Informational theory of consciousness. *Informatica: An International Journal of Computing and Informatics, 21,* 3. Retrieved May 4, 2002, from ftp://ftp.arnes.si/magazines/informatica/vol21_3.97

> Adamson, Marilyn. (2006, October 2). Is there a god? *Everystudent.com.* Retrieved October 2, 2006 from http://everystudent.com/features/isthere.html

g. Gopher

> Jordan, Z. P. (1995, July 7). Telecommunications green paper. *The ministry of posts, telecommunications and broadcasting.* Retrieved July 17, 2002, from gopher://gopher.anc.org.za/00/govdocs/green_papers/telecoms .txt%09%09%2B

h. Government website

> Library of Congress. (1999, July 9). *Official U.S. executive branch web sites.* Retrieved April 6, 2002, from http://www.loc.gov/global/executive/fed.html

10b

i. Electronic mailing list (Listserv)

Pyatt, E. J. (2001, September 24). Re: Everson typography. *The Celtic Linguistics List.* Retrieved January 5, 2002, from http://listserv.linguistlist.org/cgi-bin/wa?A2=ind0109&L=celtling&D=1&F=&S=&P=83

j. MOOs and MUDs (synchronous communication)

Miami University, Oxford, OH. Basic MOO building commands. Retrieved September 15, 2002, from http://miavx1.muohio.edu/~mandellc/moo/build_commands.html

k. Online book

Green, E. C. (1997). *Southern strategies: Southern women and the woman suffrage question.* Chapel Hill, NC: University of North Carolina Press. Retrieved October 3, 2002, from http://www.questia.com/PageManagerHTMLMediator.qst?action=openPageViewer&docId=8033348

l. Online database

Thomson, D. (2001, December 23). Dietrich at 100: The camera's truest lover. *The New York Times.* Retrieved September 4, 2002, from http://proquest.umi.com/pqdweb?Did=000000096537415&Fmt=3&Deli=1&Mtd=1&Idx=2&Sid=1&RQT=309

m. Online dictionary

Pawky. (1998). *Webster's new world dictionary.* Retrieved on June 4, 2002, from http://ask.elibrary.com/getrefdoc.asp?pubname=Webster~Q~s_NewWorld_Dictionary&puburl=0&querydocid=28317849@urn:bigchalk:US~;Lib&dtype=0~0&dinst=0&author=&title=pawky++&date=01%2D01%2D1988&query=pawky&maxdoc=1&idx=0

n. Online encyclopedia

Boswell, James. (1997). *The Columbia encyclopedia,* 5th ed. Retrieved July 4, 2002, from http://ask.elibrary.com/getrefdoc.asp?pubname=The_Columbia_Encyclopedia,_Fifth_Edition&puburl=http~C~~S~~S~icm.lhs.com~S~&

10b

querydocid=28432006@urn:bigchalk:US;Lib&dtype=0~0&dinst=0&author=&

title=Boswell%2C+James++&date=01%2D01%2D1993&query=Boswell

%2C+James&maxdoc=1&idx=0

o. Online magazine article—author listed

Peterson, S. (2001, December 18). Business: The smaller the better. *ZDNet*

News. Retrieved April 5, 2002, from http://www.zdnet.com/zdnn/stories/

comment/0,5859,2833529,00.html

NOTE: APA does not place quotation marks around the titles of articles or essays within larger works, and it capitalizes only initial letters and proper nouns. The title of the magazine is capitalized and italicized.

If the article you are citing has been published in print, but you've only consulted the electronic version, put *Electronic version* in brackets immediately after the title. A period follows the closing bracket:

Levine, J. (2001, May). The mind's eye [Electronic version]. *Psychology Today,*

34, 14. Retrieved May 10, 2002, from http://web5.infotrac-college.com/

wadsworth/session/585/376/17219801/9!xrn_1_0_A73537471

p. Online magazine article—no author listed

Consumers Union of U.S., Inc. (2000, September). Herbal Rx for prostate

problems. *Consumer Reports.* Retrieved January 4, 2002, from http://

www.consumerreports.org/main/detail.jsp?CONTENT%3C%3Ecnt_

id=31427&FOLDER%3C%3Efolder_id=31255&bmUID=1010083701919

q. Telnet

Asimov, I. (1991, May 22). Of butterflies and the origin of the species. *San Francisco*

Chronicle. Retrieved January 5, 2002, from telnet://nyplgate.nypl.org

r. Usenet

Peterson, B. (1994, January 11). Re: Bob Marley discography. Message posted

to http://groups.gÁoogle.com/groups?q=Bob+Marley&selm=1994Jan11

.112121.29935%40nomina.lu.se&rnum=2

NOTE: APA discourages the citation of newsgroup postings because they have not been subjected to peer review. Instead it recommends treating those messages like personal communications.

10b

s. Website—author listed

Sauve, D. (1998). Charles Bukowski's novels. *Charles Bukowski.* Retrieved

January 3, 2002, from http://www.levee67.com/bukowski/

t. Website—no author listed

Jamaica Tourist Board. (2000- 2001). *Official site of the Jamaica Tourist Board.*

Retrieved May 3, 2002, from http://www.jamaicatravel.com/

u. Message posted to a group

The Internet offers a wealth of online discussion groups, forums, newsgroups or electronic mailing lists, and postings that bring together people of similar interests. Care should be taken in citing these electronic discussion sources, because as a rule they are not subject to the scrutiny of formal publication, have not been peer reviewed, and often lack scholarly content. Moreover, they usually have a brief life span. Any posted message you cite should have scholarly content and should be retrievable. If it is not retrievable, then you should cite it as a personal communication.

Here are some guidelines to follow:

☐ List the author's full name—last name first, followed by initials.

☐ Provide the exact date of the posting.

☐ Follow the date with the subject line of the message (also called "thread"), not in italics. Provide any additional identifier in brackets after the subject.

☐ Finish the reference with *Message posted to* followed by the address of the group.

Osborne, D. (2006, September 12). Help in recruiting AV helpers [weekly

forum]. Message posted to http://www.Northerncaliforniaconference.org/

worshipforum/html

10b-6 Sample references to nonprint materials

The following are citation models for other common nonprint sources.

a. Motion picture

When citing a film, name the producer (title in parentheses), followed by the director (title in parentheses), and then the date of production (in parentheses). Always specify the medium in brackets so that the material cannot be confused with a book or some other source:

Cotton, D. H. (Producer), & Correll, J. B. (Director). (1980). *The management of*

hypertension in pregnancies [Motion picture]. Houston: University of Texas.

b. Audio recording (cassette, record, tape, compact disc)

When citing a recording, name the primary contributor (Speaker, Narrator, Panel chair, Forum director, and so on), followed by the date of production. If the recording has a number, list it in parentheses after the kind of recording. Otherwise, list the kind of recording in brackets after the title. Finally, list the place of publication and the publisher, supplying an exact address if one is available:

> Bronowski, J. (Speaker). (1983). *The mind* (Cassette audio recording No. BB
>
>> 4418.01). Los Angeles: Pacifica Tape Library, 5316 Venice Blvd., Los Angeles,
>>
>> CA 90019.
>
> Corley, O. R. (Interviewee). (1997). My problems with obesity (Compact disc
>
>> in private library of Luigi M. DeLucia, M.D.). North Hollywood.

10b-7 Sample references to special items

Sources come in such varied forms that a sample cannot be supplied for every possibility. When citing a source for which there is no exact model, provide enough information for your reader to find it. In general, follow this order: (1) person or organization responsible for the work; (2) year the work was published, produced, or released; (3) title of the work; (4) identifying code, if applicable; (5) place of origin; and (6) publisher. Study the following samples.

a. Government documents

(i) Congress

> U.S. Cong. House. (1977). *U.S. assistance programs in Vietnam.* 92nd Cong.,
>
>> 2nd sess. Washington, DC: U.S. Government Printing Office.
>
> U.S. Cong. Joint Committee on Printing. (1983). *Congressional directory.*
>
>> 98th Cong., 1st sess. Washington, DC: U.S. Government Printing
>>
>> Office.
>
> U.S. Cong. Senate. (1970). *Separation of powers and the independent agen-*
>
>> *cies: Cases and selected readings.* 91st Cong., 1st sess. Washington, DC:
>>
>> U.S. Government Printing Office.

(ii) Executive branch

> Executive Office of the President. (2006). *Environmental trends.* Washington, DC:
>
>> U.S. Government Printing Office.

Bush, G. W. (2007). *State of the union address.* Washington, DC: U.S. GPO.

NOTE: U.S. Government Printing Office can be abbreviated as U.S. GPO.

b. Legal references

The only legal references that a student paper is likely to cite are references to court cases or statutes. Because legal references can be complex, consult *The Bluebook: A Uniform System of Citation,* 18th ed. (Cambridge, Mass.: Harvard Law Review Association, 1996) if your paper relies heavily on legal references. For common kinds of citations, follow the sample entries below:

(i) Court case

In general use the following order when citing court decisions: (1) plaintiff v. defendant (in roman); (2) volume, name, and page of law report cited; and (3) the name of the court that decided the case (in parentheses):

Clark v. Sumner. 559 S.W.2d 914 (Tex. Civ. App. 1977).

The case can be found in the second series, volume 559, beginning on page 914, of the *South Western Reporter.* The case was decided by the Texas Civil Court of Appeals in 1977.

(ii) Statute

When citing commonly known statutes or laws, the simpler the better:

U.S. Const. Art. III, sec. 2.

Securities Act of 1933, U.S. Const. Art. III, sec. 2. 15 U.S.C. § 78j. (1964).

For lesser-known statutes, supply additional information:

90 U.S. Statutes at Large. 505 (1976).

Nuclear Waste Policy Act, Part I, sec. 112 (a).

Energy Conservation and Production Act, Title I, Part A, sec. 101, 42 USC 6901,

1976.

(iii) Treaty

Technical Cooperation Agreement Between the Government of the Royal Kingdom

of Saudi Arabia and the Government of the United States of America. (1976).

Treaties and Other International Agreements. Vol. 26, Part 1, TAIS No. 8072.

Washington, DC: U.S. Government Printing Office.

10b

c. A report

> Organization for Economic Cooperation and Development. (1983). *Assessing*
>
> *the impacts of technology on society* (Report). Washington, DC: U.S.
>
> Government Printing Office.

Place *Report* or other identifying words, such as *NIH Publication,* in parentheses after the title. If a code has been assigned to the report, add it also:

> (Report No. CSOS-R-292).

If the publisher is the same as the author, place the word *Author* where you would normally place the name of the publisher:

> California Postsecondary Education Commission. (1982). *Promises to keep:*
>
> *Remedial education in California's public colleges and universities*
>
> (Report). Sacramento, CA: Author.

10c Writing the abstract

An abstract—a summary of the major ideas contained in your research paper—is used for papers written in the APA style. Although the abstract replaces an outline, we suggest for the sake of logical progression and balance in the paper that you write from an outline, even if you are not required to submit one. Writing the abstract in coherent paragraphs is relatively easy if you have outlined your paper. To produce a smooth abstract you need only link and condense the main ideas of the outline with appropriate commentary.

In writing the abstract, use no more than 120 words. (Remember that the whole point of abstracting is to condense.) The abstract always falls on page 2, the page after the title page. It should have a running head and page number. Center the title "Abstract" (without quotation marks) one inch from the top of the page.

The abstract should observe the following conventions:

1. Reflect accurately the purpose and content of your paper
2. Explain briefly the central issue or problem of your paper
3. Summarize your paper's most important points
4. Mention the major sources used
5. State your conclusions clearly
6. Be coherent so that it is easy to read
7. Remain objective in its point of view

0c

Here is an example from a student paper:

Vitamins   2

Abstract

Until recently, the official view on healthful eating was that anyone who ate a normally balanced diet did not need vitamin supplements. However, recent research by a team at Trinity College in England and at Brigham and Women's Hospital in Boston concludes that certain vitamins, especially the vitamins A, B, C, D, and E (also called antioxidants), can help prevent such serious diseases as heart failure, diabetes, depression, flu, and eye problems. The conclusion of this research is that although vitamins cannot substitute for good eating habits, plenty of exercise, and not smoking, the findings do strengthen the argument for adding vitamins as a nutritional supplement.

10d Finished form of the paper

Before you submit your final paper, we strongly advise that you check the particular formatting requirements of your instructor. With that warning, we look now at the conventional requirements of the finished APA paper.

10d-1 Two kinds of APA papers: The theoretical and the empirical

Research papers written in the APA style are divided into two kinds—(1) the theoretical paper and (2) the empirical paper. The theoretical paper is the one most students in college will write. It is organized much like the MLA or CMS papers. The empirical paper, which consists of original research, will be used more in graduate studies or in professional writing.

REQUIREMENTS OF THE THEORETICAL PAPER

- The introduction should establish the problem and present the writer's thesis.
- The body of the paper should give proof of the problem by citing experts who have commented on the issues involved.
- The conclusion should present a possible solution to the problem, perhaps even suggesting further work to be done.

REQUIREMENTS OF THE EMPIRICAL PAPER

- The introduction should establish the subject to be examined, including a rationale and hypothesis that serve as the launching pad for the study.

10d

☐ The body of the paper should contain the following two headings: (1) *Methods* (explaining the design of the study), (2) *Results* (listing in detail the statistical findings of the study).

☐ The conclusion of the paper (with the heading *Discussion*) should interpret the results and findings of the paper and relate them to the paper's thesis.

10d-2 Appearance of the final copy

The paper should be neat and crisp, as it most likely will be if you use a computer to write it. Don't submit a handwritten paper without specific permission. Use 8½ × 11-inch paper that is heavy enough to withstand the instructor's marginal corrections and comments. Don't staple the pages together or submit the paper inside a folder: Simply paper clip the pages together. Do not use half sheets or strips of paper taped or stapled to the pages as these can get lost in handling.

☐ *Margins and spacing:* Allow one-inch margins all around. Use a ragged right margin: Do not justify the text. Double-space everything in the paper, including long quotations. The result should be no more than 27 lines of text per page.

☐ *Font:* APA recommends Times New Roman in a 12-point size.

☐ *Page numbers and headers:* Number pages, including the first, consecutively in the upper right-hand corner of the paper. Use Arabic numerals (1, 2, 3). Preceding the page number is a header, which is a shortened form of the title—the first two or three words of the title is the APA's suggestion. Type five spaces after the header, and then the page number. No hyphens, parentheses, periods, or other characters follow the numbers.

☐ *Paragraphing and indents:* Use normal paragraphing throughout the paper, with five-space or half-inch indentation at the start of the new paragraphs. Also indent long quotations—without quotation marks.

a. Outline

APA does not specifically require an outline. If you want to write from an outline, see 4b on how to prepare one, and 4c on using it to write the paper.

b. Title page

The first page is a title page with the following elements, as illustrated in Figure 10-2.

1. *Page header and number:* At the top right of this and every page are the page number and header, as described above.

2. *Running head:* In APA format you provide this shortened form (no more than 50 characters) of the paper's title that could be used as an identifier on each page of a journal publication of your paper. It appears in all-capital letters after the words "Running head" and a colon, which start flush left at the left margin on the first line below the page header and number.

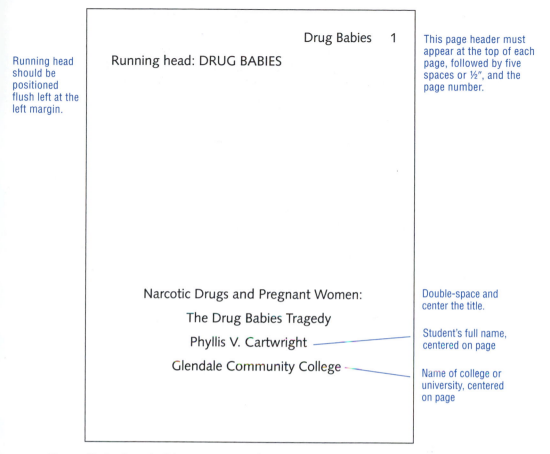

Running head should be positioned flush left at the left margin.

Running head: DRUG BABIES

Drug Babies   1

This page header must appear at the top of each page, followed by five spaces or ½", and the page number.

Narcotic Drugs and Pregnant Women:

The Drug Babies Tragedy

Phyllis V. Cartwright

Glendale Community College

Double-space and center the title.

Student's full name, centered on page

Name of college or university, centered on page

Figure 10-2   Sample title page, APA style

NOTE: Because the page header is limited to two or three words, it may be shorter than the running head.

1. *Title of the paper:* Center in upper- and lowercase letters just above your name.
2. *Name and academic affiliation of the writer:* Center and place at the bottom of the page.

c. Abstract

The second page is an abstract that concisely summarizes the gist of the paper in a block of words not exceeding 120 words. Center the title *Abstract* one inch down from the top of the page, and don't indent the first line of the abstract. See 10c.

10d

d. Text

The text of your paper always begins on page 3. Repeat the title of your paper, centered, and start the text on the next double-spaced line, with a paragraph indent.

If your paper contains sections, use headings centered on the page. Use upper- and lowercase style; for example, "Section Headings in Your Paper." Separate headings from the last line of the previous section by quadruple-spacing.

NOTE: A heading should always have at least two lines of text following it. If not, start the heading at the top of the next page.

e. Content notes and endnotes

Content notes (see 9c) and endnotes are double-spaced between notes but may be single-spaced within notes (see Figure 11-1). Use elevated (superscript) numerals in the text to refer to content notes or footnotes (and endnotes). When possible, the numbers should come at the end of a sentence, after the punctuation mark. But more important than conventional placement or size is that the reader knows to what the note refers. (See 11a-2 for more on placing superscript numerals.) Unless otherwise indicated by your instructor, start each content note or footnote at the bottom of the page on which its reference number occurs. Indent the first line of each note five spaces or one-half inch; second and subsequent lines align with the left margin. To add an explanation to a table or other illustration, use the word *Note,* in italics, followed by a period (*Note.*), and place the note directly under the illustration.

1. Double-space the endnotes.

2. Triple-space between the heading and the first note.

f. Illustrations: Tables and figures

Papers in many fields use tables, graphs, charts, maps, drawings, paintings, photographs, and other illustrations. A table presents information systematically, usually in columns, and is always labeled "Table." Any other kind of illustration is labeled "Figure." The general rule is that illustrations should appear as close as possible to the part of the text they illustrate. Or if the material requires an entire page, it should be placed in an appendix.

(i) Tables

Tables should be titled and numbered in Arabic numbers above the table. Capitalize only the word "Table," and the first word of the title. Do not use all capital letters. Place the table source in full as part of the general note (beginning *Note.*) flush left at the bottom of the table. If you don't list a source, a reader will assume that the table is your original work. Notes to specific parts of tables are indicated with superscript letters (lowercase) or symbols (asterisks and daggers, for significance levels in statistics), to avoid confusion with notes to the text. Figure 10-3 shows a sample table.

Table 2

Significance of Differences Between Mean Grade Point Averages of Male

Achievers and Underachievers From Grades 1 Through 11

| | Mean grade point average | | | | | |
Grade	Under- achievers	Achievers	F	P	t	P
1	2.81	2.56	1.97	n.s.*	1.44	n.s.
2	2.94	2.64	1.94	n.s.	1.77	n.s.
3	3.03	2.58	1.49	n.s.	2.83	.01†
4	3.19	2.72	1.03	n.s.	2.96	.01†
5	3.28	2.75	1.02	n.s.	3.71	.01†
6	3.33	2.67	1.33	n.s.	4.46	.01†
7	3.25	2.56	1.02	n.s.	5.80	.01†
8	3.36	2.50	1.59	n.s.	6.23	.01†
9	3.25	2.14	1.32	n.s.	10.57	.01†
10	3.13	1.87	1.30	n.s.	10.24	.01†
11	2.81	1.85	4.05	02‡	5.46	01†

*No significance.

† Yields significance beyond the .01 level.

‡ Yields significance beyond the .02 level but below the .01 level.

Figure 10-3   Sample table, APA style

10d

(ii) Figures

Illustrations other than tables should be labeled "Figure" and numbered with Arabic numerals: Figure 3. Give each figure a title. Capitalize only the first word or proper nouns. Place the title under the illustration:

Figure 12. The development of the Syrian alphabet

Put any notes and the source flush left immediately below the illustration. Indicate notes to illustrations with superscript letters or symbols to avoid confusion with other note numbers in the text. Figures 10-4 through 10-8 on the following pages show several kinds of text illustrations.

If your illustrative material takes up a good share of the page, you may choose to place it on a separate page titled "Appendix." In your text you would simply write "See appendix." On the appendix page, center the word "Appendix" and place the illustration under it.

g. Use of numbers

In dealing with numbers, most scholars observe the following rules:

- ☐ Use Arabic numerals for volumes, books, parts, and chapters of works; acts, scenes, and lines of plays; cantos, stanzas, and lines of poetry.

- ☐ Use Arabic numerals to express all numbers ten and above (13; 2,346; the 18th experiment; the expected 40%). Write as Arabic numerals any number below ten that cannot be spelled out in one or two words (e.g., $4\frac{1}{2}$ or 9.555).

- ☐ In using numbers that indicate a range, give the second number in full for numbers through 99 (e.g., 4–8, 16–23, 80–99). In APA, when using three digits or more, give all numbers (e.g., 120–320, 345–1450).

- ☐ Place commas between the third and fourth digits from the right, the sixth, etc. (e.g., 2,400; 5,000,000). Exceptions are page and line numbers, addresses, the year, and zip codes.

- ☐ Use the number 1, not the lowercase letter *l* or the uppercase letter *I*.

- ☐ In the following cases, use words to express numbers in your text:
  - ☐ Numbers less than ten not used in measurements: five soldiers, six research papers.
  - ☐ Common fractions: one-fourth of the student body, a one-third majority.
  - ☐ Any number beginning a sentence: Three bulls galloped down the street.
  - ☐ 0 and 1 when used alone: He had zero dollars left; only one answer counted (but 1 out of 15 patients improved).

- ☐ Combine words and numerals for large numbers: He retired with an income of $5 billion.

h. Using the right tense

Verb tense differentiates the APA paper from MLA or CMS papers. Whereas the MLA or CMS paper usually refers to cited works in the present tense ("Williams's book on style *suggests* that . . ."), the APA paper refers to cited works in the past or in the past perfect tense ("The interviews by Beckwith *showed* that . . . ," or, "Wilson and Fernando *have suggested* that . . ."). However, the APA paper uses the present tense in discussing the results of a study ("Bernard's study *concludes* . . . ," or, "This kind of therapy *offers* hope for children afflicted by autism because . . .").

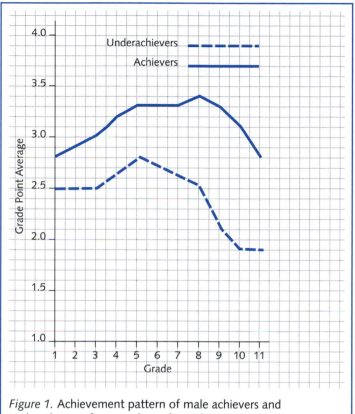

Figure 1. Achievement pattern of male achievers and underachievers from grades 1 through 11

Figure 10-4 Sample line graph

Figure 2. The Chinese characters that make up the verb "to listen"
Note. From Understanding Human Communication (7th ed.), (p. 120), R. B. Adler and G. Rodman, 2002, New York: Oxford University Press.

Figure 10-5 Sample drawing

10d

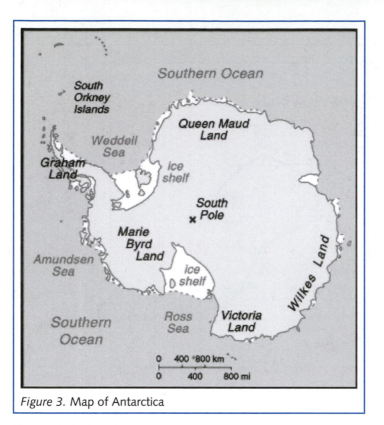

Figure 3. Map of Antarctica

Figure 10-6 Sample map

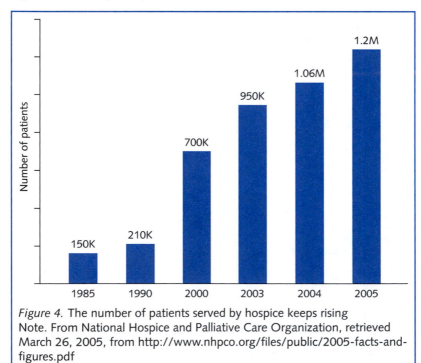

Figure 4. The number of patients served by hospice keeps rising
Note. From National Hospice and Palliative Care Organization, retrieved
March 26, 2005, from http://www.nhpco.org/files/public/2005-facts-and-
figures.pdf

Figure 10-7 Sample bar graph

10d

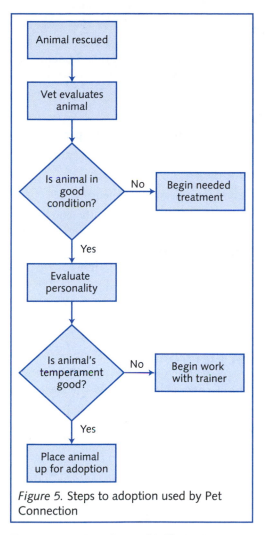

Figure 5. Steps to adoption used by Pet Connection

Figure 10-8   Sample graphic illustration

10d

i. Bibliography (titled "References")

The bibliography appears on a separate page at the end of your paper, under the centered heading "References." APA uses hanging indentation for bibliographic entries. For a sample "References" entry and page, see Figure 10-1 and the APA student paper in Chapter 12.

10e Peer review checklist

Because two pairs of eyes usually are better than one, ask another student with good writing skills to go over your paper for clarity, consistency, focus, and mechanics. Here is a checklist the peer reviewer can use:

PEER REVIEW CHECKLIST

_____ 1. Does the title give the reader a clue to the subject of the paper?

_____ 2. Is the thesis clear and positioned properly (in the opening paragraph)?

_____ 3. Do the paragraphs support the thesis?

_____ 4. Does the paper move coherently from beginning to end?

_____ 5. Are sources introduced properly and cited correctly in the body of the paper?

_____ 6. Are quotations woven smoothly into the text?

_____ 7. Is the paper free of grammatical or mechanical errors?

NOTE: Just before you print out your final copy, always run the spelling checker too.

10f Submitting your paper electronically

Some instructors allow students to submit papers electronically—as an e-mail attachment, on a floppy disk, on a CD, or even on a web page. If you have the expertise to use any of those systems, always follow your instructor's directions carefully. Don't get so taken up by the allure of electronic publishing that you overlook your primary aim—to produce a readable paper.

The atomic bomb becomes the threat of world obliteration.

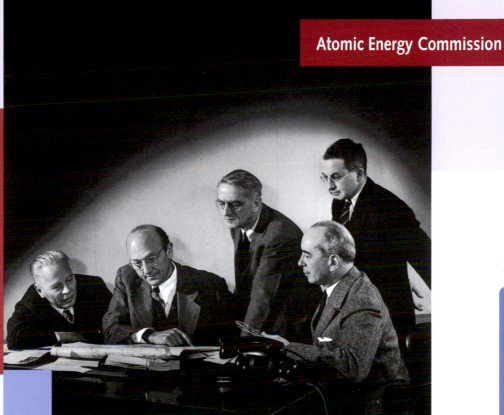

Atomic Energy Commission

J. Robert Oppenheimer, an American physicist, directed the development of the first atomic bomb. The introduction of such a stupendous weapon of destruction, made necessary by Japan's determination never to surrender to the US, even today stands out as a lesson in the catastrophic consequences of research. On April 6, 1945, in the face of Japan's vow to fight to the death, the U.S. dropped an atomic bomb on the Japanese city of Hiroshima, and three days later on Nagasaki. The devastating results proved that mankind, through research, had invented the power of self-destruction. The neighborhoods of the bombed areas became contaminated with radioactive materials damaging to living tissue. In 1946, because of the cataclysmic possibilities of nuclear energy, the Atomic Energy Commission was created by the Atomic Energy Act. This body continues to be charged with the development and control of atomic energy. It is regarded as one of the world's most important watchdogs. Although nuclear energy can be used to increase society's urgent energy needs, it remains a threat to world stability.

11 The Traditional System of Documentation (CMS)

11a Footnotes and endnotes

11b Subsequent references in footnotes and endnotes

11c Electronic sources

11d Finished form of the paper

11e Peer review checklist

11f Submitting your paper electronically

FAQ

1. What is the difference between a footnote and an endnote? *See 11a.*

2. What is the difference in the format of an endnote and a footnote? *See 11a-1.*

3. What is the meaning of the Latin term ibid.? When is this term used in a CMS paper? *See 11a-1, 11b.*

4. Where in the text do I insert the superscript numeral that indicates the presence of a footnote or endnote? *See 11a-2.*

5. How do I document a double reference—a quotation within a cited work—under the CMS system? *See 11a-3, 11a-4, 11-b.*

6. How do I footnote a reference to a periodical? *See 11c.*

7. How do I document subsequent references in the CMS format? *See 11b.*

8. How does the CMS system document electronic sources? *See 11c.*

9. Does the CMS format require an abstract? *See 11d-1.*

10. Is there a difference in the spacing of a footnote and an endnote? *See 11d-2.*

11a Footnotes and endnotes

The Chicago Manual of Style, from which the guidelines of this chapter are drawn, has functioned as an essential guide for writers, editors, and publishers since 1969. It covers everything aspiring authors need to know—from manuscript preparation and copyediting to composition, printing, and binding. In this chapter we have extracted the rules of CMS for writing research papers using footnotes or endnotes. Instructors in the fine arts, history, philosophy, religion, and theology may require this traditional style of note documentation. Be sure to check with your instructor to find out which style you are expected to follow.

Notes—whether footnotes or endnotes—serve two purposes in a research paper: (1) They acknowledge the source of a summary, paraphrase, or quotation; and (2) they add explanatory comments that would interrupt the flow of the text. Explanatory notes are often called content notes (see 9c).

Some instructors want notes to appear at the bottom of the page on which a source is cited (footnotes); others prefer that all notes appear in a separate listing at the end of the paper (endnotes).

NOTE: Papers using endnotes or footnotes do not require a bibliography unless the instructor specifies one.

The examples in this section follow CMS guidelines for documentation. It is possible that your instructor will want you to use a documentation style that differs in some ways from these examples. To avoid extra work, consult your instructor before presenting your paper in its final form.

11a-1 Formatting of notes

The format for footnotes is shown in Figure 11-1. Figure 11-2 shows the format for endnotes. Remember that the endnotes are grouped together at the end of the paper.

Endnotes should be prepared as follows:

- ☐ Begin the endnotes on a new page with the heading "Notes" (centered).
- ☐ Indent the first line of each note five spaces or one-half inch. Subsequent lines should be flush with the left margin.
- ☐ Number each note consecutively, with a space after the number. Use a full-sized number followed by a period.
- ☐ Double-space throughout the list, and number all pages.

A partial endnote page can be seen on page 222.

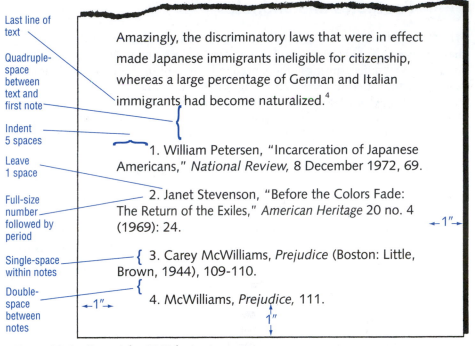

Last line of text

Quadruple-space between text and first note

Indent 5 spaces

Leave 1 space

Full-size number followed by period

Single-space within notes

Double-space between notes

Amazingly, the discriminatory laws that were in effect made Japanese immigrants ineligible for citizenship, whereas a large percentage of German and Italian immigrants had become naturalized.[4]

1. William Petersen, "Incarceration of Japanese Americans," *National Review,* 8 December 1972, 69.

2. Janet Stevenson, "Before the Colors Fade: The Return of the Exiles," *American Heritage* 20 no. 4 (1969): 24.

←1"→

3. Carey McWilliams, *Prejudice* (Boston: Little, Brown, 1944), 109-110.

4. McWilliams, *Prejudice,* 111.

←1"→   1"

Figure 11-1   Format for CMS footnotes

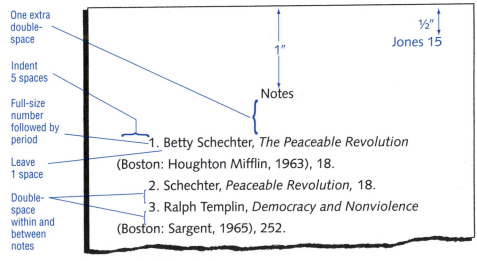

One extra double-space

Indent 5 spaces

Full-size number followed by period

Leave 1 space

Double-space within and between notes

½"
Jones 15

1"

Notes

1. Betty Schechter, *The Peaceable Revolution* (Boston: Houghton Mifflin, 1963), 18.

2. Schechter, *Peaceable Revolution,* 18.

3. Ralph Templin, *Democracy and Nonviolence* (Boston: Sargent, 1965), 252.

11a

Figure 11-2   Format for CMS endnotes

Notes

1. Edith Hamilton, "Comparing Sophocles to Aeschylus," *Readings on Sophocles,* ed. Bruno Leone and Scott Barbour (San Diego: Greenhaven, 1997), 78-81.

2. Richard Lacayo, "The Deadly Hunt," *Time,* 14 January 2002, 20-24.

3. Hamilton, "Comparing Sophocles," 85.

4. William Zinsser, *On Writing Well* (New York: Harper & Row, 1980), 35.

5. Ibid., 39.

6. Ibid.

NOTE: The Latin term *Ibid.* ("in the same place"), not underlined or italicized, and followed by a comma and a page number, may be used when you cite the same work again immediately. If the page number is the same, use *Ibid.* alone (see examples above).

11a-2   Rules for numbering the notes

In the text, use elevated (superscript) numbers for note references. (See the font menu in your word-processing software.) All notes should be numbered consecutively throughout the paper (1, 2, 3, and so on). Most word processors do the numbering automatically.

Note numbers are not followed by periods or enclosed in parentheses. They follow all punctuation marks except the dash, with no space before the number.

Whenever possible, the note should come at the end of a sentence. Numbers set between the subject and verb in a sentence are distracting. The primary rule: Place the note number as near as possible to the end of cited material.

Wrong   William Faulkner[12] used Yoknapatawpha County as a microcosm of the South as a whole.

Right   William Faulkner used Yoknapatawpha County as a microcosm of the South as a whole.[12]

If you use a quotation, the note number should always follow the quotation, whether the quotation is short and run into the text or long and set off from the text.

Wrong   In *A Matter of Life* Bertrand Russell emphasizes that law "substitutes a neutral authority for private bias," and he believes this to be the main advantage of the law.[9]

Right   In *A Matter of Life* Bertrand Russell emphasizes that law "substitutes a neutral authority for private bias,"[9] and he believes this to be the main advantage of the law.

11a

But if cited material is followed by material quoted or paraphrased from another source, then each note should be placed immediately after the material to which it refers:

> Whereas Herbert Read suggests passive resistance as "the weapon of those who
>
> despair of justice,"[14] Ralph Templin warns that nonviolence must never overlook
>
> evil for the sake of peace.[15]

In this example, note 14 cites quoted material from one source, and note 15 cites paraphrased material from another source.

Finally, never place notes immediately after an author's name, or immediately after the verb or colon that introduces a documented passage. Instead place the note at the end of the quotation or sentence:

Wrong   Justice Abe Fortas[1] states, for example, that civil disobedience should

                     be directed only against "laws or practices that are the subject of

                     dissent."

Wrong   Justice Abe Fortas states,[1] for example, that civil disobedience should

                     be directed only against "laws or practices that are the subject of

                     dissent."

Right   Justice Abe Fortas states, for example, that civil disobedience should

                     be directed only against "laws or practices that are the subject of

                     dissent."[1]

11a-3 Sample footnote references to books

The accepted format for footnotes (or endnotes) consists of the following: the author's name in normal order, the title of the work in italics or underlined, full publication information within parentheses, and appropriate page numbers. The first line of the note is indented five spaces or one-half inch.

The examples of the most common notes given below do not anticipate every kind of citation. If you need to cite a source for which this book provides no model, use your common sense, bearing in mind that the purpose of documentation is to allow a reader to reconstruct your research and thinking. The prime requirement is that you provide enough information to enable a reader to locate any cited source.

All the examples are given in footnote format, with single-spacing. They can easily be converted to endnotes by double-spacing within each note and between notes. Study each entry carefully to determine the proper punctuation, spacing, and use of italics or underlining. We prefer italics, but consistency is the important rule. Don't mix underlining with italics.

11a

a. Single author

> 1. Lester D. Langley, *The Americas in the Age of Revolution: 1750-1850* (New Haven: Yale University Press, 1996), 87.

b. More than one author

> 2. John C. Bollens and Grant B. Geyer, Yorty: Politics of a Constant Candidate (Pacific Palisades: Palisades, 1973), 73.

For up to three authors, list each author exactly as the name appears. The first and second names are followed by a comma, the second and third names by a comma plus the word *and*. For more than three authors, give the name of the first author followed by *et al.*, with no comma in between. (See 11a-4.)

c. Work in several volumes or parts

In a reference to a multivolume work in its entirety, state the number of volumes after the title:

> 3. T. Walter Wallbank and Alastair M. Taylor, *Civilization Past and Present.* 2 vols. (New York: Scott, 1949).

Because the reference is to the entire work, no page is cited.

If the reference is to a specific page in a specific volume, the number of volumes is still given after the title. Then the volume number is listed again in Arabic numerals after the facts of publication, separated from the page number(s) by a colon:

> 4. T. Walter Wallbank and Alastair M. Taylor, *Civilization Past and Present,* 2 vols. (New York: Scott, 1949), 2:217.

For multivolume works published over a number of years, show the total number of volumes and the range of years as well as information on the specific volumes used:

> 5. LeRoy Edwin Froom, *The Prophetic Faith of Our Fathers,* 4 vols. (Washington: Review and Herald, 1950-1954), 1:16-17.

For individual volumes of a multivolume work with separate titles, use the following format:

> 6. Paul Jacobs, Saul Landen, and Eve Pell, *Colonials and Sojourners,* vol. 2, *To Serve the Devil* (New York: Random House, 1971), 37-39.

11a

d. Collections: Anthologies, casebooks, and readers

For a work included in a casebook, anthology, collection of essays, or the like—that is, a collection of different pieces by different authors—use the following format:

> 7. Eudora Welty, "The Wide Net," in *Story: An Introduction to Prose Fiction,* ed. Arthur Foff and Daniel Knaff (Belmont, CA: Wadsworth, 1966), 166.

e. Double reference—a quotation within a cited work

Use the following form to refer to a quotation in a cited work:

> 8. Lin Piao as quoted in Jean Daubier, *A History of the Chinese Cultural Revolution,* trans. Richard Seaver (New York: Random House, 1974), 83.

f. Edition

The word *edition* can mean three different things: (1) a revised printing of a work, (2) a collection of items edited by one or several authors, or (3) the edited version of one or more works by an editor or editors. The proper forms to use in each of these cases are as follows:

(i) Revised edition

> 9. Porter G. Perrin and Jim W. Corder, *Handbook of Current English,* 4th ed. (Glenview, IL: Scott, 1975), 304-305.

In this note *ed.* Means "edition."

(ii) Edited collection

> 10. Charles Clerc, "Goodbye to All That: Theme, Character and Symbol in *Goodbye, Columbus,"* in *Seven Contemporary Short Novels,* ed. Charles Clerc and Louis Leiter (Glenview, IL: Scott, Foresman, 1969), 107.

The reference here is to an editorial critique of one of the novels in the collection. And here *ed.* means "edited by."

(iii) Work of an editor

> 11. Hardin Craig and David Bevington, eds., *The Complete Works of Shakespeare,* rev. ed. (Glenview, IL: Scott, Foresman, 1973), 31-38.

Because the reference is to the editorial work of Craig and Bevington, the names of the editors are listed in place of the author's. But when the paper deals with the work of the original author rather than with the work of an editor or translator, the author's name must be listed first:

11a

12. Sylvia Plath, *Letters Home,* ed. Aurelia Schober Plath (New York: Harper & Row, 1975), 153-154.

g. Translation

13. Benvenuto Cellini, *Autobiography of Benvenuto Cellini,* trans. John Addington Symons (New York: Washington Square, 1963), 75-79.

11a-4 Sample footnotes for periodicals

The format for periodicals varies somewhat. The following are typical formats. Notice that the title of an article is always placed within quotation marks, but the title of the periodical is italicized or underlined (don't mix italics and underlining in a paper).

a. Anonymous author

Many periodical articles are written by unidentified correspondents:

14. "Elegance Is Out," *Fortune,* 13 March 1978, 18.

b. Single author

15. Matt Rees, "Showdown," *Time,* 17 December 2001, 46-50.

c. More than one author

16. Clyde Ferguson and William R. Cotter, "South Africa—What Is to Be Done?" *Foreign Affairs* 56 (1978): 254.

The format of a citation to a multiple-authored magazine article is the same as for a multiple-authored book. For three authors, list the names of the authors exactly as they appear in the article. Separate the first and second names by a comma, and the second and third by a comma followed by the word *and.* For more than three authors, list the name of the first author followed by *et al.* with no comma in between.

d. Journal with continuous pagination in the annual volume

17. Anne Paolucci, "Comedy and Paradox in Pirandello's Plays," *Modern Drama* 20 (1977): 322.

Because there is only one page 322 throughout volume 20 (1977), it is unnecessary to add the month.

NOTE: Use a colon before the page numbers of a journal, but a comma before page numbers of magazines or books.

11a

e. Journal with separate pagination for each issue

Addition of the month is necessary because each issue of these journals is paged anew, so every page occurs in all issues of every volume:

> 18. Claude T. Mangrum, "Toward More Effective Justice," *Crime Prevention Review* 5 (January 1978): 7.

Some journals use numbers to distinguish different issues. The following example refers the reader to issue 4 of volume 20. Follow the style of the individual journal.

> 19. Janet Stevenson, "Before the Colors Fade: The Return of the Exiles," *American Heritage* 20, no. 4 (1969): 24.

The journal cited in the next footnote is published quarterly and in volumes that do not coincide with the year. Adding the season of publication makes the source easier to locate.

> 20. Robert Brown, "Physical Illness and Mental Health," *Philosophy and Public Affairs* 7 (Fall 1977): 18-19.

NOTE: CMS capitalizes seasons used in place of a month or issue number.

f. Monthly magazine

> 21. John L. Eliot, "Polar Bears in Hot Water," *National Geographic,* December 2005, 48-57.

Sometimes the page reference to a magazine is split because the article begins on one page and continues many pages later, to another. In that case the page references would look like this: 100, 140–141.

g. Weekly magazine

> 22. Mark Singer, "I Pledge Allegiance," *New Yorker,* 26 November 2001, 54-61.

h. Newspaper

> 23. Thomas Elias, "New Machines Lead to New Election Distrust," *Chico (CA) Enterprise Record,* 6 September 2006, p. 8A, cols. 2-3.

Listing the columns as well as the page makes the article easier to locate, but listing the column(s) is optional.

NOTE: If the first word of a newspaper's title is an article, the article is deleted. For example, *The Wall Street Journal* becomes *Wall Street Journal.*

> 24. Jim Mann, "East and West Still Divided Despite Summit," *Los Angeles Times,* 1 November 1997, Valley edition, sec. A1, p. 9.

11a

Supply the edition or section when available.

i. Editorial

Signed:

> 25. William Futrell, "The Inner City Frontier," editorial, *Sierra* 63, no. 2 (1978): 5.

Unsigned:

> 26. "Criminals in Uniform," editorial, *Los Angeles Times,* 7 April 1978, sec. B2, p. 6.

Listing the section as well as the page makes this newspaper article easier to locate.

j. Letter to the editor

> 27. Ellen B. Cutler, letter to the editor, *Vanity Fair,* June 1997, 50.

11b Subsequent references in footnotes and endnotes

Subsequent citations to an already identified source are given in abbreviated form. The rule is to make subsequent citations brief but not cryptic. Ordinarily the author's last name and a shortened title, followed by a page number, will do.

First reference:

> 1. John W. Gardner, *Excellence* (New York: Harper & Row, 1961), 47.

Subsequent reference:

> 3. Gardner, *Excellence,* 52.

If two or more sequential references cite the same work, use *Ibid.* and insert the correct page numbers:

> 5. Gardner, *Excellence,* 83.

> 6. Ibid., 198.

If two of the cited authors share the same last name, subsequent references should supply the full name of each author:

> 7. Henry James, *Substance and Shadow,* 10.

> 8. William James, *Pragmatism,* 23-24.

11b

For a subsequent reference to an anonymous article in a periodical, use a shortened version of the title.

First reference:

> 9. "The Wooing of Senator Zorinsky," *Time,* 27 March 1978, 12.

Subsequent reference:

> 10. "Zorinsky," 13.

For subsequent references to unconventional or special sources, you may need to improvise.

11c Electronic sources

CMS acknowledges that a massive volume of documents exists on computer systems but has to date offered no guidelines for citing these sources—a lack applauded by many instructors who think electronic sources too unreliable to be used in a formal research paper. CMS suggests that you consult the International Standards Organization (ISO) for uniform standards and guidelines if you wish to cite electronic sources in your papers. This organization stresses consistency, but it also allows individual discretion in the choice of punctuation used to separate elements. If your instructor insists on using the standards of CMS, ask about the documentation of electronic sources.

If the final decision is left up to you, we suggest you consult the MLA guidelines in 9b-6 and 9b-7 for the elements of electronic source notes, and put the information into CMS note style. For example, here is the CMS version of the 9b-7k reference to an online book:

> 1. Elna C. Green, *Southern Strategies: Southern Women and the Woman Suffrage Question* (Chapel Hill: University of North Carolina Press, 1997), http://www.questia.com/PageManagerHTMLMediator.qst?action=openPageViewer&docId=8033348 (accessed 3 January 2005).

Here is the CMS version of the 9b-7o reference to an online journal article:

> 2. Scot Peterson, "Business: The Smaller the Better," *ZDNet News,* 18 December 2001, http://www.zdnet.com/zdnn/stories/comment/0,5859,2833529,00.html (accessed 5 January 2002).

NOTE: Information on citations to electronic documents may be requested from the ISO at the following address:

11c

ISO

Secretariat: Office of Library Standards

National Library of Canada

Ottawa, K1A ON4

11d Finished form of the paper

No matter what documentation system you use, it is a universal requirement that research papers be neat and clean and printed out unless you have some special excuse approved by your instructor that compels you to submit handwritten work. Before you submit a final version of your paper, you should make sure that you have complied with all your instructor's formatting requirements.

Your paper should be double-spaced and written in paragraphs with the first line indented five to seven spaces. It should use one-inch margins all around. The pages should not be stapled or bound, but should simply be held together by a paper clip. CMS requires no title page, but on the first page, indented 1 inch from the top with type flush against the left margin, put your name, the name of your professor, the class for which you've written the paper, and the date of writing. See Figure 11-3 and the sample student paper in 12c.

CMS requires
no title page.

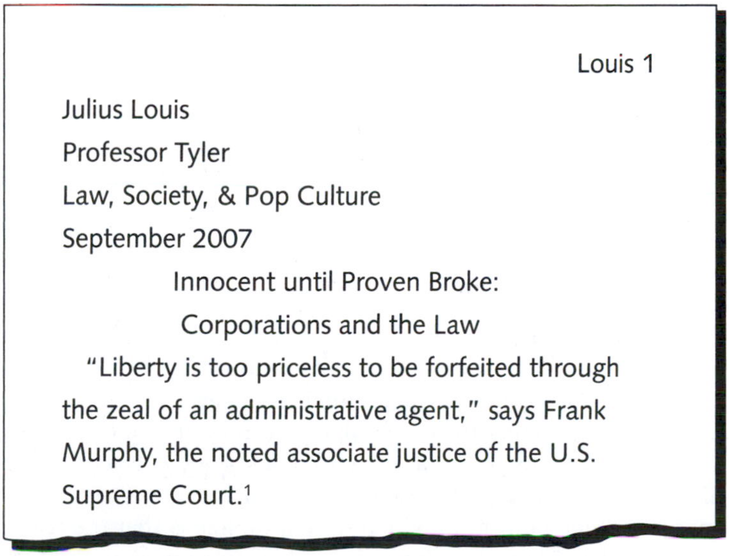

> Louis 1
>
> Julius Louis
>
> Professor Tyler
>
> Law, Society, & Pop Culture
>
> September 2007
>
> Innocent until Proven Broke:
>
> Corporations and the Law
>
> "Liberty is too priceless to be forfeited through the zeal of an administrative agent," says Frank Murphy, the noted associate justice of the U.S. Supreme Court.[1]

Figure 11-3   Opening page, CMS format

11d

11d-1 Abstract

CMS does not require an abstract.

11d-2 Pagination and text format

Number pages, including the first, consecutively in the upper right-hand corner of the paper. Use Arabic numerals (1, 2, 3). The numbers are part of the headers. CMS uses your last name followed by a space and the page number. No hyphens, parentheses, periods, or other characters follow the numbers. Endnotes begin on new pages but are numbered in sequence from the body of the paper (similar to the MLA student paper in 12a). Use lowercase roman numerals (i, ii, iii) to paginate the outline (if required by your instructor) and any other material that precedes the body of the paper. The CMS title page (if required) is not numbered but is counted as "i" if an outline follows, as "1" if no outline follows. If the title page is not separate, then CMS counts the front page as "1."

- ☐ *Margins:* Allow one-inch margins all around. Use a ragged right margin: Do not justify the text.
- ☐ *Spacing:* Double-space the text, including quotations. Footnotes are double-spaced between notes but single-spaced within; endnotes are double-spaced throughout (see Figures 11-1 and 11-2).
- ☐ *Font:* CMS recommends an easy-to-read font such as 12-point Times Roman.
- ☐ *Paragraphing:* Use normal paragraphing throughout the paper, with a five-space or half-inch indentation at the start of new paragraphs. Also indent long quotations—without quotation marks.
- ☐ *Headings:* If your paper contains sections, use headings either centered on the page or aligned with the left margin. Underline but do not capitalize headings. Separate headings from the last line of the previous section by quadruple-spacing.

NOTE: A heading should always have at least two lines of text following it. If not, start the heading at the top of the next page.

11d-3 Content or reference notes

Footnotes or endnotes and their use as explanatory or source notes are discussed in detail in 11a. This section summarizes how to incorporate them in your paper.

Use elevated (superscript) numerals in the text to refer to content notes or source notes, whether the notes appear as footnotes or endnotes. When possible, the numbers should come at the end of a sentence, after the punctuation mark. CMS recommends that the superscript within the text be in small font. But more important than conventional placement or size is that the reader know to what the note refers. (See 11a-2 for more on placing superscript numerals.)

Start each footnote at the bottom of the page on which its reference number occurs, unless otherwise indicated by your instructor. Indent the first line of each note five spaces or one-half inch; second and subsequent lines align with the left margin. CMS prefers a full-sized number followed by a period. See Figure 11-1.

If you are using endnotes, as CMS allows, follow this style:

1. Begin notes on a new page at the end of the text.
2. Write the word "Notes," centered and placed one inch from the top of the page.
3. Indent the first line of each note five spaces or one-half inch. For CMS use an Arabic numeral, followed by a period.
4. Double-space the endnotes.
5. Quadruple-space between the heading and the first note.

See Figure 11-2.

11d-4   Illustrations: Tables and figures

Papers in many fields use tables, graphs, charts, maps, drawings, paintings, photographs, and other illustrations. A table presents information systematically, usually in columns, and is always labeled "Table." Any other kind of illustration is labeled "Fig." or "Figure." The general rule is that illustrations should appear as close as possible to the part of the text they illustrate. Or if the material requires an entire page, it should be placed in an appendix.

a. Tables

Tables should be titled and numbered in Arabic numerals above the table. Capitalize only the word "Table" and the first word of the title. Do not use all capital letters. Place the table source and accompanying notes flush left at the bottom of the table. If you don't list a source, a reader will assume that the table is your original work. Indicate notes to tables with superscript letters (lowercase) or symbols (asterisks and daggers) to avoid confusion with notes to the text. (Use one or the other consistently.) Figure 11-4 (page 234) shows a sample table.

b. Other illustrative materials

Other illustrations should be labeled "Fig." or "Figure" and numbered with Arabic numerals: Figure 3. Give each figure a title. Capitalize only the first letter of the title and any proper noun. Place the title under the illustration:

Fig. 12. The development of the Syrian alphabet

Put any notes and the source flush left immediately below the caption. If no source is cited, a reader is going to assume that the illustration is your original work. Indicate notes to illustrations with superscript letters or symbols to avoid confusion with other note numbers in the text.

If your illustrative material takes up a good share of the page, you may choose to place it on a separate page titled "Appendix." In your text you would simply write "See appendix." On the appendix page, center the word "Appendix" and place the illustration under it.

Table 11

Medicare prescription drug plans

Plan Name and ID Numbers	Company Name (Co-brand)	Monthly Drug Premium	Annual Deductible	Drug Cost Sharing	Coverage in the Gap*
WellCare Classic	WellCare (Epic; Hoosier Rx; Walgreens)	$12.20	$265	$2 25%-33%	No gap coverage
Humana PDP Standard	Humana Insurance Company (State Farm; Wal-Mart)	$13.00	$265	25%	No gap coverage
AARP MedicareRx Plan-Saver	United-Healthcare	$18.60	$265	$5-$46.05 25%	No gap coverage
Cignature Rx Value Plan	Cignature Rx	$18.90	$265	$0-$60 30%	No gap coverage
Humana PDP Enhanced	Humana Insurance Company (State Farm; Wal-Mart)	$20.10	$0	$5-$60 25%	No gap coverage

Source: U.S. Department of Health and Human Services, Medicare Prescription Drug Plan Finder, http://www.medicare.gov.
*Gap: The period when beneficiary normally pays 100% of costs.

Figure 11-4   Sample Table

11d-5 Use of numbers

In dealing with numbers, most scholars observe the following rules:

- ☐ Use Arabic numerals for volumes, books, parts, and chapters of works; acts, scenes, and lines of plays; cantos, stanzas, and lines of poetry.

- ☐ For a nontechnical subject, generally spell out numbers one through one hundred, and use numerals for 101 and up, with the exception of larger round numbers (four hundred, two hundred million).

- ☐ For technical and number-intensive topics, use Arabic numerals to express all numbers ten and above.

☐ In both the technical and nontechnical styles, write as Arabic numerals any number below ten that cannot be spelled out in one word (e.g., 4½ or 9.555).

☐ In using numbers that indicate a range, give the second number in full for numbers through ninety-nine (e.g., 4–8, 16–23, 80–99). In the CMS format, when using three digits or more, cite only the last two in the second number unless more digits are needed for clarity (e.g., 65–197, 120–30, but 3877–3906; also, 101–8).

☐ Place commas between the third and fourth digits from the right, the sixth, etc. (e.g., 2,400; 5,000,000). Exceptions are page and line numbers, addresses, the year, and zip codes.

☐ Use the number 1, not the lower-case letter *l* or the upper-case letter *I*.

☐ In the following cases, use words to express numbers in your text:

  ☐ Numbers less than ten (or 101 in nontechnical papers) not used in measurements: five soldiers, six research papers.

  ☐ Common fractions: one-fourth of the student body, a one-third majority.

  ☐ Any number beginning a sentence: Three bulls galloped down the street.

  ☐ 0 and 1 when used alone: He had zero dollars left; only one answer counted (but 1 out of 15 patients improved).

☐ Use words for large numbers: He retired with an income of five billion dollars.

11d-6 Bibliography

CMS does not require a separate bibliography since all the publication details on a source are given in the footnotes or endnotes.

11e Peer review checklist

Because two pairs of eyes usually are better than one, ask another student with good writing skills to go over your paper for clarity, consistency, focus, and mechanics. Here is a checklist the peer reviewer can use:

PEER REVIEW CHECKLIST

_____ 1. Does the title give the reader a clue to the subject of the paper?

_____ 2. Is the thesis clear and positioned properly (in the opening paragraph)?

_____ 3. Do the paragraphs support the thesis?

_____ 4. Does the paper move coherently from beginning to end?

_____ 5. Are sources introduced properly and cited correctly in the body of the paper?

_____ 6. Are the transitions from paragraph to paragraph smooth?

_____ 7. Are quotations woven smoothly into the text?

_____ 8. Is the paper free of grammatical or mechanical errors?

NOTE: Just before you print out your final copy, always run the spelling checker too.

11f Submitting your paper electronically

Some instructors allow students to submit papers electronically—as an e-mail attachment, on a floppy disk, on a CD, or even on a web page. If you have the expertise to use any of those systems, always get your instructor's approval and directions. If you are interested in creating an electronic paper, talk with your instructor about the institutional support available for the process, and make sure you keep on schedule.

11f

The computer is the ultimate research tool with infinite possibilities in cyberspace.

There is a rich, complex history underlying the invention of the computer and the development of cyberspace. In 1930, Vannevar Bush built the first general-purpose analog computer, and in 1944, Howard Aiken built the first digital computer. These two computers were followed by the Electronic Numerical Integrator and Computer (ENIAC), which used thousands of electron tubes that were eventually replaced by transistors. Later, Bill Gates and associates were credited for developing Microsoft Windows, and Steve Jobs and Steve Wozniak were recognized as being the pioneers behind the creation of the Apple computer. These—and many more—steps in the development of the computer have resulted in a device that is increasingly more compact, easier to use, and more capable of completing complex calculations while storing, retrieving, and processing data. The Internet, for its part, has been evolving and growing by leaps and bounds since the 1960s. Today, most college students cannot remember the days when typewriters and library stacks were the foundation of college research papers. Instead, the focus has shifted to cyberspace, allowing today's researchers to access a vast cyber-storehouse of information from the comfort of their own homes or a single library carrel—a boon that early writers never imagined.

12 Sample Student Papers

12a Paper using author-work documentation (MLA)

12b Paper using author-date documentation (APA)

12c Paper using footnote documentation (CMS)

Arakelian 1

Geghard Arakelian

Glendale Community College

English 312

August 7, 2009

The Badge of Islamic Ideology: A Look into the Implications of Hijab

The word *hijab* refers to apparel considered pious and regulatory by the Qur'an. An example of hijab is the chador/headscarf or the cloak covering of a woman's body from head to feet. Hijab, or more specifically the image of a woman wearing a chador, has become synonymous with the image of Iranian women.[1] Its use happens to be deeply rooted in Islamic law and ideology. These scarves worn by Iranian women are the result of a religious decree meant to unify, oppress, and reform the role of women within the Islamic republic. An overview of how Iranian law is based on Islam, the religious implications of the chador, and a brief review of how conservatives oppose social reform in Iran will reveal a political cause which undermines women and will also highlight the symbolic nature of hijab as a tool of oppression and as a badge of inferiority.

On June 13, 2009, the Interior Ministry of Iran announced that Mahmoud Ahmadinejad was reelected to office to serve as Iran's president for another four years. According to official reports by the Ministry, he won 63 percent of the votes, a clear win over the liberal Mir-Hossein Mousavi by a margin of 11 million votes. According to pre-election poles, the difference in the number of votes between the two candidates was quite narrow and differed from those announced by the Interior Ministry. Mousavi's party suspected that the votes had been tampered with and corrupted. What followed were six days of intensive

---

elevated
ber
erscript)
his page
two other
rscripts
d on
wing
es will be
enced
er "Notes"
separate
e at the
of the
er.

In the paper's upper left-hand corner, place your full name, your instructor's name or your college affiliation, the name of the course, and the date on which you submitted the paper.

Do not italicize the title of the paper. Give page numbers in the upper right-hand corner. Precede the number by your last name. Use the header feature of your word processor if it has one.

The best position for your thesis statement is the last sentence of your opening paragraph, as in this student paper.

This paper follows the MLA style, which calls for double spacing throughout the paper. MLA does not require a separate title page.

12a

Arakelian 2

street protests and demonstrations sponsored by the liberal candidate, which resulted in the deaths of ten to fifteen people.[2] What did these protests reveal about the Iranian people? Were all Iranian citizens entrapped and socially imprisoned by their government? Certainly not. In the matter of voting for a leader, many citizens clearly showed that they would not be bullied by the government.

The contrary can be argued for women, whose social liberties are often smothered by Islamic law. In order to better understand the precarious circumstances of women in present-day Iran, one must scrutinize the social reforms within the Islamic republic throughout the past decades rather than merely observe the civil strife that engulfed the country in June of 2009. A review of the role women play in Iran, in conjunction with an understanding of the aggregate sum of political and social changes the country has undergone, can begin to give the reader a clear idea of the purpose, impact, and cause of hijab.

Unlike the United States of America, church and state are not separate in Iran. The Islamic republic behaves like a theocracy, where the church operates in conjunction with the state. So the decree that a woman must wear a chador is the product of Iranian politics working with the values of Shiite clerics. Understanding how the country operates within the legal sphere of Islam can help in understanding why women are judged as inferior to men within the republic. Although Iran's political structure is complex, it can be summed up by three core bodies: the Majlis, the Guardian Council, and the supreme leader. The Majlis is a parliament that is most active in bringing about social reform to the country and is made up of a body of elected deputies. The Guardian Council is a small cohort of ultra-conservative men elected by the supreme leader whose job is to interpret and dispute jurisprudence and

---

Indent all paragraphs 5 spaces or ½ inch.

Notice that the first four paragraphs require no documentation because they summarize the author's own observations concerning hijab.

12a

Arakelian 3

any change the Majlis wish to bring to the state. The members of the Guardian Council can be thought of as similar to the justices of the U.S. Supreme Court, with the exception that the Guardian Council members often work in favor of their supreme leader rather than being guided by impartial standards. The supreme leader is the highest ranking political and religious authority of the nation. Unlike the president, who deals with the economy and foreign affairs, the supreme leader of Iran is the director of the national radio and television network, is the final authority over military operations, and is the president's superior.

The Iranian revolution of 1979 brought the Ayatollah Khomeini into power. The social reforms brought about by the country's first supreme leader were based on laws taken from the Qur'an and were considered virtues of the Islamic faith, since Islam is based on the teachings of the Qur'an. To summarize, the revolution established Islam as the set of social and political rules and regulations in Iran. This system of beliefs acted both as a religion and standard of law. As Azar Tabari states in *The Enigma of the Veiled Iranian Woman,* "Islam is not simply a religion in the limited sense of a set of concepts and practices related to man and god. It is, above all, an overarching political system, with a set of legal, economic and moral policies according to which the Islamic community is governed" (24). Such examples of Islam can be observed in the passing of laws based on religious beliefs within the social, political, and legal spectrums of the republic. Here are two examples of such laws: 1) "Adaptation of Medical Services to Religious Law," which imposed gender segregation in the field of medicine, and 2) "Banning the Exploitation of Women's Images and the Creation of Conflicts between Men and Women by Propagating Women's Rights outside the Legal and Islamic Frame Work," which prohibited press debate on women's rights. Both laws were passed in 1998, though they

Following the proper MLA style, the student paper has included the author as well as the title of the book from which the student is quoting. The quotation is introduced and placed within quotation marks. The page reference follows the quotation, is placed within parentheses, and is followed by a period.

Italicize titles of books. Use quotation marks for smaller works, such as titles of chapters, articles, poems, or titles of laws.

12a

Arakelian 4

were difficult to implement. Also, according to Ziba Mir-Hosseini, in *The Conservative: Reformist Conflict Over Women's Rights in Iran,* the first law passed imposing the chador as a mandatory dress code in 1983 can be found in Article 102 of "Islamic Punishments," which "made appearing in public without hijab an offence against public morality, punishable by the "Islamic" penalty of up to seventy-four lashes" (42). What is considered "moral" in this clause is ascribed to wearing a chador. Hijab is a subject of morality only in the Qur'an. Hence, it and the other laws cited are examples of how Iran policy is based on religion.

Most of the extremist laws passed during the early post years of the revolution have been overturned, but those that have not are still in practice in a manner which disadvantages women. For example, while women are encouraged to serve in the armed forces, they are restricted in what they can study in school. Women have been elected to the Majlis, but are required to wear a cloak and they still ride in the back of buses, segregated from men. Furthermore, abortion is not permissible in terminating an unwanted pregnancy except when the pregnancy might endanger the health of the mother. Even in such a case the fetus must be aborted within the first 120 days, before it is considered to have a soul. Moreover, only with judicial permission and the consultation of a physician can the abortion be carried out. A passage from *Women in Iran: The Revolutionary Ebb and Flow* sums up women's present-day circumstances in Iran: "Although Article 20 provides 'equal protection of the law' for men and women, it states that 'all human, political, economic, social and cultural rights will be based upon Islamic precepts,' thus placing women in an unequal position with regard to polygny [sic], divorce and child custody" (Ramazi 411). In maintaining the law based on the precepts of Islam, the republic subordinates women to their male counterparts.

Margin notes:

A quotation within a quotation is placed within single quotation marks. Note 'Islamic'.

2a If you cite the title of the book in your text, place only the author and page within parentheses, followed by a period.

Arakelian 5

Laws are enacted and then revamped to the degree that they become paradoxical. Women are treated with equality so long as they behave according to the rules and regulations of Islam; however, the irony is that according to Islam, men are by religious decree superior to women. Even if she is a member of parliament, a woman must wear a chador; she must remain segregated from men in education or in public; and she can have an abortion only after scrutinizing requirements are met. Yet there are no such dress codes or prohibitions imposed on men, who are the dominants. Three conclusions can be drawn from the above: 1) The republic is a fusion of law and religion that empowers men but demeans women. 2) Post-revolutionary Iranian social ideology is derived from the Islamic faith. 3) The religion of Islam uses the Qur'an as its source of gender policies.

> To clarify and stress his summary, the student writer has numbered each point.

In order better to understand the origin of the chador, let us examine what the Qur'an teaches. Tabari cites two verses from the Qu'ran in her text: One verse tells men, "Your women are tillage for you; so come unto your tillage as you wish, and forward for your souls" (25). Another verse states that "Men are the managers of the affairs of women, for that God has preferred in bounty one of them over another, and for that they have expended of their property. Righteous women are therefore obedient . . . And those you fear may be rebellious admonish banish them to their couches, and beat them" (Tabari 25). The female is obviously considered the lesser of the two species. Yet the woman is also considered the pinnacle of honor in any Islamic household. Haleh Afshar confirms this view in *Women, State and Ideology,* as follows:

> Introduce long quotations (four lines or more) and separate them from the text by indenting them ten spaces or one inch from the left margin. If you quote only one paragraph, do not indent the first line more than the rest. If you quote more than one paragraph, indent the first line of each paragraph. Avoid long quotations when possible.

> Women expected the new revolutionary government to guarantee their legal independence and give them the dignity and honor that Islam bestows on all women. . . . What they failed to see was that the dignity so obtained made them the custodian of the family

12a

honour. Women have in fact become the most vulnerable members of the household, assumed to be in need of constant paternalistic control and protection (256).

A connection can be made between the Qu'ran's view of women and the ideology of Islamic men. A male superiority complex has trickled down from the Qu'ran to Islam and into post-revolutionary Iran. The verses from the Qu'ran's teachings have been applied as a social norm. Here is Afshar's wording of this concept: "Hijab has been identified by the regime as the very cornerstone of its revolution. It is described as 'basic to Islamic ideology' and prescribed by God Himself as a 'duty' for women" (265). Afshar then goes on to describe the purpose of hijab: "But in reality this 'trench of modesty' is imposed, not to protect women, but to prevent the endangered male species from total annihilation at the mere sight of women" (266). In the Iranian regime the only threats to male "sanity and rationality are anger and sexual arousal--the latter incurred exclusively through women" (Afshar 266). A paradoxical image of women begins to emerge from all the above. A woman bears her family's honor and so she must appear modest in person by being covered. In other words, hijab serves not only to assist women in their custodial roles, but also to stop their fallible natures from corrupting the male spirit. Anywhere outside of a domestic role women are seen as a danger to themselves and those around them. Hence the chador can be interpreted as both a badge of honor and a badge of inferiority. The chador is ultimately a reflection of how Islamic men view women, and it is a constant reminder of women's limitations in the social sphere. As Afshar says, "The 'natural' and 'biological' inferiority of women is described as a fundamental law governing all social and political activities" (259). It can be concluded from the implications of the chador that the republic

2a

Arakelian 7

attempts to domesticate women and maintain an image of inferiority through what is masked as a badge of honor, but what in reality merely serves as a reminder of women's secondary role in the regime.

Up to this point, we have examined how the Iranian republic establishes its social laws and what it considers moral in Islam. Hence, women in Iran can be viewed as domestic fodder in light of Islamic jurisprudence, which works in conjunction with the biased gender roles Islam has set forward in the name of religion. These gender roles can be observed in the wearing of the chador by Iranian women, since hijab serves to impose a domestic or secondary role on all women, irrespective of their willingness or refusal to participate in such a system. It is also used as a means of protecting men with the religious belief that women are inherently inclined to corrupt. Now, let us examine how the republic has engineered a social ladder where women are made inferior to men through laws and social stigmas designed to maintain the law of compulsory hijab. Let us also consider the unwillingness of Iranian conservative political leaders to budge in the face of continual attempts at reform. By citing examples of how conservatives stave off reform and the reformist movement, aimed at liberating women, we can reach a better understanding of how the republic continues to engineer a plan for women's subordination.

When Mohammad Khatami won the presidential election in 1997, the reformist movement was born. A liberal candidate and an advocate of women's rights, he presided over the apex of conservative/reformist conflicts. Mir-Hosseini comments on the internal political strife that took place, saying, "The dividing line this time is between Conservatives, who insist on keeping intact the ideological discourse of the Revolution, and Reformists, who want to reconcile it with the discourse of human rights and democracy" (38). This passage is an accurate summation of the past

12a

and present. Keeping intact the "ideological discourse of the revolution" is, in other words, maintaining the status quo since conservative Islam is inclined to abide by religion as opposed to democracy. For example, in June of 1998, Interior Minister Abdolla Nuri, serving under Khatami, was impeached by conservative men of authority for criticizing the Guardian Council, the judiciary, and the police forces. Nuri's vice was being an "outspoken critic of hijab who pointed out the futility of making an ideology of one's lifestyle and imposing it on the rest of society" (Mir-Hosseini 44). The second testament to the conservatives' resistance to reform came when Nuri's criticism of anti-reformists became bolder. Gaining popularity, a conservative body then put him on trial for spreading reformist writings before the February 2000 Majlis elections, which he stood a good chance of winning. His writings mainly spoke out against hijab. During his trial in November of 1999, the Special Court for the Clergy brought five charges against him. Evidence of his offense was brought to the court in the form of an article he had written, titled "Morality, Gaiety, and Life-Style," published in <u>Khordad</u> on May 30, 1999. The charges brought against him are significant because they reflect the intent of the conservative movement to maintain Islamic fundamentalism. One of the charges insisted that Nuri's publication implied that "people have freedom in taste and lifestyle and can choose what to eat and wear; nobody has the right to interfere. This kind of thinking is in open contradiction with the Islamic duty of 'promotion of virtue and prohibition of vice'" (Mir-Hosseini 45). This can be observed as an axiom of conservative ideology in Iran: autonomy is sacrilegious and therefore against the law. Another charge read as follows: "By separating lifestyle from religion and allowing people to choose, and by placing issues such as observing hijab, listening to music, mingling of the sexes, wearing a beard and so on in the realm of 'lifestyle,' this article is implicitly propagating

2a

Arakelian 9

social corruption and immorality in society" (Mir-Hosseini 45). This accusation can be interpreted as meaning that anything not in uniformity with the clergy is a crime.

In 2000, reformists enjoyed a victory with the election for the Sixth Majlis, which implied a loss of conservative popularity. In retaliation for their loss in popularity, the conservatives attacked the reformists during a conference organized by the Heinrich Boll Foundation in Berlin.[3] A number of reformists invited to the conference were met by the arrival of a girl performing an erotic Persian dance and a woman who appeared in her bikini (Mir-Hossein 46). Moments of interruptions were selectively filmed and aired on a conservative TV station in Iran. As a result, the judiciary had over twenty reformist newspapers and journals closed down overnight and prosecuted journalists along with some participants of the conference for reporting on their theories of how conservative saboteurs were to blame for the interruptions (Mir-Hossein 46). This offensive by the conservatives was aimed at debilitating the reformist platform and making it unavailable to its supporters (Mir-Hosseini 46). This event serves as an example of how far the conservatives would go to maintain the status quo. The struggle between reformists and conservatives has been in motion for over a decade. Most recently, the protests in Iran resulted from what reformists claim to be tampering with the election results by conservative operatives--a sabotage meant to bring conservative incumbent Ahmadinejad into power. So long as conservative gender roles reign, the chador will be enforced. Reformist rhetoric is centered on women's rights and argues against compulsory hijab. The conservatives'refusal to budge on hijab and their reluctant track record on granting women more civil liberties is a gauge of how Islamic ideology aims at keeping women in a position of subordination.

12a

Arakelian 10

By examining Islamic law and its effects on Iran's society, the purpose of imposing hijab, and the attempts by conservatives to snuffle reformist policies, we can better understand how the Islamic Republic of Iran continues to engineer a political code that tramples women's rights and enforces the chador. The beliefs of Islam, in conjunction with state law and the conservatives' *modus operandi,* funnel into the effect of the chador. By observing how wearing the chador is engineered and maintained by the state, it is reasonable to interpret such apparel as a badge meant to oppress women and unify men.

Present-day Iran is not facing a dilemma so much as it is facing a civil strife between two opposing parties: one which interprets the government as a democratic avenue to liberty and the other which sees the government as the means to maintain the ethos of the Islamic Revolution, which is based on religion. Of the many distinctions the republic has, none is more prominent than the dominance given to men over women. The problem is made cosmetic and noticeable to the public eye because of compulsory hijab, which not only forces a role of subordination on many women, but also serves as a reflection of the religious belief that women are born different from men, both spiritually and biologically. In present-day Iran, the chador is a malfunctioning shackle. Since the Revolution, women have reclaimed positions in law, medicine, and politics. The religious implication of the traditional cloak is beginning to be eradicated by the dawn of women's growing accomplishments within the country. In light of the headway women are making, maintaining the ethos of the Islamic Revolution may falter and give way to a more democratic Iran. If the chador is slowly becoming the only apparent distinguisher between men and women, then it would mean that Islam is the only threshold standing between freedom and antiquity.

The final paragraph serves to point out what hijab has caused in the past, but it also offers a glimpse of hope for future equality between the men and women of Iran. It neatly wraps up the thesis of the paper.

2a

Arakelian 11

Notes

1. The woman portrayed in the image below is wearing a typical Iranian chador.

Imagestate Media Partners Limited-Impact Photos/ Alamy

2. This election was heavily televised on United States news channels and was followed intensely by the American audience, who threw their popular support behind Mousavi.

3. The Heinrich Boll Foundation in Berlin was established in 1989 to honor Heinrich Theodor Boll (1933-1985), one of Germany's foremost post-World War II writers. During the war Boll served reluctantly in Hitler's Wehrmacht and was eventually caught by the American army and made to serve as a prisoner of war in an American camp. His many novels reflect his World War II experience and won him the 1972 Nobel Prize for Literature. Boll was a strong proponent of human rights, including the rights of women in places like India and Iran. Today the Boll Foundation supports projects that work toward equality and justice in social and international relations.

Content notes are gathered on a new page at the end of the paper under the heading "Notes." Each note must correspond to a superscript in the body of the paper. Number the note page as if it were part of the paper. Double-space throughout the page.

12a

"Works Cited" must begin on a new page and is double-spaced throughout. MLA stipulates that authors cited be listed alphabetically by last name, followed by first name and an initial, unless the author is listed otherwise in the original source.

Proper entry for an online encyclopedia. Notice that the medium of the source must be stated—in this case "Print." (See 9b-i).

Proper entry for a translated work.

Each entry begins with a hanging indentation (5 spaces or ½ inch for second and subsequent lines).

Proper entry for a journal.

Proper entry for an electronic source. The medium is "Web."

12a

Arakelian 12

Works Cited

Afshar, Haleh. "Women, State and Ideology in Iran." *Third World Quarterly* 7.2 (1985): 256-278. Print.

"Heinrich Boell Foundation." *Wikipedia,* 2001. Web. 15 Aug. 2009.

The Qur'an: A New Translation. Trans. Tarif Khalidi. New York: Viking, 2008. Print.

Mir-Hosseini, Ziba. "The Conservative: Reformist Conflict over Women's Rights in Iran." *International Journal of Politics, Culture, and Society* 16.1 (2002): 37-53. Print.

Olivier, Roy. "The Crisis of Religious Legitimacy in Iran." *Middle East Journal* 53.2 (1999): 201-216. Print.

Ramazani, Nesta. "Women in Iran: the Revolutionary Ebb and Flow." Middle East Journal 47.3 (1993): 409-428. Print.

Tabari, Azari. "The Enigma of the Veiled Iranian Woman." *MERIP Reports* 103 (1982): 22-27. Print.

Viorst, Milton. "The Limits of the Revolution." *Foreign Affairs* 74.6 (1995): 63-76. Print.

Wright, Robin. "Iran's New Revolution." *Foreign Affairs* 79.1 (2000): 133-145. Print.

Ziabari, Kourosh. "Another Iranian Revolution?" *Foreign Policy Journal.* 23 June 2009. Web 20 July, 2009. <http://www.foreignpolicyjournal.com/2009/06/23/another-iranian-revolution/>.

12b   Paper using author-date documentation (APA)

Children from Poverty   1

Running head: CHILDREN FROM POVERTY: CAN THEY SUCCEED?

Page header, including a shortened version of the running header, followed by the page number.

Running head, written in capital letters, should not exceed 50 characters, counting everything from spaces to punctuation.

Children from Poverty: Can They Succeed?

Shelley Taylor

Academic Instruction and Intervention--CPS 688

State University of New York—Oswego

Full title of paper.

Student author's byline (your name).

Name of class for which the paper is written.

Name of college or university and the city in which it is located.

12b

The abstract should be no longer than three-fourths of a page. It should state the problem presented, the observations made (including examples), and the solutions proposed. Center the word "Abstract" on the page.

Abstract

The question of whether or not children from low socioeconomic groups can raise their level of achievement and success should be of vital concern to today's society. This problem greatly impacts our educational system, even though all students are theoretically offered equal learning opportunities. Several reasons why children from impoverished homes often do poorly in school are explored in this article. Some of these factors include health concerns, lack of cognitive stimulation, physical environment, attitudes and values of parents and other family members, mobility rate, and low teacher-expectations. Much can be done to help these at-risk children and thus to minimize the negative effects that their condition creates for society in general. Good early childhood education programs can be very beneficial.

2b

Children of Poverty: Can They Succeed?

A problem that should be of deep concern to society is the question of how children from low socioeconomic groups can raise their status and success level by hard work and higher education. On the surface it would seem that our schools offer equal learning opportunities for all students. Yet, as a counselor and a teacher, I have seen children from this class who, while initially having lofty goals, follow in the same path as their parents and grandparents before by failing to achieve them. It seems as if social class mobility is very rare and that the lower class tends to perpetuate itself from generation to generation. In this paper, I have looked at some of the reasons for this phenomenon and explored possible actions that can be taken to help remedy the situation.

The fact is that poverty does exist in this country. Some studies have shown that 21.5% of our children are living in poverty (Bracey, 1999). Other studies have found that the ratio is currently one child in every four (Kelly, 1994). This percentage is very high, compared with that of many other countries. According to Adrian White, an analytic social psychologist, the happiest nations in the world are those that are "healthy, wealthy, and wise"--meaning that they make sure that the number of poor in their country is low, that good health care is provided, and that everyone has access to education (Komenov, 2006).

So why can't America's children take hold of the educational opportunities available to them and change their social and economic status for the better? Several environmental factors decrease the possibility of this happening. Perhaps the first matter to consider is the characteristics of the family system itself. Families commonly seek *homeostasis*--the tendency of any group of relationships to continually strive to preserve the principles of its existence. The family strives for a kind of balance in order to foster the

---

Full title of the paper.

The purpose of this paper is stated in one full sentence at the end of the first paragraph. This sentence is also the thesis of the paper.

Notice that the paper uses the correct APA tense. The opening sentence of the paragraph uses the present tense ("*does exist*") to indicate a conclusion, but past perfect tense in citing references ("Some studies *have shown* . . ." "Other studies *have found* . . .").

This paragraph begins to answer the question of why students from poverty cannot take hold of the educational opportunities offered them.

12b

continuity needed to maintain its identity. In other words, families tend to resist change. The creative thinker who disturbs the balance will often be ignored or rejected (Friedman, 1985).

In their study concerning the effects of poverty on children, Guang Guo and Kathleen Mullan Harris (2000) have demonstrated that poverty has a measurable effect on children's development and school achievement, bringing with it risk factors that can predispose children to perform poorly. A recent study has isolated five such factors: the child's ill health at birth, poor health in childhood, cognitive stimulation, parenting style, and physical environment (Guo & Harris, 2000).

Poor mothers are much more likely to have minimal prenatal care, if any at all, in sharp contrast with mothers from a higher economic plane. They do not know about nutrition and other factors that will affect their babies. Poor nutrition and lack of health care, along with a higher chance of exposure to lead and other contaminants, attack the healthy development of the growing child (McLoyd, 1998).

Studies on children residing in economically shattered neighborhoods independently predict lower scores on intelligence tests, lower levels of school achievement, and more socio-emotional problems. The results of these studies also coincide negatively with completed years of schooling. The cognitive stimulation that is so vital to developing children is often absent in poor homes (McLoyd, 1998). According to one study, enriched learning experiences are crucial during the "windows of opportunity" which occur in the young growing child, and if these critical times are not taken advantage of, the child is not even adequately prepared for preschool (Begley, 1996).

Parents from these homes are often driven by stress, and they tend to be harsh and punitive with their children (Guo & Harris, 2000). These parents face many more stressful life events and have less social support

The parenthetical reference includes the last name of the author, followed by a comma and the date of publication. All references must be cited in correct APA form.

Notice that scientific papers rely heavily on studies conducted in the field.

When two authors are cited in parentheses, the names are connected with an ampersand.

12b

than do parents who have more money. There is often a single parent in the home, but even when both parents are present, they usually have to work long hours for minimal wages and can spend little time with their children. Sometimes they lack basic skills of literacy and math and cannot supply the training that children need when entering kindergarten (McLoyd, 1998).

The physical environment in which poor children find themselves can be one of abuse and alcoholism. Also, poverty contributes to a high incidence of teenage pregnancies, drug abuse, and pervasive violence within the neighborhood. This makes every child a victim. Many children are so afraid that they actually stay home from school, adding truancy to the problem (Kelly, 1994).

Another real factor is the issue of housing. Our nation has one of the highest mobility rates of all developed countries--annually about one-fifth of our people move. This especially affects low-income families who are often displaced when rents increase or rental markets tighten. According to one study in 1994, 41% of all third-graders from low-income families have attended at least two schools. And nearly 20% of all third-graders have attended three or more schools. Children who move frequently face disruption in their lives and their education. And many times they are not helped to adjust to this disruption. The rates of family mobility correlate directly with student underachievement. Children who have moved often are more likely to have behavioral problems as well (Kaptur, 2001).

Constantly having to move and be displaced definitely affects children in poor urban areas who can be an isolated group, deprived of supportive relationships and consistency in their lives. Rural poverty, however, is also an increasing problem. "By 1986, the poverty rate in rural areas was 50% higher than the urban rate" (Huang & Howley, 1991, p. 1). Rural poverty tends to be more deep-seated than that in urban areas.

A page number accompanies the quotation. This reference is to ERIC ("Educational Resources Information Center"), a clearinghouse for articles and reports, and often used by psychologists. Giving the page number will assist the reader in locating the source.

12b

Often rural households have two parents in the family. A larger part of the rural poor are Caucasian, contrasting with the wider ethnic mix that is found in cities. More of the parents work, but often for lower pay and no insurance benefits. Characterizing the rural economy are features like dependence on natural resources, a narrow industrial base, and emphasis on low-skill labor. Because of specialization, rural economies are less "elastic" than urban economies. Many of these communities neither attract outside investment nor launch new economic development. There is lack of demand for a highly educated work force, so those who are better educated tend to leave rural areas (Huang & Howley, 1991).

In addition, mental health assistance in the rural community may be limited to a small local mental health center that serves a wide geographic area. Often, the school is the primary resource of professional assistance and physical facilities in an entire community. The school becomes the "hub" of the community, so to speak (Fasko & Fasko, 1998).

As one psychologist bluntly explained, "The fate of our country depends on our ability to successfully educate young people. Education is the key to reversing many trends" (Kelly, 1994, p. 120). Yet poverty does affect educational performance. If math achievement scores in our country had been based on well-funded schools in districts with low levels of poverty, we would have earned an achievement score better than the second-ranked nation, the Netherlands. However, had we been represented only by schools in high-poverty districts, our achievement scores would have fallen below other industrialized nations and would be nearly on a par with Nigeria and Swaziland (Bracey, 1999).

The school curriculum that is now offered seems to benefit white males and students of high socioeconomic status. Usually, children from other classes start school with positive attitudes, but differences

When referencing a quotation, the period is placed after the closing parenthesis.

12b

Children from Poverty 7

in race, gender, and social class begin to be present in elementary schools and increase by high school and college. Affective orientations, material resources, and instructional policies of schools contribute to economic group differences in children's school achievement (Jones & Watson, 1990).

Also to be taken into consideration is the attitude of the teachers. It appears that all students do *not* receive equal preparation in schools. Teachers of high-risk students tend to use ineffective instructional approaches. They have negative attitudes and low expectations for these students (Jones & Watson, 1990). According to McLoyd (1998), instructing teachers about normative behaviors such as speech patterns among lower class children and affirming the legitimacy of those behaviors may be prerequisites to raising teachers' expectancies of these children.

Because of changing value systems, family disintegration, and economic issues, education for children is far down on the list of priorities for low-income families (Kelly, 1994). Parents must deal with too many major issues regarding simple survival to be particularly concerned about the education their children are receiving, or how they are performing academically. They are less involved with the school and with their children's educational needs. They may have a sense of low self-efficacy about their ability to influence their children's learning. In fact, many times they feel intimidated by the school system in general, and are very uncomfortable meeting individually with teachers and administrators to consider the specific needs of their children. This is unfortunate, because it has been shown that parental involvement is critical to the success of the child (McLoyd, 1998).

Perhaps one of the biggest factors in the failure of children from low-income families to succeed is low or nonexistent self-esteem. This is a crucial factor because a positive self-image is directly correlated with

The words "one of the biggest factors" indicate that at this point the paper focuses on one of the most difficult problems facing children from poverty. This transition adds readability through coherence.

12b

Children from Poverty   8

academic success. Teachers, parents, and other significant adults in their lives have low expectations for these children because of their backgrounds (Jones & Watson, 1990). They see the plight of their parents, and they don't think that they are capable of bettering themselves or of achieving high goals. This can cause a vicious circle of failure and despair.

Looking ahead to higher education, it can be seen that these factors do much to cause attrition, a major problem for our colleges and universities. Efforts to retain students are complicated by an increasing number of enrollees who fit the socioeconomic and demographic profile of "high-risk" students. This attrition affects funding, facility plans, and long-term academic curricula. It also affects the future labor market because students are unprepared for jobs and responsibilities. So attrition and risk are costly, both directly and indirectly, to society and to the individual (Jones & Watson, 1990).

To help counteract this, institutions of higher education need to make a financial commitment to high-risk students in the form of guaranteed financial assistance until the end of their degree program (Jones & Watson, 1990). This commitment is not present in most instances. At the same time, elementary and high schools have a marked lack of government support to serve children and families in need. This sort of widespread neglect of our young people at the federal, state, and community level decreases the quality of education and of society in general (Kelly, 1994).

How is the general educational field addressing these problems? Bracey (1999) felt that we were not doing nearly enough. In response to the feeling among some educators that poverty is no excuse for academic failure, he wrote the following:

> Poverty, like gravity, is a fact, a condition. Gravity acts on people
> in profound ways. So does poverty. . . . To overcome the effect of

Long quotations are set apart by indentation. No quotation marks are needed.

12b

gravity and fly requires great effort. Men tried for centuries without success. To overcome the effects of poverty will require great effort, an effort we are not now making. (Bracey, 1999, p. 330)

What, then, can be done to stem the tide of the perpetuation of poverty in our society and to give those children and youth who come from lower socio-economic groups a better chance to succeed? The first step is to pay more attention to our early childhood education opportunities. It is hard for young children who come from disadvantaged homes, without the benefit of healthful and safe environments, competent parenting or other care, and stimulating learning experiences to catch up with their more affluent peers. Feldman (2001) made the following perceptive statement:

> It is clear that a critical part of closing this achievement gap is
> to get it right from the start. That's why we not only need
> full-day kindergarten available to all children, but also a national
> commitment to make high-quality, preschool education,
> universally available--not compulsory, but accessible and affordable
> to all--with first priority given to needy children. (p. 2708)

This strengthens the case for implementing programs such as Head Start. The existing Head Start program has been helpful, but we need to expand beyond Head Start "to create a universal program of quality early childhood learning and care" (Feldman, 2001, p. 2708).

Also, parent involvement is critical to children's success. Research shows that, as parents become more involved in their children's education, academic achievement improves. "Many parents desperately want their children to do well in school but don't know how to help them" (Kelly, 1994, p. 120). Schools can aid in this process by helping communities support parent involvement, working with teachers to improve parent-teacher relationships, offering staff meetings on effective parent conferences, and

By asking a question at this point, the paper begins to offer solutions to the problems presented.

Since the name of the author is given in the text, only the date of publication appears in parentheses.

12b

providing workshops for teachers on parent communication. Home visits may also be appropriate for parents who lack the transportation necessary to attend school functions (McLoyd, 1998).

An effective program is the Parent and Child Education Program (PACE), which is designed to help both parents and children to improve literacy. Parents work on their own reading skills and study for the GED, thus becoming models for their children. These parents also learn positive ways to interact with their children. This program has four components: (1) early childhood education, (2) adult education, (3) parent time, and (4) parent-child interaction time. Adults are more likely to remain in programs when their children are involved. At the culmination of this program, adults have improved their skills by an average of 1.5 grade levels and children have improved academic performance by at least ten percentile points. This suggests strongly that successful academic experience should enhance the self-efficacy of the adults as well as the children (McLoyd, 1998).

One aspect of our educational system that has had a positive influence on higher education for disadvantaged youth is the creation and support of community colleges. More and more of these colleges have adopted as their mission the objective of breaking the poverty cycle. Program administrators of community colleges have opened their doors to at-risk and "nontraditional" students while many four-year colleges and job training programs have not. In addition, they are creating sustainable developmental projects reaching beyond job training programs. They are asking the students, "What would make it possible for you to get a college education?" and coming up with viable answers (Newberry, 2000).

Another positive innovation has been the development of planned mentoring programs, which link youth with older, more experienced adults.

2b

This is essential to those children and adolescents who are deprived of supportive adult relationships elsewhere. The definition of a mentoring relationship is the following: "A supportive relationship between a youth or young adult and someone more senior in age and experience, who offers support, guidance, and concrete assistance as the younger partner goes through a difficult period, enters a new area of experience, takes on an important task, or corrects an earlier problem" (Ascher, 1988, p. 1).

During mentoring, mentees identify with their mentors; as a result, they become more able to do for themselves what their mentors have done for them. Mentoring includes both psychosocial and instrumental aspects. In psychosocial roles, mentors are counselors and role models, giving confirmation, clarification, and emotional support. In instrumental roles, mentors are teachers, advisors, coaches, advocates, and dispensers of concrete resources. A critical ingredient of a working mentor program is the establishment of trust between the mentor and the mentee. If this is attained, mentoring can improve the social chances of adolescents by leading them to new resources and by providing them with much-needed support and encouragement (Ascher, 1988).

Finally, school counselors and psychologists have a crucial role to play in working with these disadvantaged youth and facilitating change in the schools and in the community. With their specialized training, they are in a position to help close the gaps in services for children. They also have the opportunity to examine existing systemic interventions in the school and suggest improvements and initiate new interventions. They can work with teachers and principals in managing and implementing these changes. They can also educate the community about the change process by being aware of community services that may be available, making referrals to them, and coordinating those services with school services. Counselors and

12b

psychologists can help design strategies to reduce tensions, help people recognize and attain success, and help them feel in control of their lives. Additionally, the counselor can be a much-needed source of strength and support for students (Kelly, 1994).

It is still too early to determine the long-term effectiveness of these interventions. Yet, it is safe to say that families are becoming empowered. Agencies are working together better to address the needs of poor students, and these children are learning the value of education and literacy. They have improved their academic performance and their parents have improved their literacy skills. Thus the self-efficacy of both parent and child has improved greatly (McLoyd, 1998).

This study has helped me to clarify the problems and barriers our children and youth from low-income homes face environmentally and educationally. We have made some strides toward helping to solve some of these problems, but much remains to be done. Those of us who work directly with such children can make a real difference in their lives. Although faced with an uphill battle, these children can succeed. That would be a legacy of which all Americans could be proud.

The paper ends with the writer's personal opinion on what she has gained from her research.

12b

Children from Poverty   13

References

Ascher, C. (1988). *The mentoring of disadvantaged youth.* Washington,

   D.C: Office of Educational Research and Improvement, U.S.

   Department of Education. (ERIC Document Reproduction Service

   No. ED306326)

Begley, S. (1996, February 19). Your child's brain. *Newsweek, 55-61.*

Bracey, G. W. (1999). Poverty and achievement. *Phi-Delta-Kappan, 4,*

   330-331.

Fasko, S. N., & Fasko, D., Jr. (1998). A systems approach to self-efficacy

   and achievement in rural schools. *Education, 119,* 292-296.

Feldman, S. (2001). Building blocks. *National Journal, 36,* 2708.

Friedman, E. H. (1985). *Generation to Generation.* New York: Guilford Press.

Guo, G., & Harris, K. (2000). The mechanisms mediating the effects of

   poverty on children's intellectual development. *Demography, 37,*

   431-447.

Huang, G., & Howley, C. (1991). *Recent trends in rural poverty: A summary*

   for educators. Washington, D.C: Office of Educational Research and

   Improvement. (ERIC Document Reproduction Service No. ED335180)

Jones, D. J., & Watson, B. C. (1990). *High risk students and higher*

   education: Future trends. George Washington University: ERIC

   Clearinghouse on Higher Education. (ERIC Document Reproduction

   Service No. ED325033)

Kaptur, M. (2001). The link between housing and education. *Journal of*

   Housing and Community Development, 58(6), 6.

Kelly, C. (1994). *School psychologists: Leaders for change building a*

   secure future for children. Washington, D.C: Office of Educational

   Research and Improvement. (ERIC Document Reproduction Service

   No. ED366879)

The references begin on a new page, with the title "References" centered on the page. Notice that the pagination continues.

Citation for a weekly magazine article.

Citation for a book.

Citation for ERIC. The specific number of the ERIC report must be given.

The APA style requires that authors be listed by their last names, followed by a comma and the authors' initials.

12b

Children from Poverty 14

Komenov, M. (2006). Rating countries for the happiness factor. Retrieved

October 25, 2006, from http://www.travel.aol.com/travel/

departmentpage?id=1000182

Mamlin, N., & Harris, K. R. (1998). Elementary teachers' referral to special

education in light of inclusion and prereferral: "Every child is here to

learn . . . but some of these children are in real trouble." *Journal of

Educational Psychology, 90,* 385-396.

McLoyd, V. C. (1998). Socioeconomic disadvantage and child

development. *American Psychologist, 53,* 185-204.

Newberry, E. (2000). Where credit is due: How many colleges does it take

to change a community? *Sojourners, 29*(4), 12.

Reynolds, Maynard C. (1994). Child disabilities: Who's in, who's not.

Journal of School Health, 64, 238-242.

Citation for an
electronic source
from the Internet.

Citation for a
journal article by
two authors.

Citation for a
journal.

2b

12c Paper using footnote documentation (CMS)

Julius Louis

Professor Tyler

Law, Society, & Pop Culture

September 2007

Innocent until Proven Broke: Corporations and the Law

"Liberty is too priceless to be forfeited through the zeal of an

administrative agent," says Frank Murphy, the noted associate justice of

the U.S. Supreme Court.[1]

The legal system, as portrayed by the popular culture, is not a fair

system. Countless numbers of proverbs, books, movies, editorials, and the

like express this popular view of disapproval and skepticism toward the legal

system. This opinion is nothing new. In 1764, the writer Oliver Goldsmith

wrote, "Law grinds the poor, and rich men rule the law."[2] Is it surprising that

more than two centuries later, the popular culture sings the same lament?

The uneven treatment of the wealthy has been the cry of the masses before

the birth of Christ, and that cry is still heard today--especially concerning the

lopsided advantage possessed by corporations in a court of law.

If there is a great equalizer in the American system, it is supposed

to be the courtroom. Indeed, no principle is made more explicitly clear in

the Constitution than that in a court of law we are all equal. Lawyers of all

stripes, even corporation lawyers, openly proclaim this belief. Yet common

sense tells us that corporations--with their batteries of lawyers--possess such

    1. *Oklahoma Press Publishing Co. v. Walling*, 326 U.S. 186, 219
(1946).
    2. Robert Andrews, Mary Biggs, and Michael Seidel, eds., *The
Columbia World of Quotations* (New York: Columbia University Press,
1996), http://www.bartleby.com/66/38/25538.html (accessed 24 July
2002).

CMS requires no title page.

In the footnotes at the bottom of the page the student uses a regular number followed by a period—CMS format—rather than the superscript and no period that MLA prefers.

Notice also that legal case names are italicized, including the *v.*

12c

Louis 2

an enormous and unfair advantage over the rest of us as to actually pose a grave danger to our legal system. True, our judicial system does provide a legal process that allows all to be judged by a jury of unbiased peers. Intended to nullify any lingering racial and social inequalities, the system has more or less accomplished this aim. But it does not take into account a dangerous loophole in this just and commendable process: namely, the economic inequality that exists between the individual litigant and powerful, affluent corporations.

Popular culture has criticized this aspect of the law repeatedly in its analysis of the court-appointed attorney. Such attorneys are usually represented in popular culture as incompetent, weak, and apathetic. This portrayal is grounded in economic logic as well. A good attorney (assuming greed as a motive in the capitalist system) would surely want to work for a high-paying private firm. Were our economic system a socialist or even a communist system, the world would indubitably have more faith in not only lawyers provided by the court but lawyers in general. Yet, all human beings are granted equal rights to liberty, to property, and to equal protection under the laws. Does not the right to property make cloudy the right to liberty, if such economic advantages of property can be used to assure unequal representation before equal protection of the law? The power of this ideology--our belief in the fairness and naturalness of the right to property--masks the reality that the acquisition of a wealthy lifestyle for a few rests on the misery of the many.

Lois Tyson, in *Critical Theory Today,* writes that "undesirable ideologies promote repressive political agendas and, in order to ensure their acceptance among citizenry, pass themselves off as natural ways of seeing

12c

Louis 3

the world instead of acknowledging them as ideologies."[3] Tyson's Marxist analysis of the American Dream--or the right to the accumulation of wealth-- reveals the oversight of material and historical conditions that brought about the system. Our legal system attempts to counter these imperfections by enforcing a bar of ethics, which only permits entrance to morally and ethically sound individuals. But as French moralist Marquis de Vanvenargues said, "Law has no power to equalize men in defiance of nature."[4] If our system, as Marx and Tyson claim, is allegedly constructed in oversight of nature and in the unnatural process of hoarding wealth, then according to Vanvernargues, the law has no power to equalize that fundamental inequality.

Indeed, the law has no power to equalize--especially when our current system recognizes a corporation as an individual when it is not. Edward Thurlow once asked, "Did you ever expect a corporation to have a conscience, when it has no soul to be damned and no body to be kicked?"[5] A century earlier Sir Edward Coke had echoed the same theme when he said, "Corporations cannot commit treason, nor be outlawed, nor excommunicated, for they have no souls."[6]

Since the legal system's ethics stem from a system or code of morals, it has a duty to distinguish the soul of an individual from the plethora of souls that constitute a corporation. Corporations have advantages over individuals in a number of different arenas, which include the realms of

3. Lois Tyson, *Critical Theory Today: A User-Friendly Guide* (New York: Garland, 1998), p. 76.

4. W. Gurney Benham, *Putnam's Complete Book of Quotations, Proverbs and Household Words* (New York: Putnam, 1927), p. 87.

5. *The Oxford Dictionary of Quotations* (Oxford, England: Oxford University Press, 1979), p. 550.

6. Quoted in Elizabeth Frost-Knappman and David S. Shrager, *The Quotable Lawyer*, rev. ed. (New York: Checkmark, 1998), p. 29.

CMS allows the use of *p.* or *pp.* before page numbers if you choose to use them, but be consistent.

12c

politics, justice, business, and so on. Corporations have the lobbying might--to influence and change the law--that cannot be matched by an individual's effort. "Liberty is the soul's right to breathe and, when it cannot take a long breath, laws are girdled too tight."[7]

Our society enters the courtrooms to find the truth, but finding the truth takes time. Ideally, the legal process should go on as long as it takes for both the defendant and the plaintiff to argue their case with whatever hard evidence they have until justice is served. Unfortunately, what really happens in many cases is summed up in a quip often used among bar members: innocent until proven broke. At the root of this quip is a grim acknowledgment of the economic inequality in our legal system.

These arguments concerning the legal system's treatment of corporations are endless, and the length of this assignment limits my response, but the reader must know that it is possible to "pierce the corporate veil." The corporation's veil is its ability to be treated as an individual in the courts.

Howell Walsh said, "A corporation cannot blush. It is a body, it is true; has certainly a head--a new one every year; arms it has very long ones, for it can reach at anything;... a throat to swallow the rights of the community, and a stomach to digest them! But who ever yet discovered, in the anatomy of a corporation, either bowels or a heart?"[8]

7. *Good Will Hunting,* Dir. Gus Van Sant Jr.; perf. Robin Williams and Matt Damon (Los Angeles: Miramax, 1997).

8. Quoted in *International Encyclopedia of Prose and Political Quotations* (New York: Holt, Rinehart & Winston, 1951), p. 289.

List of Complications
Julius Louis

☐ **The instructor's help:** I find that when I write a paper for a professor that I like, I do better work. In this case, I really liked my professor and thought him a very good teacher. He allowed us to choose our own topics, and he was very informative and helpful in helping us make the right choice.

☐ **Choosing a sequence:** The most difficult task for me when I write a paper is choosing the right sequence of topics and subtopics to cover. I don't know why I find this so difficult, but I'm constantly juggling subtopics and points as I write. Eventually everything comes out more or less the way I want it to, but only after much effort.

☐ **The audience:** Another point of difficulty when I write is to see beyond the professor as the audience. I'm aware that I am writing for the professor but that I should be writing for any informed and intelligent reader. Sometimes I tend to tailor my work to fit the professor I'm writing for, which is not a good tactic. It may work in this specific instance, but overall it is better for my development as a writer if I aim my writing at an educated audience.

☐ **Balance:** I get carried away sometimes in my passion for my topic, which leads me to ignore the other side of the argument and write an unbalanced paper. In this particular paper, my passionate anti-corporate stance began leading me astray very early on and forced me to revise what I had written. This is definitely one of my weaknesses as a writer.

☐ **The title:** Finally, there's the problem of finding a good title. I always have trouble with titles and have learned never to title an essay too early. Sometimes the best titles occur to me when I'm on my way to drop off the paper at my professor's office, when it is too late. Oh, well, I guess every writer has problems.

A — Mechanics

A1 Numbers and dates

A2 Titles

A3 Italic and underlining

A4 Names of people

A5 Hyphenating words

A6 Spaces and punctuation marks

A7 Foreign-language words

A8 Abbreviations

A9 Spelling

A1 Numbers and dates

The rule of thumb on the use of numbers is this: Use a numeral only if the number cannot be spelled out in two words or less. MLA and APA prefer that numbers from one to nine be spelled out and that numerals be used for all numbers 10 and above. CMS suggests spelling out numbers through one hundred. For the Roman numeral *one*, use a capital *I*; for the Arabic numeral *one*, use the number *1* on your keyboard.

Dates and page numbers usually are not spelled out: Use *November 19* or *19 November,* and *page 36.* But spell out any number at the beginning of a sentence:

Wrong   25,000 voters hailed the passage of the bill.
Right   Twenty-five thousand voters hailed the passage of the bill.

Or rewrite the sentence like this:

Right   The passage of the bill was hailed by 25,000 voters.

A1-a Percentages and amounts of money

According to MLA style, the use of numbers in percentages and amounts of money is governed by the rule above: Figures or amounts that can be written out in two words or less may be spelled out; otherwise, they must be expressed as numerals.

Both APA and CMS suggest that numerals should always be used for specific percentages or amounts of money:

6 percent   6%

$6   £6

A1-b   Inclusive numbers

When using inclusive numbers—a range of pages, for example—give the second number in full for all numbers from 1 through 99. For numbers from 100 on, MLA suggests giving only the last two figures of the second number if it is within the same hundred or thousand:

4-5

15-18

106-07

486-523

896-1025

1860-1930

1860-75

1,608-774

13,456-67

13,456-14,007

APA and CMS tend to show all digits of the second number, in all cases.

A1-c   Roman numerals

Use capital Roman numerals for major divisions of an outline (see 4b-1), and for people in a series—monarchs, for example—who share a common name:

Henry VIII, king of England

Do not use capital Roman numerals for volumes, books, and parts of major works, or for acts of plays.

Use lowercase Roman numerals for pages from prefaces, forewords, or introductions to books. Do not use lowercase Roman numerals for chapters of books, scenes of plays, cantos of poems, or chapters of books from the Bible.

A1-d   Dates

Consistency is the prime rule governing the treatment of dates in the paper. Write either *19 November 1929* or *November 19, 1929,* but not a mixture of both. Month and year should look like this:

June 2007

All three styles prefer no comma between the month and year (or after the year in this construction).

Here are some other rules about dates:

☐ Use a number, not a word, for the day of the month:

Right   November 19
Wrong   November nineteenth

☐ Centuries are expressed in lowercase letters:

in the thirteenth century

☐ Add a hyphen when the century is used as an adjective:

twelfth-century literature

seventeenth- and eighteenth-century philosophy

☐ Decades can either be written out:

during the thirties

or expressed in numerals:

during the 1930s   during the '30s

☐ The term B.C. ("before Christ") follows the year; A.D. (*anno Domini*, "in the year of the Lord") precedes the year. The MLA recommends omitting the periods in these abbreviations; CMS advocates periods. In books, these often print in a small-cap style of the text font, as in this paragraph, but you may type them in all capital letters.

in 55 BC   in AD 1066

NOTE: Use A.D. only when a discussion makes reference to a B.C. date.

☐ When using both a Western and a non-Western date, place one or the other in parentheses:

1912 (Year One of the Republic)

☐ Both *in 1929–30* and *from 1929 to 1930* are correct, as is *from 1929–30 to 1939–40*. However, do not write *from 1951–72*. Instead write *from 1951 to 1972*.

A2   Titles

The rules that follow apply to titles used in your text. For how to handle titles in notes or the bibliography, consult the chapter (9, 10, or 11) on the style you are using. The APA, for example, has a special way of handling titles.

A2-a   Titles in italic

Certain titles must be italicized (MLA, APA, and CMS) in your final copy:

Published books:

> *A Farewell to Arms*

Plays:

> *The Devil's Disciple*

Long poems:

> *Enoch Arden*

Pamphlets:

> *The Biology of Cancer: A Guide to Twelve College Lectures*

NOTE: Again, these are in-text titles. APA style changes in documentation.

Newspapers:

> *Los Angeles Times*
>
> but
>
> Stoneham *Gazette*

NOTE: Italicize only those words that appear on the masthead of the paper.

Magazines and journals:

> *U.S. News & World Report*
>
> *Shakespeare Quarterly*

Classical works:

> *Plutarch's Parallel Lives*

Films:

APA   *Gone With the Wind*

NOTE: APA capitalizes all words of four or more letters in in-text titles.

MLA, CMS   *Gone with the Wind*

Television and radio programs:

> *60 Minutes* (CBS)
>
> *The Music of Your Life* (KNXT)

Ballets:

> *The Sleeping Beauty*

Operas:

> *Carmen*

Instrumental music listed by name:

> Brahms's *Rinaldo*

NOTE: Instrumental music listed by form, number, and key is not italicized

> Brahms's Piano Concerto no. 1, opus 15 in D minor

Paintings:

> Regnault's *Three Graces*

Sculptures:

> Michelangelo's *Madonna and Child*

Ships:

APA   U.S.S. *Charr*

MLA, CMS   USS *Charr*

Aircraft:

> the presidential aircraft *Air Force One*

NOTE: An initial *A*, *An*, or *The* is italicized, and capitalized when it is part of the title:

> *The Grapes of Wrath*

The full title of Henry James's work is *The Portrait of a Lady*. But after the use of the possessive case, you would delete an initial *A*, *An*, or *The* in a title:

> Henry James's *Portrait of a Lady*

A2-b   Titles in quotation marks

The following titles should be placed in quotation marks.

Short stories:

> "The Black Cat"

Short poems:

> "The Road Not Taken"

Songs:

> "A Mighty Fortress Is Our God"

Newspaper articles:

> "It's Drag Racing without Parachutes"
>
> NOTE: APA would capitalize *without*.

Magazine or journal articles:

> "How to Cope with Too Little Time and Too Many Meetings"
>
> NOTE: APA would capitalize *with*.

Encyclopedia articles:

> "Ballet"

Subdivisions in books:

> "The Solitude of Nathaniel Hawthorne"

Appendix A

Unpublished dissertations:

"The Local Communications Media and Their Coverage of Local Government in California"

NOTE: Published dissertations are treated like books.

Lectures:

"The Epic of King Tutankhamen: Archaeological Superstar"

Television episodes:

"Turnabout," from the program *The World of Women*

Sacred writings, series, editions, societies, conventional titles, and parts of books are not italicized and are not enclosed in quotation marks.

Sacred writings:

the Bible	the Gospels
the Douay Version	the Talmud
the New Testament	the Koran
Matthew	the Upanishads

Series:

Masterpiece Theatre

the Pacific Union College Lyceum Series

Editions:

the Variorum Edition of Spenser

Societies:

L'Alliance française

the Academy of Abdominal Surgeons

Conventional titles:

Kennedy's first State of the Union Address

Parts of books:

MLA, APA, CMS   preface

table of contents

appendix

chapter 5

An exception is that APA capitalizes *Table* and *Figure:*

APA   Table 3

Figure 4

A2-c Titles within titles

If a title enclosed by quotation marks appears within an italicized title, the quotation marks are retained. If an italicized title appears within a title enclosed by quotation marks, the italic is retained:

Book   *"The Sting" and Other Classical Short Stories*

Article   "Textual Variants in Sinclair Lewis's *Babbitt*"

In all styles, use single quotation marks with a title requiring quotation marks that appears in another title also requiring quotation marks:

Article   "Jonathan Swift's 'Journal to Stella'"

A title that normally would be italicized but that appears as part of another title is neither italicized nor placed in quotation marks. For example, the title of the book *The Great Gatsby* usually would be italicized. But when the title forms part of the title of another book—for example, *A Study of* The Great Gatsby, only *A Study of* is italicized:

A Study of The Great Gatsby

A2-d Frequent references to a title

If you refer to the same title throughout your paper, use the full title at first mention and then use a shortened title in subsequent references. In shortening the title, always use a key word. Use the same method for book titles:

Return (for *Return of the Native*)

Tempest (for *Tempest in a Teapot*)

and for titles in quotation marks:

"Bishop" (for "The Bishop Orders His Tomb at Saint Praxis")

For the citation of titles in subsequent references in notes, see 11b; for the use of acronyms, see A8-b, c.

A3 Italic and underlining

The tradition in typewritten work was to use underlining to indicate italics (typewriters can't italicize). But with the popularity of the computer and word-processing programs has come a preference for italics over underlining. MLA, APA, and CMS all now recommend italics.

☐ Italicize phrases, words, letters, or numerals cited as linguistic examples:

One cannot assume that the Victorian word *trump* is an amalgamation of *tramp* and *chump*.

☐ Italicize foreign words in English texts:

It seems clearly a case of *noblesse oblige*.

He used the *post hoc ergo propter hoc* fallacy.

NOTE: Exceptions to the rule include quotations entirely in another language, titles of articles in another language, and words anglicized through frequent use, such as *detente, laissez-faire, gestalt,* and *et al.* In papers dealing with the arts, foreign expressions commonly used in the field—*hubris, mimesis, leitmotif, pas de deux,* for example—should not be italicized.

☐ Use italics sparingly (if at all) for emphasis.

See A2-a for the use of italics in titles.

A4   Names of people

☐ In general, omit formal titles (Mr., Mrs., Miss, Ms., Dr., Professor) when referring to people, living or dead, by their last names. However, convention dictates that certain people be referred to by title:

Mme de Staël

Mrs. Humphry Ward

☐ It is acceptable to use simplified names for famous people:

Dante (for Dante Alighieri)

Michelangelo (for Michelangelo Buonarroti)

Vergil or Virgil (for Publius Vergilius Maro)

☐ It also is acceptable to use an author's pseudonym rather than the author's real name:

George Sand (for Amandine-Aurore-Lucie Dupin)

Mark Twain (for Samuel Clemens)

Molière (for Jean-Baptiste Poquelin)

☐ The particles in foreign names (*von, van, van der, de*) usually are not included in surname-only references to people:

Frontenac (Louis de Frontenac)

Goethe (Hans Wolfgang von Goethe)

Ruysdael (Salman van Ruysdael)

NOTE: CMS generally retains the particle for names of people in English-speaking countries.

□ But certain names keep the particle:

Van Dyck

de Gaulle

Von Braun

O'Neill

> **Spelling tip**
>
> **When in doubt about the spelling of a name, consult a biographical dictionary or encyclopedia. A practical source is the one-volume** *New Columbia Encyclopedia.*

A5 Hyphenating words

The hyphenation of words that end a line, formerly a tiresome chore, now is handled automatically by word processors. But writers still must cope with compound words that sometimes require hyphens and sometimes do not depending on how they are used:

She stepped up when her name was called.

Her job was on a stepped-up schedule.

If you're not sure whether or not to hyphenate words, check your dictionary.

de-ter-mined   haz-ard-ous

i-vo-ry   grad-u-al

con-clud-ing   dress-er

Correct syllabification of words can be found in a dictionary.

□ Never hyphenate a one-syllable word, such as "twelfth," "screamed," or "brought."

□ Do *not* end or begin a line with a single letter:

a-mend, bur-y

□ Make *no* division that might cause confusion in either the meaning or pronunciation of a word:

sour-ces, re-creation

□ Divide hyphenated words only at the hyphen:

editor-in-chief, semi-retired

□ Do not divide proper names, such as "Lincoln" or "Italy."

□ Do not end several consecutive lines with a hyphen.

A6   Spaces and punctuation marks

☐ Use just one space after all end punctuation marks.

☐ Separate the initials of personal names—which are always punctuated by a period—by one space:

A. A. Winkler

M. J. Fibiger

W. E. B. Du Bois

NOTE: Certain people are known by their initials, used without punctuation: JFK (for John F. Kennedy), FDR (for Franklin Delano Roosevelt).

☐ Use two hyphens to indicate a dash. No extra space before or after the hyphens:

Wrong   The movie was horrible—not fit to be seen.
Right   The movie was horrible—not fit to be seen.

☐ Within common abbreviations punctuated by periods, do not use a space after the first period:

i.e.

a.m.

See A8-a for a list of common abbreviations.

☐ Use a space before and after the slash that separates lines of a quoted poem:

Last night / a snail / crawled / out my ear

☐ A hyphen takes no space before or after unless it is meant as a minus sign, in which case a space is used before and after. If the hyphen is meant to signify a negative number, then a space comes before but not after:

a self-made man

$5x - 9x = -4x$

☐ Use a single space after all other punctuation marks.

A7   Foreign-language words

Words or phrases in a foreign language must be reproduced with all of their accent marks. If you have no accent marks in your program or on your keyboard, insert the accent by hand on the final copy of the paper. Pay special attention to the following:

☐ It is not necessary to accent the capital letters of French and Spanish words:

énormément

but

Enormément

or

ENORMEMENT

- For German words with the umlaut, use two dots instead of an *e*, even for initial capitals:

  Überhaupt, fröhlich

  not

  Ueberhaupt, froehlich

- Proper names retain their conventional spelling:

  Boehm, Dürrenmatt

  not

  Böhm, Duerrenmatt

- Digraphs (two letters that represent one sound) can be printed without connection (ae, oe), can be written in by hand (æ, œ) or can be connected at the top ($\overline{ae}$, $\overline{oe}$). In American English, the digraph *ae* is often abandoned:

  archeology, medieval, esthetic

  not

  archaeology, mediaeval, aesthetic

A8 Abbreviations

Following is a list of abbreviations commonly encountered in research. The MLA favors dropping periods whenever possible.

A8-a   Commonly used abbreviations

AD, A.D.	*anno Domini,* "in the year of the Lord." Usually prints in small caps in books; no space between the letters; precedes numerals (AD 12).
a.m. (MLA and APA)	*ante meridiem* (before noon). CMS uses lowercase (a.m.) or small caps without periods (AM)
anon.	anonymous
app.	appendix
art., arts.	article(s)
assn.	association
assoc.	associate, associated
b.	born
BC, B.C.	before Christ. Usually prints in small caps in books, no space between the letters; follows numerals (23 BC).

bibliog.	bibliography, bibliographer, bibliographical
biog.	biography, biographer, biographical
bk., bks.	book(s)
©	copyright (© 1997)
c., ca.	circa, "about." Used with approximate dates (c. 1851).
cf.	confer, "compare." Do not use *cf.* if *see* is intended.
ch., chs.	chapter(s). CMS uses *chap(s).*
chor., chors.	choreographed by, choreographer(s)
col., cols.	column(s)
comp., comps.	compiled by, compiler(s)
cond.	conducted by, conductor
Cong.	Congress
Cong. Rec.	*Congressional Record*
d.	died
dir., dirs.	directed by, director(s)
diss.	dissertation
E., Eng.	English
ed., eds.	edited by, editor(s), editions(s)
e.g.	*exempli gratia,* "for example." Preceded and followed by a comma. Avoid this abbreviation in your text; use it only within parentheses.
enl.	enlarged (as in "rev. and enl. ed.")
esp.	especially (as in "124–29, esp. 125")
et al.	et alii, "and others"
etc.	et cetera, "and so forth." Do not use in text.
ex., exs.	example(s)
f., ff.	and the following (with no space after a numeral) page(s) or line(s). Exact references are preferable: *89–90* instead of *89f.; 72–79* instead of *72ff.*
facsim., facs.	facsimile
fig., figs.	figure(s)

fol., fols.	folio(s)
Fr.	French
front.	frontispiece
Ger.	German
Gk.	Greek
GPO, G.P.O.	Government Printing Office
hist.	history, historian, historical
ibid.	*ibidem,* "in the same place," i.e., in the just-cited title. Avoid using. Used in CMS notes only. In text, cite the author's last name and the page number.
i.e.	*id est,* "that is." Preceded and followed by a comma. Do not use in text.
illus.	illustrated (by), illustrator, illustration(s)
intro., introd.	introduced by, introduction
ips	inches per second (used on labels of recording tapes)
It.	Italian
jour.	journal
L., Lat.	Latin
l., ll.	line(s). MLA now uses *line* or *lines;* CMS suggests that it is better not abbreviated.
lang., langs.	language(s)
LC, L. C.	Library of Congress. Leave a space between the letters when periods are used.
loc. cit., l.c.	*loco citato,* "in the place (passage) cited." Avoid using; instead repeat the citation in shortened form.
MA, M.A.	Master of Arts. No space between the letters.
mag.	magazine
ME	Middle English
ms, mss;	manuscript(s). Capitalized and followed by a period in
ms., mss.	reference to a specific manuscript.
MS, M.S.	Master of Science. No space between the letters.
n., nn.	note(s)

narr., narrs.	narrated by, narrator(s)
NB, N.B.	*nota bene,* "take notice, mark well." No space between the letters.
n.d.	no date (in a book's imprint). No space between the letters.
no., nos.	number(s)
n.p.	no place (of publication); no publisher. No space between the letters.
n. pag.	no pagination. Leave space between. CMS uses *n.p.*
NT	New Testament
OE	Old English
op.	opus (work)
op. cit.	*opere citato,* "in the work cited." Avoid using; instead repeat the citation in shortened form.
OT	Old Testament
p., pp.	page(s)
par., pars.	paragraph(s)
pass.	passim, "throughout the work, here and there" (84, 97, and pass.). Frequently not abbreviated.
PhD., Ph.D.	Doctor of Philosophy. No space between.
philos.	philosophical
pl., pls.	plate(s); plural
p.m. (MLA and APA)	*post meridiem* (after noon). CMS uses lowercase (p.m.) or small caps without periods (PM)
pref.	preface
prod., prods.	produced by, producer(s)
pseud.	pseudonym
pt., pts.	part(s)
pub., pubs.	published by, publication(s)
qtd.	quoted
rept., repts.	reported by, report(s)
rev.	revised (by), revision; review, reviewed (by). Spell out *review* if there is any possibility of ambiguity.

rpm, r.p.m.	revolutions per minute (used on recordings)
rpt.	reprinted (by), reprint
sc.	scene
sec., secs.	section(s)
ser.	series
sic	"thus," "so." Put between square brackets to signal an editorial interpolation.
soc.	society
Sp.	Spanish
st., sts.	stanza(s)
St., Sts.	Saint(s)
supp., supps.	supplement(s)
tech rep.	technical report
TLS(s)	typed letter(s) signed
trans. (tr.)	translated by, translator, translation
ts.	typescript. Cf. "ms."
U.S.	United States. Use as adjective only: They flew the U.S. flag.
v., vs.	versus, "against." Cf. "v., vv."
v., vv.; vs., vss.	verse(s)
vol., vols.	volume(s)

A8-b   The Bible

Use the following abbreviations in notes and parenthetical references; do not use them in the text (except parenthetically).

OLD TESTAMENT (OT)

Gen.	Genesis	Eccl. or Eccles.	Ecclesiastes
Exod.	Exodus	Song Sol.	Song of Solomon
Lev.	Leviticus	(also Cant.)	(Canticles)
Num.	Numbers	Isa.	Isaiah
Deut.	Deuteronomy	Jer.	Jeremiah
Josh.	Joshua	Lam.	Lamentations
Judg.	Judges	Ezek.	Ezekiel
Ruth	Ruth	Dan.	Daniel

1 Sam.	1 Samuel	Hos.	Hosea
2 Sam.	2 Samuel	Joel	Joel
1 Kings	1 Kings	Amos	Amos
2 Kings	2 Kings	Obad.	Obadiah
1 Chron.	1 Chronicles	Jon.	Jonah
2 Chron.	2 Chronicles	Mic.	Micah
Ezra	Ezra	Nah.	Nahum
Neh.	Nehemiah	Hab.	Habakkuk
Esth. or Esther	Esther	Zeph.	Zephaniah
Job	Job	Hag.	Haggai
Ps.	Psalms	Zech.	Zechariah
Prov.	Proverbs	Mal.	Malachi

SELECTED APOCRYPHAL AND DEUTEROCANONICAL WORKS

1 Esd.	1 Esdras	Bar.	Baruch
2 Esd.	2 Esdras	Song 3	Song of the Three
Tob.	Tobit	Childr.	Holy Children
Jth.	Judith	Sus.	Susanna
Esth.	Esther	Bel and Dr.	Bel and the Dragon
(also Apocr.)	(Apocrypha)	Pray. Man. or	Prayer of Manasseh
Wisd. Sol.	Wisdom of Solomon	Pr. of Man.	(or Manasses)
(also Wisd.)	(Wisdom)	1 Macc.	1 Maccabees
Ecclus. (also Sir.)	Ecclesiasticus (Sirach)	2 Macc.	2 Maccabees

NEW TESTAMENT (NT)

Matt.	Matthew	1 Tim.	1 Timothy
Mark	Mark	2 Tim	2 Timothy
Luke	Luke	Tit. or Titus	Titus
John	John	Philem.	Philemon
Acts	Acts	Heb.	Hebrews
Rom.	Romans	Jas. or James	James
1 Cor.	1 Corinthians	1 Pet.	1 Peter
2 Cor.	2 Corinthians	2 Pet.	2 Peter
Gal.	Galatians	1 John	1 John
Eph.	Ephesians	2 John	2 John
Phil.	Philippians	3 John	3 John
Col.	Colossians	Jude	Jude
1 Thess.	1 Thessalonians	Rev. (Apoc.)	Revelation
2 Thess.	2 Thessalonians		(Apocalypse)

SELECTED APOCRYPHAL WORKS

G. Thom.	Gospel of Thomas
G. Heb.	Gospel of the Hebrews
G. Pet.	Gospel of Peter

A8-c   Shakespeare

Ado	*Much Ado about Nothing*	*MM*	*Measure for Measure*
Ant.	*Antony and Cleopatra*	*MND*	*A Midsummer Night's Dream*
AWW	*All's Well That Ends Well*	*MV*	*The Merchant of Venice*
AYL	*As You Like It*	*Oth.*	*Othello*
Cor.	*Coriolanus*	*Per.*	*Pericles*
Cym.	*Cymbeline*	*PhT*	*The Phoenix and the Turtle*
Err.	*The Comedy of Errors*	*PP*	*The Passionate Pilgrim*
F1	*First Folio ed. (1623)*	*Q*	*Quarto ed.*
F2	*Second Folio ed. (1632)*	*R2*	*Richard II*
Ham.	*Hamlet*	*R3*	*Richard III*
1H4	*Henry IV, Part 1*	*Rom.*	*Romeo and Juliet*
2H4	*Henry IV, Part 2*	*Shr.*	*The Taming of the Shrew*
H5	*Henry V*	*Son.*	*Sonnets*
1H6	*Henry VI, Part 1*	*TGV*	*The Two Gentlemen of Verona*
2H6	*Henry VI, Part 2*	*Tim.*	*Timon of Athens*
3H6	*Henry VI, Part 3*	*Tit.*	*Titus Andronicus*
H8	*Henry VIII*	*Tmp.*	*The Tempest*
JC	*Julius Caesar*	*TN*	*Twelfth Night*
Jn.	*King John*	*TNK*	*The Two Noble Kinsmen*
LC	*A Lover's Complaint*	*Tro.*	*Troilus and Cressida*
LLL	*Love's Labour's Lost*	*Ven.*	*Venus and Adonis*
Lr.	*King Lear*	*Wiv.*	*The Merry Wives of Windsor*
Luc.	*The Rape of Lucrece*	*WT*	*The Winter's Tale*
Mac.	*Macbeth*		

A8-d   Days and months

Sun.	Jan.
Mon.	Feb.
Tues.	Mar.
Wed.	Apr.
Thurs.	May
Fri.	June
Sat.	July
	Aug.
	Sept.
	Oct.
	Nov.
	Dec.

Appendix A

A8-e   States and U.S. territories

AL	Alabama	MT	Montana
AK	Alaska	NE	Nebraska
AS	American Samoa	NV	Nevada
AZ	Arizona	NH	New Hampshire
AR	Arkansas	NJ	New Jersey
CA	California	NM	New Mexico
CO	Colorado	NY	New York
CT	Connecticut	NC	North Carolina
DE	Delaware	ND	North Dakota
DC	District of Columbia	OH	Ohio
FL	Florida	OK	Oklahoma
GA	Georgia	OR	Oregon
GU	Guam	PA	Pennsylvania
HI	Hawaii	PR	Puerto Rico
ID	Idaho	RI	Rhode Island
IL	Illinois	SC	South Carolina
IN	Indiana	SD	South Dakota
IA	Iowa	TN	Tennessee
KS	Kansas	TX	Texas
KY	Kentucky	UT	Utah
LA	Louisiana	VT	Vermont
ME	Maine	VA	Virginia
MD	Maryland	VI	Virgin Islands
MA	Massachusetts	WA	Washington
MI	Michigan	WV	West Virginia
MN	Minnesota	WI	Wisconsin
MS	Mississippi	WY	Wyoming
MO	Missouri		

NOTE: CMS recommends using full names in text and allows traditional abbreviations in reference notes (e.g., Calif., Hawaii, Maine, Mass., N.Y., N.Dak.).

A8-f   Publishers' names

Here are some guidelines for shortening the names of publishers:

☐ Omit articles (*A, An, The*), business abbreviations (*Co., Corp., Inc., Ltd.*), and words that describe the business (*Books, House, Press, Publishers*).[1] When listing a university press, however, always leave the word *Press* or use the abbreviations *U* and *P* (MLA) because the university may publish independently of its press.

---

1. Both APA and CMS recommend leaving the word that describes the business if an entry would be ambiguous without it—for example, *Free Press*.

◻ If a publisher's name includes the name of one person (Alfred A. Knopf, W. W. Norton, William B. Eerdmans), list only the surname (Knopf, Norton, Eerdmans). If more than one surname is involved (Harcourt Brace Jovanovich; Farrar, Straus and Giroux; McGraw-Hill; Prentice-Hall), MLA lists only the first surname (Harcourt, Farrar, McGraw, Prentice).

◻ If the publisher's name is a well-known abbreviation—MLA or GPO, for example—MLA suggests you use it.

Below is a list of shortened versions of well-known publishers' names. Use it only as a guide, bearing in mind that a publisher can change its name or stop publishing even though its imprint remains on title and copyright pages.

CMS okays the use of "&" or "and" as long as you are consistent. We believe that most instructors support consistency in matters of style, such as italics versus underlining or "p.m." versus "P.M."

Allyn	Allyn & Bacon
Barnes	Barnes and Noble Books
Basic	Basic Books
Beacon	Beacon Press
Bedford	Bedford Books
Bobbs	Bobbs-Merrill
Bowker	R. R. Bowker
Cambridge UP[2]	Cambridge University Press
Citadel	Citadel Press
Collier	Collier Books
Columbia UP	Columbia University Press
Dell	Dell Publishing
Dodd	Dodd, Mead
Dorset	Dorset Press
Doubleday	Doubleday
Farrar	Farrar, Straus, and Giroux
Free Press	Free Press
GPO	U.S. Government Printing Office

---

2. CMS spells out "Press"; "University" may be abbreviated (Univ.).

Harcourt	Harcourt Brace Jovanovich
Harper	Harper & Row
Harvard UP	Harvard University Press
Heath	D. C. Heath
Holt	Holt, Rinehart & Winston
Houghton	Houghton Mifflin
Knopf	Alfred A. Knopf
Lippincott	J. B. Lippincott
Little	Little, Brown
Longman	Addison, Wesley, Longman
Macmillan	Macmillan
McGraw	McGraw-Hill
MLA	Modern Language Association
Norton	W. W. Norton
Oxford UP	Oxford University Press
Prentice	Prentice-Hall
Putnam	G. P. Putnam's Sons
St. Martin's	St. Martin's Press
Scott	Scott, Foresman
Scribner's	Charles Scribner's Sons
Simon	Simon & Schuster
State U of New York P	State University of New York Press
U of Chicago P	University of Chicago Press
UP of Florida	University Press of Florida
Washington Square P	Washington Square Press

NOTE: CMS and APA may use fuller forms of the publishers' names than the abbreviations listed.

For any publisher not listed above, use the guidelines for abbreviation offered at the beginning of this list.

A8-g   Abbreviations

An *acronym* is a word formed from the initial letters of a name or title; for example, NATO and AIDS. Another type of abbreviation (called an *initialism*) is formed the same way but is pronounced as a series of letters instead of a word. We've used the initialisms *MLA* and *APA* throughout this book, for example, to abbreviate the names of the Modern Language Association and the American Psychological Association.

The first time you use any abbreviation in your paper, define it parenthetically:

First Reference   The United Nations Educational, Scientific, and Cultural Organization (UNESCO) is headquartered in . . .

Second Reference   UNESCO is responsible for . . .

Exceptions to this rule are words that are widely known in their abbreviated form, such as TV, AIDS, and IQ.

 Spelling

Spelling matters. Always use your word processor's spelling checker. If in doubt, consult your dictionary. If the dictionary offers more than one way to spell a word, generally use the first but be consistent. The exception is when you are quoting. In that case you must retain the original spelling whether or not it is correct. Also be consistent about your use of hyphenation and accents throughout the paper. If you are using sources from a foreign language, be sure that you reproduce all accents and other marks exactly as they appear in the original.

> **Spelling tip**
>
> We suggest that you keep a style sheet on which you note any special spelling or treatment of words that you have looked up. Such a style sheet will have two benefits: (1) You will be consistent, (2) you will not need to look things up several times.

Appendix A

B General and Specialized References, an Annotated List

B1 A list of general references

B2 A list of specialized references

B1 A list of general references

This section lists common but useful general references. General references cover information available on a variety of subjects; specialized references cover information on specific subjects.

B1-a Sources that list books

The very best work on the part of diligent bibliographers cannot hope to produce a list of all the books currently in print. Still, many sources catalog the publication of books. The following are the prime sources for information about existing books.

(1) For books currently in print

Amazon.com: Earth's Biggest Bookstore. Seattle: Amazon.com, 1995–present. Online at www.Amazon.com (7 February 2007). A wonderful resource for locating currently available books and for finding a variety of book reviews, both professional and nonprofessional.

Books in Print (BIP). New York: Bowker, 1948–present. Also on microfiche. Published annually in September. Many vendors have mounted the tapes for BIP on their online systems.

Books in Print Plus. New York: Bowker Electronic, 1986–present. CD-ROM. Published bimonthly. A very helpful resource containing reviews of books.

Forthcoming Books. New York: Bowker, 1966–present. Published bimonthly.

(2) Bibliographies

Cumulative Book Index. New York: Wilson, 1908–present. Eleven issues published a year. A world list of books in the English language.

This appendix was updated by Deborah Anne Broocker, a reference librarian at Georgia Perimeter College, Dunwoody, Georgia. URLs were updated by Mary Fibiger.

A few library catalogs come closer to achieving bibliographic universality than do most other listings. The following union catalogs (alphabetized lists of the contents of more than one catalog or library) are the most pertinent sources for students:

National Union Catalog. New York: Rowan and Littlefield; Ann Arbor, MI: Edwards, 1958–1983. Published in five-year cumulations. Monthly, quarterly, and annual volumes published by Library of Congress.

National Union Catalog. Books. Washington, DC: Library of Congress, 1983–present. Microfiche. Published monthly.

The National Union Catalog, Pre-1956 Imprints: A Cumulative Author List Representing Library of Congress Printed Cards and Titles Reported by Other American Libraries. 754 vols. London: Mansell, 1968–1981.

WorldCat. Dublin, OH: Online Computer Library Center (OCLC). Online at www.worldcat.org (29 March 2007). This union catalog of all materials cataloged by member libraries is the world's largest. Now available to the public through OCLC's FirstSearch, this database holds more than 1 billion records.

For information on incunabula—books published before 1501—see the following:

Stillwell, Margaret Bingham. *The Beginning of the World of Books, 1450 to 1470; a Chronological Survey of the Texts Chosen for Printing during the First Twenty Years of the Printing Art, with a Synopsis of the Gutenberg Documents.* New York: Bibliographical Society of America, 1972.

(3) Book industry journals

Publishers Weekly. New York: Bowker, 1872–present. Weekly record of books published in the United States. Semiannual issues announce books scheduled for publication.

(4) Indexes of book reviews

Book Review Digest. New York: Wilson, 1906–present. Published monthly (except February and July) with annual cumulations. Lists and digests book reviews from English-language periodicals. Helpful for finding reviews on older books.

Book Review Index. Detroit: Gale, 1965–present. Published three times a year with annual cumulation. Indexes book reviews.

B1-b   Sources that list periodicals and newspapers

Since its beginning in the eighteenth century, periodical literature—whether published weekly, monthly, or in serial form—has become increasingly important for scholarly research, especially in fields where up-to-date information is crucial. Millions of articles are published annually, making a complete index nearly impossible. But the following sources about periodicals are especially useful.

(1) Directories

Ayer Directory of Publications. Philadelphia: IMS, 1880–1982. An annual list of newspapers and periodicals published in the United States. Organized geographically with indexes.

Editor & Publisher International Year Book. New York: Editor & Publisher, 1959–present. Provides information on newspapers, advertising agencies, and syndicates, and other aspects of journalism in the United States, Canada, and other countries.

E. W. Scripps's International On-line Newspaper Listings. Athens, OH: Ohio University School of Journalism. Online at www.scripps.ohiou.edu/lasher/int-nwsp.htm (7 February 2007). Listings of daily newspapers from countries around the world that are available online.

Gale Directory of Publications and Broadcast Media. Detroit: Gale, 1990–present. Supersedes the *Ayer Directory of Publications*.

Ulrich's International Periodicals Directory. New York: Bowker, 1932–present. Supplemented by *Ulrich's Update*. The most commonly used listing of periodicals published worldwide.

Ulrich's Plus. New York: Bowker Electronic. CD-ROM. Published quarterly.

(2) Indexes

An *index* lists topics of periodical and newspaper articles, giving each article's title and bibliographic citation. William Poole, working with a group of dedicated librarians, compiled the first American index in 1802. His index is still in use, as are the other sources listed.

Academic Search Premier. Ipswich, MA: EBSCO, 1984–present. CD-ROM and on-line. Provides abstracts and indexing, as well as full text for more than 3,200 scholarly journals and general magazines. Audience is general, student, and research. Provides information on a broad range of subject categories. Access is usually through a library.

General Periodicals Index. Foster City, CA: Information Access. CD-ROM.

Index to U.S. Government Periodicals. Chicago: Infordata International, 1970–1987.

National Newspaper Index. Foster City, CA: Information Access, 1979–present. Indexes the *New York Times, Wall Street Journal, Christian Science Monitor, Washington Post, Los Angeles Times*, and others.

NewsBank. New Canaan, CT: NewsBank, 1970–present. Also on CD-ROM.

Poole's Index to Periodical Literature: An Alphabetical Index to Subjects, Treated in the Reviews, and Other Periodicals, to Which No Indexes Have Been Published. 1848. Rev. ed., 1882–1908.

Readers' Guide to Periodical Literature. Minneapolis: Wilson, 1901–present. Also on CD-ROM. This library standard is still in print; an augmented edition includes abstracts and full text.

Social Sciences & Humanities Index. New York: Wilson, 1966–1974. Split into *Social Sciences Index* and *Humanities Index,* the list continues from 1974 to the present.

UnCover: CARL Journal Database. Denver: CARL Systems. Online at www .ingenta.com (7 February 2007). A periodical index covering more than 17,000 multidisciplinary journals since 1988, including brief descriptive information for some articles.

U.S. Government Periodicals Index. Bethesda, MD: Congressional Information Service, 1994–present. Also on CD-ROM.

(3) Union lists

Union lists catalog and record the collections of periodical and newspaper titles available in various libraries. The following are among the most prominent union lists:

American Newspapers, 1821–1936: A Union List of Files Available in the United States and Canada. New York: Wilson, 1937. Catalog files of newspapers in nearly 6,000 libraries and private locations.

Brigham, Clarence Saunders. *History and Bibliography of American Newspapers, 1690–1820.* 2 vols. Worcester, MA: American Antiquarian Society, 1947. The best list for finding articles in old newspapers.

———. *History and Bibliography of American Newspapers, 1690–1820: Including Additions and Corrections, 1961.* Worcester, MA: American Antiquarian Society, 1961.

LexisNexis Academic Universe. An online database that contains approximately 5,000 publications, all full text, including newspapers in English and many other languages. Coverage can go back twenty years. Other areas of coverage include public affairs and government publications. Access by subscription only or through a subscribing library.

Magazines for Libraries. New York: Bowker, 1969–present. Kept up to date with supplements. A standard reference for librarians and library users, with good annotations describing each publication.

Milner, Anita Cheek. *Newspaper Indexes: A Location and Subject Guide for Researchers.* Metuchen, NJ: Scarecrow, 1977–1982. Three volumes have been published so far.

Newspapers in Microform. Ann Arbor, MI: UMI, 1995–present. Annual. UMI is the major vendor for available microforms, making this sales catalog a very informative listing.

Newspapers in Microform. United States. 1948–1983. 2 vols. Washington, DC: Library of Congress, 1984.

Union List of Serials in Libraries of the United States and Canada. 3rd ed. 5 vols. New York: Wilson, 1965.

B1-c   Sources about general knowledge

Internet Public Library. Ann Arbor, MI: School of Information and Library
Studies, 1995. Online at www.ipl.org (7 February 2007). An amazing
source, modeled after a traditional library, with links to a large variety
of online reference materials.

B1-d   Encyclopedias

An encyclopedia is a great source for general knowledge and a good place to begin your research on almost any topic. Although they do not treat subjects thoroughly, encyclopedias are usually factual and current.

Academic American Encyclopedia. 21 vols. Danbury, CT: Grolier, 1997.
Britannica Online. Chicago: Britannica Online. Online at www.eb.com (7 February
2007). Provides good links to credible Internet sources.
Columbia Encyclopedia. Ed. Paul Lagasse. 6th ed. New York: Columbia UP, 2000.
Also on CD-ROM.
Compton's Multimedia Encyclopedia. Vers. 2.00. Carlsbad, CA: Compton's New-
Media, 1994. CD-ROM.
Encarta. Redmond, WA: Microsoft, annual. CD-ROM. A multimedia encyclope-
dia with more than 26,000 articles, including the text of *Funk & Wagnalls
New Encyclopedia;* several hours of sound, including spoken language;
illustrations; video clips and animations; maps; MindMaze game; and an
illustrated timeline of world history.
Encyclopedia Americana. International ed. 30 vols. Danbury, CT: Grolier, 1998.
Also on CD-ROM.
Encyclopedia Americana Online. Danbury, CT: Grolier, 1997. Online at ea.grolier
.com (7 February 2007).
Encyclopaedia Britannica. 15th ed. Chicago: Encyclopaedia Britannica, 1998.
Webster's Interactive Encyclopedia. Chatsworth, CA: Cambrix, 1998. CD-ROM.
Year 2000 Grolier Multimedia Encyclopedia. Danbury, CT: Grolier Electronic,
1999. CD-ROM version of *Academic American Encyclopedia.*

B1-e   Sources about words: Dictionaries

Dictionaries originally were a translation tool: They listed equivalent words in two
languages. Sumerian clay tablets, for example, showed Sumerian words beside their
Assyrian equivalents. By the seventeenth century, *dictionary* had come to mean a
book that explains the etymology (origin), pronunciation, meaning, and correct usage of words. Nathan Bailey's *Universal Etymological English Dictionary,* published in
1721, was the first comprehensive dictionary in English.

Modern dictionaries provide information about the meaning, derivation, spelling, and syllabication of words. Some include usage and dialectical variations as

well as synonyms, antonyms, rhymes, slang, and colloquialisms. Unabridged dictionaries purport to contain complete information about words; abridged dictionaries, with a nod to portability, condense the information.

(1) General dictionaries

American Heritage Dictionary of the English Language. 4th ed. Boston: Houghton Mifflin, 2000.

Merriam-Webster's Collegiate Dictionary. 11th ed. Springfield, MA: Merriam-Webster, 2003.

Merriam-Webster Online: Collegiate Dictionary. Springfield, MA: Merriam-Webster, 1996–present. Online at www.m-w.com/netdict.htm (7 February 2007).

Oxford Dictionary of New Words: A Popular Guide to Words in the News. 2nd ed. New York: Oxford UP, 1998.

Oxford English Dictionary. 2nd ed. 20 vols. New York: Oxford UP, 1989. An essential, authoritative resource for the study of origins and evolution of words.

Oxford English Dictionary: On Compact Disc. 2nd ed. New York: Oxford UP, 1999.

Random House Webster's Concise Dictionary. 2nd ed. New York: Random House, 1997.

Webster's Third New International Dictionary of the English Language, Unabridged. Ed. Philip Babcock Grove & the Merriam-Webster editorial staff. Springfield, MA: Merriam-Webster, 1993.

(2) Specialized dictionaries

The Barnhart Concise Dictionary of Etymology. New York: HarperCollins, 1995.

Bartlett's Roget's Thesaurus. 1st ed. Boston: Little, Brown, 1996. A compilation of synonyms grouped according to concepts.

The Concise Oxford Dictionary of English Etymology. Ed. T. F. Hoad. New York: Oxford UP, 1993.

A Dictionary of American English on Historical Principles. 4 vols. Chicago: U Chicago P, 1938–1944.

Dictionary of American Regional English. 3 vols to date. Ed. Frederick G. Cassidy. Cambridge, MA: Belknap, 1985– .

A Dictionary of Slang and Unconventional English: Colloquialisms and Catch Phrases, Fossilised Jokes and Puns, General Nicknames, Vulgarisms, and Such Americanisms as Have Been Naturalised. 8th ed. London: Routledge, 1984.

Merriam-Webster's Rhyming Dictionary. Springfield, MA: Merriam-Webster, 2002.

The Oxford Dictionary and Thesaurus. Ed. Sara Hawker and Maurice Waite. 2nd ed. New York: Oxford UP, 2007.

Partridge, Eric. *A Concise Dictionary of Slang and Unconventional English.* New York: Macmillan, 1990.

The Right Word III: A Concise Thesaurus. Boston: Houghton Mifflin, 1990.

Roget's International Thesaurus. Ed. Barbara Anne Kipfer. 6th ed. New York: HarperCollins, 2001.

Spears, Richard A. *NTC's Dictionary of American Slang and Colloquial Expressions.* 4th ed. Lincolnwood, IL: National Textbook, 2006.

Webster's Dictionary of Synonyms and Antonyms. New York: Smithmark, 1996.

Webster's Dictionary of Word Origins. New York: Smithmark, 1995.

B1-f Works about places

Reference works on places come in two forms: atlases and gazetteers.

(1) Atlases

Britannica Atlas. Chicago: Encyclopaedia Britannica, 1994.

Concise Atlas of the World. Washington, DC: National Geographic Society, 1997.

Goode, J. Paul. *Goode's World Atlas.* 21st ed. Chicago: Rand McNally, 2005.

Hammond World Atlas. 4th ed. Maplewood, NJ: Hammond World Atlas, 2003. Also on CD-ROM.

National Geographic Atlas of the World. 8th ed. Washington, DC: National Geographic Society, 2005.

Rand McNally Commercial Atlas & Marketing Guide [year]. Chicago: Rand McNally, 1876–present.

Times *Atlas of the World.* 11th comprehensive ed. London: Times Books, 2003.

USA State Factbook on CD-ROM. Minneapolis: Quanta, 1992–present.

(2) Gazetteers

Cambridge World Gazetteer: A Geographical Dictionary. Ed. David Munro. New York: Cambridge UP, 1990.

Canby, Courtlandt. *The Encyclopedia of Historic Places.* New York: Facts On File, 1984.

Modern Geography: Over One Million Named Places in the U.S.: An Encyclopedic Survey. New York: Garland, 1991.

Place-Name-Index. Mineral, VA: Buckmaster, 1992. CD-ROM.

Worldmark Encyclopedia of the Nations. 11th ed. 5 vols. Detroit: Gale, 2004.

B1-g Works about people

(1) General biographies of deceased persons

Cambridge Biographical Dictionary. Ed. David Crystal. New York: Cambridge UP, 1990.

Cambridge Biographical Dictionary. New York: Cambridge UP, 1996. Shorter paperback edition.

De Ford, Miriam Allen. *Who Was When? A Dictionary of Contemporaries.* 3rd ed. New York: Wilson, 1976.

Encyclopedia of World Biography. 20th-century supp. Palatine, IL: Heraty, 1987.

Great Lives from History. American Women Series. Ed. Frank N. Magill. 5 vols. Pasadena, CA: Salem, 1995.

Great Lives from History. Ancient and Medieval Series. Ed. Frank N. Magill.
    5 vols. Pasadena, CA: Salem, 1988.
Great Lives from History. Renaissance to 1900 Series. Ed. Frank N. Magill. 5 vols.
    Pasadena, CA: Salem, 1989.
Great Lives from History. Twentieth Century Series. Ed. Frank N. Magill. 5 vols.
    Pasadena, CA: Salem, 1990.
*The McGraw-Hill Encyclopedia of World Biography; an International Reference
    Work.* 2nd ed. 25 vols. New York: McGraw-Hill, 1998–2005.
Slocum, Robert B. *Biographical Dictionaries and Related Works: An International
    Bibliography of More Than 16,000 Collective Biographies.* 2nd ed. 2 vols.
    Detroit: Gale, 1986. This work lists all major biographical sources. An
    excellent place to begin finding biographies.
Thinkers of the Twentieth Century. Ed. Roland Turner. 2nd ed. Chicago: St. James,
    1987.

(2) General biographies of living persons

Biographical Books, 1876–1949. New York: Bowker, 1983.
Biographical Books, 1950–1980. New York: Bowker, 1980.
Current Biography. New York: Wilson, 1940–present.
Current Biography. Cumulated index. New York: Wilson, 1973–present.
The International Who's Who. London: Europa, 1935–present.
The New York Times *Biographical Edition.* New York: New York Times and Arno,
    1974–present.
Who's Who in the World. Wilmette, IL: Marquis, 1971/1972–present.
Wilson Current Biography. New York: Wilson; Norwood, MA: SilverPlatter Infor-
    mation, 1997–present. CD-ROM. Profiles and obituaries that have appeared
    in *Current Biography Yearbook* since 1940.

(3) Biographies of deceased persons, American and British

Appleton's Cyclopaedia of American Biography. 7 vols. New York: Appleton,
    1887– 1900.
Concise Dictionary of American Biography. 5th ed., complete through 1980.
    2 vols. New York: Scribner's, 1997.
Dictionary of American Biography. Comprehensive index, complete through sup-
    plement 10. New York: Scribner's, 1996.
Dictionary of American Biography. Supp. New York: Scribner's, 1973–present.
*Dictionary of American Biography, under the Auspices of the American Council of
    Learned Societies.* 22 vols. New York: Scribner's, 1928–1958.
The Dictionary of National Biography: From the Earliest Times to 1900. Ed. Sir Leslie
    Stephen and Sir Sidney Lee. 22 vols. London: Oxford UP, 1998. Supplements
    have been published irregularly since 1921 to the present.
Notable American Women, 1607–1950; a Biographical Dictionary. Ed. Edward T.
    James. 3 vols. Cambridge, MA: Belknap, 1971.

Notable American Women: The Modern Period: A Biographical Dictionary. Cambridge, MA: Belknap, 1980.

Webster's American Biographies. Springfield, MA: Merriam-Webster, 1984.

Who Was Who: A Companion to Who's Who, Containing the Biographies of Those Who Died during the Decade. New York: St. Martin's Press, 1897–present.

Who Was Who: A Cumulated Index, 1897–1990. New York: St. Martin's Press, 1991.

Who Was Who in America, a Companion Volume to Who's Who in America. Chicago: Marquis, 1943–present.

(4) Biographies of living persons, American and British

The National Cyclopaedia of American Biography, Being the History of the United States as Illustrated in the Lives of the Founders, Builders, and Defenders of the Republic, and of the Men and Women Who Are Doing the Work and Moulding the Thought of the Present Time. 63 vols. New York: White, 1893–1984.

Who's Who. London: Black, 1849–present.

Who's Who in America. Chicago: Marquis, 1899–present. Regional supplements— *Who's Who in the East, Who's Who in the West, Who's Who in the Midwest,* and *Who's Who in the South and Southwest*—are all issued by Marquis.

Who's Who of American Women: A Biographical Dictionary of Notable Living American Women. Chicago: Marquis, 1958–present.

NOTE: Many countries and professions publish Who's Who directories as well. Ask your librarian about specific titles that are appropriate to your research.

(5) Indexes to biographical material

Almanac of Famous People: A Comprehensive Reference Guide to More Than 30,000 Famous and Infamous Newsmakers from Biblical Times to the Present. 6th ed. 2 vols. Detroit: Gale, 1998.

Bio-base. Detroit: Gale, 1978–present. Microfiche. A cumulative master index to several major biographical sets.

Biography and Genealogy Master Index. Detroit: Gale, through 1999. CD-ROM.

Biography and Genealogy Master Index: A Consolidated Index to More Than 3,200,000 Biographical Sketches in over 350 Current and Retrospective Biographical Dictionaries. 2nd ed. 8 vols. Detroit: Gale, 1980. Kept up to date by annual supplements (1981/1982–present) and by quinquennial cumulations.

Biography index. New York: Wilson, 1946–present. A cumulative index to biographical material in books and magazines. Also on CD-ROM.

Historical Biographical Dictionaries Master Index: A Consolidated Index to Biographical Information Concerning Historical Personages in over 35 of the Principal Retrospective Biographical Dictionaries. Detroit: Gale, 1980.

The New York Times *Obituaries Index.* vol. 1, *1858–1968*; vol. 2, *1969–1978*. New York: New York Times, 1970–1980.

New York Times *Obituary Index*. Westport, CT: Meckler, 1990–present. This companion publication to the *Obituaries Index* covers the *New York Times* and other newspapers.

B1-h   Resources about government publications

The largest publisher in the world is the U.S. Government Printing Office (GPO), which issues all the works of the national government and its various divisions. Because the government is so complex, almost every subject area is covered. Sources about those documents include the following:

NOTE: Other nations' governments, as well as the United Nations, publish valuable resource materials too.

Ames, John G. *Comprehensive Index to the Publications of the United States Government, 1881–1893*. 2 vols. Washington, DC: 1905. Continuation of Benjamin Perley Poore's catalog of government publications.

Anzinger, Gunnar. *Governments on the WWW.* 1995–1997. Online at www.gksoft .com/govt (7 February 2007). Comprehensive database of government institutions on the World Wide Web. Entries include parliaments, ministries, offices, law courts, embassies, city councils, political parties, public broadcasting institutions, and more, from 192 countries and territories.

Catalog of the Public Documents of the Congress and of All Departments of the Government of the United States: Being the Comprehensive Index Provided for by the Act Approved Jan. 12, 1895. 25 vols. Washington, DC: GPO, 1896–1919.

Checklist of United States Public Documents, 1789–1909, Congressional: to Close of Sixtieth Congress, Departmental to End of Calendar Year 1909. 3rd ed., rev. and enlarged. Washington, DC: GPO, 1911.

CIS Index to Publications of the United States Congress. Washington, DC: Congressional Information Service, 1970–present. CD-ROM.

Congressional Series of United States Public Documents. Washington, DC: GPO, 1789–1969.

FedWorld. Online at www.fedworld.gov (7 February 2007). An agency of the U.S. Department of Commerce, FedWorld is an online locator of information dispersed by the federal government.

Government Infomine. Riverside, CA: Library of the University of California, Riverside, 1996–present. Online at infomine.ucr.edu/cgi-bin/search?govpub (7 February 2007).

Government Resources on the Web. Ann Arbor, MI: University of Michigan Library, Documents Center. Online at www.lib.umich.edu/govdocs (7 February 2007).

GPO Access: Pathway Services. Washington, DC: GPO. Online at www.access.gpo .gov/su_docs/gils/pathway.html (30 March 2007).

GPO Monthly Catalog. Dublin, OH: OCLC, 1990–present. CD-ROM.

Hoffmann, Frank W. *Guide to Popular U.S. Government Publications*. 5th ed. Englewood, CO: Libraries Unlimited, 1998.

LinxNet U.S. Government Index—Agencies, Policies and Laws. LinxNet. Online at www.linxnet.com/gov.html (7 February 2007).

Monthly Catalog of United States Government Publications. Washington, DC: GPO, 1951–present.

Morehead, Joe. *Introduction to United States Government Information Sources.* 6th ed. Englewood, CO: Libraries Unlimited, 1999.

Pokorny, Elizabeth J. *U.S. Government Documents: A Practical Guide for Nonprofessionals in Academic and Public Libraries.* Englewood, CO: Libraries Unlimited, 1989.

Poore, Benjamin Perley. *A Descriptive Catalogue of the Government Publications of the United States, September 5, 1774–March 4, 1881.* 1885. Reprint, Buffalo, NY: Hein, 2003.

THOMAS—U.S. Congress on the Internet. Washington, DC: Library of Congress. Online at thomas.loc.gov (30 March 2007).

Zwirn, Jerrold. *Accessing U.S. Government Information: Subject Guide to Jurisdiction of the Executive and Legislative Branches.* Rev. and expanded ed. Westport, CT: Greenwood, 1996.

B1-i Sources about nonbooks (nonprint materials)

Nonprint materials form an important and integral part of library collections. Materials stored on microfiche, microfilm, videotape, sound recordings, and computer files can be very valuable to student-researchers.

(1) General guides

Audiovisual Materials. Washington, DC: Library of Congress, 1979–1982.

AV Market Place. New York: Bowker, 1989–present.

Media Resource Catalog from the National Audiovisual Center. Capitol Heights, MD: The Center, 1986–2006.

Media Review Digest. Ann Arbor, MI: Pierian, 1973/1974–present.

The Video Source Book. Syosset, NY: National Video Clearinghouse, 1979–present.

(2) Indexes of microforms

Bibliographic Guide to Microform Publications. Boston: Hall, 1987–1993. Lists nonserial microforms cataloged by the research libraries of the New York Public Library and the Library of Congress.

Dissertation Abstracts International. Series A, *The Humanities and Social Sciences;* Series B, *The Sciences and Engineering.* ProQuest (formerly UMI) Database. Online by subscription only or through a subscribing library. Coverage, 1861–present; updated monthly.

An Index to Microform Collections. Ed. Anne Niles. Westport, CT: Meckler, 1984.

Newspapers in Microform. Washington, DC: Library of Congress, 1973–1983.

Newspapers in Microform. Ann Arbor, MI: UMI, 1984/1985–1991/1992. Merged with *Serials in Microform* to form *Serials & Newspapers in Microform.*

Newspapers in Microform. Ann Arbor, MI: UMI, 1995–to present.

Newspapers in Microform. United States. Washington, DC: Library of Congress, 1973–present. Continues *Newspapers on Microfilm*, 1948–1972.

Serials & Newspapers in Microform. Ann Arbor, MI: 1992/1993–present. Formed by the union of *Serials in Microform* and *Newspapers in Microform*.

(3) Guides to films

The American Film Institute Catalog of Motion Pictures Produced in the United States. Berkeley: U of California P, 1971–1993. Covers feature films in the periods 1911–1920, 1921–1930, 1931–1940, and 1961–1970. (AFI catalog continues as an electronic resource.)

American Folklore Films and Videotapes: A Catalog. 2nd ed. New York: Bowker, 1982–present.

Aros, Andrew A. *A Title Guide to the Talkies, 1964 through 1974*. Metuchen, NJ: Scarecrow, 1977.

———. *A Title Guide to the Talkies, 1975 through 1984*. Metuchen, NJ: Scarecrow, 1986.

Bowker's Complete Video Directory. New York: Bowker, 1990–present.

Dimmitt, Richard B. *A Title Guide to the Talkies; a Comprehensive Listing of 16,000 Feature-Length Films from October, 1927, until December, 1963*. 2 vols. New York: Scarecrow, 1965.

The Film File. Minneapolis: Media Referral Service, 1981–present.

Films and Other Materials for Projection. 8 vols. Washington, DC: Library of Congress, 1973–1978.

Halliwell's Film & Video Guide. New York: HarperPerennial, 1997.

Halliwell's Film Guide. 11th ed. New York: Scribner's, 1995.

International Film Guide. 26 vols. London: Tantivy Press; New York: Barnes, 1964–1988.

International Motion Picture Almanac. New York: Quigley, 1956–present.

Leonard Maltin's 2003 Movie and Video Guide. New York: New American Library, 2003. Published annually.

Library of Congress Catalog. Motion Pictures and Filmstrips. 9 vols. Washington, DC: Library of Congress, 1955–1973.

Marill, Alvin H. *Movies Made for Television, 1964–2004*. Lanham, MD: Scarecrow, 2005.

Motion Picture Guide CD-ROM. New York: Cinebooks, 1994–present.

Nash, Jay Robert. *The Motion Picture Guide*. Chicago: Cinebooks, 1987.

Nowlan, Robert A. *The Films of the Eighties: A Complete, Qualitative Filmography to over 3400 Feature-Length English Language Films, Theatrical and Video-Only, Released between January 1, 1980, and December 31, 1989*. Jefferson, NC: McFarland, 1991.

Variety *International Film Guide*. London: Andre Deutsch; Hollywood: Samuel French, 1989–present.

Variety's *Video Directory Plus*. New York: Bowker, 1986–1998. CD-ROM. Includes *Variety's* complete home video directory and reviews from the critical media.

(4) Guides to sound recordings: Music

Bibliography of Discographies. 3 vols. Vol. 1, *Classical Music, 1925–1975;* vol. 2, *Jazz;* vol. 3, *Popular music.* New York: Bowker, 1977–1983.

CD Guide. Optical ed. Hancock, NH: WGE.

CD Review Digest Annual. 3 vols. Voorheesville, NY: Peri, 1987–1989.

CD Review Digest Annual. Classical. 5 vols. Voorheesville, NY: Peri, 1988–1994.

CD Review Digest Annual. Jazz, Popular, etc. 5 vols. Voorheesville, NY: Peri, 1988–1990.

Harris, Steve. *Film, Television, and Stage Music on Phonograph Records: A Discography.* Jefferson, NC: McFarland, 1988.

Library of Congress Catalog: Music and Phonorecords. Washington, DC: Library of Congress, 1953–1972.

March, Ivan. *The Penguin Guide to Compact Discs and Cassettes.* New ed., rev. and updated. New York: Penguin, 1996.

Music, Books on Music, and Sound Recordings. Washington, DC: Library of Congress, 1973–1989.

The Music Catalog on CD-ROM. Washington, DC: Library of Congress, Cataloging Distribution Service, 1994–present.

Music Library. Musical sound recordings. Dublin, OH: OCLC, 1990–present. CD-ROM.

Popular Music: An Annotated Index of American Popular Songs. Detroit: Gale, 1974–2004.

Rust, Brian A. L. *The American Record Label Book.* New Rochelle, NY: Arlington, 1978.

Schwann. Boston: ABC Consumer Magazines, 1986–present.

Schwann CD Review Digest. Santa Fe: Stereophile, 1995–present.

Schwann Opus. Santa Fe: Stereophile, 1992–2001.

Schwann Spectrum. Santa Fe: Stereophile, 1992–2001.

Tudor, Dean. *Popular Music: An Annotated Guide to Recordings.* Littleton, CO: Libraries Unlimited, 1983.

(5) Guides to sound recordings: Speeches, readings, and oral history

Hoffman, Herbert H. *International Index to Recorded Poetry.* New York: Wilson, 1983.

On Cassette. 3 vols. New York: Bowker, 1989–1991. Merged with *Words on Tape* to form *Words on Cassette.*

The Oral History Collection of Columbia University. Ed. Elizabeth B. Mason and Louis M. Starr. New York: Oral History Research Office, 1979.

Perks, Robert. *Oral History: An Annotated Bibliography.* London: British Library National Sound Archive, 1990.

Smith, Allen. *Directory of Oral History Collections.* Phoenix: Oryx, 1988.

Words on Cassette. 12 vols. New Providence, NJ: Bowker, 1992–2003.

Words on Tape. Westport, CT: Meckler, 1984–1991. Merged with *On Cassette* to form *Words on Cassette.*

(6) Sources about computer files

With the explosion of computers and the Internet, computerized information sources have become common. The following are representative of some of the better sources:

AltaVista: Main Page. Digital Equipment Corporation, 1997. Online at www
.altavista.com (7 February 2007).
Gale Directory of Databases. Detroit: Gale, 1993–present.
NetFirst. Dublin, OH: OCLC. Available online at firstsearch.oclc.org (7 February 2007).
WebCrawler: Lightning Fast Web Search. America Online, 1994–present. Online at www.webcrawler.com (7 February 2007).
Yahoo! Sunnyvale, CA: Yahoo, 1994–present. Online at www.yahoo.com (29 March 2007). Searches a directory of web links rather than keywords.

B2   A list of specialized references

The sources in this section cover specific subject areas. Because a complete listing of all the specialized references on popular subjects easily would fill an entire volume, we have been selective here, choosing examples of the better works in given subject areas.

B2-a   Art

American Art Directory. New York: Jaques Cattell; New York: Bowker, 1952–present.
Art & Architecture Thesaurus. 2nd ed. 5 vols. New York: Oxford UP, 1994.
Artbibliographies Modern. Santa Barbara: ABC-Clio, 1969–present.
Art Index. New York: Wilson, 1929/1932–present. Also on CD-ROM.
Arts & Humanities Search. Philadelphia: Institute for Scientific Information. Online through Dialog, Datastar, and OCLC. Ask your librarian. Covers 1980 to the present.
Atkins, Robert. *Artspeak: A Guide to Contemporary Ideas, Movements, and Buzzwords, 1945 to the present.* 2nd ed. New York: Abbeville, 1997.
———. *Artspoke: A Guide to Modern Ideas, Movements, and Buzzwords, 1848–1944.* New York: Abbeville, 1993.
Bibliography of the History of Art: BHA. Santa Monica: J. Paul Getty Trust; Vandoeuvre-les-Nancy, France: Centre national de la recherche scientifique, 1996–present. CD-ROM.
Chiarmonte, Paula L. *Women Artists in the United States: A Selective Bibliography and Resource Guide on the Fine and Decorative Arts, 1750–1986.* Boston: Hall, 1990.
Contemporary Artists. 5th ed. Ed. Sara Pendergast and Tom Pendergast. Detroit: St. James, 2002.

Contemporary Designers. 3rd ed. Detroit: St. James, 1997.

Denvir, Bernard. *The Thames and Hudson Encyclopaedia of Impressionism.* London: Thames and Hudson, 1990.

Ehresmann, Donald L. *Fine Arts: A Bibliographic Guide to Basic Reference Works, Histories, and Handbooks.* 3rd ed. Englewood, CO: Libraries Unlimited, 1990.

Encyclopedia of Architecture: Design, Engineering & Construction. Ed. Joseph A. Wilkes. 4 vols. New York: Wiley, 1988–1989.

Encyclopedia of World Art. 17 vols. New York: McGraw-Hill, 1959–1987.

Fleming, John. *The Penguin Dictionary of Architecture.* 5th ed. New York: Penguin, 1999.

———. *The Penguin Dictionary of Decorative Arts.* New ed. New York: Viking, 1989.

Gardner's Art through the Ages. Ed. Fred S. Kleiner, Christin J. Mamiya, and Richard G. Tansey. 12th ed. Belmont, CA: Thomson/Wadsworth, 2005.

International Dictionary of Architects and Architecture. 2 vols. Detroit: St. James, 1993.

International Dictionary of Art and Artists. 2 vols. Chicago: St. James, 1990.

Jones, Lois Swan. *Art Information: Research Methods and Resources.* 3rd ed. Dubuque: Kendall/Hunt, 1990.

Julier, Guy. *The Thames and Hudson Encyclopaedia of 20th Century Design and Designers.* New York: Thames and Hudson, 1993.

Livingston, Alan. *The Thames and Hudson Encyclopaedia of Graphic Design and Designers.* New ed. New York: Thames and Hudson, 2003.

Modern Arts Criticism. 4 vols. Detroit: Gale, 1991–1994.

Norman, Geraldine. *Nineteenth-Century Painters and Painting: A Dictionary.* Berkeley: U California P, 1977.

The Oxford Companion to the Decorative Arts. New York: Oxford UP, 1985.

The Oxford Companion to Twentieth-Century Art. Ed. Harold Osborne. New York: Oxford UP, 1981.

The Oxford Dictionary of Art. Ed. Ian Chilvers. 3rd ed. New York: Oxford UP, 2004.

The Pelican History of Art. Harmondsworth, England: Penguin, 1953–present.

Petteys, Chris. *Dictionary of Women Artists: An International Dictionary of Women Artists Born before 1900.* Boston: Hall, 1985.

RILA (Répertoire international de la littérature de l'art), International Repertory of the Literature of Art. New York: College Art Association of America, 1975–1989. Merged with *Répertoire d'art et d'archaeologie* to form *Bibliography of the History of Art.*

RILA (Répertoire international de la littérature de l'art), International Repertory of the Literature of Art. Santa Monica, CA: J. Paul Getty Trust, 1989–1996. Also on CD-ROM.

Who's Who in American Art. New Providence, NJ: Marquis Who's Who, 1936/1937–present.

World Artists, 1950–1980: An H. W. Wilson Biographical Dictionary. New York: Wilson, 1981.

World Artists, 1980–1990: An H. W. Wilson Biographical Dictionary. New York: Wilson, 1991.

Thousands of art museums have sites on the web, some official, some not. On those sites you may find images of artwork, narrative sound files, and text commentary, most often in English. Many Internet search engines have a classified listing of museums. A few examples follow:

Guggenheim Museum Home Page. New York: Solomon R. Guggenheim Foundation, 1996, 1997. Online at www.guggenheim.org (7 February 2007).

Kyoto National Museum. Kyoto, Japan: Kyoto National Museum, 1997. Online at www.kyohaku.go.jp (7 February 2007).

Los Angeles County Museum of Art—LACMAweb Home Page. Los Angeles: Museum Associates dba the Los Angeles County Museum of Art, 1996. Online at www.lacma.org (7 February 2007).

Louvre Museum. [Paris: Musée du Louvre]. Online at www./louvre.fr/llv/commun/home_flash.jsp (30 March 2007). A related but unofficial multimedia site is *Le WebLouvre;* use a search engine to reach it.

National Gallery of Art. Washington, DC: National Gallery of Art, 1997. Online at www.nga.gov (7 February 2007).

Welcome to the Metropolitan Museum of Art. New York: Metropolitan Museum of Art, 1997. Online at www.metmuseum.org (7 February 2007).

B2-b   Business and economics

ABI/INFORM. ProQuest (formerly UMI) Database, 1971–present. Online by subscription only or through a subscribing library. ABI/INFORM is a database covering business, management, economics, and a wide range of related fields. It provides abstracts from 1971 onward and full text from 1987, though not all journals are available in full text.

Accountant's Handbook. Ed. D. R. Carmichael and Paul Rosenfield. 10th ed. 2 vols. New York: Wiley, 2003.

Business Dateline. Ann Arbor, MI: UMI. Computer file.

Business Periodicals Index. New York: Wilson, 1958/1959–present.

Business Periodicals Index. New York: Wilson, 1987–present. CD-ROM.

D&B—Dun's Electronic Business Directory. Parsippany, NJ: Dun's Marketing Services. Computer file.

D&B—Dun's Market Identifiers. Parsippany, NJ: Dun's Marketing Service. Computer file.

D&B Million Dollar Directory: America's Leading Public & Private Companies. Bethlehem, PA: Dun & Bradstreet, 1997–present.

D&B Million Dollar Disc. Murray Hill, NJ: Dun & Bradstreet. CD-ROM.

A Dictionary of Business. 3rd ed. New York: Oxford UP, 2002.

Economic Literature Index (EconLit). Pittsburgh: American Economic Association: EBSCO Information Services. 1969–present. Online by subscription only or through a subscribing library.

Encyclopedia of American Business History and Biography. New York: Facts On File, 1988–present.

Encyclopedia of Banking & Finance. Ed. Charles J. Woelfel. 10th ed. Chicago: Probus, 1994.

Encyclopedia of Business Information Sources. 16th ed. Detroit: Gale, 2002.

F&S Index Plus Text. International ed. New York: SilverPlatter Information. CD-ROM.

Freed, Melvyn N. *Business Information Desk Reference: Where to Find Answers to Business Questions.* New York: Macmillan, 1991.

Handbook of Labor Statistics. Washington, DC: U.S. Department of Labor, Bureau of Labor Statistics, 1924–1989.

Handbook of U.S. Labor Statistics: Employment, Earnings, Prices, Productivity, and Other Labor Data. Lanham, MD: Bernan, 1997–present.

Ingham, John N., and Lynne B. Feldman. *Contemporary Business Leaders: A Biographical Dictionary.* New York: Greenwood, 1990.

International Marketing Handbook: Detailed Marketing Profiles for 141 Nations, Supplemented by Customs Information, International Marketing Advisories to Assist in Developing an Export Marketing Program, and Basic Importation Data. 3rd ed. Detroit: Gale, 1988–present.

Mattera, Philip. *Inside U.S. Business: A Concise Encyclopedia of Leading Industries.* Burr Ridge, IL: Irwin, 1994.

The MIT Dictionary of Modern Economics. Ed. David W. Pearce. 4th ed. Cambridge, MA: MIT Press, 1992.

Moody's Handbook of Common Stocks. New York: Moody's Investors Service, 1965–1999.

Moody's Handbook of Corporate Managements. New York: Moody's Investors Service, 1967–present.

Moody's Handbook of Nasdaq Stocks. New York: Moody's Investors Service, 1992–2001.

Moody's Industrial Manual. New York: Moody's Investors Service, 1954–present.

The New Palgrave Dictionary of Money & Finance. 3 vols. London: Macmillan; New York: Stockton, 1992.

The Oxford Handbook of International Business. Ed. Alan M. Rugman and Thomas L. Brewer. New York: Oxford UP, 2001.

Rand McNally Commercial Atlas & Marketing Guide [year]. Chicago: Rand McNally, 1876–present.

Rosenberg, Jerry Martin. *Dictionary of Banking.* New York: Wiley, 1993.

Rosenberg, Jerry Martin. *Dictionary of Business and Management.* New York: Wiley, 1993.

———. *Dictionary of Investing.* New York: Wiley, 2004.

———. *Dictionary of Marketing and Advertising.* New York: Wiley, 1995.

———. *McGraw-Hill Dictionary of Business Acronyms, Initials, and Abbreviations.* New York: McGraw-Hill, 1992.

Shim, Jae K. *Encyclopedic Dictionary of Accounting and Finance.* New York: M.F.J. Books, 1996.

Small Business Sourcebook. Detroit: Gale, 1983–present. Updated with supplements.

Terry, John V. *International Management Handbook.* Fayetteville, AR: U Arkansas P, 1992.

Thomas Register of American Manufacturers. New York: Thomas, 1905/1906– present. Also online at www.thomasregister.com (7 February 2007).

Who's Who in Economics. Ed. Mark Blaug and Howard R. Vane. 4th ed. Northampton, MA: Elgar, 2003.

Who's Who in Economics: A Biographical Dictionary of Major Economists, 1700–1986. Ed. Mark Blaug and Paul Sturges. 2nd ed. Cambridge, MA: MIT Press, 1986.

Wilson Business Abstracts. New York: Wilson, 1991–present. CD-ROM.

There is a wealth of information about individual businesses on the World Wide Web. Many companies have their own website, on which you'll find a description of the company, the disclosure of at least some financial information, and a directory of corporate personnel. Sites that are not published by a company itself may contain comparative performance measures and news stories. A good research strategy is to do a well-planned query on a search engine, paying close and critical attention to the results.

B2-c Dance

American Dance Directory. New York: Association of American Dance Companies, 1979/1980–present.

Cohen-Stratyner, Barbara Naomi. *Biographical Dictionary of Dance.* New York: Schirmer; London: Collier Macmillan, 1982.

The Dance Anthology. Ed. Cobbett Steinberg. New York: New American Library, 1980.

Kirstein, Lincoln. *Four Centuries of Ballet: Fifty Masterworks.* New York: Dover, 1984.

Koegler, Horst. *The Concise Oxford Dictionary of Ballet.* 2nd ed., updated. New York: Oxford UP, 1982.

Lawson, Joan. *A Ballet-Maker's Handbook: Sources, Vocabulary, Styles.* London: A & C Black; New York: Theatre Arts Books/Routledge, 1991.

Robertson, Allen. *The Dance Handbook.* Boston: Hall, 1988.

Studwell, William E. *Ballet Plot Index: A Guide to Locating Plots and Descriptions of Ballets and Associated Material.* New York: Garland, 1987.

Appendix B

B2-d   Ecology

Dorgan, Charity Anne. *Statistical Record of the Environment.* Detroit: Gale, 1995.

Ecological Abstracts. Norwich, England: Geo Abstracts, 1974–present.

Encyclopedia of Global Change: Environmental Change and Human Society. Ed. Andrew S. Goudie. New York: Oxford UP, 2002.

Energy Statistics Yearbook. New York: United Nations, 1993–present.

Environment Abstracts Annual. New York: EIC Intelligence, 1980–present.

Environment Abstracts on CD-ROM. Bethesda, MD: Congressional Information Service, 1994–present.

Environmental Periodicals Bibliography. Baltimore: National Information Services, 1990–present. CD-ROM.

The Global Ecology Handbook: What You Can Do about the Environmental Crisis. Boston: Beacon, 1990.

Hazardous Substances Resource Guide. Ed. Richard P. Pohanis and Stanley Greene. 2nd ed. Detroit: Gale, 1997.

Introduction to Environmental Geology. Ed. Edward A. Keller. 4th ed. Upper Saddle River, NJ: Pearson Education, 2007.

Mason, Robert J. *Atlas of United States Environmental Issues.* New York: Macmillan, 1990.

Pollution Abstracts. Bethesda, MD: Cambridge Scientific Abstracts, 1970–present.

Sax's Dangerous Properties of Industrial Material. 11th ed. New York: Wiley, 2004. CD-ROM.

Stevenson, L. Harold. *The Facts On File Dictionary of Environmental Science.* New ed. New York: Facts On File, 2006.

U.S. Environmental Protection Agency. Online at www.epa.gov (7 February 2007).

Water Encyclopedia. Ed. Jay Lehr, et al. 5 vols. Hoboken, NJ: Wiley, 2005.

B2-e   Education

Barrow, Robin. *A Critical Dictionary of Educational Concepts: An Appraisal of Selected Ideas and Issues in Educational Theory and Practice.* 2nd ed. New York: Teachers College Press, Teachers College, Columbia University, 1990.

Bibliographic Guide to Education. Boston: Gale, 2000–present.

Current Index to Journals in Education (CIJE). New York: CCM Information, 1969–1974.

Current Index to Journals in Education (CIJE). Phoenix: Oryx, 1975–present.

Dejnozka, Edward, L. *American Educators' Encyclopedia.* Rev. ed. New York: Greenwood, 1991.

Directory of American Scholars. Lancaster, PA: Science, 1942–1982.

Educational Directory Online. Shelton, CT: Market Data Retrieval. Online at www .prebot.com/prebot.cgi?modlist=engweb&q=online%20education (7 February 2007).

Education Index. New York: Wilson, 1997–present. CD-ROM.

Appendix B

Education Index. New York: Wilson. Online at www.educationindex.com
(7 February 2007). Also available through telnet, dial-up access, and
OCLC's First Search.

*The Education Index: A Cumulative Author and Subject Index to a Selected List of
Educational Periodicals, Books, and Pamphlets.* New York: Wilson, 1932–present.

The Encyclopedia of Education Information. Lakeville, CT: Grey House, 1999–
present.

The Encyclopedia of Higher Education. Ed. Burton R. Clark. 4 vols. New York:
Pergamon, 1992.

ERIC (Educational Resources Information Center). Washington, DC: U.S. Department of Education. Online at www.eric.ed.gov or through library subscription
service. The ERIC collection of educational documents dates back to 1966,
and online documents to 1993 or earlier. There are several modes of delivery
for the various documents. For journal articles, use CIJE (*Current Index to
Journals in Education*). For other documents published on microfiche, several
online services offer access to the computer index, but the OCLC interface
(www.oclc.org) is one of the easiest to use.

The International Encyclopedia of Education. 2nd ed. Oxford, England: Pergamon;
New York: Elsevier, 1994.

The Mental Measurements Yearbook. Highland Park, NJ: Mental Measurements
Yearbook, 1941–present.

O'Brien, Nancy P. *Education: A Guide to Reference and Information Sources.* 2nd ed.
Englewood, CO: Libraries Unlimited, 2000.

PC-TESS: The Educational Software Selector. Hampton Bays, NY: EPIE Institute,
1994–2002. Computer file.

Peterson's College Database. Wellesley Hills, MA: SilverPlatter Information
Services. CD-ROM.

World Education Encyclopedia: A Survey of Educational Systems Worldwide. Ed.
Rebecca Marlow-Ferguson. 2nd ed. 3 vols. Detroit: Gale/Thomson, 2002.

B2-f   Ethnic studies

(1) General

Cashmore, Ernest. *Dictionary of Race and Ethnic Relations.* 4th ed. New York:
Routledge, 1996.

Documentary Archives: Multicultural America. Woodbridge, CT: Primary Source
Media, 1997. Computer file.

Dictionary of American Immigration History. Ed. Francesco Cordasco. Metuchen,
NJ: Scarecrow, 1990.

Dictionary of Multicultural Education. Ed. Carl A. Grant. Phoenix: Oryx, 1997.

Guide to Multicultural Resources: 1985–1997/1998. Fort Atkinson, WI: Highsmith,
1997.

Immigration in American Today: An Encyclopedia. Ed. James Loucky, Jeanne
Armstrong, and Larry J. Estrada. Westport, CT: Greenwood, 2006.

Weinberg, Meyer. *Racism in the United States: A Comprehensive Classified Bibliography.* New York: Greenwood, 1990.

Woll, Allen L. *Ethnic and Racial Images in American Film and Television: Historical Essays and Bibliography.* New York: Garland, 1987.

World Directory of Minorities. London: Minority Rights Group International, 1997.

(2) African-American studies

The African American Almanac: A Reference Work on the African American. 6th ed. Detroit: Gale, 1994–present.

Black Americans: A Statistical Sourcebook. Palo Alto, CA: Information Publications, 2005.

Black Americans Information Directory. 3 vols. Detroit: Gale, 1990–1993. Biennial. Continued by *African Americans. Information Directory.* Updated twice a year. Ceased in 1999.

Black Leaders of the Nineteenth Century. Ed. Leon Litwack. Urbana, IL: U Illinois P, 1988.

Black Leaders of the Twentieth Century. Ed. John Hope Franklin. Urbana, IL: U Illinois P, 1982.

Black Newspapers Index. Ann Arbor, MI: UMI, 1987–present.

The Black Resource Guide. Washington, DC: Ben Johnson, 1981–present.

Cantor, George. *Historic Landmarks of Black America.* Detroit: Gale, 1991.

Contemporary Black Biography. Detroit: Gale, 1992–present.

Dictionary of Afro-American Slavery. Ed. Randall M. Miller. Westport, CT: Praeger, 1997.

Hornsby, Alton. *Chronology of African American History: From 1492 to the Present.* 2nd updated ed. Detroit: Gale, 1997.

Index to Black Periodicals. Boston: Hall, 1988–present.

Who's Who among African Americans. Detroit: Gale, 1996–present.

Who's Who among Black Americans. 8 vols. Detroit: Gale, 1975/1976–1994/1995.

(3) Asian-American studies

Asian Americans: Comparative and Global Perspectives. Pullman, WA: Washington State UP, 1991.

Asian Americans Information Directory. 2 vols. Detroit: Gale, 1992–1994.

Chan, Sucheng. *Asian Americans: An Interpretive History.* Boston: Twayne, 1991.

Haseltine, Patricia. *East and Southeast Asian Material Culture in North America: Collections, Historical Sites, and Festivals.* New York: Greenwood, 1989.

UXL Asian American Reference Library: Cumulative Index. Detroit: UXL, 2004.

(4) Hispanic-American studies

Graham, Joseph Stanley. *Hispanic-American Material Culture: An Annotated Directory of Collections, Sites, Archives, and Festivals in the United States.* New York: Greenwood, 1989.

The Hispanic-American Almanac: A Reference Work on Hispanics in the United States. Ed. Sonia Benson. 3rd ed. Detroit: Gale, 2003.

Hispanic American Periodicals Index (HAPI). Los Angeles: UCLA Latin American Center Publications, University of California, 1970/1974–present.

Hispanic Americans: A Statistical Sourcebook. Ed. Manthi Nguyen. 2004 ed. Palo Alto, CA: Information Publications, 2004.

Hispanic Americans Information Directory. 3 vols. Detroit: Gale, 1990–1994.

Marvis, Barbara J. *Contemporary American Success Stories: Famous People of Hispanic Heritage.* 9 vols. Childs, MD: Mitchell Lane, 1996–1998.

Meier, Matt S. *Mexican American Biographies: A Historical Dictionary, 1836–1987.* New York: Greenwood, 1988.

Meyer, Nicholas E. *The Biographical Dictionary of Hispanic Americans.* 2nd ed. New York: Checkmark, 2001.

Statistical Handbook on U.S. Hispanics. Ed. Frank L. Schick and Rene Schick. Phoenix: Oryx, 1991.

(5) Native-American studies

Bibliography of Native North Americans on Disc. Santa Barbara: ABC-Clio, 1992–present.

Brumble, H. David. *American Indian Autobiography.* Berkeley: U California P, 1988.

Encyclopedia of American Indian Civil Rights. Ed. James S. Olson. Westport, CT: Greenwood, 1997.

Handbook of North American Indians. Ed. William C. Sturtevant. Washington, DC: Smithsonian Institution: 1978–2004.

Hoxie, Frederick E. *Native Americans: An Annotated Bibliography.* Pasadena, CA: Salem, 1991.

Klein, Barry T. *Reference Encyclopedia of the American Indian.* 6th ed. West Nyack, NY: Todd, 1993.

LePoer, Barbara A. *A Concise Dictionary of Indian Tribes of North America.* 2nd rev. ed. Algonac, MI: Reference Publications, 1991.

The Marshall Cavendish Illustrated History of the North American Indians. 6 vols. New York: Marshall Cavendish, 1991.

Murdock, George Peter. *Ethnographic Bibliography of North America.* 4th ed. 5 vols. New Haven: Human Relations Area Files, 1975. A supplement was published in 1990.

North American Indians. St. Paul: Quanta, 1991. CD-ROM.

Waldman, Carl. *Who Was Who in Native American History: Indians and Non-Indians from Early Contacts through 1900.* New York: Facts On File, 1990.

B2-g High technology

Computer Literature Index. Phoenix: Applied Computer Research, 1980–present.

Computers and Computing Information Resources Directory. Detroit: Gale, 1987–present.

Computer Sourcebook. New York: Random House, 1997–present.

Cortada, James W. *A Bibliographic Guide to the History of Computer Applications, 1950–1990*. Westport, CT: Greenwood, 1996.

Downing, Douglas. *Dictionary of Computer and Internet Terms*. 9th ed. Hauppauge, NY: Barron's, 2006.

Encyclopedia of Artificial Intelligence. 2nd ed. 2 vols. New York: Wiley, 1992.

Encyclopedia of Computer Science. Ed. Anthony Ralston. 4th ed. Hoboken, NJ: Wiley, 2003.

Encyclopedia of Microcomputers. New York: Dekker, 1988–2000.

Freedman, Alan. *The Computer Glossary: The Complete Illustrated Dictionary*. 9th ed. New York: American Management Association, 2001.

Gibilisco, Stan. *TAB Encyclopedia of Electronics for Technicians and Hobbyists*. New York: McGraw-Hill, 1997.

Handbook of Theoretical Computer Science. 2 vols. New York: Elsevier; Cambridge, MA: MIT Press, 1990.

Hordeski, Michael F. *The McGraw-Hill Illustrated Dictionary of Personal Microcomputers*. 4th ed. New York: McGraw-Hill, 1995.

INSPEC. Dublin, OH: OCLC. Available online through OCLC's FirstSearch. Corresponds to the print publications *Science Abstracts,* Series A, *Physics Abstracts,* and Series B, *Electrical and Electronics Abstracts;* and *Computer & Control Abstracts*. It also includes Section D of the INSPEC database (covering information technology), which has no print equivalent, and the complete *INSPEC Thesaurus*.

INSPEC Ondisc. Ann Arbor, MI: UMI, 1991–present. CD-ROM.

Microcomputer Abstracts. Medford, NJ: Learned Information, 1994–present.

Microcomputer Index. Santa Clara, CA: Microcomputer Information Services, 1980–1993. *Microcomputer Abstracts* continues the index.

Microsoft Press Computer Dictionary. 4th ed. Redmond, WA: Microsoft, 1999.

The Software Encyclopedia. New York: Bowker, 1985–present.

SuperTech Abstracts Plus. New York: Bowker Electronic, 1991–present. CD-ROM.

White, Ron. *How Computers Work*. 6th ed. Indianapolis: Que, 2002.

B2-h History

(1) World history

Barzun, Jacques. *The Modern Researcher*. 6th ed. Belmont, CA: Thomson Wadsworth, 2004.

Boorstin, Daniel J. *The Discoverers*. 2 vols. New York: Abrams, 1991.

The Cambridge Ancient History. 3rd ed. 14 vols. New York: Cambridge UP, 1970–2006.

Cook, Chris. *Dictionary of Historical Terms*. 2nd ed. New York: Gramercy Books, 1998.

———. *1000 Years of World History: A Dictionary of Historical Terms*. 2nd ed. New York: Gramercy, 1998.

Dictionary of Historic Documents. Ed. George C. Kohn. New York: Facts On File, 2003.

Dictionary of the Middle Ages. Ed. Joseph R. Strayer. 13 vols. New York: Scribner's, 1982–1989.

DISCovering World History. Detroit: Gale, 1997. CD-ROM.

Durant, Will. *The Story of Civilization.* New York: Simon & Schuster, 1939.

Encyclopedia of Asian History. 4 vols. New York: Scribner; London: Collier Macmillan, 1988.

Fritze, Ronald H. *Reference Sources in History: An Introductory Guide.* 2nd ed. Santa Barbara: ABC-Clio, 2004.

Great Historians of the Modern Age: An International Dictionary. Ed. Lusian Boia. New York: Greenwood, 1991.

Grove, Noel. *National Geographic Atlas of World History.* Washington, DC: National Geographic Society, 1997.

Hammond Concise Atlas of World History. Ed. Geoffrey Barraclough. 6th rev. ed. Union, NJ: Hammond, 2002.

Historical Abstracts: Bibliography of the World's Historical Literature. Part A, *Modern History Abstracts, 1775–1914;* Part B, *Twentieth-Century Abstracts, 1914–2000.* Santa Barbara: ABC-Clio, 1971–present.

Historical Abstracts on Disc. Santa Barbara: ABC-Clio, 1991–present.

The New Cambridge Modern History. 2nd ed. Cambridge, England: Cambridge UP, 1990.

Palmowski, Jan. *A Dictionary of Twentieth-Century World History.* 2nd ed. Oxford, England: Oxford UP, 2003.

Penn, James R. *Encyclopedia of Geographical Features in World History: Europe and the Americas.* Santa Barbara: ABC-Clio, 1997.

Ritter, Harry. *Dictionary of Concepts in History.* Westport, CT: Greenwood, 1986.

Steinberg, S. H. *Historical Tables: 58 BC–AD 1990.* 12th ed. London: Garland, 1991.

World History by the World's Historians. Boston: McGraw-Hill, 1998.

(2) American history

Album of American History. 6 vols. New York: Scribner's, 1981.

Album of American History. Supp. 1968–1982. New York: Scribner's, 1985.

America, History and Life. Santa Barbara: ABC-Clio, 1964–present. Also online and on CD-ROM from ABC-Clio. Article abstracts and citations of reviews and dissertations covering the United States and Canada.

The American Civil War. Minneapolis: Quanta, 1992. CD-ROM.

American Reformers: An H. W. Wilson Biographical Dictionary. Ed. Alden Whitman. New York: Wilson, 1985.

Ambrose, Stephen E. *American Heritage New History of World War II.* New York: Viking, 1997.

The Annals of America. 22 vols. Chicago: Encyclopaedia Britannica, 1976–1987.

Dictionary of American History. Ed. Stanley I. Kutler. 3rd ed. New York: Scribner's, 2003.

Documents of American History. Ed. Henry Steele Commager and Milton Cantor. 10th ed. 2 vols. Englewood Cliffs, NJ: Prentice-Hall, 1988.

Encyclopedia of North American History. New York: Marshall Cavendish, 1999.

Encyclopedia USA: The Encyclopedia of the United States of America Past & Present. Gulf Breeze, FL: Academic International, 2001.

Historical Atlas of the United States. Rev. ed. Washington, DC: National Geographic Society, 1993.

Historical Times Illustrated Encyclopedia of the Civil War. New York: HarperPerennial, 1991.

Hochman, Stanley. *The Penguin Dictionary of Contemporary American History, 1945 to the Present.* 3rd ed. New York: Penguin Reference, 1997.

Kane, Joseph Nathan. *Facts about the Presidents: A Compilation of Biographical and Historical Information.* 6th ed. New York: Wilson, 1993.

The New York Public Library American History Desk Reference. 2nd ed. New York: Hyperion, 2003.

U.S. History on CD-ROM. Parsippany, NJ: Bureau Development, 1990.

U.S. Presidents: A History of the Presidents of the United States of America. Minneapolis: Quanta, 1992–present.

USA Wars: Civil War. Minneapolis: Quanta, 1992. CD-ROM.

USA Wars: Desert Storm with Coalition Command. Carlsbad, CA: Compton's New Media, 1992. CD-ROM.

USA Wars. Korea. St. Paul: Quanta, 1992. CD-ROM.

USA Wars. Vietnam. St. Paul: Quanta, 1989. CD-ROM.

USA Wars. World War II. Carlsbad, CA: Compton's NewMedia, 1993. CD-ROM.

B2-i   Literature

(1) General

Abrams, M. H. *A Glossary of Literary Terms.* 8th ed. Boston: Thomson, Wadsworth, 2005.

Black Literature Criticism: Excerpts from Criticism of the Most Significant Works of Black Authors over the Past 200 Years. Ed. Jeffrey W. Draper. Detroit: Gale, 1999.

Blain, Virginia. *The Feminist Companion to Literature in English: Women Writers from the Middle Ages to the Present.* New Haven: Yale UP, 1990.

Bracken, James K. *Reference Works in British and American Literature.* 2nd ed. Englewood, CO: Libraries Unlimited, 1998.

Columbia Dictionary of Modern European Literature. Ed. Jean-Albert Bede. 2nd ed. New York: Columbia UP, 1980.

The Columbia Dictionary of Modern Literary and Cultural Criticism. Ed. Joseph Childers. New York: Columbia UP, 1995.

The Columbia Granger's Index to Poetry in Anthologies. 13th ed. New York: Columbia UP, 2007.

Contemporary Authors; a Bio-bibliographical Guide to Current Writers in Fiction, General Nonfiction, Poetry, Journalism, Drama, Motion Pictures, Television and Other Fields. Detroit: Gale, 1962–present.

Contemporary Authors on CD. Detroit: Gale.

Contemporary Dramatists. 5th ed. Detroit: St. James, 1973–present.

Contemporary Literary Criticism. Detroit: Gale, 1973–present.

Contemporary Novelists. New York: St. James, 1972–present.

Contemporary Poets. 7th ed. New York: St. James, 2001.

Dictionary of Literary Biography (DLB). Detroit: Gale, 1978–present.

Dictionary of Literary Biography Yearbook. Detroit: Gale, 1981–present.

Drama Criticism. Detroit: Gale, 1991–present.

Encyclopedia of World Literature in the 20th Century. Ed. Steven R. Serafin. 3rd ed. 4 vols. Detroit: St. James, 1999.

Essay and General Literature Index. New York: Wilson, 1900/1933–present. Also on CD-ROM (Norwood, MA: SilverPlatter Information; New York: Wilson).

European Writers. 14 vols. New York: Scribner's, 1983–1991.

Good Reading: A Guide for Serious Readers. 23rd ed. New York: Bowker, 1990.

Harmon, William. *A Handbook to Literature.* 10th ed. Upper Saddle River, NJ: Prentice-Hall, 2006.

Hispanic Writers: A Selection of Sketches from Contemporary Authors. Ed. Scot Peacock. 2nd ed. Detroit: Gale, 1999.

Kuntz, Joseph Marshall. *Poetry Explication: A Checklist of Interpretation Since 1925 of British and American Poems Past and Present.* 3rd ed. Boston: Hall, 1980.

Literature Criticism from 1400 to 1800. Detroit: Gale, 1984–present.

Magill's Literary Annual. Pasadena, CA: Salem, 1977–present.

Masterplots Complete CD-ROM. Pasadena, CA: Salem, 1997.

Masterplots II. Drama Series. 4 vols. Rev. ed. Pasadena, CA: Salem, 2004.

———. Poetry Series. Rev. ed. 8 vols. Pasadena, CA: Salem, 2002.

———. Short Story Series. 10 vols. Rev. ed. Pasadena, CA: Salem, 2004.

———. Women's Literature Series. 6 vols. Pasadena, CA: Salem, 1995.

———. World Fiction Series. 4 vols. Pasadena, CA: Salem, 1987.

MLA International Bibliography. New York: Wilson. CD-ROM.

MLA International Bibliography. New York: Modern Language Association of America. Online by subscription only or through a subscribing library.

Peacock, Scott. *Black Writers: A Selection of Sketches from Contemporary Authors.* 3rd ed. Detroit: Gale, 1999.

Poetry Criticism: Excerpts from Criticism of the Works of the Most Significant and Widely Studied Poets of World Literature. Detroit: Gale, 1991–present.

Research Guide to Biography and Criticism. 6 vols. Washington, DC: Research Pub., 1985–1991.

The Routledge Dictionary of Literary Terms. Ed. Peter Childs and Roger Fowler. Rev. and enlarged ed. New York: Routledge, 2005.

Short Story Criticism. Detroit: Gale, 1988–present.

Spanish American Women Writers: A Bio-bibliographical Source Book. New York: Greenwood, 1990.

Walker, Warren S. *Twentieth-Century Short Story Explication.* Hamden, CT: Shoe String, 1989–2004. A new series with checklists of books and journals used.

World Authors. New York: Wilson; Norwood, MA: SilverPlatter Information. CD-ROM.

World Authors, 1900–1950. 4 vols. New York: Wilson, 1996.
———. *1950–1970.* New York: Wilson, 1975.
———. *1970–1975.* New York: Wilson, 1980.
———. *1975–1980.* New York: Wilson, 1985.
———. *1980–1985.* New York: Wilson, 1991.
———. *1985–1990.* New York: Wilson, 1995.
———. *1990–1995.* New York: Wilson, 1999.
———. *1995–2000.* New York: Wilson, 2003.

(2) American literature

American Literary Scholarship. Durham, NC: Duke UP, 1965–present. Online at als.dukejournals.org (29 March 2007).
American Women Writers: A Critical Reference Guide from Colonial Times to the Present. Ed. Taryn Benbow-Pfalzgraf. 2nd ed. 4 vols. Detroit: St. James, 2000.
Bibliography of American Literature, 1588–1918. New York: Facts On File, 1991–present.
Blanck, Jacob. *Bibliography of American Literature.* 9 vols. New Haven: Yale UP, 1955–1991.
The Cambridge Handbook of American Literature. Ed. Jack Salzman. New York: Cambridge UP, 1986.
Columbia Literary History of the United States. Ed. Emory Elliot. New York: Columbia UP, 1988.
Concise Dictionary of American Literary Biography. Detroit: Gale, 1987–1999.
DiscLit: American Authors. Dublin, OH: OCLC, 1991. CD-ROM.
DiscLit: American Authors. Twayne's United States Authors Series and OCLC American Authors Catalog. Dublin, OH: Hall and OCLC, 1991. CD-ROM.
Gerhardstein, Virginia Brokaw. *Dickinson's American Historical Fiction.* 5th ed. Metuchen, NJ: Scarecrow, 1986.
Kellman, Steven G. *The Modern American Novel: An Annotated Bibliography.* Pasadena, CA: Salem, 1991.
Leitch, Vincent B. *American Literary Criticism from the Thirties to the Eighties.* New York: Columbia UP, 1988.
Literary History of the United States. 4th ed., rev. New York: Macmillan, 1974.
Ludwig, Richard M. *Annals of American Literature, 1602–1983.* New York: Oxford UP, 1986.
Notable Women in the American Theatre: A Biographical Dictionary. Ed. Alice M. Robinson. New York: Greenwood, 1989.
The Oxford Companion to African American Literature. Ed. William L. Andrews. Oxford, England: Oxford UP, 1997.
Reference Guide to American Literature. Ed. Thomas Riggs. 4th ed. Detroit: St. James, 2000.
Winship, Michael. *Bibliography of American Literature: A Selective Index.* Golden, CO: North American, 1995.

(3) British literature

British Novelists, 1890–1929: Modernists. Ed. Thomas F. Staley. Detroit: Gale, 1985.

British Novelists, 1890–1929: Traditionalists. Ed. Thomas F. Staley. Detroit: Gale, 1985.

British Novelists, 1930–1959. Ed. Bernard Oldsey. 2 vols. Detroit: Gale, 1983.

British Novelists Since 1960. Ed. Jay L. Halio. 2 vols. Detroit: Gale, 1983.

British Novelists Since 1900. Ed. Jack I. Biles. New York: AMS, 1987.

British Writers. 7 vols. New York: Scribner's, 1979–1984.

The Cambridge Guide to English Literature. New York: Cambridge UP, 1983.

The Cambridge Guide to Literature in English. Ed. Dominic Head. 3rd ed. New York: Cambridge UP, 2006.

The Cambridge Guide to Theatre. Ed. Martin Banham. New ed. New York: Cambridge UP, 1995.

The Cambridge History of English Literature. 15 vols. Cambridge, England: Cambridge UP, 1918–1930.

A Chronology of English Literature. Ed. Michael Cox. 2 vols. Oxford, England: Oxford UP, 2002.

Concise Dictionary of British Literary Biography. 8 vols. Detroit: Gale, 1991–1992. A series of monographs about authors.

Critical Essays on British Literature. New York: Hall. A series of books devoted to analysis of works of various British authors.

DiscLit: British Authors. Twayne's English Authors Series and OCLC British Authors Catalog. Dublin, OH: Hall and OCLC, 1992. CD-ROM.

English Novel Explication. Supp. Hamden, CT: Shoe String, 1976–1997. A new supplement is in progress.

English Novel Explication: Criticisms to 1972. London: Bingley, 1973.

Kunitz, Stanley. *European Authors, 1000–1900: A Biographical Dictionary of European Literature.* New York: Wilson, 1967.

Magill Book Reviews. Pasadena, CA: Salem, 1986/1987–present. Also on CD-ROM.

Marcuse, Michael J. *A Reference Guide for English Studies.* Berkeley: U California P, 1990.

The New Cambridge Bibliography of English Literature. Ed. Joanne Shattock. 3rd ed. 4 vols. Cambridge, England: Cambridge UP, 1999–present.

The New Moulton's Library of Literary Criticism. Ed. Harold Bloom. 11 vols. New York: Chelsea House, 1985–1990.

The Oxford History of English Literature. Oxford, England: Clarendon, 1945–present.

B2-j   Music

Anderson, James. *The Harper Dictionary of Opera and Operetta.* New York: Harper & Row, 1990.

Annals of the Metropolitan Opera: The Complete Chronicle of Performances and Artists: Chronology 1883–1985. 2 vols. New York: Metropolitan Opera Guild; Boston: Hall, 1989.

Baines, Anthony. *The Oxford Companion to Musical Instruments*. New York: Oxford UP, 1992.

Bordman, Gerald Martin. *American Musical Theatre: A Chronicle*. 3rd ed. New York: Oxford UP, 2001.

Cohen, Aaron I. *International Encyclopedia of Women Composers*. 2nd ed., rev. and enlarged. 2 vols. New York: Books & Music USA, 1987.

Cohen-Stratyner, Barbara Naomi. *Popular Music, 1900–1919: An Annotated Guide to American Popular Songs, Including Introductory Essay, Lyricists and Composers Index, Important Performances Index, Chronological Index, and List of Publishers*. Detroit: Gale, 1988.

Contemporary Musicians. Detroit: Gale, 1989–present.

Duckles, Vincent H. *Music Reference and Research Materials: An Annotated Bibliography*. 5th ed. New York: Schirmer, 1997.

Ewen, David. *Composers Since 1900; a Biographical and Critical Guide*. New York: Wilson, 1969.

———. *Composers Since 1900*. First supp., *A Biographical and Critical Guide*. New York: Wilson, 1981.

———. *Great Composers, 1300–1900; a Biographical and Critical Guide*. New York: Wilson, 1966.

Gammond, Peter. *The Oxford Companion to Popular Music*. New York: Oxford UP, 1991.

The Harmony Illustrated Encyclopedia of Country Music. 3rd rev. ed. New York: Crown, 1994.

The Harmony Illustrated Encyclopedia of Rock. 7th ed. New York: Harmony, 1992.

Heintze, James R. *Early American Music: A Research and Information Guide*. New York: Garland, 1990.

International Who's Who in Music and Musical Gazetteer. New York: Current Literature, 1918–present.

Kuhn, Laura D. *Music Since 1900*. 6th ed. New York: Schirmer, 2001.

LePage, Jane Weiner. *Women Composers, Conductors, and Musicians of the Twentieth Century: Selected Biographies*. 3 vols. Metuchen, NJ: Scarecrow, 1980– 1988.

Musical America. International Directory of the Performing Arts. Great Barrington, MA: ABC Leisure Magazines, 1974–2005.

The Music Index. Warren, MI: Harmonie Park, 1949–present. Available online through www.harmonieparkpress.com/MusicIndex.asp (29 March 2007).

The New Grove Dictionary of American Music. Ed. H. Wiley Hitchcock. 4 vols. New York: Grove's Dictionaries, 1986.

The New Grove Dictionary of Jazz. 2nd ed. 2 vols. London: Macmillan; New York: Grove's Dictionaries, 2001.

New Oxford History of Music. 10 vols. New York: Oxford UP, 1954–1990.

The Oxford Companion to Music. Ed. Alison Latham. New York: Oxford UP, 2002.

The Oxford History of Music. 2nd ed. rev. 8 vols. New York: Cooper Square, 1973.

The Oxford History of Opera. Ed. Roger Parker. New York: Oxford UP, 1996.

Pollack, Bruce. *Popular Music: An Annotated Guide to American Popular Songs, Including Introductory Essay, Lyricists and Composers Index, Important Performances Index, Chronological Index, Awards Index, and List of Publishers.* Detroit: Gale, 1986–present.

———. *Popular Music, 1980–1984.* Detroit: Gale, 1986.

———. *Popular Music, 1980–1989: An Annotated Guide to American Popular Songs, Including Introductory Essay, Lyricists and Composers Index, Important Performances Index, Chronological Index, Awards Index, and List of Publishers.* Detroit: Gale, 1995.

Sadie, Stanley. *The New Grove Dictionary of Music and Musicians.* 2nd ed. New York: Grove, 2001.

———. *The New Grove Dictionary of Musical Instruments.* 3 vols. London: Macmillan; New York: Grove's Dictionaries, 1984.

———. *The New Grove Dictionary of Opera.* 4 vols. New York: Grove's Dictionaries, 1992.

Slonimsky, Nicolas. *Baker's Biographical Dictionary of Musicians.* Centennial ed. 6 vols. New York: Schirmer, 2001.

———. *Baker's Biographical Dictionary of Twentieth-Century Classical Musicians.* New York: Schirmer, 1997.

Stedman, Preston. *The Symphony: A Research and Information Guide.* New York: Garland, 1990.

This Business of Music: The Definitive Guide to the Music Industry. 10th ed. New York: Watson-Guptill, 2007.

Thomsett, Michael C. *Musical Terms, Symbols, and Theory: An Illustrated Dictionary.* Jefferson, NC: McFarland, 1989.

Zaimont, Judith Lang. *The Musical Woman: An International Perspective.* New York: Greenwood, 1991.

B2-k   Mythology, classics, and folklore

Ancient Writers: Greece and Rome. Ed. T. James Luce. 2 vols. New York: Scribner's, 1982.

Bell, Robert E. *Women of Classical Mythology: A Biographical Dictionary.* New York: Oxford UP, 1993.

Brumble, H. David. *Classical Myths and Legends in the Middle Ages and Renaissance: A Dictionary of Allegorical Meanings.* Westport, CT: Greenwood, 1998.

Bulfinch, Thomas. *Bulfinch's Mythology.* New York: Meridian, 1995.

Civilization of the Ancient Mediterranean: Greece and Rome. 3 vols. New York: Scribner's, 1988.

Classical and Medieval Literature Criticism. Detroit: Gale, 1988–present.

Folklore: An Encyclopedia of Beliefs, Customs, Tales, Music, and Art. 2 vols. Santa Barbara, CA: ABC-Clio, 1997.

Frazer, James George, Sir. *The Golden Bough: A Study in Magic and Religion.* New York: Oxford UP, 1998.

Grant, Michael. *Atlas of Classical History.* 5th ed. New York: Oxford UP, 1994.

Hamilton, Edith. *Mythology.* Boston: Little, Brown, 1942.

Howatson, M. C. *The Oxford Companion to Classical Literature.* 2nd ed. New York: Oxford UP, 1989.

Lenardon, Robert J. *A Companion to Classical Mythology.* White Plains, NY: Longman, 1997.

Man, Myth & Magic: The Illustrated Encyclopedia of Mythology, Religion, and the Unknown. Ed. Richard Cavendish. New ed. 21 vols. New York: Marshall Cavendish, 1997.

Mythical and Fabulous Creatures: A Source Book and Research Guide. Ed. Malcolm South. New York: Greenwood, 1987.

New Larousse Encyclopedia of Mythology. New ed. New York: Crescent, 1989.

Room, Adrian. *Brewer's Dictionary of Phrase and Fable.* 16th ed. New York: Harper & Row, 1999.

Rosenberg, Donna. *Folklore, Myths, and Legends: A World Perspective.* Lincolnwood, IL: NTC, 1997.

Walker, Barbara G. *The Woman's Dictionary of Symbols and Sacred Objects.* New ed. London: Pandora, 1995.

B2-l   Philosophy

Brehier, Emile. *The History of Philosophy.* Trans. Joseph Thomas. 7 vols. Chicago: U Chicago P, 1963–1969.

The Concise Encyclopedia of Western Philosophy and Philosophers. New ed., completely rev. New York: Routledge, 1991.

Copleston, Frederick Charles. *A History of Philosophy.* 9 vols. Westminster, MD: Newman Bookshop, 1946–1975.

Directory of American Philosophers. Bowling Green, OH: Philosophy Documentation Center, Bowling Green State University, 1963–present.

The Encyclopedia of Eastern Philosophy and Religion: Buddhism, Hinduism, Taoism, Zen. Boston: Shambhala, 1989.

The Encyclopedia of Ethics. Ed. Lawrence Becker and Charlotte Becker. 2nd ed. New York: Routledge, 2001.

The Encyclopedia of Philosophy. Ed. Paul Edwards. 8 vols. New York: Macmillan, 1967.

Grimes, John A. *A Concise Dictionary of Indian Philosophy: Sanskrit Terms Defined in English.* New and rev. ed. Albany, NY: State U of New York P, 1996.

The Handbook of Western Philosophy. Ed. G. H. R. Parkinson. New York: Macmillan, 1988.

Handbook of World Philosophy: Contemporary Developments Since 1945. Ed. John R. Burr. Westport, CT: Greenwood, 1980.

International Directory of Philosophy and Philosophers. Bowling Green, OH: Philosophy Documentation Center, Bowling Green University, 1965–present.

Kersey, Ethel M. *Women Philosophers: A Bio-critical Source Book.* New York: Greenwood, 1989.

List, Charles J. *Library Research Guide to Philosophy.* Ann Arbor, MI: Pierian, 1990.

Mautner, Thomas. *The Penguin Dictionary of Philosophy.* Rev. ed. London: Penguin, 1997.

The Oxford Companion to the Mind. Ed. Richard L. Gregory. New York: Oxford UP, 2004.

The Philosopher's Index. Bowling Green, OH: Philosophy Documentation Center, Bowling Green University, 1967–present.

Routledge Encyclopedia of Philosophy. Ed. Richard Craig. 10 vols. New York: Routledge, 1998.

Sparkes, A. W. *Talking Philosophy: A Wordbook.* New York: Routledge, 1991.

Stanford Encyclopedia of Philosophy. Palo Alto, CA: Center for the Study of Language and Information, 1996. Online at plato.stanford.edu (7 February 2007).

Tice, Terrence N. *Research Guide to Philosophy.* Chicago: American Library Association, 1983.

World Philosophy: Essay-Reviews of 225 Major Works. Ed. Frank N. Magill. 5 vols. Englewood Cliffs, NJ: Salem, 1982.

B2-m Psychology

The Cambridge Encyclopedia of Human Growth and Development. New York: Cambridge UP, 1998.

Campbell, Robert Jean. *Psychiatric Dictionary.* 8th ed. New York: Oxford UP, 2004.

Child Development Abstracts and Bibliography. Washington, DC: Committee on Child Development, National Research Council, 1928–2001.

Dictionary of Biological Psychology. Ed. Philip Winn. New York: Routledge, 2001. Pacific Grove, CA: Brooks/Cole, 1995.

The Encyclopedia of Human Development and Education: Theory, Research, and Studies. Ed. R. Murray Thomas. New York: Pergamon, 1990.

International Encyclopedia of Psychiatry, Psychology, Psychoanalysis, & Neurology. Ed. Benjamin B. Wolman. New York: Aesculapius, 1983–present.

The Mental Measurements Yearbook. Lincoln, NE: Buros Institute of Mental Measurements, University of Nebraska, 1955–present. Also on CD-ROM.

Psychological Abstracts. Washington, DC: American Psychological Association, 1927–present.

PsycINFO. Washington, DC: American Psychological Association. Online by subscription only or through a subscribing library. Database of psychological abstracts, 1887–present.

Reid, William H. *The Treatment of Psychiatric Disorders.* 3rd ed. Bristol, PA: Brunner/Mazel, 1997.

Roeckelein, Jon E. *Dictionary of Theories, Laws, and Concepts in Psychology.* Westport, CT: Greenwood, 1998.

Stuart-Hamilton, Ian. *Dictionary of Developmental Psychology.* Rev. ed. Bristol, PA: J. Kingsley, 1996.

Sutherland, N. S. *The International Dictionary of Psychology.* 2nd ed. New York: Crossroad, 1996.

———. *The Macmillan Dictionary of Psychology.* 2nd ed. Houndmills, Basingstoke, England: Macmillan, 1995.

B2-n   Religion

The Anchor Bible. Garden City, NY: Doubleday, 1964–2006.

The Anchor Bible Dictionary. Ed. David N. Freedman. 6 vols. New York: Doubleday, 1992.

The Cambridge History of Islam. Ed. P. M. Holt. 2 vols. Cambridge, England: Cambridge UP, 1970.

The Cambridge History of Judaism. Ed. W. D. Davies and Louis Finkelstein. New York: Cambridge UP, 2006.

The Cambridge History of the Bible. 3 vols. Cambridge, England: Cambridge UP, 1963–1970.

Encyclopaedia Judaica. Ed. Fred Skolnik. 2nd ed. 22 vols. Jerusalem: Encyclopaedia Judaica; Detroit: Keter, 2007.

Encyclopaedia Judaica. Decennial Book, 1983–1992: Events of 1982–1992. Jerusalem: Encyclopaedia Judaica, 1994.

Encyclopaedia Judaica. Yearbook. Jerusalem: Encyclopaedia Judaica, 1973–present.

The Encyclopaedia of Islam. New ed. 12 vols. Leiden, The Netherlands: Brill; London: Luzac, 1960–2005.

The Encyclopedia of Religion. Ed. Lindsay Jones. 15 vols. Detroit: Macmillan Ref. USA, 2005.

An Encyclopedia of Religions in the United States: One Hundred Religious Groups Speak for Themselves. Ed. William B. Williams. New York: Crossroad, 1992.

Illustrated Dictionary & Concordance of the Bible. Ed. Geoffrey Wigoder. New York: Macmillan, 1986.

The International Standard Bible Encyclopedia. 4 vols. Grand Rapids: Eerdmans, 1979–1988.

MacGregor, Geddes. *Dictionary of Religion and Philosophy.* New York: Paragon House, 1989.

Mead, Frank Spencer. *Handbook of Denominations in the United States.* New 12th ed. Nashville: Abingdon, 2005.

Melton, J. Gordon. *The Encyclopedia of American Religions.* 6th ed. Detroit: Gale, 1999.

____. *Religious Leaders of America: A Biographical Guide to Founders and Leaders of Religious Bodies, Churches, and Spiritual Groups in North America.* Detroit: Gale, 1991–present.

Mercer Dictionary of the Bible. Ed. Watson E. Mills. Macon, GA: Mercer UP, 1990.

New Catholic Encyclopedia. 2nd ed. Detroit: Thomson/Gale; Washington DC: Catholic University of America, 2003.

The Oxford Dictionary of the Christian Church. Ed. F. L. Cross. Rev. ed. New York: Oxford UP, 2005.

The Oxford Dictionary of the Jewish Religion. New York: Oxford UP, 1997.

Peters, F. E. *Judaism, Christianity, and Islam: The Classical Texts and Their Interpretation.* Princeton, NJ: Princeton UP, 1990.

Prebish, Charles S. *Historical Dictionary of Buddhism.* Metuchen, NJ: Scarecrow, 1993.

Religion Index One: Periodicals: A Subject and Author Index to Periodical Literature. Rev. and expanded ed. of *The Index to Religious Periodical Literature.* Chicago: American Theological Library Association, 1985–present. Also on CD-ROM.

Sullivan, Bruce M. *Historical Dictionary of Hinduism.* Lanham, MD: Scarecrow, 1997.

Who's Who in Religion. Chicago: Marquis, 1975/1976–1994.

Wilson, Epiphanius. *Sacred Books of the East: With Critical and Biographical Sketches.* Rev. ed. New York: Wiley, 1945.

B2-o   Science

American Men & Women of Science. 19th ed. New Providence, NJ: Bowker, 1989–present. Also on CD-ROM (SciTech Reference Plus).

Annual Review of Information Science and Technology. Medford, NJ: Learned Information, 1966–present.

Asimov, Isaac. *Asimov's Chronology of Science and Discovery.* New York: HarperCollins, 1994.

Biological & Agricultural Index. New York: Wilson, 1964/1965–present. Also on CD-ROM (Norwood, MA: SilverPlatter; New York: Wilson, 1983) and online at www.hwwilson.com/Databases/bioag.cfm (7 February 2007).

The Cambridge Dictionary of Scientists. 2nd ed. New York: Cambridge UP, 2002.

DePree, Christopher. *Van Nostrand's Concise Encyclopedia of Science.* 2 vols. Hoboken, NJ: Wiley, 2003.

Dictionary of Scientific Biography. 18 vols. New York: Scribner's, 1980–1990.

Encyclopedia of Physical Science and Technology. 3rd ed. 18 vols. San Diego: Academic, 2002.

General Science Index. New York: Wilson, 1978–present. Also on CD-ROM (Norwood, MA: SilverPlatter Information).

Grzimek, Bernhard. *Grzimek's Animal Life Encyclopedia.* 2nd ed. 17 vols. Detroit: Gale, 2003.

Grzimek's Encyclopedia of Mammals. 5 vols. New York: McGraw-Hill, 1990.

Herzenberg, Caroline L. *Women Scientists from Antiquity to the Present: An Index: An International Reference Listing and Biographical Directory of Some Notable Women Scientists from Ancient to Modern Times.* West Cornwall, CT: Locust Hill, 1986.

Lincoln, Roger J. *The Cambridge Illustrated Dictionary of Natural History.* New York: Cambridge UP, 1987.

Magill's Survey of Science. Applied Science Series. 7 vols. Pasadena, CA: Salem, 1993–1998.

Magill's Survey of Science. Earth Science Series. Ed. James A. Woodhead. Pasadena, CA: Salem, 2001.

Magill's Survey of Science. Physical Science Series. Ed. Frank N. Magill. 7 vols. Pasadena, CA: Salem, 1992.

The Marshall Cavendish Ilustrated Encyclopedia of Plants and Earth Sciences. Ed. David M. Moore. 10 vols. New York: Marshall Cavendish, 1988.

McGraw-Hill Encyclopedia of Science & Technology. 9th ed. 20 vols. New York: McGraw-Hill, 2002.

Parkinson, Claire L. *Breakthroughs: A Chronology of Great Achievements in Science and Mathematics, 1200–1930.* Boston: Hall, 1985.

Science Citation Index. Philadelphia: Institute for Scientific Information, 1961–present. Also on CD-ROM.

The Weather Almanac: A Reference Guide to Weather, Climate, and Related Issues in the United States and Its Key Cities. Ed. Richard Wood. 11th ed. Detroit: Gale, 2003.

B2-p   Social sciences

Annual Review of Sociology. Palo Alto, CA: Annual Reviews, 1975–present.

Barker, Robert L. *The Social Work Dictionary.* 5th ed. Washington, DC: NASW Press, 2003.

Encyclopedia of Sociology. 2nd ed. 5 vols. New York: Macmillan, 2000.

International Handbook of Sociology. Ed. Stella R. Quah. Thousand Oaks, CA: Sage, 2000.

A London Bibliography of the Social Sciences. 47 vols. London: Mansell, 1929–1989.

PAIS/EBSCO CD-ROM. Peabody, MA: EBSCO.

PAIS International in Print. New York: Public Affairs Information Service, 1991–present. Formerly (1986–1990), *PAIS Bulletin.*

The Social Science Encyclopedia. 3rd ed. New York: Routledge, 2004.

The Social Sciences: A Cross-Disciplinary Guide to Selected Sources. Ed. Nancy L. Herron. 3rd ed. Englewood, CO: Libraries Unlimited, 2002.

Social Sciences Index. New York: Wilson, 1974–present.

Social SciSearch. Philadelphia: Institute for Scientific Information, 1972–present. Computer file.

The Social Work Reference Library. Washington, DC: National Association of Social Workers, 1995–present. Contains the full text of the most recent editions of *Encyclopedia of Social Work; Social Work Dictionary;* and *Social Work Almanac.*

Sociological Abstracts. San Diego: Cambridge Scientific Abstracts, 1953–present. Also on CD-ROM; information online at www.silverplatter.com/catalog/soci .htm (7 February 2007).

B2-q   Women's studies

Handbook of American Women's History. Ed. Angela M. Howard and Frances M. Kavenik. 2nd ed. Thousand Oaks, CA: Sage, 2000.

Humm, Maggie. *The Dictionary of Feminist Theory.* 2nd ed. Columbus, OH: Ohio State UP, 1995.

Jackson-Laufer, Guida M. *Women Who Ruled.* Santa Barbara: ABC-Clio, 1990.

Notable American Women: A Biographical Dictionary Completing the Twentieth Century. Ed. Susan Ware. Cambridge, MA: Belknap, 2004.

Notable Black American Women. Ed. Jessie Carney Smith. 3 vols. Detroit: Gale, 1992–2003.

Palgrave Macmillan Dictionary of Women's Biography. Ed. Jennifer S. Uglow. 4th ed. New York: Palgrave Macmillan, 2005.

Statistical Record of Women Worldwide. Ed. Linda Schmittroth. 2nd ed. New York: Gale, 1995.

Watson, G. Llewellyn. *Feminism and Women's Issues: An Annotated Bibliography and Research Guide.* 2 vols. New York: Garland, 1990.

Women's Resources International. Baltimore: National Information Services, 1996–present. Online at www.nisc.com (7 February 2007).

Women's Studies Encyclopedia. Ed. Helen Tierney. Rev. and expanded ed. 3 vols. Westport, CT: Greenwood, 1999.

Credits

Text Credits

Chapter 3

Figure 3-1, page 22: Screen capture of the homepage of the Georgia State University Pullen Library. Reprinted by permission.

Figure 3-2, page 23: Screen capture of a library database search for "Winkler, Rhetoric Made Plain." Reprinted by permission of the Georgia State University.

Figure 3-3, page 26: Reproduced with permission from copyright 2007 on the Internet Public Library Consortium (http://www.ipl.org). All rights reserved.

Chapter 5

Figure 5-1, page 54: Excerpt from *Readers' Guide to Periodical Literature,* reprinted by permission of the H. W. Wilson Company. © 2006. Material reproduced with permission of the publisher.

Figure 5-2, page 55: List of documents found for: New York Times; Late Edition (East coast); New York, NY, April 12, 2007. Board of Regents of the University Systems of Georgia.

Figure 5-3, page 56: Image produced by ProQuest-CSA LLC. © 2007, ProQuest-CSA LLC; all rights reserved. Inquiries may be made to: ProQuest-CSA LLC, 789 E. Eisenhower Parkway. P.O. Box 1346, Ann Arbor, MI 48106-1346 USA. Telephone (800) 521-0600; (734) 761-4700; E-mail: info@proquest.com; Web page: www.il.proquest.com.

Figure 5-4, page 59: Sample bibliography card. Social Sciences Index, April 1991–March 1992. Reproduced by permission.

Figure 5-5, page 66: Sample note card containing a summary in Book Review Index, January–April 1992 by Gale Group. Copyright © 1992 Gale Group. Reprinted by permission of Thomson Gale.

Figure 5-7, page 68: Sample note card containing a quotation, Psychological Abstract, March 1991. Reproduced by permission.

Figure 5-8, page 68: Sample note card containing a paraphrase and quotations, Social Sciences Index, April 1991–March 1992. Reproduced by permission.

Chapter 7

Page 112:   Table POP9.C, Exposure to environmental tobacco smoke, 2003. U.S. Environmental Protection Agency, Indoor Environmental Management of Asthma and Children's Exposure to Environmental Tobacco Smoke.

Page 114:   Graph showing share of homebuyers who are first-time homebuyers. Accountability Report, U.S. Department of Housing and Urban Development.

Chapter 9

Figure 9-6, page 180:   Line Graph Health 7: Death rates among infants by detailed race and Hispanic origin, 1983–2003. Childstats.gov. Centers for Disease Control and Prevention, National Center for Health Statistics.

Figure 9-7, page 181:   American Museum of American History.

Figure 9-9, page 182:   "Average educational debt for indebted medical school graduates 1994–2003." AAMC Graduate Questionnaire. Copyright © 2007 American Medical Student Association. Reproduced by permission.

Figure 9-10, page 182:   John Sibbick/National Geographic Image Collection.

Chapter 10

Figure 10-5, page 245:   Adapted from *Understanding Human Communication,* Seventh Edition, by Ronald B. Adler and George Rodman, © 2002, New York: Oxford University Press.

Figure 10-6, page 216:   Courtesy of the Central Intelligence Agency (CIA).

Figure 10-7, page 216:   "The Number of Patients Served by Hospice Keeps Rising." Statistics provided by The National Hospice and Palliative Care Organization, November, 2006. Reproduced by permission.

Chapter 11

Figure 11-4, page 234:   "Medicare Prescription Drug Plans," www.medicare.gov.

Photo Credits

Chapter 1 tab: Copyright © North Wind/North Wind Picture Archives—All rights reserved.

Chapter 2 tab: Copyright © North Wind/North Wind Picture Archives—All rights reserved.

Chapter 3 tab: © Associated Press.

Chapter 4 tab: © dpa/Landov.

Index

Page numbers in italics refer to figures and tables.

Abbreviations
  in acronyms, 291
  for books of the Bible, 285–286
  for *compiler*, 282
  for days, 287
  definition of, for first-time use,
    190, 291
  for *dissertation*, 282
  for *edition* and *revised edition*, 282
  for *editor/s*, 282
  for *figure*, 282
  list of, 281–285
  for months, 287
  for *page/s*, 187, 192, 284
  for publishers' names, 288–290
  for *quoted in*, 151, 284
  for Shakespeare's plays, 287
  spacing of, 280
  for states and U.S. territories, 288
  for *translator*, 285
  of U.S. Government Printing
    Office, 171
  for *volume*, 143, 285
Abstracts
  APA style, 208–209, 211
  CMS style and, 232
  criteria and conventions for, 208–209
  length of, 208
  MLA style and, 177
  of periodical articles, 53
  in "References" (APA style), 201
  of research paper, 115, 177
  samples of, 115, 209
  in "Works Cited" (MLA style), 160
Acronyms, 190, 291. *See also*
  Abbreviations

Active voice of verbs, 126–127
Addresses and lectures, in "Works
  Cited" (MLA style), 158, 162–163
African-American studies, 313
Afterwords, in "Works Cited" (MLA
  style), 153
Aircraft, italics or underlining for titles
  of, 275
Alphabetization
  of corporate authors, 145
  initial article in title and, 145, 191
  of multiple authors, 144
  of "References" (APA style), 191,
    192, 197
  of "Works Cited" (MLA style),
    144–145
AltaVista search engine, 41, 306
Amazon.com, 21, 293
American National Biography
  (database), 24
American Psychological Association
  (APA) style
  abstracts, 208–209, 211
  appearance of finished paper, 210–211
  avoiding clutter in text with, 193
  compared with MLA style, 187, 214
  content notes, 212
  electronic submission of paper, 218
  empirical paper, 218
  endnotes, 212
  finished form of APA paper, 209–217
  graphics, 212–214, 215–217
  headings in research paper, 210
  italics, 188, 195, 198, 199,
    201, 212
  long quotations, 95–97

American Psychological Association
(APA) style (*continued*)
  numbers, 214
  parenthetical documentation
    (author-date), 187–193
  peer review checklist and, 218
  publishers' names, 290
  "References" format, 193–208
  running head, 210–211
  sample of APA paper, 251–264
  tense style of, 214
  title page, 210–211, *211*
  theoretical paper, 209
  See also "References" (APA style)
Ampersand for multiple authors, 188,
  195, 198
Angle brackets for URL, 159
Annuals, in "Works Cited" (MLA
  style), 151
Anonymous works
  footnotes/endnotes for, 227
  parenthetical documentation (APA
    style) for, 191
  parenthetical documentation (MLA
    style) for, 142
  in "Works Cited" (MLA style),
    150, 155
Anthologies. *See* Collections
  (anthologies, casebooks and readers)
APA. *See* American Psychological
  Association (APA) style
Appendix, graphics in, 212, 214, 233
Arabic numerals
  APA style of, 214
  CMS style of, 234–235
  for edition in "Works Cited" (MLA
    style), 143
  MLA style of, 183
  in parenthetical documentation, 143
  for series number, 147
  words versus numerals for, 234–235
Art Abstracts, 56
Articles (*a, an the*). *See* Initial articles
Art Index, 56

Artworks
  italics or underlining for titles of, 275
  reference works on, 306–308
  in "Works Cited" (MLA style), 163, 167
Asian-American studies, 313
Ask (search engine), 42
Atlases and gazetteers, 53, 299
Audio recordings
  in "References" (APA style), 206
  reference works on, 305–306
  in "Works Cited" (MLA style), 165–166
Audiovisual room in library, 25
Author-date style of documentation. *See*
  American Psychological Association
  (APA style)
Authors
  alphabetization of, in "Works Cited"
    (MLA style), 144–145
  of books in "References" (APA style),
    188–191
  of books in "Works Cited" (MLA
    style), 146–153
  of electronic sources in "Works
    Cited" (MLA style), 158
  in footnotes/endnotes, 225, 227
  parenthetical documentation (APA
    style) for, 187–192
  parenthetical documentation (MLA
    style) for, 139–144
  of periodical articles in "References"
    (APA style), 198
  of periodical articles in "Works
    Cited" (MLA style), 153, 155
  See also Anonymous works;
    Corporate authors; Multiple authors
Author-work style of documentation.
  See Modern Language Association
  (MLA) style

Ballets
  italics or underlining for titles of, 274
  reference works on, 310
  in "Works Cited" (MLA style), 164,
    166–167

Bell, Alexander Graham, 49
Bible
    abbreviations for books of, 285–286
    references to, not italicized or
        underlined, 276
    in "Works Cited" (MLA style), 167
    See also Religion
Bibliographies
    for avoiding plagiarism, 70
    bibliography cards, 58–60
    of books, 293–294
    definition of, 58
    as not required by CMS, 221, 235
    working bibliography, 58–60
    See also "References" (APA style);
        "Works Cited" (MLA style)
Biographical sources
    for deceased persons, 299–301
    indexes to, 301–302
    for living persons, 300–301
    online reference works, 24
    reference works on, 293–294
    spelling of names in biographical
        sources, 279
Biography, in Dewey Decimal System, 29
Blogs, 40–41
Book industry journals, 294
Book Review Digest, 53, 63
Book review indexes, 294
Books
    bibliographic references to, 4
    bibliographies of, 293–294
    classification of, in library, 27–31
    in CMS footnote/endnote references,
        224–227
    footnotes/endnotes for, 224–227
    incunabula, 294
    in-print books, 293
    italics or underlining for titles of,
        274
    microform indexes for, 24
    online books, 159, *159*, 161, 203
    online full-text databases of, 23–24
    online purchase of, 21

parenthetical documentation (APA
    style), 188–193
parenthetical documentation (MLA
    style), 139–145
parts of, as not italicized, 276
publication information, 148–149
quotation marks for subdivisions
    in, 275
rare books, 23
in "References" (APA style),
    193–197
reference works on, 151, 293–294
reserve books, 25
sample references to in "Works
    Cited" (MLA style), 149–153
skimming of, 60–61
in "Works Cited" (MLA style),
    145–153
Books in Print, 21
Brackets
    for anonymous and pseudonymous
        authors, 150
    in quotations, 94
    for *sic*, 99
    for translated title in "Works Cited"
        (MLA style), 153
    for translated title in "References"
        (APA style), 196
Brief direct quotations, 94–95
Brochures, in "Works Cited" (MLA
    style), 169
Bulletin boards (Usenet), 38, 42
Business reference works, 308–310

Capitalization
    excessive capitalization, 92
    of *figure* and *table*, 212, 213, 276
    of foreign-language book titles,
        152
    of titles of illustrations, 213
    of titles of works, 152
    of words *volume*, *book*, *part*, *act*
        and *chapter* in parenthetical
        documentation, 143

Card catalogs, 21. *See also* Classification systems; Online catalogs; OPAC (online public-access catalog)
Carrels in library, 27
Carver, George Washington, 19
Casebooks. *See* Collections (anthologies, casebooks and readers)
catalog.loc.gov (Library of Congress Online Catalog), 23
CD-ROMs
  indexes on, 53
  in "References" (APA style), 201
  reference works on, 13, 14, 51, 52
  topic selection and, 13
  in "Works Cited" (MLA style), 160
CD sound recordings
  in "References" (APA style), 206
  in "Works Cited" (MLA style), 165–166
Census statistics, 110
Chapters of books
  parenthetical documentation for, 143
  in "Works Cited" (MLA style), 150
Charts, in "Work Cited" (MLA style), 173–174. *See also* Graphics
Chicago Manual of Style (CMS)
  abbreviations for U.S. states and territories, 288
  abstract, 232
  bibliography not required by, 235
  books in footnote references, 224–227
  content notes, 232–233
  electronic sources, 230–231
  electronic submission of paper, 236
  finished form of CMS paper, 231–235
  footnotes and endnotes, 221–229
  foreign names of people, 278
  graphics, 233, 234
  italics, 277
  long quotations, 95–97
  numbers, 235, 271–273
  pagination and text format, 232
  peer review checklist and, 235
  periodicals in footnote references, 227–229
  publishers' names, 288–290
  sample of CMS paper, 265–269
  subsequent references in footnotes and endnotes, 229–230
  tense style of, 108–109
"Children from Poverty" (Taylor), 251–264
Citations, plagiarism and, 69–70. *See also* Documentation; Parenthetical documentation
Classical works
  italics or underlining for titles of, 274
  reference works on, 322–323
  in "Works Cited" (MLA style), 167–168, 169, 170
Classification systems, 27–33
Closed stacks in library, 24–25
CMS. See Chicago Manual of Style
CNN Interactive, 27
Coherence principle, 106–108
Collections (anthologies, casebooks, and readers)
  footnotes/endnotes for, 226
  parenthetical documentation for, 142
  in "Works Cited" (MLA style), 150–151
Columbia Encyclopedia, 51, 279
Compilers
  abbreviation for, 147
  in "Works Cited" (MLA style), 147
Computer programs
  in "References" (APA style), 202
  in "Works Cited" (MLA style), 160
Computer room in library, 27
Computers
  email submission of research papers, 37, 184, 218, 236
  invention of, 37
  in libraries, 21–24, 27
  note cards versus, 37
  for note-taking, 64
  outline and, 88
  over-revision and, 92
  reference works on, 306
  remote access to libraries through, 21–23

for research, 37–48
voice recognition software, 37
for writing rough draft, 91–92
Concerts, in "Works Cited" (MLA style),
166
Congressional publications
in "References" (APA style), 206
in "Works Cited" (MLA style), 171
Congressional Record, 171
Content notes
APA style of, 212
CMS style, 232–233
indentation of, 212
MLA style of, 174–176
numbers for, 212
sample of, 249
spacing of, 212
Copernicus, Nicholas, 1
Copy machine for note-taking, 65
Copyright date, 148
Corporate authors
acronyms for, 190
alphabetization of, 145
parenthetical documentation (APA
style), 190
subdivision of parent body, 145
in "Works Cited" (MLA style),
145, 149
in "References" (APA style),
196–197
Corporate websites
in "References" (APA style), 202
in "Works Cited" (MLA style), 160
Correspondence. *See* Email; Letters to
the editor; Personal communication
Court cases. *See* Legal documents
CQ Weekly (website), 27
Critical reviews
in "References" (APA style), 200
in "Works Cited" (MLA style), 157
CSPAN Online, 27
Curie, Marie, 137
Curriculum vitae of expert, 57
Cutter-Sanborn Author Marks,
29–30

Dance reference works, 310
Dashes, 280
Databases
Bible concordance, 47
definition of, 39
Galileo system, 22, 39
indexes to periodical articles,
53–54
InfoTrac College, 39
online full-text databases, 24, 38
OPACs, 13, 21–23, 22, 23
in "References" (APA style), 203
reference works on, 306
state-supported databases, 39
in "Works Cited' (MLA style),
158–159, 161
Date of publication. *See* Copyright date
Dates
abbreviations for days and
months, 287
numbers in, 272
Days, abbreviations for, 287
Decimal outline notation, 86
Dewey Decimal System, 28–29
Diction
accuracy and exactness of,
131–132
definition of, 130
revision of, 130–134
rules for, 134–135
Dictionaries
general dictionaries, 298
hyphenation of words in, 279
information in, 53
online dictionary, 47, 203
in "References" (APA style), 203
specialized dictionaries, 298–299
in word-processing programs, 91
in "Works Cited" (MLA style), 151,
161
Dictionary.com, 53
Directories of periodicals and
newspapers, 295
Directory of Open Access Journals,
(DOAJ), 39

Direct quotations
    brief direct quotations, 94–95
    double reference (quotation within
      cited work), 143, 147
    ellipsis for omission in, 99–102
    indirect quotations compared with,
      93–94
    interpolations in, 99
    long quotations, 95–97
    from poetry, 97–98
    punctuation of, 98–99
    within another quotation, 98
Discussion groups (Internet)
    description of, 38, 42
    in "References" (APA style), 205
Dissertations
    abbreviation for, 282
    quotation marks for titles of, 276
    in "Works Cited" (MLA style), 168
DOAJ (Directory of Open Access
  Journals), 39
Documentation
    for avoiding plagiarism, 69–72, 140
    items requiring, 140
    See also American Psychological
      Association (APA style); *Chicago
      Manual of Style* (CMS); Footnotes;
      Modern Language Association (MLA
      style); Parenthetical documentation
Double reference (quotation within
  cited work)
    footnotes/endnotes for, 226
    parenthetical reference for, 143
    in "Works Cited" (MLA style), 151
Double–spacing. *See* Spacing
Drafts of research paper, 6–9. *See also*
  Rough draft
Dragon NaturallySpeaking, 37
DVDs, in "Works Cited" (MLA style),
  163–164

E-books/online books, 39, 159, *159*,
  161, 230
Ecology reference works, 311
Economic reference works, 308–310

Edison, Thomas, 35
Editions
    abbreviations for, 282
    definition of, 148
    footnotes/endnotes for, 226–227
    in "References" (APA style), 196
    titles of, not italicized or underlined,
      276
    in "Works Cited" (MLA style),
      147, 152
Editorials
    footnotes/endnotes, 229
    in "References" (APA style), 200
    in "Works Cited" (MLA style), 157
Editors and edited works
    abbreviation for *editor/s*, 147
    electronic sources in "Works Cited"
      (MLA style), 158
    in "References" (APA style), 195–196
    in "Works Cited" (MLA style),
      147, 152
Education
    reference works, 54, 56, 311–312
    search engines on, 42
Education Index, 54
Einstein, Albert, 185
Electronic journals, 39
Electronic mailing list
    in "References" (APA style), 203
    in "Works Cited" (MLA style), 161
Electronic/online sources
    blogs, 40–41
    CMS style of, 230
    databases, 23–24, 39
    electronic journals, 39
    evaluation of, 43–44
    full-text databases, 23–24, 38, 39
    for graphics, 110
    newspapers, 26–27
    OPAC (online public-access
      catalog), 13, 21–23, *22, 23*, 39–40
    plagiarism from, 72
    in "References" (APA style),
      200–205
    reference works, 13, 14, 23–24, 306

sample references to, in "Works Cited" (MLA style), 158–162
in "Works Cited" (MLA style), 158–162
social networks, 40–41
See also Sources; *headings beginning with Online; other electronic sources*
Electronic submission of research paper, 37, 184, 218, 236
Ellipses
    misuse of, 99–100
    period and, 100
    in quotations, 99–102
    rules for, 100
E-mail
    parenthetical documentation (APA style), 192–193
    as part of Internet, 38
    in "References" (APA style), 202
    as source of information, 57–58
    for submission of research papers, 37, 184, 218, 236
    in "Works Cited" (MLA style), 160
Emphasis principle, 108
Empirical paper, 209–210
Encarta (encyclopedia), 52
Encyclopedia Britannica (database), 24
Encyclopedia.com, 14, 47
Encyclopedias
    on CD-ROM, 52
    list of, 297
    online encyclopedias, 14, 47, 52, 203–204
    quotation marks for articles in, 275
    in "References" (APA style), 203–204
    in "Works Cited" (MLA style), 151
    See also specific subject areas
Endnotes
    APA style of, 212
    for books, 224–227
    citation of, in "Works Cited" (MLA style), 168
    CMS, style of, 221, 222
    ibid, in, 223, 229
    indentation for, 221

numbering of, 223–224
    for periodicals, 227–229
    spacing of, 221
    subsequent references in, 229–230
et al, for multiple authors, 142, 146, 149, 156, 225, 227
Ethnic studies, 312–314
Evaluation of sources, 43–46, 61–63
Evidence. *See* Sources
Executive branch publications
    in "References" (APA style), 206
    in "Works Cited" (MLA style), 171
Experts
    corresponding with, by email, 57–58
    interviews of, 57

Facebook, 40
Federal government. *See headings beginning with government*
Fiction, in Dewey Decimal System, 29
Figures (graphics)
    abbreviation for *figure*, 233
    APA style of, 213–214, 276
    CMS style of, 233
    guidelines and rules for, 110
    labels and numbers for, 212–213
    MLA style of, 178–182
    samples of, 180–182
    tables versus, 178–179
File transfer protocol (FTP), 38
Films
    italics or underlining for titles of, 274
    in "References" (APA style), 205
    reference works on, 304
    in "Works Cited" (MLA style), 163–164
First-person point of view, 128–129
Fleming, Alexander, 89
Folklore reference works, 322–323
Fonts
    for APA research paper, 210
    for CMS research paper, 232
    for MLA research paper, 178
    for rough draft, 92

Footnotes
    APA style of, 212
    for books, 224–227
    citation of, in "Works Cited" (MLA
        style), 168
    CMS style of, 222
    computer formatting and placement,
        37
    for content notes (MLA style), 174
    ibid, in, 229
    for illustrations, 173
    indentation for, 212
    MLA style of, *178*
    numbering, 223–224
    for periodicals, 227–229
    spacing, 174
    subsequent references in, 229–230
Foreign-language books
    capitalization of titles of, 152
    translation of titles of, 153
    in "Works Cited" (MLA style), 152
    in "References" (APA style), 196
    format of, 280–281
Freud, Sigmund, 73
FTP (file transfer protocol), 38
FTP sources
    in "References" (APA style), 202
    in "Works Cited" (MLA style), 160

Galileo system (database), 22, 39, 54
Gazetteers and atlases, 53
General indexes, 53–54
Geographical reference works, 53, 299
Google search engine, 41, 42, 52
Gophers
    description of, 42
    in "References" (APA style), 202
    in "Works Cited" (MLA style), 160
Government information, 110
Government publications
    indexes of, 302–303
    in "References" (APA style), 206–207
    reference works on, 302–303
    in "Works Cited" (MLA style),
        171–172

Government websites
    in "References" (APA style), 202
    in "Works Cited" (MLA style), 161
Graphics
    APA style of, 212–214
    in Appendix, 212, 214, 233
    CMS style of, 233, 234
    electronic resources for, 110
    explanation of, 109–110
    figures, 213–214
    footnotes for, 173
    guidelines and rules for, 109–110
    in-text reference (MLA style) for, 173
    maps, 173–174, 178–180, *181, 216*
    MLA style of, 178–183
    parenthetical documentation (APA
        style) or, 212–214
    photographs, *113–114*
    samples of, *111–114*
    tables, *112*, 173–174, *179*, 212–213,
        213, 234
    titles and numbering of illustrations,
        178–180
    in "Works Cited" (MLA style),
        173–174
Graphs
    samples of, *180, 182, 215, 216*
    in "Works Cited" (MLA style),
        173–174
    See also Graphics
Grove Dictionary of Art Online, 24
Gutenberg, Johannes, 11

Hatred of research paper, 3
Headings
    of APA research paper, 210
    of CMS research paper, 232
    of MLA research paper, 177
Health information, 110
HighWire Press (database), 24
Hispanic-American studies, 313–314
History reference works, 315–317
Hosts on Internet, 38
HTTP (hypertext transfer protocol), 38
Humanities Index, 54

Hypertext transfer protocol (HTTP), 38
Hyphenation
    spacing with, 280
    of words, 279

ibid., 223, 229
Illness information, 110
Illustrations, book of, in "Works Cited"
    (MLA style), 153, 173–174. *See also*
    Graphics
Incunabula, 294
Indentation
    of APA research paper, 210
    for CMS paper, 221, 224, 231, 232
    for content notes, 212
    for footnotes/endnotes, 221
    for long quotations, 95–97
    for "References" (APA style), 194, 210
    for "Works Cited" (MLA style), 146,
        146
In-depth information, 52
Indexes
    electronic indexes, 53–54, *54*
    of biographical sources, 301–302
    of book reviews, 294
    definition of, 53
    general indexes, 53–54
    of government publications, 302–303
    Internet searches for, 54
    microform indexes, 24
    newspaper indexes, 53–54, *56*,
        295–296
    specialized indexes, 54, 56
Indirect quotations, 93–94. *See also*
    Quotations
Information
    email correspondence, 57–58
    evaluation of, 43–46, 61–63
    finding information for research paper,
        51–63
    general information, 51
    indexes to, 53–56
    Internet search for, 37–48
    interviews and surveys, 57
    single-face information, 51

skimming of sources for, 60–61
statistics, 63
types of, 51–52
working bibliography of, 58–60
    See also Indexes; Library; Reference
        works; Sources
InfoTrac College (database), 39
Initial articles
    of publishers' names, 288
    of titles of works, 147, 191, 275
"Innocent until Proven Broke" (Louis),
    29–34
Instrumental music
    italics or underlining for titles of, 274
    in "Works Cited" (MLA style), 164
Interlibrary loan, 22–23
International Standards Organization
    (ISO), 230–231
Internet
    address or URL, 43–44
    definition of, 38
    evaluation of sources, 43–46
    gopher, 42
    hosts on, 38
    library use, 21–23
    links on, 160–161
    Listserv, 42
    newspapers, 26–27, *26*
    purchase of research papers on, 14
    references to, in "Works Cited"
        (MLA style), 158–162
    reference works, 24
    remote access to libraries, 21–23
    running search on, 46–47
    search engines for, 41–42
    social networks, 40–41
    Telnet, 42
    topic selection and, 13–14
    useful sites, 47–48
    Usenet, 38, 42
    World Wide Web versus, 38
    See also Computers; Electronic/
        online sources; Reference works;
        Websites
Internet Public Library (IPL), 26, 47

Interpolations in quotations, 99
Interviews
    as information source, 57
    published interview in "Works
        Cited" (MLA style), 157
    in "Works Cited" (MLA style), 164
In-text citations. *See* American
    Psychological Association (APA
    style); Footnotes; Modern Language
    Association (MLA style); Parenthetical
    documentation
Introductions
    to parenthetical documentation, 144
    in "Works Cited" (MLA style), 153
"I" or "we" point of view, 128–129
IPL (Internet Public Library), 26, 47
ISO (International Standards
    Organization), 230–231
Italics
    APA style of, 188, 195, 198, 199,
        277–278
    for emphasis, 278
    in footnotes (CMS style), 277
    in foreign words in English texts,
        277–278
    in "References" (APA style), 188,
        195, 198, 199
    for titles, 277–278
    for words, letters or numerals used
        as linguistic examples, 277
IxQuick search engine, 47

Jargon, 131
Journals. *See* Periodicals

Laws. *See* Congressional publications;
    Legal documents
LCSH (Library of Congress Subject
    Headings), 30–31
Lectures
    quotation marks for titles of,
        276
    in "Works Cited" (MLA style), 158
Legal documents
    alphabetization of, 145

parenthetical documentation (APA
    style) for, 207–208
    in "References" (APA style), 207
    in "Works Cited" (MLA style), 145,
        171–172
Letters. *See* E-mail; Personal
    communications
Letters to the editor
    in footnotes/endnotes, 229
    in "References" (APA style), 200
    in "Works Cited" (MLA style), 157
Library
    audiovisual room in, 25
    card catalogs, 21
    carrels in, 27
    CD-ROMs, 13
    computers and computer room in,
        21–24, 27
    Cutter-Sanborn Author Marks, 29–30
    Dewey Decimal System, 28–29
    interlibrary loan, 22–23
    layout of, 21–27
    Library of Congress Classification
        System, 14, 30–31
    main desk in, 25
    microform indexes and microform
        room in, 24, 26
    newspaper racks in, 26
    nonbooks in, 32, 33
    online full-text databases, 23–24
    OPAC (online public-access
        catalog), 13, 21–23, 22, 23, 39–40
    organization of library collections,
        27–33
    reference librarians, 25
    reference room, 25
    remote access to, through personal
        computers, 22–23
    reserve desk, 25
    stacks in, 24–25
    topic choice and, 13
    See also Reference works
Library classification of periodicals, 31
Library of Congress Classification
    System, 14, 30–31

Library of Congress Exhibitions (website), 110
Library of Congress online catalog, 23
Library of Congress search engine, 52
Library of Congress Subject Headings (LCSH), 30–31
Links on Internet
    abstracts online or on CD-ROM, 160, 201
    alphabetization of, 158
    anonymous works, 158
    CD-ROMs in, 160, 201
    computer programs in, 160, 202
    corporate websites in, 160, 202
    databases in, 203
    electronic sources, 158–162, 200–205
    electronic mailing lists in, 161, 203
    e-mail in, 160, 202
    FTP sources in, 160, 202
    gophers in, 160, 202
    government websites in, 160, 202
    MOOs or MUDs in, 161, 203
    online books in, 161, 203
    Telnet in, 162
    Usenet in, 162
    websites in, 162
Listserv
    definition of, 42
    in "Reference" (APA style), 203
Literature reference works, 317–320

Magazine Index, 54
Magazines
    footnotes/endnotes for, 228
    indexes to, 53, 296
    italics or underlining titles of, 274
    online magazines, 204
    quotation marks for articles in, 275
    in "References" (APA style), 199, 204
    union lists of, 296
    in "Works Cited" (MLA style), 154, 156
    See also Periodicals

Main desk in library, 25
Manuscripts
    in "References" (APA style), 197
    in "Works Cited" (MLA style), 168–169
Maps
    samples of, *181, 216*
    in "Works Cited" (MLA style), 173–174, 178–180
    See also Graphics
Margins
    of APA research paper, 210
    of CMS research paper, 232
    of MLA research paper, 176–178
    of "Works Cited" (MLA style), 146
Meaningless words and phrases, 133
Media center, 25. *See also* Library
Medium of publication, 149, 155, 159
Merlot: Multimedia Educational Research for Learning and Online Teaching (database), 24
Merriam-Webster website, 47
MetaCrawler search engine, 42
Microfiche, 24, 26
Microfilm, 24, 26
Microforms
    indexes of, 24, 303–304
    library room, 26
    types of 24, 26
MLA. See Modern Language Association (MLA) style
Modern Language Association (MLA) style
    abbreviations, 273
    appearance of finished paper, 176
    content notes in, 174–176
    electronic submission of paper, 184
    finished form of MLA paper, 176–184
    font, 178
    footnotes, 168
    graphics, 178–183
    headings in research paper, 177
    introductions to parenthetical documentation, 144

Modern Language Association (MLA)
style (*continued*)
  long quotations, 96
  margins of research paper, 176–178
  numbers, 183
  pagination of research paper, 177
  parenthetical documentation
    (author-work), 4, 139–144
  peer review checklist, 184
  publishers' names, 289
  running head, 176–177
  sample of MLA paper, 239–250
  spacing of text, 178
  tense style of, 108
  "Works Cited" format in,
    144–174
  See also "Works Cited" (MLA style)
Money amounts, 271–272
Months, abbreviations for, 287
MOOs (synchronous communication)
  in "References" (APA style), 203
  in "Works Cited" (MLA style), 161
Motion pictures. *See* films
MUDs (synchronous communication)
  in "References" (APA style), 203
  in "Works Cited" (MLA style), 161
Multiple authors
  alphabetization of, in "Works Cited"
    (MLA style), 145
  ampersand for, in "References" (APA
    style), 188, 195, 198
  of books in "References" (APA style),
    195
  of books in "Works Cited" (MLA
    style), 149
  et al. for, 142
  footnotes/endnotes for, 225
  parenthetical documentation (APA
    style) for, 188–189
  parenthetical documentation (MLA
    style) for, 142
  of periodical articles in "References"
    (APA style), 198
  of periodical articles in "Works
    Cited" (MLA style), 155

  punctuation for in "Works Cited"
    (MLA style), 142
Multivolume works
  footnotes/indexes for, 225
  parenthetical documentation for, 143
  publication dates for, 148, 197
  in "References" (APA style), 197
  with separate titles, 150
  in "Works Cited" (MLA style), 148,
    150
  See also Volume numbers
Museum reference works, 308
Music
  italics or underlining for titles of, 274
  quotation marks for titles of songs,
    275
  reference works on, 205, 320–322
  in "Works Cited" (MLA style), 164
MySpace, 40
Mythology reference works, 322–323

Names of people, 278–279
Names of publishers, 288–290
National Institutes of Health (website),
  110
Native-American studies, 314
n.d., 148
Newsgroups
  description of, 42
  in "References" (APA style),
    204–205
Newspapers
  directories of, 295
  editorials in, 157, 200, 229
  footnotes/endnotes for, 228–229
  indexes to, 53–54, *56*
  italics or underlining for titles of, 274
  letters to editor in, 159, 200, 229
  in library, 26–27
  online sources, 26–27
  parenthetical documentation (APA
    style), 199–200
  place names for, 155
  quotation marks for articles in, 275
  racks for, in library, 26

in "References" (APA style),
    199–200
reference works on, 294–296
union lists of, 296
in "Works Cited" (MLA style),
    154–155, 157
See also Databases
Newspapers.com, 27
New York Times Index, 54, 55
Nonbooks
    catalog cards for, 32
    in library, 25–27, 33
Nonprint materials
    in "References" (APA style),
        205–208
    reference works on, 303–306
    in "Works Cited" (MLA style),
        162–167
Nonsexist language, 129–130
Note cards, 37, 59–60, 63
Note-taking
    for avoiding plagiarism, 69–70
    cards for, 63
    complete sentences for, 72
    computer for, 64
    copy machine for, 65
    formatting note cards, 63–64
    organizing notes for rough draft, 92
    paraphrase, 66, 67
    personal comments, 68, *69*
    quotation, 66–67, *68*
    quotation marks in, 67
    sorting notes for rough draft, 92
    summary on note card, 65–66, *66*
    types of, 65–69
    use of notes in research paper, 63–69,
        92–104
n.p., 148–149
n. pag., 148–149
Numbers
    APA style of, 214
    CMS style of, 234–235
    commas within, 183
    for content notes and endnotes/
        footnotes, 212
    dates, 272
    for edition in "Works Cited" (MLA
        style), 148–149
    for footnotes and endnotes,
        223–224
    for illustrations, 180, 214
    inclusive, 272
    MLA style of, 183
    in parenthetical documentation, 183
    percentages and amounts of money,
        271–272
    Roman numerals, 272
    series number in "Works Cited"
        (MLA style), 183
    words versus numerals for, 271
    See also Page numbers

Objective point of view, 128–129
OCLC (Online Computer Library
    Center), 23
Omission in quotations, ellipsis for,
    99–102
Online abstracts
    in "References" (APA style), 201
    in "Works Cited" (MLA style), 160
Online books
    CMS style of, 230
    in "References" (APA style), 203
    in "Works Cited" (MLA style), 159,
        159, 161
Online catalogs, 13, 21–23
Online Computer Library Center
    (OCLC), 23
Online databases, 161. *See* Databases
Online dictionaries
    Internet sites for, 53
    in "References" (APA style), 203
    in "Works Cited" (MLA style), 161
Online encyclopedias
    for choice of research paper
        topic, 14
    information found in, 51–52
    Internet site for, 52
    in "References" (APA style), 203
    in "Works Cited" (MLA style), 162

Online magazines
    in "References" (APA style), 204
    in "Works Cited" (MLA style), 162
    See also Magazines; Online
        periodicals; Periodicals
Online periodicals
    CMS style for periodical articles, 230
    electronic journals, 39
    full-text databases of, 23–24
    in "References" (APA style), 204
    in "Works Cited" (MLA style), 162
    See also Periodicals
Online resources. *See* Computers;
    Electronic/online sources; Internet;
    other headings beginning with Online
OPAC (online public-access catalog),
    13, 21–23, 22, 23, 39–40
Opening paragraph
    rough draft and revision, 120–124
    samples, 120–124
Open stacks in library, 24–25
Operas
    italics or underlining for titles of, 274
    in "Works Cited" (MLA style), 164, 166
Oppenheimer, J. Robert, 219
Oral history reference works, 305
Outline
    choosing form of, 87–88
    computer used for, 88
    decimal outline notation, 86
    definition of, 81
    equal ranking in online entities, 82
    paragraph outline, 85–86
    parallelism in outline entries, 82–83
    sentence outline, 84–85
    topic outline, 83–84
    types of, 83–86
    visual conventions of, 81–82
    writing outline for rough draft, 91
Oxford English Dictionary (database), 24

PACs (public-access catalogs), 21
Page numbers
    abbreviation for *page/s*, 187, 192, 284
    of APA research papers, 210

in CMS footnote style, 224
missing information, 148
in parenthetical documentation
    (APA style), 187
in "Works Cited" (MLA style), 149
See also Numbers; Pagination
Pagination
    CMS style and, 232
    of periodical articles, 155
    of periodicals, 154, 198–199,
        227–228
    of research paper (MLA style), 177
    of "Works Cited" (MLA style), 154,
        155
    See also Page numbers
Paintings
    italics or underling for titles of, 275
    in "Works Cited" (MLA), 163
    See also Artworks
Pamphlets
    italics or underlining for the titles
        of, 274
    in "Works Cited" (MLA style), 169
Paragraph outline, 85–88
Paragraphs
    body paragraphs, 123–124
    opening paragraph, 120–124
    revision of, 120–124
    sequence of, compared with thesis,
        122–124
    transitions between, 107–108, 124
Parallel constructions, 106, 126
Paraphrase
    definition, 92
    on note cards, 66
    parenthetical documentation of, 93
    quotations versus, 93
    in rough draft, 92–93
    sample of, 93
Paraphrase notes, 67
Parenthetical documentation
    APA style of, 187–193
    Arabic numerals in, 143
    avoiding clutter in text with, 139, 193
    bibliography entry for, 139

citation as part of parenthetical comment, 193
guidelines for, 140–144
introductions to, in text, 144
MLA style of, 4, 139–144
of paraphrase, 141
period after parenthetical reference, 4
for volume numbers, 143
See also American Psychological Association (APA) style; Documentation; Modern Language Association (MLA) style
Passive voice, of verbs, 126–127
Peer review
of journal articles, 39
for research paper, 184, 218, 235
People's names, 278–279
Percentages, 271–272
Performances
italics for titles of, 274
in "Works Cited" (MLA style), 166–167
Periodicals
abstracts of journal articles, 53
book industry journals, 53
directories of, 295
electronic journals, 39
footnotes/endnotes for, 227–229
indexes to, 53–54, 295–296
italics or underlining for titles of, 274
in library, 31
microform indexes for, 24
online full-text databases of, 23–24
online periodicals, 23–24
pagination of articles in, 154, 198–199
pagination of volumes of, 154, 156
peer review of journal articles, 39
publication information on, 154–155
quotation marks for articles in, 275
in "References" (APA style), 197–200
reference works on, 294–296
sample reference to, in "Works Cited" (MLA style), 155–158
skimming periodical articles, 60–61

thesis of periodical articles, 24
union lists of, 296
volume and issue number of, 154–155
in "Works Cited" (MLA style), 153–158
See also Databases; Magazines; Newspapers
Personal commentary in research paper, 103–104
Personal comment notes, 68, *69*
Personal communications
parenthetical documentation (APA) for, 192–193
in "Works Cited" (MLA style), 169
Philosophy reference works, 323–324
Photographs
of artwork in "Works Cited" (MLA style), 163
samples of, *113, 114*
See also Graphics
Place of publication. *See* Publication facts
Plagiarism
definition, 69
from electronic sources, 72
items requiring documentation, 70
samples of, 70–72
techniques for avoiding, 69–72
Plays
abbreviations for Shakespeare's, 287
italics or underlining of titles for, 274
parenthetical documentation (MLA style) for, 143
in "Works Cited" (MLA style), 169–170
Poetry
italics for titles of long poems, 274
parenthetical documentation (MLA style) for, 143
quotation marks for titles of short poems, 275
quotations from, 97–98
slash for line breaks, 143
in "Works Cited" (MLA style), 170

Point of view, 128–129

Population statistics, 110

Prefaces, in "Works Cited" (MLA style), 153

Primary sources, 61

Project Gutenberg (database), 24

Pronouns
    clarity in, 106
    nonsexist pronoun *thon*, 129–130

Proofreading of research paper, 176

Pseudonymous authors
    brackets for, 150
    use of pseudonyms, 278
    in "Works Cited" (MLA style), 150

Psychological Abstracts, 56–57

Psychology reference works, 324

Public-access catalogs, 21

Publication facts
    of books in "Works Cited" (MLA style), 148–149
    copyright date, 148
    dates for multivolume works, 148, 197
    of electronic sources in "Works Cited" (MLA style), 159
    missing information, 148–149
    of periodicals in "References" (APA style), 197–198
    of periodicals in "Works Cited" (MLA style), 154–155
    place of publication, 148
    shortening of publishers' names, 148, 288–289

Public documents. *See* Government publications

Publishers' names, shortening of, 148, 288–289

Punctuation
    brackets for anonymous and pseudonymous authors, 150
    brackets for translated titles in "Works Cited" (MLA style), 153
    brackets in quotations, 94
    colon to introduce long quotations, 95
    dashes, 280
    ellipsis, 99–102
    hyphens for repeated author in "Works Cited" (MLA style), 145
    for multiple authors in "Works Cited" (MLA style), 142
    for multiple authors in "References" (APA style), 189
    numbers for footnotes/endnotes and, 223–224
    in parenthetical references, 139
    period after parenthetical references, 139
    of quotations, 98–99
    of "References" (APA style), 187–188
    spaces and punctuation marks, 280
    of subtitles, 147
    of "Works Cited" references (MLA style), 139
    See also specific punctuation marks

Questions
    thesis worded as, 78
    use of, in research paper, 121–122

Quotation marks
    for brief direct quotations, 69, 92–94
    for chapters of books, 147
    colon outside, 98
    comma inside, 98
    for direct quotations, 93–94
    for essay in collection, 142
    exclamation point and, 99
    in notes, 67
    period inside, 98
    for poetry quotations, 143
    question mark and, 99
    semicolon, 98
    single quotation marks for quotation within another quotation, 98
    single quotation marks for titles within titles, 277
    within indented long quotations, 96
    See also Quotations

Quotation notes, 66–67, 68

Quotations
　　abbreviation for *quoted in*, 151, 284
　　brackets in, 94
　　brief direct quotations, 94–95
　　direct quotations, 93–94
　　double reference (quotation within
　　　cited work), 143, 151
　　ellipsis for omission in, 99–102
　　indirect, 93–94
　　interpolations in, 99
　　long, 95–96
　　overuse of, 102–103
　　personal response to, in research
　　　paper, 103–104
　　from poetry, 97–98
　　punctuation of, 98–99
　　sic in, 99
　　as source in "Works Cited" (MLA
　　　style), 172–173
　　string-of-pearls effect and, 103
　　within another quotation, 98
　　use of in opening paragraph, 121

Radio programs
　　italics or underlining for titles of, 274
　　in "Works Cited" (MLA style), 165
Rare books, 23
Readers. *See* Collections (anthologies,
　　casebooks and readers)
Reader's Guide to Periodical Literature,
　　53–54, *54*
Redundant expressions, 133
Refdisk (website), 47
Reference libraries, 25. *See also* Library
Reference room or shelf in library, 25
"References" (APA style)
　　abstracts in, 201, 208–209
　　alphabetization of, 191, 192, 197
　　audio recordings in, 206
　　books in, 194–197
　　CD-ROMs in, 201
　　chronological listing for works by
　　　same author in, 194
　　computer programs in, 202
　　corporate websites in, 202

　　databases in, 203
　　electronic mailing list in, 203
　　electronic sources in, 200–205
　　e-mail in, 202
　　films in, 205
　　format of, 193–208
　　FTP sources in, 202
　　gophers in, 202
　　government documents in, 206–207
　　government websites in, 202
　　indentation of, 194, 210
　　italics in, 188, 195, 198, 199
　　legal references in, 207
　　manuscripts in, 197
　　MOOs and MUDs (synchronous
　　　communication) in, 203
　　newspapers in, 199–200
　　nonprint materials in, 205–208
　　online books in, 203
　　periodicals in, 197–200, 204
　　punctuation of generally, 187–188
　　reports in, 208
　　sample of, *194*, 195–197
　　spacing of, 210
　　Telnet in, 204
　　Usenet in, 204
　　websites in, 205
Reference works
　　art, 306–308
　　atlases and gazetteers, 53, 299
　　biographical sources, 299–302
　　books, 293–294
　　business, 308–310
　　on CD-ROMs, 13
　　classics, 322–323
　　computer files, 306
　　computer technology, 314–315
　　dance, 310
　　dictionaries, 297–299
　　ecology, 311
　　economics, 308–310
　　education, 311–312
　　encyclopedias, 297
　　ethnic studies, 312–314
　　films, 304

Reference works (*continued*)
  folklore, 322–323
  government publications, 302–303
  history, 315
  indexes, 295–296
  list of general reference works,
    293–306
  list of specialized reference works,
    306–328
  literature, 317–320
  microforms, 24, 303–304
  music, 305, 320–322
  mythology, 322–323
  newspapers, 294
  nonprint materials, 303–306
  online full-text databases, 23–24
  online reference works, 14
  periodicals, 294
  philosophy, 323–324
  psychology, 324
  religion, 325–236
  science, 326–327
  social sciences, 327
  sound recordings, 305
  technology, 314–315
  union lists, 296
  women's studies, 327–328
  in "Works Cited" (MLA style), 151
  See also Library
Religion
  abbreviations for books of the Bible,
    285–286
  reference works on, 325–326
  titles of sacred writings, 167, 276
  See also Bible
Repetition of key words, 106
Reports
  in "References" (APA style), 208
  in "Works Cited" (MLA style), 173
Reprints, in "Works Cited" (MLA style),
    152
Research paper
  abstract of, 115–116, 177, 211
  APA paper in finished form, 209–217

appearance of, 176, 210–211
CMS paper in finished form, 231–235
definition of, 3–4
drafts of, 6–9
electronic submission of, 37, 184,
    218, 236
empirical paper, 209–210
font for, 178, 210
format of, 4
graphics in, 109, 178–183, 212
hatred of, 3
headings of, 210
impact of computer on, 37
library research for, 21–33
mechanics of, 271–291
MLA paper in finished form, 176–184
note-taking, 63–69
opening paragraph of, 120–124
outline of, 81–88, 210
pagination of, 177, 210
peer review of, 184, 218, 235
plagiarism and avoiding plagiarism,
    69–72
proofreading, 176
reasons for, 5
rough draft, 6–8, 91–115
sample using APA style, 251–264
sample using CMS footnotes, 265–269
sample using MLA style, 239–250
schedule for, 8, 9
spacing of text, 178, 210
steps in, 9–10
theoretical paper, 209–210
thesis in, 75–80
thesis paper compared with, 5–6
titles of, 80–81, 211
title page of, 176–177
topic choice for, 3, 13–15
working bibliography for, 58–60
See also American Psychological
    Association (APA) style; *Chicago
    Manual of Style* (CMS); Computers;
    Graphics; Modern Language
    Association (MLA) style; Rough draft

Reserve desk in library, 25
Reviews. *See* Critical reviews
Revised editions. *See* Editions
Revision
    active voice of verbs and, 126–127
    of body paragraphs, 123–124
    checking paragraphs for sequence of
      topics in thesis, 122–123
    of meaningless words and phrases,
      133
    of opening paragraph, 120
    of overuse of phrases from subjects
      instead of nouns, 132–133
    of paragraphs, 120–124
    of paragraph transitions, 124
    parallel constructions and, 126
    of point of view (first-person versus
      objective), 128–129
    principle of, 119
    reading paper aloud and, 134
    of redundant expressions, 133
    rules for, 134–135
    of sentence length, 125
    of sentences for variety and style,
      125–126
    of sexist language, 129–130
    of snobbish diction, 134
    subordinate clauses and, 126
    of words, 130–134
Rhetorical principles
    coherence, 106–108
    emphasis, 108
    unity, 105
Roman numerals, 272. *See also* Numbers
Rough draft
    abstract and, 91
    checklist for, 91
    coherence in, 106–108
    computer for writing, 91–92
    diction of, 130–134
    emphasis in, 108
    graphics in, 109–114
    opening paragraph of, 120–124
    over-revision, 102

paraphrases in, 92–93
personal commentary in, 103–104
quotations in, 93–104
reading aloud for revision of, 134
revision of, 119–135
samples of, 6–8
sentence variety and style in,
    125–126
sequence of paragraphs in, 122–123
spell-checker for, 92
summaries in, 92–93
tense of, 108–109
unity in, 105
use of notes in, 92–104
writer's block and, 91
Routledge Encyclopedia of Philosophy, 24
Running head
    APA style of, 210–211
    MLA style of, 176–177

Sacred writings, 167, 276
Schedule for research paper, 8, 9
Science reference works, 326–327
Sculptures
    italics or underlining of titles, 275
    in "Works Cited" (MLA style), 163
    See also Artworks
Search engines
    AltaVista, 41
    Ask, 42
    definition of, 41
    education search engines, 42
    finding, 42
    Google, 41, 42, 53
    hits (results of search), 41
    instructions for, 41
    IxQuick, 47
    MetaCrawler, 42
    online full-text databases, 23–24
    running search, 46–47, 52
    types of, 42
    Windweavers, 42
    Yahoo!, 41, 42
Sentence outline, 84–85

Sentences
  active voice, 126–127
  length of, 125
  overuse of phrases for subjects of, instead of single nouns, 132–133
  parallel constructions in, 106, 126
  revision of, for variety and style, 125–126
  rules for, 134–135
  subordinate clauses in, 126
Serials. *See* Magazines; Newspapers; Periodicals
Series
  numbered series, 151
  titles of, not italicized or underlined, 276
  unnumbered series, 152
  in "Works Cited" (MLA style), 147–148, 151–152
Sexist language, 129–130
Shakespeare's plays, abbreviations for, 287
Ships, italics or underlining for titles, 275
Short stories, quotation marks for titles of, 275
sic, 99
Single-fact information, 51
Single quotation marks, 98
Skimming of sources, 60–61
Slash for line breaks in poetry, 143
Snobbish diction, 134
Social networks, 40–41
Social Sciences Citation Index, 57
Social Science Index, 327
Social sciences reference works, 327
Societies' names, 276
Songs. *See* Music
Sound recordings, 305. See Audio recordings
Sources
  bibliography cards for, 58–60
  date of evidence in, 63
  email correspondence, 57–58
  evaluation of, 43–46, 61–63
  general information, 51, 297

in-depth information, 52
  indexes to, 53–56
  Internet search for, 37–48
  interviews and surveys, 57
  library search for, 21–34
  point of view, 62
  primary sources, 61
  secondary sources, 61
  single-fact information, 51
  skimming for selection of, 60–61
  statistics, 63
  working bibliography, 58–60
  See also Electronic/online sources Internet; Library; Reference works
Spacing
  of APA research paper, 210
  of CMS research paper, 232
  of content notes, 175
  of footnotes and endnotes, 221
  hyphenation and, 280
  margins (MLA style), 176, 177, 178
  MLA style of, 178
  punctuation marks and, 280
  of "References" (APA style), 194
  of "Works Cited" (MLA style), 146
Specialized indexes, 54, 56
Specialized reference works, 306–328
Speech reference works, 305
Spelling and spell-checker, 92, 291
Stacks in library, 24–25
States (U.S.), abbreviations for, 288
Statistical Abstract of the United States, 63
Statistics
  parenthetical documentation (APA style) for, 192
  population statistics, 110
  resources, 63
Statutes. *See* Congressional publications; Legal documents
Steps and schedule for research paper, 9
Subordinate clauses, 126
Subtitles, in "Works Cited" (MLA style), 147

Summary
    definition, 92
    on note cards, 65–66
    quotations versus, 93
Summary notes, *66*
Surveys, 57

Tables
    APA styles of, 212, *213*, 276
    CMS styles of, 233
    figures versus, 178–179
    guidelines and rules for, 110
    labels, titles and numbers for, 276
    MLA style of, 178–179, *179*
    parenthetical documentation (APA
      style) for, 189
    samples of, 213
    in "Works Cited" (MLA style),
      173–174
    See also Graphics
Technology, reference works on,
      314–315
Telephone conversations, parenthetical
  documentation for, 192
Television
    italics or underlining for programs
      on, 274
    quotation marks for episodes on, 276
    in "Works Cited" (MLA style), 165
Telnet
    description of, 42
    in "References" (APA styles), 204
    in "Works Cited" (MLA style), 162
Tense of research paper, 108–109, 214
Theoretical paper, 209–210
Thesaurus, 92
Theses. *See* Dissertations
Thesis in research paper
    body paragraphs in, 123–124
    checking sequence of paragraphs
      with, 122–123
    definition of, 75
    formulation of, 76–77
    functions of, 75–76

    placement of, 79–80
    rules for wording, 77–79
    samples, 75–80
Thesis of periodical articles, 61
Thesis paper, 5–6
Third-person point of view, 128–129
thon (nonsexist pronoun), 129–130
Title of research paper
    APA style of, 210–211, *211*
    MLA style and, 176–177
Titles of works
    books in "References" (APA style),
      194
    books in "Works Cited" (MLA style),
      147
    capitalization of, 147
    electronic sources in "Works Cited"
      (MLA style), 158
    foreign-language books, 152
    frequent references to, 277
    initial article in, 147, 181, 275
    italics or underlining for, 273–275,
      278
    multivolume works, 150
    periodical articles in "References:
      (APA style), 194
    periodical articles in "Works Cited"
      (MLA style), 154
    in quotation marks, 275–276
    single quotation marks for titles
      within titles, 277
    subtitles with, 147
    within titles, 277
Topic of research paper
    avoidance of certain types of, 15–16
    choice of, 3, 13–15
    narrowing of, 17
    OPAC and, 13
Topic outline, 83–84
Traditional documentation. *See Chicago
    Manual of Style* (CMS); Endnotes;
    Footnotes
Transitional markers, 106–107
Transitional sentence, 107–108

Translations and translators
  abbreviation for *translator*, 147
  footnotes/endnotes for, 227
  in "References" (APA style), 196
  in "Works Cited" (MLA style),
    147, 153
Treaties, 207
Twitter, 40
Typescripts, 168–169

Underlining
  for titles, 277–278
  of words, letters or numerals used as
    linguistic example, 277
UNESCO Statistical Yearbook, 63
Uniform resource locator (URL), 38, 159
Union lists, 296
United Nations *Demographic Yearbook*, 63
Unity principle, 105
Unpublished manuscripts. *See*
        Manuscripts
URL (uniform resource locator), 38, 159
USA.gov (website), 110
U.S. Census Bureau website, 110
Usenet
  definition, 38, 42
  in "References" (APA style), 204
  in "Works Cited" (MLA style), 162
U.S. Government Printing Office,
  abbreviation of, 207
U.S. News Online, 27

Variety of sentences, 125–126
Verbs
  active versus passive voice, 126–127
  in parallel constructions, 126
  tense of, in research paper, 108–109
Videotapes, in "Works Cited" (MLA
  style), 163–164
Voice recognition software, 37
Volume numbers
  abbreviation for *volume*, 143, 285
  of books in "Works Cited" (MLA
    style), 148
  of periodicals in "Works Cited"
    (MLA style), 154

Weblogs. *See* Blogs
Websites. *See also* Electronic/online
  sources; Internet; *specific websites*
Who's Who, 53, 63
Wikipedia, 44
Windweavers, 42
Women's studies, 327–328
Word-processing programs
  dictionary in, 91
  fonts for, 92
  over-revision of rough draft and, 92
  spell-checker in, 92, 291
  thesaurus in, 91
Words
  conciseness of, 131–132
  in dates, 273
  foreign-language words, 280–281
  hyphenation of, 279
  italics or underlining of, 277–278
  jargon, 131
  as linguistic examples, 277
  meaningless words and phrases, 133
  numerals versus, 214, 271–273
  overuse of phrases versus use of
    single nouns, 132–133
  redundant expressions, 133
  revision of, 130–134
  rules for, 134–135
  snobbish diction, 134
  spelling of, 291
Working bibliography, 58–60
"Works Cited" (MLA style), 144–174
World Almanac, 63
WorldCat, 40
World Wide Web, 38. *See also* Internet
Wright, Orville and Wilbur, 117
Writer's block, 91
Writing rough draft. *See* Rough draft

Yahoo! search engine, 41
YouTube, 40